Marijke Steegstra

Resilient Rituals

Modernity and Belonging

edited by

Peter Geschiere and Birgit Meyer
(University of Amsterdam)

Band 3

LIT

Marijke Steegstra

Resilient Rituals

Krobo initiation
and the politics of culture in Ghana

LIT

Cover Illustration: 'Priestesses during Dipo' by Marijke Steegstra

Publication was made possible in part by grants from the J. E. Jurriaanse Foundation and the Dr. L. A. Buma Foundation

Bibliographic information published by Die Deutsche Bibliothek
Die Deutsche Bibliothek lists this publication in the Deutsche Nationalbibliografie; detailed bibliographic data are available in the Internet at http://dnb.ddb.de.

ISBN 3-8258-7786-8
Zugl.: Nijmegen, Univ., Diss., 2004

© LIT VERLAG Münster   2004
Grevener Str./Fresnostr. 2   48159 Münster
Tel. 0251-23 50 91   Fax 0251-23 19 72
e-Mail: lit@lit-verlag.de   http://www.lit-verlag.de

Distributed in North America by:

Transaction Publishers
New Brunswick (U.S.A.) and London (U.K.)

Transaction Publishers   Tel.: (732) 445 - 2280
Rutgers University   Fax: (732) 445 - 3138
35 Berrue Circle   for orders (U. S. only):
Piscataway, NJ 08854   toll free (888) 999 - 6778

Contents

Maps

Figures

Acknowledgements

In this book I have written down some of the knowledge and insights I acquired about changes in Krobo society regarding religion and culture through my study of the *dipo* rites for Krobo women. Acknowledging that 'What I don't know would make a whole new world', borrowing a popular phrase from my dear friend and story-teller Thérèse Folkes-Plair, I hope that I have nevertheless contributed to an appreciation of the creativity and dynamics of Krobo history and culture, which is an important part of Ghana as a whole and remains understudied up to this very day.

'Ghana' has become part of me. When I listen back to tapes I recorded during my stays or look at pictures and videotapes I took in Ghana, vivid memories come back to me of voices and faces that have become so familiar. These records do not only give information about the people in Ghana with whom I lived, they also tell much about myself, as no other periods in my life have been documented as well as my visits to Ghana. They are among the most important markers in my life. For example, when I try to recall certain events or structure my life until now, I use the period before or after 'my first time in Ghana' (end of 1992) or 'my first fieldwork' (1994) as my frame of reference. Now a new phase is about to start, now that I have completed this project. There are many people I feel indebted to for helping me to accomplish this.

Two of the most important people involved in this project are my supervisors Frans Hüsken and Birgit Meyer. Before, during and especially after the fieldwork, I felt they supported me. Birgit Meyer's stimulating critical remarks and never-ending enthusiasm kept me motivated. Her belief that I could still do better encouraged me to continue and improve. Although any mistakes in this book are my responsibility, I knew that with her I was in safe hands and I greatly admire her ambition and skills and see her as a great example. As the Krobo proverb says: 'The one who follows an elephant never gets wet on dewy paths' (*Noko kpε suo nε e wu bo*). Even though at times it was in the background, I always felt the presence of Frans Hüsken's trust and confidence. He showed me the way into the academic world. I think the Krobo proverb 'You cannot guide yourself, somebody must guide you' (*Epi milemi kaa nko maale ni pe mine*) is very true and expresses how important he is to me.

Historian Veit Arlt also needs a honourable mention. We met in the archives of the Basel Mission in the summer of 1997, where Veit was an assistant archivist and investigated into Krobo history as well. He made me realize how enormous the range and richness was of the historical material available in Basel and encouraged me to explore it in greater detail than I had intended to. By coincidence, we had planned our fieldwork in Ghana almost exactly at the same time between 1998-1999, during which period we were almost neighbours in

Krobo, about five kilometres from each other. During our research activities, but also when drinking cool beers at our favourite bar in Somanya, while riding on Veit's motorbike to the swimming pool of the four-star Volta hotel in Akosombo when we needed a break from the heat and dust of Odumase, and while dancing to (old!) highlife music at Bywell's in Accra, we shared research experiences, exchanged information and made memories for life. I also thank Veit for being my host in London during my brief research into the British colonial archives, reading and commenting on several chapters, and making the beautiful maps of the Krobo area I use in this book.

In Ghana, particularly in Odumase where I lived, I especially appreciate all the efforts of my very good friend Juliana (Julie) Baidoo and her mother Lako Sakite. When I think of their welcoming, beautiful smiles, it makes me feel warm inside. I admire women like Julie who seem to be jacks-of-all-trades, as they manage to do so many different things at the same time. I am very grateful to Abraham Adjoka's family for providing me with accommodation and letting me know there always is a place for me in their house. I also thank Julie's husband, Samuel Sakite, who introduced and accompanied me to several traditional rulers and priests. I thank all of the latter for contributing to my research, the Klowɛki priests and priestesses in particular. One special person among them I would like to acknowledge is the late Tetteh Gaga from Plau, Somanya. He was a true friend and a great informant. Unfortunately, he did not live to see the end of this project. I want to thank all the Manya and Yilo Krobo chiefs, queen mothers and elders I talked to. In particular kono̱ Nene Sakite II, manyɛ Maku from Kpong, paramount queen mothers Nana manyɛ Mamle Okleyo and Nana manyɛ Korlekwor Adjado III, and all the queen mothers of the Manya Krobo Queen Mothers Association. In addition, I would like to thank all those other people in Odumase and its surroundings who helped me in any way, but who are too numerous to mention.

A big thank you goes to Padi Odonkor, without whose translations there would have hardly been any direct quotes from Krobo language in this book. My friend and colleague Dzodzi Tsikata's study-cum-guestroom on the campus of Legon university felt like an oasis to me and I thank her for offering me a place where I could relax every now and then, and for all the stimulating talks. I also have fond memories of my outings to Accra's vibrant nightlife with Juliet Amoah. I thank Kodjo Senah and Adwoa Asiedu for visiting me in Odumase, all their good advice, and the many cold Star beers in Accra.

I thank my friends and family back home for all the mail I received. At a time when hand-written letters are becoming an anomaly, they probably do not realize how grateful I was for all the mail I received throughout the time I lived in Ghana. I wish they all could have seen how anxiously I went for the mailbox twice a week in Odumase, and returned very happily when there was a letter for me. It gave me the feeling people back home had not forgotten about me, and it kept me longing for home in a healthy way. I thank Suzanne van Stratum and

Irene Terstappen for visiting me 'in the field' and Martine Leuveld for picking me up at the airport and taking good care of my apartment during my absence.

I was fortunate enough to meet Hugo Huber, who wrote the first published ethnography on the Krobo people (1963), in his home in Switzerland. I want to thank him for his words of encouragement. His love for Krobo life and culture can be felt through his little notes and in his letters to this very day. His 'Krobo bible' offered a wealth of information to me, and provided a bottom line. I look forward to presenting him with my very own book now.

I thank my colleagues and members of the 'promovendi-overleg' at the Nijmegen Department of Anthropology and Development Studies. It is always good to know that you never suffer alone. Especially Gerben Nooteboom and Janine Klungel acted as good sounding boards in the last few years, as well as my dear colleague and neighbour Catrien Notermans. I also thank Iris Shiripinda for her sense of humour and ability to put things in perspective. This brings me to the various other members of the 'post-doc group' of Women's Studies of the University of Nijmegen. I thank all of them and the above who gave critical comments on earlier drafts of papers and chapters. I also thank the various members of the Ghana Study Group for our discussions and their stimulating critiques during our regular meetings at the African Studies Centre in Leiden and beyond, especially Rijk van Dijk, Malika Kraamer and Felix Ameka.

I am greatly indebted to the Netherlands Foundation for the Advancement of Tropical Research (WOTRO) for generously sponsoring this research and making it all possible. I also learned much from my participation in the sessions of the WOTRO 'Globalisation and the construction of communal identities' research programme. I thank CERES for educational support and the University of Nijmegen for all their support and facilities. I would also like to thank Peter Davies for correcting the English in the final text and Antoine van Hemelrijk for his help in digitalising the photos in this book. And I also thank Rene van der Haar for his help with my bibliography.

'My' people in Ghana have told me more than once that I should consider Odumase my 'second home'. My stay in Ghana has made me realize how important it is to have a home and a family, and how much it shapes your identity. Last but certainly not least, I am therefore very grateful to my parents for giving me the security that I always have a place I can call home and I would like to dedicate this book to them: *heit en mem, foar jimme*.

A note on orthography

Dangme is the indigenous language of different Dangme groups in the Southeast of Ghana, and therefore includes various dialects. Sometimes the language 'Ga' and 'Dangme' are combined as 'Ga-Dangme', but as the linguist Kropp-Dakubu notes:

> (...) because of their obviously close relationship, many have tended to regard Dangme and Ga as 'the same', or anyway as variants of one language. However, Ga and Dangme are not mutually intelligible to speakers of one who have never been exposed to the other, and the languages are structurally different in many interesting ways, so that there is no question that greater attention to the linguistics of Dangme is long overdue (Kropp-Dakubu 1987: 3).

As a standard Dangme orthography was only introduced in 1970, different spellings of Dangme are used in the sources I consulted. I have not always used the standard orthography for Dangme terms that I mention in this book. However, I have used the same spelling for each Dangme term throughout the book. Instead of the symbol ŋ, I use 'ng' and 'ngm' replaces 'ŋg'. In some of the sources 'dz' is used where now 'j' has replaced it. I use o̱ to indicate the vowel sound as in 'rock', whereas 'o' is pronounced as in 'go'. The 'r' does not exist, except in a few cases. However, in different spellings 'or' is sometimes used where 'o̱' is meant. The symbol ɛ is used to indicate that an 'e' is pronounced as in the French 'è'. There is no grammatical gender.

I use 'Krobo' instead of 'Klo', which would be the proper Dangme term, because this name is more common outside Krobo and the Krobo use it in English writing and speaking as well. I use 'Krobo' for both singular and plural, rather than adding an 's' to indicate plural words. For a long time 'Adangme' or also 'Adangbe' rather than 'Dangme' was the accepted spelling for both the ethnonym and the language. However, 'Dangme' is the proper term in standard orthography.

Dangme is a tonal language, which means that relative pitch is an essential aspect of the syllables of a word. There are three tones, low, mid and high. However, since indicating tones by using accent signs is not standard practice in printed Dangme, I have not marked tones and nasalisation.

Interlude

The medicine men have an imposing temple, or *lati pso*, in every community of any size. The more elaborate ceremonies required to treat very sick patients can only be performed at this temple. These ceremonies involve not only the thaumaturge but a permanent group of vestal maidens who move sedately about the temple chambers in distinct costume and headdress.

(…) The supplicant entering the temple is first stripped of all his or her clothes. In every-day life the Nacirema avoids exposure of his body and its natural functions. Bathing and excretory acts are performed only in the secrecy of the household shrine, where they are ritualised as part of the body-rites. Psychological shock results from the fact that body secrecy is suddenly lost upon entry into the *lati pso*. A man, whose own wife has never seen him in an excretory act, suddenly finds himself naked and assisted by a vestal maiden while he performs his natural functions into a sacred vessel. This sort of ceremonial treatment is necessitated by the fact that the excreta are used by a diviner to ascertain the course and nature of the client's sickness. Female clients, on the other hand, find their naked bodies are subjected to the scrutiny, manipulation and prodding of the medicine men (Miner 1956: 505-506).

This is an excerpt from a brilliantly ironic article called *Body ritual among the Nacirema*, which appeared in *The American Anthropologist*. Readers with a sharp eye may have noticed that Nacirema is 'American' spelled backward, or may even have seen through the description that admittance to a hospital (*lati pso*) is behind it. By referring to a hospital as a temple, nurses as vestal maidens, the bathroom as the household shrine, medical doctors as a diviner and medicine men, and the aid of a nurse in using a bedpan ('sacred vessel') as a ceremonial treatment, Miner depicts the admittance to a hospital as exotic and renders the familiar strange (cf. Grimes 2000: 270). The effect is two-fold. First, it makes us realise we are just as exotic as anybody else in this world. Everybody thinks what they do is normal and what everybody else does is weird. Secondly, by applying the rhetoric of ritual to our own society we become aware of our tendency to label any activity of 'others', which we do not understand, as 'ritual' and 'sacred'. Miner's article reminds us that anthropological representations bear as much on the representer's world as on who or what is represented. This excerpt shows that we have to remain critical of our tendency to exoticise 'the other', while anthropology can hold up a mirror in which to look at ourselves. During the writing of this book, I tried to keep these messages in the back of my mind.

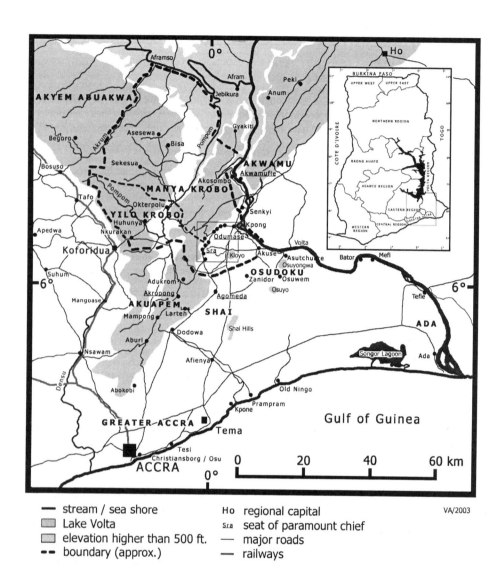

Map 1: The Krobo area

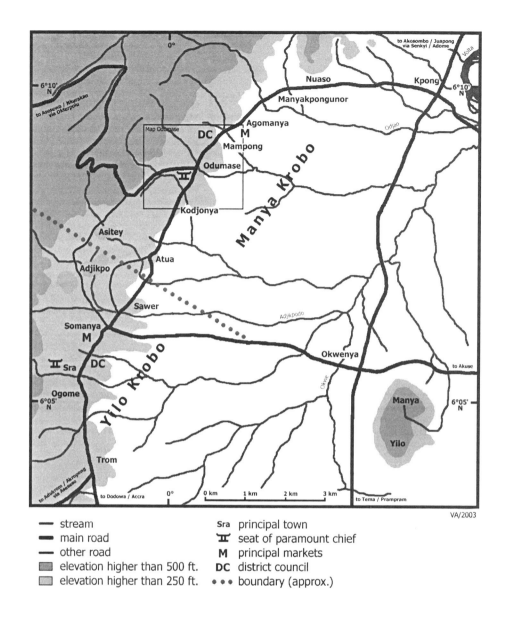

Map 2: The hometowns 'in the valley' (d*o*m)

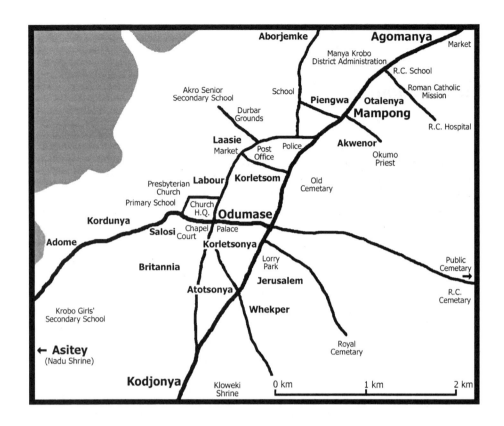

Map 3: Odumase and its environment

Introduction

In this anthropological and historical study I describe and analyse the performance, resilience and dynamics of girls' initiation rites among the Krobo and the
insights this process of resilience offers into local responses to global processes
of change. The Krobo are the largest group among the patrilineal Dangme
speaking people in what is today the Eastern Region of Ghana and they number
about a quarter of a million people.[1] Every year between March and May, their
initiation rites called *dipo* are performed for a few thousand Krobo girls between
two and eighteen years old. They are probably the best known and certainly the
most enduring girls' initiation rites in Ghana.[2] The *dipo* rites can be classified as
rites of passage, or life cycle rituals. Rites of passage encompass the rituals and
symbols that accompany the transition from one life stage to another, such as
birth, puberty, marriage and death. Female initiation rites are embedded in cultural notions about cleanliness, pollution, and what it means to be a woman in,
and to be part of, a particular society. Girls in many parts of Africa, the Middle
East and Southeast Asia undergo clitoridectomy, labial excision and/or vaginal
infibulation as part of the ritual procedures (Lutkehaus & Roscoe 1995: xiii).
These procedures have attracted the attention of Western feminists and are often
condemned as 'female genital mutilation'. Margaret Field, who served as official government anthropologist in the Gold Coast from 1938 to 1944, concluded

---

[1] Other Dangme-speaking peoples in the South of Ghana are the Shai, the Osudoku, and the coastal
Ningo and Ada people. Together with the culturally and linguistically related Ga speaking people, who
inhabit Accra (the current capital of Ghana) and its environs, the Dangme numbered 1,387,217 people
according to the '2000 Population and Housing Census' by the Ghana Statistical Service (GSS).
Ghana currently has a total population of around 19 million inhabitants, with a growth rate of 2.7%.
According to the census figures, the Ga-Dangme comprise 8.0% of the total population in Ghana,
which makes them the fourth largest ethnic group, after the matrilineal Akan (49.1%), among whom
the Asante (also written as 'Ashanti') and the Fanti stand out in size, the Mole-Dagbon (16.5%) who
live in the north, and the Ewe (12.7%). The Ewe are located further east of the Dangme. The Dangme
alone, however, include 4.3 %, which amounts to 748,014 people (GSS 2002c: table 4: 'Ethnic grouping of Ghanaians by birth by region'). The census does not make any further ethnic distinctions and
does not specify how someone's ethnicity was determined other than that the classification of ethnic
groups that was used was officially provided by the Bureau of Ghanaian languages. 'Birthplace' also
seems to have been a significant factor to determine ethnicity, which was normally the locality of
usual residence of the mother, or otherwise the actual town or village of physical birth (GSS 2002c: ix,
1, 5).
[2] Similar rites also called *dipo* are performed by neighbouring smaller groups of Dangme speaking
people, particularly the Shai and the Osudoku.

prematurely in her report on the Krobo *dipo* rites that clitoridectomy was part of the rites (Field 1941c).[3] Even though these practices are not part of them, the *dipo* rites are also highly debated in Ghana and criticised by Christians in particular.

Throughout my fieldwork, I had numerous conversations with Krobo people about the tensions felt between Christianity and *dipo*. I often encountered the views – held by Krobo Christians from different denominations – that *dipo* is not celebrated today as 'in the olden days', and that *dipo* has become 'more pagan' and is deemed 'outmoded' and 'immoral'. *Dipo* is seen as inimical to 'development' in a world where Christianity is linked with 'enlightenment' and 'modernity'. Christianity has become the dominant religion in Southern Ghana where most people now call themselves Christians. A few old Presbyterian families originating from the first Krobo converts have abstained from *dipo* since generations and strict Christian church members do not want to be associated with *dipo*. The rites represent 'paganism' and therefore local Christian churches do not allow their followers to participate in the rites. Nowadays, especially adherents of Pentecostal churches criticise the rites. At the same time, the Ghanaian government has developed initiatives for the enunciation of a national cultural policy, and therefore a national identity, advocating the protection of and respect for 'cultural traditions' such as *dipo*. In this way it seeks to propagate a national culture, of which the key symbol is the concept of *sankofa*. The *sankofa* bird turns its head and looks back in the direction of its origin, meaning 'return to the roots' or 'go back and take it'. The state therefore sees the *dipo* rites as part of a rich cultural heritage. Many Krobo people also apply the national rhetoric by saying that *dipo* 'is our culture'. In such a usage, 'culture' becomes 'thing-like', objectified, a rhetorical instrument for claims to identity (cf. Keesing 1994: 30). The negative attitudes towards the *dipo* rites originate from the time of the first encounters between the Krobo and Western missionaries and British colonial agents, who perceived the rites as an obstacle to 'civilisation' and 'development'. In their reports, they used *dipo* again and again to show the barbarous and pagan state of the Krobo in order to prove the necessity of conversion to Christianity and the need for the incorporation of Krobo society into the 'civilised' colonial nation state. The Christianisation of the Krobo already began in the late 1830s with the arrival of Protestant missionaries of the Evangelical Mis-

---

[3] Genital 'mutilation' was thought to be normal in female initiation (in Africa). It has been argued that female initiation rituals are more likely to be found among matrilocal than among patrilocal societies. Therefore ethno-psychiatric and psycho-analytical explanations such as Field's claimed that female initiation rites subjecting initiates to extreme pain in the form of a genital operation or extensive tattooing, exist in patrilocal societies where conditions of child rearing supposedly foster a conflict in sex identity (also e.g. Brown 1963). However, there is no evidence that clitoridectomy has ever been part of the *dipo* initiation rites. Field's theory that 'the excision of the clitoris removes the girl's tendency to wanton unchastity' sounds fairly inconceivable, as the *dipo* initiation rites rather provided and still form the approved entry into sexual relationships for Krobo girls.

2

sionary Society of Basel (*Evangelische Missionsgesellschaft zu Basel*), commonly known as the 'Basel Mission' (hereafter abbreviated as BM). When in 1891, Christian Kölle, one of the Basel missionaries, was stationed in Krobo area for the first time, he expressed the common missionary view about *dipo* as part of Heathendom in his quarterly report:

> Nowhere else [on the Gold Coast] did I find the people as much entangled in superstition, sorcery, fetishism and sin as here in this particular place. (...) That this custom [*dipo*], or better said this vice, holds our Krobo back the most from their acceptance of the gospel, speaks for itself. Yet, even though this custom is still so deeply enrooted, and this stronghold of the Devil stands as firm as Krobo Mountain itself, it will loosen itself, stagger, and has to fall, according to the promise of the Godly Word.[4] (Original in German, my translation)

The Basel missionaries thought it would be a matter of time until 'superstition' or 'Heathendom' would cease to exist. 'Pagan' practices such as the *dipo* initiation rites were perceived as a matter of 'the past' that should be left behind, while Christianity was part of the modern future.

With the missionary and colonial accounts a tradition of thinking about non-Western people as being 'stuck in tradition' has been established that still influences Western perceptions of the 'otherness' of African cultures until today, as images of Africans in, for example, advertisements for tourism show. The *dipo* rites seemingly possess all the earmarks of so-called 'African traditional culture', such as ancestral rites, traditional dances and songs, animal sacrifices, ritual taboos, loincloths and naked breasts. Nowadays, images of *dipo* girls in their finery printed on postcards and in tourist brochures easily create a romantic fantasy of exotic people practising mysterious rituals. This is exactly the effect that photographers Carol Beckwith and Angela Fisher generate in their recent two-volume book *African Ceremonies*, in which (beautiful) photographs of *dipo* girls occupy a prominent place. In their introduction Beckwith and Fisher explain their: '(...) desire to create a book that would be a visual exploration of the meaning and power of traditional rituals and ceremonies in Africa before they disappeared forever' (Beckwith & Fisher 1999: 11). Beckwith and Fisher create an impression of peoples in remote areas, some of whom, they claim, have never seen a book before, and of traditions in imminent danger of being lost, that are threatened by external (Western) forces.

However, since my first acquaintance with the Krobo in 1994 I have been intrigued by the great importance Krobo people attach to their initiation rites, notwithstanding all kinds of more or less elaborate criticisms, and by the fact that the great majority of their girls passes through these rites in practice. There-

---

[4] BMA, D-1,54; Station Odumase, C. Kölle, 25.9.1891, p. 167. See References for an explanation of the archival sources used.

fore it would be a mistake to join the chorus of those who claim that the 'traditional' practice of *dipo* is on the wane. Indeed, how is it possible that despite the fact that the process of Christianisation and 'modernisation' has been taking place for over 150 years, *dipo* is still annually celebrated nowadays? The very same Krobo people who go to school, church, work in an office, or sometimes have attended university, also – albeit secretly - visit shrines, and have *dipo* performed for their daughters. Obviously, the stereotype that the participation in ritual practices, such as the initiation of girls into womanhood, is something 'traditional' that will automatically disappear with modernisation in the form of capitalism, world religions and modern nationalism, does not coincide with actual developments in Africa today, as recent studies about witchcraft in Cameroon (Geschiere 1997) and masquerades in Senegal (De Jong 2001), for example, also demonstrate. Discourses on 'tradition' and 'culture' are intertwined with modern changes. Regular media and political attention show the preoccupation with 'traditional customs' in modern Ghana.

Both in the Christian and in the romanticised perspective, 'African culture', with its keywords 'traditional' and 'custom', is regarded as a matter of the past, as opposed to modernity. Depending on the perspective taken, this 'matter of the past' should be abandoned or it will be considered to be in danger of being lost. The examples I just mentioned indicate that *dipo* can only be discussed within a framework of particular discursive constructions of 'culture', and never on its own merits. Even though Krobo people themselves often talk about *dipo* as 'pagan' or as an 'outmoded custom' or 'culture', this does not withhold them from partaking in the rites. The point is to understand how Krobo people relate to *dipo* as Christians, and why they continue to perform these rites. In order to do so it is necessary to study the contemporary meaning of *dipo* as it is experienced in practice, and the way its performance has changed. Why have these rites remained important for both Krobo women and men ever since they were contested by Christianity and the colonial state? This study aims to unearth the multidimensional nature of the initiation rites and to assess what it tells us about the field of tension the Krobo experience between Krobo culture and identity, which is perceived as 'traditional' and 'authentic', and Christianity, which is associated with modernity and progress. How has the discursive field in which *dipo* is discussed and contested evolved?

Dipo in Ghana

The *dipo* rites are performed annually between March and June for different groups of girls that are attached to different 'traditional' priests' shrines. The rites are performed by female priests and expert old ladies. According to oral tradition, the rites have been introduced by the female deity Nana Klowεki. The time of the performance of *dipo* for an individual girl is not determined by her first menstruation. However, there is a relation with her fertility, as it is a strong taboo for a girl to become pregnant before the rites. In case she gets pregnant, she is regarded as unclean and will become a social outcast. After *dipo* a woman is allowed to enter into sexual relationships and have children. The rites last about ten days, and mostly take place in two subsequent weekends.

In the first weekend the girl is marked as a *dipo* girl by changing her dress and shaving part of her hair. In between the first and the second weekend the girls can only eat 'traditional' Krobo food and are not allowed to drink tap water. They learn how to dance in a very feminine way. The dances are accompanied with songs that are often proverbial in character and considered part of Krobo cultural heritage. The second weekend several rituals are performed to cleanse the girls and others that have to test whether they are pregnant. The different stages are marked by changing dresses and appearance. After the final rites, the girls 'come out', dressed up beautifully, and dance in public for everybody to see that they have entered womanhood now and they are considered as 'pure Krobo', both in a literal and figurative sense.

In the past, the initiation period lasted much longer, especially the period of confinement. Below I will quote Lako Sakite, an old 'traditional' priestess in her eighties, who told me about her *dipo* initiation, which probably took place in the (mid-) 1930s:

> My *dipo* was extraordinary. [First], as the only female among six siblings it was bound to be special. Secondly, my grandmother's daughters gave birth to only men and I happened to be the only woman among my grandmother's daughters' children. You will realise I occupied a position of some pride at home. (…) I was in *dipo* confinement for a year right in this room. We were forty who were in confinement, all [great-]grandchildren of King Sakite. I was the elder. (…) We engaged in dance performances called *nohuɛ*.[5] After learning the dance, we took a break to cook, we cleaned the house and its surroundings. We swept and cleaned the rooms of our grandmothers, and especially scrubbed the bed-stead. We did almost everything in the home. Some days we went to Kojonya, Agomanya and other places, with our hats and bangles on, to perform the *dipo* dance (Original in Dangme, August 5, 1998, Odumase).[6]

Lako Sakite's *dipo* was special, not only because she was the only female among brothers, but also because she was destined to become a priestess, and therefore

---

[5] *Nohuɛ* songs are melodious, sorrowful songs, usually sung by women who clap their hands or little bamboo sticks as accompaniment. The dancers dance with well controlled rhythmic movements. *Dipo* girls used to sing such songs during their initiation period when, while residing on Krobo Mountain in particular, they felt homesick for their lovers (Huber 1993: 213).

[6] It is hard to estimate when Lako Sakite was born and the exact year of her *dipo* performance. However, from some estimations I could make on the basis of what she told me and other information, it is likely that she was born around, but probably before, 1920, and her *dipo* performance was in the mid to late 1930s. Lako Sakite said she was the eldest among the other initiands, but she was probably not over twenty years old.

had to be in confinement for so long. According to other old women's stories, their initiation in the 1930s used to last for about three weeks, whereas before 1892, the rites could last from about three months until one year. Due to colonial and missionary interference, this has changed, as will be elucidated in the next chapters.

Although for many Krobo *dipo* eventually did not constitute an obstacle to conversion to Christianity, the ambivalence towards *dipo* is still part and parcel of contemporary local discourse. While some people initially told me that they, as Christians, did not approve of these 'pagan' rites, the reactions of Krobo people to my research were usually positive. Many Krobo people are familiar with the work of Hugo Huber, a Catholic missionary of the Divine Word Congregation (SVD) and anthropologist, who, between 1951-1957, conducted research on Krobo 'traditional social and religious life' (Huber 1993 [first published in 1963]). They expected me to be likewise interested in 'traditional culture' and therefore the topic of *dipo* seemed a logical choice. They thought I would want to study the 'authentic *dipo*', and therefore often directed my attention to the fact that, in their view, *dipo* has been adulterated. They complained that some of the 'traditional' priests 'only are into it for the money' they earn by performing 'unnecessary' rites. They felt that things have changed for the worse, because, in contrast with 'the olden days', girls are sometimes even initiated at the age of two. Therefore *dipo* has 'lost its function', they say, and the rites have become 'more pagan' and provoke immorality.

Krobo women are confronted with several stereotypes relating to supposed immorality, which is often associated with the *dipo* rites. They are considered beautiful and among non-Krobo groups in Ghana they are imagined to be sexually permissive. The high HIV prevalence in the area seems to support the characterisation.[7] Often promiscuous behaviour (and consequently a high rate of HIV infection) is linked with the *dipo* rites.[8] The fact that a girl is allowed to enter into sexual relationships after *dipo* goes against Christian morality, which situates such relationships firmly within matrimony. Therefore, many (Christian) Krobo see the rites as the catalyst of teenage pregnancies, prostitution and further 'immoral behaviour'. However, during the course of my research I found that, despite all the objections, in practice, it is inconceivable for the majority of the Krobo people that girls may not pass through the *dipo* rites of passage.

---

[7] As will be explained in greater detail in the next chapter, the creation of the Volta Lake for hydroelectricity in the 1960s, which exacerbated land shortage, has contributed to significant migrations into the urban sector within Ghana and other West African countries (such as Ivory Coast and Nigeria). The high migration rate shows a correspondence with high HIV prevalence rates, as many women working in prostitution in Abidjan returned to their hometowns with the HIV virus.

[8] See for example the booklet of Jamie Hampton (1991).

It is interesting that views on *dipo* are expressed largely through an idiom of conflict between tradition and Christianity. Different local publications about *dipo* also specifically deal with the topic of 'conflicting religions'. Titles of booklets such as *Dipo Custom and the Christian Faith*, written by a Krobo Presbyterian reverend (Teyegaga 1985) and *The Ongoing Encounter Between Christianity and African Culture: A Case Study of Girls' Nubility Rites of the Krobos*, written by a lecturer in the Department for the Study of Religions at the University of Ghana (Omenyo 2001), speak for themselves. Both writers feel that the *dipo* rites, at least in their current form, are incompatible with Christianity. The latter is of the opinion that the rites have changed in character:

> Emphasis of *dipo* has shifted from its sociological to its religious dimensions. Although the religious bias was strong from the outset, social change has undermined its social aspect considerably. (…) The conflict between Christianity and the *dipo* custom is more glaring because it is religion versus religion (Omenyo 2001: 43).

With 'religion versus religion', Omenyo opposes Christianity to '(*dipo* as part of) traditional religion', like the Basel missionaries opposed Christianity to 'Heathendom'. A number of unpublished BA and MA theses written at the University of Ghana likewise deal with *The Impact of Christianity on the Dipo custom of the Krobos* (Narh 1998), or use the idea that there is 'a conflict of Christianity with traditional religion' to analyse the rites in terms of being obsolete and pagan (Ofoe 1979; Tettey 1977). Elsewhere in Africa, rites of passage have been approached in the same way as a recent edited volume on *Rites of Passage in Contemporary Africa* (Cox 1998) shows. The contributors are mainly theologians and scholars of religious studies who mostly deal with cases from Southern Africa. They regard 'Christianity' and 'African Traditional Religions' as separate traditions that may or may not come into contact with each other and whereby conflicts can arise over the performance of 'traditional' rites of passage.

The Basel Mission Church's successor, the Presbyterian Church, formally still rejects participation in *dipo*, but realizes that their members have developed strategies 'to combine the two' in practice. The rejection of 'traditional religion', however, has gained a renewed vigour through the rising popularity of Pentecostal churches in Ghana in the last two or three decades. The Krobo case illustrates the dilemmas of Christians who must let their daughters pass through the traditional *dipo* rituals, including ancestor worship and sacrifice, which offend Christian principles and prevents them from being Christians in good standing. It also shows the struggle to renegotiate the meaning of *dipo* and accommodate Christianity when 'tradition' will not conveniently disappear.

Throughout this study the relationship between Christianity and *dipo*, which often was a topic of discussion with Krobo people during my research, will be a central topic. In order to fully understand the origin of the contemporary views on *dipo* that are often expressed in the idiom of conflict between

Christianity and tradition, we have to delve into history. How did colonial intervention and missionary influence change the perception of *dipo*? This study will investigate how and why the Basel Missionaries perceived *dipo* to be 'pagan' and therefore decided that it had to be abandoned upon conversion. It will also pay attention to the combined missionary and colonial action in 1892 that influenced Krobo society significantly until this very day.

Female initiation

The question of the importance of the *dipo* rites of course is linked to debates on female initiation as a rite of passage. As the *dipo* rites are often called 'puberty rites' and female initiation is a somewhat neglected theme in anthropology, we have to investigate how far they can help us to understand their meaning. It is relatively extraordinary that the Krobo initiation rites for girls are performed in groups, and take place every year, whereas Krobo male initiation is absent these days, apart from a rather unceremonious circumcision. As the Human Relations Area Files (HRAF) show, female initiation involving *groups* of initiands only occurs in around ten percent of societies compared to around thirty percent for male initiation (Schlegel & Barry III 1979: 201), while rites focused on female individuals take place in fifty to sixty percent of societies compared to just thirty to forty percent for males (Brown 1963: 845-847; Lutkehaus & Roscoe 1995: xiv; Young 1965: 14). In many cases female initiations are small-scale affairs, and this is one reason why they have received scarce ethnographic attention. Although the *dipo* rites are not small-scale affairs, the fact that they are often called 'puberty rites' (Ayi 1966; Narh 1998; Ofoe 1979; Tettey 1977) misrepresents the complexity and significance of *dipo*. All in all, until now no comprehensive study of *dipo* has been conducted.

Authors such as La Fontaine (1985: 14-15, 162-163) define puberty rites as individual transitions to (sexual) maturity usually concerning girls and closely linked to events in the life cycle, such as the development of the breasts or the onset of menstruation, whereas initiation is defined as collective, based on 'social' transitions. Such a distinction is often artificial and therefore *dipo* rites could be classified both as 'puberty rites' and as 'initiation'. However, although there is a relation with sexual maturity and nubility, I prefer to classify *dipo* as an 'initiation', as there is no link with the first menstruation, girls are initiated in groups and their ages may range from around two to about eighteen years. Moreover, the term 'puberty' or 'adolescence' is problematic, as it mainly is an etic term which foregoes indigenous classification (cf. Roscoe 1995: 230). Nevertheless, distinguishing between female puberty ceremonies and initiation is not as relevant as acknowledging that both types of rituals are but one in a series of life-cycle events that a society celebrates as part of the cultural process through which an individual achieves personhood. In addition, it is important to understand how the concern of female rites with the body and physiological functions is also 'a preoccupation with broader social concerns of morality, politics, and the regeneration of life' (Lutkehaus 1995: 19). The question how *dipo* relates to other life cycle rituals and Krobo ideas of personhood will be addressed in this study. The wider importance of *dipo* to Krobo society is a central concern throughout.

Although rites of passage and more specifically initiation, have been a classical topic in anthropology since Van Gennep's influential study (1960 [1909]), and developments in feminist theory have inspired a large amount of literature on women in Sub-Saharan Africa, relatively little has been written by anthropologists about female initiation (La Fontaine 1985: 162). One obvious reason may still be that often only female researchers can gain full access to their performance. Jean la Fontaine explains the neglect of female initiation by the relative scarcity of these rites, but both Pels (1999: 166) and Lutkehaus (1995: 4-5) point out that this is partly due to the exclusion of what are called individual 'puberty' rites, based on 'natural' changes, from initiation per se. As I pointed out above, female rites more often focus on the individual, and a related reason for the neglect could be that the 'puberty rites' are usually of a less elaborate nature than the 'initiation' ceremonies. There is a tendency to see female rites as pale imitations of male initiation rites, as Lutkehaus explains for Melanesia (Lutkehaus 1995: 5). A final important reason why little has been written on female initiation rites might be that they were considered as an obvious support for male dominance and (feminist) anthropologists were therefore presented with an ethical dilemma. This becomes particularly clear where female initiation involves female circumcision (Lutkehaus 1995: xiii). However, this should be criticised as an overemphasis on male dominance (cf. Pels 1999: 167). Many interpretations still seem to be inspired by the assumption that non-Western women must be more oppressed than European women (e.g. Hafkin & Bay 1976), and therefore these authors often tend to stress obedience to the future husband (e.g. Geisler 1997). But this is frequently not the primary relation of authority enacted in female initiation ritual (cf. Pels 1999: 168), as I will also show in this study.

Another reason why male domination in female initiation has been emphasised is because of functionalist analyses that assume that male domination contributes to the maintenance of social order and therefore to the maintenance of local structures of power that privilege men (La Fontaine 1985: 179; Lincoln 1991: 93). Lincoln, for example, argues that female initiation is mostly about creating productive workers, docile faithful wives and nurturant mothers. He regards society as a series of competing interest groups and states that:

> Women's initiations, as practised by 'society as a whole', have not always served women very well. More specifically, at those points where the collective interests of women *as women* diverge from those of 'society as a whole', these rituals not only

serve the latter interests, but make it very difficult for women to struggle against them (1991: 117).

The fact that it is assumed that women's rituals tend to be celebrated for individuals, whereas rituals for men are usually corporate affairs, is seen as having clear consequences. Whereas

> ... group solidarity, which serves men exceedingly well in the political arena, is ritually constructed for them in the course of their collective initiation, the corresponding rituals for women most often atomize the initiands, and provide them with neither bonds of solidarity nor experience in group mobilization that could be useful in later political action (1991: 117).

In such a view only the male perspective is taken into account and Lincoln does not consider differences *within* groups of women and men. Moreover, such a perspective also seems to imply that 'group solidarity' in a society where women are collectively initiated and where there are no initiation rites for men, would empower women or that women then would have a more than usual importance in their society. This seems too simplistic to me. This study tries to show that the transformations of the Krobo female initiates are not merely 'natural' nor 'individual'. They show a combination of both 'natural' and 'social' aspects, as initiation always concerns both aspects. Moreover, women as well as men attach importance to female rites.

Many studies about female initiation focus primarily on gender relations and/or ritual efficacy (e.g. Adjaye 1999; Beidelman 1997; Kratz 1994). The notion that there are other organising principles besides gender, such as age and class, and that a single initiatory rite or set of rites can 'do' several things at once is not new (e.g. Lutkehaus 1995: 3). Indeed, as Jansen points out:

> Life cycle rituals in particular are explicit moments in which cultures create, organise, transmit, and bestow meaning. They are central means by which identity is marked, not only in terms of gender but also with regard to age, class, religion, ethnicity, or whatever social identity aspect is relevant in a given context (1997: 25).

Initiation rites can be seen as paradigmatic of almost all ritual activity (cf. Jackson & Karp 1990: 24). Like Jansen, Lutkehaus (1995: 27) argues that 'embedded in the symbolism and practices of these rituals are clues to a society's fundamental beliefs, not only about gender but also about personhood, power, and life itself' (cf. Bowie 2000: 183-184).[9] Similarly, Piot has pointed out with re-

---

[9] Fiona Bowie (2000: 183-184) clearly states that the study of ritual in general is crucial in the understanding and interpretation of 'culture': "Rituals attempt to enact and deal with the most central and basic dilemmas of human existence. These can be named as continuity and stability, growth and fertility, mortality and immortality or transcendence. Rituals have the potential to transform people and situations, which lends them their power. The conveyance of a culture's most deeply held values from

gard to Kabre initiation rites in the north of Togo that initiation ceremonies do not only play a role in the differentiation of male and female gender, but also achieve many other things:

> In addition to addressing issues of gender identity, the initiations also vitally influence household and community-wide productive activities, establish relations with the ancestor and spirit world, play an important role in selecting the next generation of community diviners, and activate relations between homesteads, clans, and communities (1999: 79-80).

Piot also demonstrates the role of initiation ceremonies in national politics and in maintaining (inter)national relations, for those Kabre who have migrated into the diaspora return to the north at the time of these ceremonies to initiate their children. De Jong (1997) similarly argues for the Jola in Senegal that their men's initiation is a central event in the reproduction of community. I regard rites of passage, and *dipo* rites in particular, as pivotal occasions at which people gather and a sense of belonging is created. The ritual symbolization of identity is an effective procedure for making collective identities matter to individuals, affectively and cognitively (Jenkins 1997: 122-123), and such ceremonies are ways to embody locality as well as locate bodies in socially and spatially defined communities (Appadurai 1995: 205). *Dipo* initiation should be considered as an important event or stage in larger social processes and cycles fundamental to the life of both individuals and the whole society. It can therefore be approached as a large corpus of rituals that celebrate not only the life cycle of a woman, but also the life cycle of Krobo society in which it is embedded (cf. Lutkehaus 1995: 28), provided that the historicity of the rites is not ignored, as such rituals have changed both in form and meaning over time.

Although the debates on 'initiation' are necessary to answer part of the question of the importance of *dipo*, to understand why it is contested, yet also so resilient, and the way the discursive field in which it is discussed evolved, we also need to look at it from a historical perspective by delving into anthropological debates about 'tradition' and 'culture'.

---

one generation to another may be facilitated by means of ritual. Symbols and sacred objects within ritual can communicate ideological messages concerning the nature of the individual, society, and cosmos. Therefore the study of ritual can provide a key to an understanding and interpretation of culture".

Imagining culture

Even though in Africanist anthropology and historical scholarship the a-historical notion of unchanging and static traditions in Africa that have been celebrated 'since time immemorial' has been contested for the past three decades or so, this idea lingers on in popular imagination. Simplistic notions especially based on the distinction between 'modernity' and 'tradition' keep on haunting contemporary African studies. 'Tradition' became a popular term in anthropology at the beginning of the twentieth century, as anthropology's object of study was often described as the customs and traditions of non-western peoples. In this usage the concept of tradition was instrumental in creating an overall contrast between the West and the Rest, in 'othering', as Otto and Pederson (2000: 4) explain: "Whereas western societies were characterized by change and development, in short by history, non-western societies were seen as static and dominated by tradition. This image of stasis was often summarized by the term 'traditional societies'."

From this point of view, many ethnographers had the idea that their description of a particular initiation ceremony would be the last, as they thought that it would disappear and be absorbed by the Western world. In their structural-functionalist analyses it is assumed that initiation rites attribute to the maintenance of social order. In his cross-cultural study of initiation rites, Young (1965), for example, argued that the degree of solidarity of a given social system determines the degree to which status transitions within it will be dramatised. One effect of such a view is that it is believed that with the advancement of modernisation and the concomitant individualisation, rituals such as *dipo*, centred on the extended family and the worship of a traditional deity, will decline (also e.g. Adjaye 1999). Audrey Richards based her book *Chisungu* on an initiation rite in a Bemba village in present-day Zambia she studied in 1931, and thought she was lucky to observe the rites that were about to disappear (1956: 13). Sarpong, writing about the girls' 'nubility rites', as he calls them, for Asante girls in Ghana, writes that: "Individualism eats its way into the former corporate spirit of the Ashanti", and that: "the ignoring of the nubility rites is an inevitable result of the introduction of new forms from outside the society" (1977: 98). Some of these authors' visions proved wrong, as in many areas in Africa initiation rites for women are still practiced or even re-emphasised (e.g. De Jong 2001; Kratz 1994; Rasing 2001),[10] whereas in other cases initiation rites for girls have declined (e.g. Olupona 1991a).

---

[10] Thera Rasing's study (2001) shows that the Chisungu rites that were studied by Richards are still widely observed in Zambia.

Unlike neighbouring ethnic groups of the Krobo, such as the Ewe and the Akan, who have mostly stopped performing initiation rites for girls,[11] the Krobo *dipo* rites prove to be very enduring. What factors have contributed to the survival of *dipo*? My study here in particular supplements the work of the already mentioned Swiss anthropologist Hugo Huber (1958; 1988; 1993 [1963]), who published the first and only ethnography to date about 'the Krobo' and pays specific attention to *dipo*. His book cover says that: "[T]he ritual introduction to womanhood occupies up to the present time a privileged place in Krobo community life." In his valuable study of the 'traditional social and religious life' of the Krobo, Huber (1993: 291-296) gives a functionalist analysis of the factors contributing to the "consciousness of their tribal unity, of their common customs and traditional lore", and attributes social and cultural change to 'acculturation'. Although his descriptions of the *dipo* rites show a great sense of detail and accuracy, he places them in a timeless, a-historical framework. We do not know when and how often the author observed the rites, and how far he, as a man, and a Roman Catholic priest, had access to every part of the ceremony. Furthermore, he did not describe any 'real persons', and we do not get much of a sense of what the actors in the ceremony think or feel and who they are.

The idea that African societies are dominated by tradition was, amongst others, fed by the study of the role of ritual. Jean and John Comaroff (1993: xv-xvi) have pointed out that this "has long been a mark, in Western social thought, of all that separates rational modernity from the culture(s) of tradition". However, in the, relatively recent, upsurge of historical anthropology, ritual has been demystified and historicized and is studied as a vital element in the processes that make and remake social facts and collective identities everywhere in the world. This study aims to complement Huber's study by placing a greater emphasis on the history of *dipo*. It does not share the romantic functionalist view of a traditional a-historical harmonious social order. Rather, conflicting ideas and arguments about the rites should be taken into account, because rituals such as *dipo*, which are a conglomeration of symbolic statements about identity, gender and social relations, are central foci in processes of change.

Ever since the pioneering work of Hobsbawm and Ranger (1983), constructions of tradition that entail claims about identity and renderings of history have been a central topic of anthropological and historical research. Many critics have unmasked and unravelled the constructedness of 'tradition' in African societies and elsewhere. A body of literature has emerged since the early 1980s that regards 'tradition' as a specific construction at a specific time for specific purposes. These 'invention-of-tradition' studies have been exploring the ways in which modernist projects of colonial rule, missionary activity and postcolonial

---

[11] See e.g. Meyer (1999: 71) about the case of the Peki Ewe, and Middleton (1983) and Gilbert (1993: 8) about the case of the Akuapem people.

state formation imposed certain 'traditions' on African societies (cf. Van Dijk & Van Rouveroy van Nieuwaal 1999: 1). In this way tradition has been studied increasingly as a contemporary interpretation of the past, rather than as something passively received, as a result therefore also emphasizing the creative and dynamic aspects of tradition and cultural identity (Borsboom & Otto 1997: 1-2). However, more recently the study of the recent emergence and 'invention' of tradition has been criticised for laying too much emphasis on 'creation' and examining present constructions of the past. The cultural continuity with the past which is emphasized by ethnic ideologists and national historians is not all make-believe and manipulative invention of the past. Ranger (1993) now prefers to speak of 'imagined' traditions, drawing on Benedict Anderson's concept of 'imagined communities' (1983) to indicate that the term 'invention', which he originally employed, exaggerates 'the mechanical, authorial aspects of the creation as well as the fictionality and rigidity of the end-product' (Lentz & Nugent 2000: 6), and that there was a desire in local society to share in the construction of new models of identity.

However, the Krobo objectify ritual practices and performances as 'traditions' or 'culture'. In their view Christianity is the modern religion and *dipo* is a matter of 'traditional religion' and 'the past'. This study tries to show why this view is so powerful and resilient. I will argue that the fixation of tradition and imagining culture as shown in particular in the *dipo* rites is part of modernity and a way of dealing with modernity. Where modernity emphasises change and rationally controlled development, tradition is its twin concept that denotes continuity with the past. I go along with De Jong (2001: 6), who reasons that casting ritual performances as 'traditional culture' paradoxically "corroborates the modernity of these performances since the conceptualization of practices *as traditions* is part of a modernist discourse, a discourse that emphasizes a break between past and present, a rupture between a world lost and a future to win".

This study will show that the conceptualisation of practices as traditions has to be understood within a specific history of encounters with colonial intervention, missionary influence, and of modern nationalism. In other words, initiation is not a remnant of the African past. The *dipo* rites are traditional in the sense that they refer to beliefs and customs which are handed down from one generation to the other. But it is important to point out that: 'the concept of tradition itself has a history; its popularity is, in fact, a product of modernity' (Otto & Pederson 2000: 3).

The idea that traditions are in imminent danger of being lost, that they are threatened by external (Western) forces, not only illustrates the view of the unchanging and static nature of traditions, but also the classic view of the world as a conglomerate of separate and internally homogeneous cultures, each with its own essence, so that intercultural contacts are understood in terms of loss of authenticity (Geschiere & Meyer 1999: 604). However, in recent years considerable attention has been given to processes of globalisation and the paradox that its homogenizing tendencies seem to imply a continued or even intensified heterogeneity in cultural terms (see e.g. Appadurai 1990; 1995; De Jong 2001; Friedman 1990; Geschiere 1997; Staring, Van der Land, & Tak 1997). There is much empirical evidence that people's awareness of being involved in open-ended global flows triggers a search for fixed orientation points and action frames, as well as determined efforts to affirm old and construct new boundaries (Geschiere & Meyer 1999: 602). Encounters on a global level engage markers of difference such as race, ethnicity, gender, class and religion (Grosz-Ngate & Kokole 1997: 8).

It is this debate on globalisation and culture,[12] which admonishes us that the premise of 'the primitive isolate', despite the long-standing debate on ethnicity in Africa,[13] and the considerable amount of research and writing in recent years that has emphasised the interplay of culture and history and the permeability of boundaries, still inspires views of globalisation in terms of 'Americanisation' or 'Westernisation' and hence as threatening to erase cultural diversity. The problem with such views is that they seem to be intrinsically related to a vision of authentic cultures that have to be protected against the onslaught of cultural imperialism. I agree with Geschiere and Meyer (1999: 604) that if we want to take the challenge of globalisation seriously, we have to surpass such notions – notably by showing how these 'endangered' cultures themselves emerged historically from the colonial enterprise and the ensuing world order. Not only

---

[12] The term 'globalisation' usually refers to the rapidly growing economic interdependence of different parts of the world and the spread of new techniques on a global scale. The idea that we live in 'a global village' has become widespread. This idea often coincides with the idea that cultures are becoming more alike and that a process of homogenisation is taking place. This has been called the 'Coca-Colaization' of the world. However, globalisation does not automatically mean westernisation. Within anthropology more attention has been paid to the cultural aspects of processes of globalisation since the 1980s. It is emphasised that globalisation rather goes together with the emergence of new differences and identities. Hannerz (1992), for example, does not speak of a global village but of a 'global ecumene'. Paradoxically, processes of globalisation seem to be connected with marking new boundaries. The idea that these processes can only correspond with processes of westernisation is also contested: modern 'cultural flows' also take place in other, non-Western, parts of the world.

[13] For the most part, models of ethnicity fall into the primordialist, the instrumental and the constructivist 'camps'. Primordial views would be objectivist theories of ethnicity that assert that ultimately there is some real, tangible foundation to ethnic identification (Barnard & Spencer 1996: 190). It assumes that groups are geographically and internally bound, and based on kinship. Geertz (1973: 259) argues that by primordial attachments are meant the 'givens', or the assumed 'givens', of social existence such as blood (kin connection), language, custom and so on which are seen to have an ineffable coerciveness in and of themselves. Instrumental theories see ethnicity as declining in significance. It is something of the pre-industrial social order. They therefore see ethnicity as essentially competitive, political, situational contingent and based on self-interest, collective and otherwise (Gorgendière 1996: 2). Constructivist theories view ethnicity as a continuing ascription which classifies a person in terms of their most general and inclusive identity, presumptively determined by origin and background (Barth 1969). The latter approach emphasizes the situational and contextual character of ethnicity, group boundaries and identity.

'modern' processes of globalisation, but also historical transformations should be taken into account.

The history of the Krobo in the last 150 years reveals that, despite repeated attempts to abolish *dipo*, the *dipo* rites show a remarkable tenacity and resilience. The way Krobo people perform and talk about the rites reflects changes and reveals sometimes competing views, but at the same time shows feelings of cultural continuity and of continuous identities. The performance of *dipo* today bears witness to the radical economic, political and religious transformation of Southern Ghana since the mid-nineteenth century. It reflects, amongst others, (Protestant) missionary activity, colonial rule, the introduction of a new political geography of hierarchically ordered chiefdoms, and the emergence of an educated elite. The history of these changes, as Lentz (1998) describes for the Dagara in a detailed and thorough study of the construction of ethnicity in North-western Ghana, can be seen as a narrative of incorporation of a local agricultural society into larger economic and political networks. British, and later Ghanaian, administration, cash crop production, migration, Christianity and school education introduced new patterns of consumption, cultural and political practices, norms and expectations which the Dagara in the north as well as the Krobo in the south nowadays share with many other people in Ghana and elsewhere. Along with this process of modernisation and homogenisation, however, images of the Krobo as a bounded ethnic group, with a unique traditional culture deeply rooted in history, have been created (cf. Lentz 1997: 35). Thomas claims (for the Pacific islands) that colonial encounters were more consequential in this process than pre-colonial contacts: 'objectification and cultural juxtaposition did occur quite independently of colonialism, but their development over the colonial and postcolonial periods involved qualitative changes and distinct arenas of differentiation' (1992: 218). 'Krobo custom' obtained a particular meaning in the encounter with Europeans, and 'tradition', 'culture' and 'tribe' become powerful resources in modern contexts by, for instance, serving the creation of a political community claiming larger returns from government (cf. Lentz 1997: 35), or by helping to attract (Western) tourists.

This study in particular links up with the idea that it is important to trace connections between the past and the present. In order to be able to understand the resilience and dynamics of the *dipo* rites, it is essential to study how they relate to social-historical and cultural developments, how *dipo* has emerged as a marker of Krobo identity from a history of encounters, and why it was this particular practice that served this purpose very well. Whatever the Krobo are, including the very name 'Krobo', as Piot (1999: 21) argues for the Kabre of North-Togo, has been fashioned within the encounter between Europe and Africa, as well as within the encounter between Krobo and various non-European others. It is important to acknowledge this process of trans-culturation (Thomas 1991), and to unravel the history and politics of the making and unmaking of boundaries, localities and 'cultures', which are shaped within a wider social field. Although the main focus of this study is the situation as I experienced it during my fieldwork in the course of fourteen months in Odumase in two periods between 1998 and 2000, the Krobo contacts with the missionaries of the Basel Mission, between 1837 and 1917, and British colonial administration, mainly between 1892 and the 1930s, will also be examined. They are decisive periods in which the preconditions evolved for current developments.

Researching dipo

In this study one objective is to continue to undermine the notion of homogeneous and bounded cultural wholes by shifting the spotlight to the historical dynamics and cultural creativity, which have characterised the Krobo over time. My aim is to achieve this goal by focussing on the neglected theme of female initiation. The point I want to illustrate is that debate and contestation over the current meaning and practical implications of cultural norms coexist with the pervasive conviction in Krobo society that the Krobo have 'a unique culture', consisting of specific institutions, rules and beliefs, which are common to all members of the community and which need to be 'preserved'. I argue that questions of ritual pollution and communal identity prove to remain very central in a globalising world, and that the resilience of *dipo* and the nature of its contestation and transformation can only be understood by using a parallel ethnographic and historical research focus.

This study will not only examine how girls in the South-east of Ghana become Krobo women through initiation, but also investigate the importance and resilience of the *dipo* initiation rites as a marker of Krobo identity. I will investigate the multidimensional and changing nature of the rites and explore how *dipo* can be so enduring and at the same time articulate different meanings in different periods in history and how conceptions of modernity, tradition and ethnic and gender identity relate to initiation. These themes are set historically in order to highlight their interconnections and the broader settings and processes of their cultural production. In this way I will try to follow the point made by Sahlins (1993: 1) and others that: "an ethnography with time and transformation built into it is a distinct way of knowing the anthropological object, with a possibility of changing the way culture is thought".[14]

Talking about 'the Krobo', there is the danger of essentialism and the suggestion of homogeneity, coherence and timelessness (cf. Abu-Lughod 1991: 152). Of course there is a wide diversity among people according to, amongst others, age, gender, religion and education. First of all, it should be kept in mind

---

[14] See also Jean and John Comaroff (1992), Meyer (1999) and Pels (1999) for examples of historical ethnographies.

that an ethnographic representation is always a 'partial truth' (Clifford & Marcus 1986: 6). Secondly, although a certain degree of generalising seems hardly avoidable, I try to focus on particular individuals and families in time and place, and make clear that there are differences within, for example, by focusing on contestation and history. 'The Krobo' consist of different individuals, clans and groups that have joined together as political and social units at some point in history. Although there are differences within, vis-à-vis other groups in Ghana, Krobo people do consider themselves, and are regarded by others, as being culturally distinctive, and it is this notion of shared culture that will be studied here. I will pay attention to the relationship between Christianity and *dipo*, which often was a topic of discussion with Krobo people during my research. In order to fully understand the origin of the contemporary views on *dipo* that are often expressed in the idiom of conflict between Christianity and tradition, we have to trace the activities of the first Pietist missionaries from Basel among the Krobo, their interaction with 'traditional religion' and their work among Krobo women. Particular questions in relation to history need to be asked. Why was *dipo* a specific focus of attention for the BM? Which role did the Basel missionaries play in identifying Krobo 'tradition' and stigmatising Krobo women? The eventual success of the BM cannot be understood without paying attention to some of the key Krobo players and their collaboration with the British colonial administration. This study investigates how the combined action of colonial administration, the Basel missionaries and their first converts led to a ban on *dipo*, causing it to go underground and resurface only fifty years later in a changed and abridged form.

The advent and development of Christianity among the Krobo has been shaped by the interaction with 'traditional religion'. I want to stress that 'traditional religion' cannot be studied 'as if Christianity was never there', rather, as outlined above, its compartmentalisation has largely been the outcome of the influence of Christianity. For lack of a more adequate term, I use the term 'traditional' to designate both the pre-Christian religion before the introduction of Christianity to the Krobo as well as the non-Christian religion existing side by side to Christianity once the latter was introduced. I consider an alternative term such as 'indigenous religion' as equally inadequate, because it implies the same hierarchy between 'world religions' such as Christianity and Islam and African religious expressions. As Meyer points out (1995a: 3), the real problem is not the term as such, but rather the politics of its use. In this study I will rather try to investigate the hegemonic relations that are expressed through this use. I want to know what comprises traditional religion today and what the place of *dipo* is in traditional religion.

I will address the question how *dipo* relates to other life cycle rituals and Krobo ideas of personhood, as *dipo* cannot be understood in isolation. How is *dipo* connected with other life cycle rituals? How do competing notions of the person and the world come to the fore in the performance of life cycle rituals?

This study aims to show that female initiation is not on the wane among the Krobo, nor is it a remnant of the African past or an exotic ceremony. I will describe how *dipo* is celebrated today by making clear that Krobo people perform these rites with pride, while the performances are characterized by joy and fun rather than by 'oppression'. At the same time, the role *dipo* plays in the reproduction of a sense of belonging, of a Krobo community, will be studied.

Finally, I want to know how Krobo people as Christians relate to cultural practices, and *dipo* in particular. How to relate to 'culture' as Christians, is a hotly debated issue in Ghana. What do the various discourses about culture look like? In what sense do they resonate the 19th century Protestant missionaries' point of view? How are debates over culture and cultural practices related to national politics of culture? How do different people strategically make use of different concepts of culture in order to either reconcile their Christian identity with participation in *dipo*, or at times step away from *dipo*?

In anthropology, the notion of culture as a bounded universe of shared ideas and customs, once taken for granted, has been under siege for some time now. Keesing (1994: 309) wants to avoid using 'culture' to avoid reification and prefers the adjective 'cultural' (cf. Appadurai 1996: 12). Abu-Lughod (1991: 148) proposes the use of 'discourse' for a similar effect and to write *'against* culture'. Instead of a self-contained, homogeneous and largely a-historical framing of the cultural unit, authors suggest to see cultural situations as always in flux (Marcus & Fischer 1986: 78) and as 'liquid', i.e., open and fluid (Fabian 1991: Ch. 10). Feminist theory in particular has problematized cleavages of gender and social inequality rather than assuming collectivity and uniformity of culturally defined beliefs, norms and experiences (e.g. Moore 1994). However, everyday contemporary talk have been heavily influenced by the anthropological concept of culture, and the essentialist, reified conception of culture, having passed into everyday Western discourse, has been adopted by non-Western people as well. 'A culture' as thing-like provides an ideal rhetorical instrument for claims to identity, phrased in opposition to modernity, Westernisation, or neo-colonialism (Keesing 1994: 30). It becomes a thing outside the individual to be contemplated, discussed and reflexively modified (Borsboom & Otto 1997: 2). In this study it is precisely the way 'culture' is debated and this popular use of 'culture' through which claims regarding specific identities are made that I will try to investigate, i.e., the politics of culture, whereby 'politics' does not refer to the domain of politics as defined by the state, but to politics at large (cf. De Jong 2001: 3).

One way of avoiding the impression of linking the notion of culture to a specific locality or regarding it as homogeneous and bounded, is to focus on connections and interconnections. As I mentioned earlier, I tried to apply this approach especially by tracing connections between the past and the present (cf. Abu-Lughod 1991: 148-149). In order to collect the material for this study I conducted fieldwork among the Krobo in Ghana. In addition I carried out historical research in the archives of the BM in Basel (Switzerland), of the Ghana National Archives (GNA) in Accra, and of the Public Records Office (PRO) in London. The historical documents from these archives make up the basis of chapters three and four of this book.

The historical documents of the BM are very extensive. In Basel, I concentrated on travel reports that are available from 1835, as well as reports collected under the section 'Odumase' from the Krobo area. The latter are available from 1857, the time of the founding of a permanent mission post in Odumase-Krobo, until 1917, when the Basel missionaries were forced to leave the Gold Coast as a result of World War I (see next chapter). The historical documents considered are, first of all, unpublished documents for the mission board that are (hand) written by German missionaries and Ga and Krobo mission workers. These documents that refer to the Krobo have hardly been the subject of academic research before, partly because they are hard to access for non-German speakers who at the same time have to decipher and transcribe the old Gothic-style handwriting. (Photocopying of these texts is not allowed). Other documents that were studied are German-written published periodicals for the supporters of the mission in local congregations in Switzerland and Germany (*Der evangelische Heidenbote*, the *Evangelisches Missionsmagazin*, and *Deutsches Kollekteblatt*), and I went through the yearbooks (*Jahresberichte*) from 1857 until 1914. All quotes from the German sources presented in this book have been translated by me. Some letters and reports by native mission workers were written in English. Whenever I quote statements from letters and reports that were originally drawn up in German I will indicate this.

In Ghana, I read through the 'ADM-files' (administration files) in the GNA, records from the former colonial administration with regard to the Krobo (with a particular focus on GNA ADM 11/1/1115 and 1116: 'Manya Krobo Native Affairs' and 'Yilo Krobo Native Affairs'). These records mainly provided information from an administrative point of view. The files also contained some letters, appeals and memoranda from Krobo about matters of local interest. To supplement the information from the Ghanaian records, I spent a short time in London to consult the Public Records Office (PRO), which used to be the Colonial Office (CO). There I adopted a more pragmatic approach and concentrated on particular events and years, and followed clues to references I had found before in Basel and Accra. The social historian Veit Arlt, who is working on Krobo history, also made many valuable documents available to me.[15]

Each of the sources has its own biases. In making use of them one has to take into account that they were produced for different audiences and were to serve different aims (Arlt 1995; Meyer 1997: 332). Despite the fact that the

---

[15] The sources are listed in full in the text.

sources from the BMA for instance, reflect the missionary bias and point of view, they need not be rejected as mere misrepresentations of pre-missionary culture and Krobo ideas and practices. By reading them 'from below' and against the background of available oral history, it is also possible to grasp an indication of the Krobo point of view (cf. Meyer 1997).

As a cultural anthropologist I conducted long-term and intensive field-work in Ghana during two periods of respectively twelve and two months in 1998/99 (from June 1998 until June 1999) and 2000 (mid-May until mid-July). I already was familiar with the Krobo after staying in Odumase for six months as part of my MA research in 1994.[16] Between 1998 and 2000 I lived with a Krobo family in the centre of Krobo-Odumase to learn about life in Krobo society through participant observation (see below and the next chapter for more details about the composition of 'my' family). The rural town of Odumase, some 80 kilometres north of Accra, is the centre of a conglomeration of towns and vil-lages, and has about 14,000 inhabitants. The total conglomeration has almost 45,000 people (see next chapter for specifications). For a number of reasons I considered Krobo-Odumase to be a suitable location for an investigation of the interaction of 'traditional' practices with Christianity. Odumase is considered to be the capital and the ritual focal point of both the Manya Krobo District and the Manya Krobo Traditional State (the Krobo are politically divided into the Yilo and the Manya Krobo, see next chapter). The seat of the local government in the form of the District Assembly is located in Agomanya, an adjacent town that is part of the conglomeration. Odumase is the seat of the traditional rulers in the per-sons of the Manya Krobo paramount Chief (*kono̱*) and Queen Mother (*manyɛ*) and their elders. Odumase is also the place where Christianity had a profound and lasting impact, as the missionaries of the BM settled here and established the first mission post on Krobo land in 1857 on the land they acquired from *kono̱* Odonkor Azu. As will become clear in the following chapters, the history of the Mission and the development of a Krobo paramountcy are inextricably intertwined. Today, the successor of the BM Church, the Presbyterian Church, is still the largest and most influential church in Odumase, maybe even in the whole of Krobo. At the same time, the conglomeration of Odumase and its adjacent towns is considered the seat of 'custom', where all the important non-Christian shrines are located. Krobo people from the villages and all over the country come down here when-ever it is time for their daughters to pass through the *dipo* rites.

Although I lived in Odumase, I also frequently visited adjacent towns such as Atua, Asite, Kodjonya, Agomanya, Manya Kponguno̱ and Nuaso, and towns under Krobo jurisdiction that were more distant such as Akuse, Kpong, Akosombo and Asesewa. I also regularly visited the Yilo Krobo town of Soma-

---

[16] Although in 1994 I intended to focus my MA research on women's clothing and adornment as ex-pressed amongst others during the *dipo* rites, I already became fascinated by the central place of these rites in Krobo society.

nya, and its adjacent towns such as Sra, Ogome and Sawer. A few times I travelled to small farming villages such as Otrokpɛ, Sekesua and Tortibu. Usually I was accompanied by a friend or assistant to introduce me to new people in the appropriate way and prevent me from making any mistake. Doing participant observation means gradually learning the 'rules' of a society first, learning how to behave, dress, eat, drink, and speak etcetera. A very basic thing one has to learn is to greet, as paying visits to greet people is seen as very important. Greetings in Krobo can be very extensive. You always start with asking about someone's 'house' (extended family) and the immediate family, before asking about the person's own well-being. In the greetings the community comes before the individual. If you enter somebody's house for the first time or after returning from a long journey, you have to sit down and are welcomed by shaking hands. Then you will be offered a glass of water, before the reason for your visit is formally asked through the question 'what is your mission?' After returning from a trip you are expected to bring along something, usually bread. Every time I returned from Accra I was asked by the people in my house: 'Did you bring bread for me?' Although I did spend a part of my research budget on bread and other presents, I also learned to give standardised answers to the standardised questions, such as: 'Next time!', or 'Tomorrow!'. Especially in the beginning I had to get used to certain standard questions because I experienced them as social control, such as: 'Where are you going?' (*Jije o yaa?*), and after returning: 'Where did you go?' After a while, I simply answered with the same routine: 'Oh, I go come!' (literally translated from: *I yaa me ba*), or: 'I have to see to something somewhere', which seemed perfectly satisfying to most people.

Apart from participating in daily life, which provided me with much useful information through informal discussions, I attended and observed many *dipo* performances. One full *dipo* performance for one group of girls usually goes on for about ten days. I witnessed one full *dipo* performance before at the Okumo priest's home in Mampong, one of the quarters of Odumase, in 1994. I observed and participated in dozens of (parts of) *dipo* performances at more than ten different places between March and June in 1999. Sometimes I just watched, sometimes I donated something to show my appreciation of the dancing of a particular *dipo* girl. I paid (part of) the expenses for a few children passing through *dipo* that were members of 'my' family. At times I took part in the dancing. I was always allowed to take photographs, and many times even asked to do so. Usually I showed my appreciation by distributing copies of photographs I took. In one particular *dipo* priestess' house, I was allowed to film the rites with my video-camera. During the ceremonies and afterwards, I asked people questions about what was happening and why. I also wanted to get background information about the girls who went through the rites, and about their families. However, my participation was not such that I went through the rites myself. I felt I would have attracted too much attention as a grown-up and white woman. And it rather would have been difficult to ask questions, as an initiand is expected to compose and humble herself. My main aim was not to study the efficacy of the rituals and therefore to feel how it is to go through the rites, but rather to study who participated, in what way, and why, what *dipo* looked like, and what were discussions concerning *dipo* and 'traditional culture' about.

During fieldwork, I further spoke with members of Christian churches, as well as with representatives of Krobo 'traditional' religion, of local and 'traditional' governments, and women and girls participating in *dipo*. I attended church services, 'traditional' shrines and celebrations, and a great number of rites of passage such as naming ceremonies, weddings and funerals. I was always allowed to take pictures and could often film, for example at 'traditional' religious celebrations. I learned a great deal about Odumase by just living there, by visiting schools and the market, and by being involved in informal conversations on the roadside, on the bus, or in people's house. I tape recorded most of the formal interviews. Although I gained a basic understanding of local Dangme language and was able to have some small talk, whenever an interview was conducted in Dangme, I was assisted by a Dangme speaking interpreter. Dangme was a difficult language for me to learn, because it is a tonal language and not many written learning tools are available. Fortunately, many people in Odumase are rather fluent in English. The recordings in Dangme language were transcribed and then translated into English by native speaker Padi Odonkor, who was then an MPhil-student in the Department of Linguistics of the University of Ghana specialising in Dangme. Some of the recordings were transcribed and translated by a primary school teacher, Juliana Sakite-Baidoo.

I spoke with so many people that it is impossible to mention them all by name. However, at this stage I will nonetheless introduce a number of people who played a key role in my research, as some of their names are frequently mentioned in the following chapters. The above-mentioned Juliana (Julie) Sakite-Baidoo was not only my guide during much of the research, she also became my friend and elder 'sister'. She is a teacher, at the time of my research in her late thirties and an active member of the Presbyterian Church. As the daughter of the senior *dipo* and 'stool' priestess in Odumase and member of the royal paramount family, she was able to introduce and accompany me to many people in the 'proper way', such as the *kono* and other chiefs and queen mothers, traditional senior priests and *dipo* priestesses. You need to know, for example, that, when visiting such people, it is customary to bring a drink to pour libation with to communicate with the ancestors. Normally in recounting history or talking about customs and installations, the names of ancestors are mentioned and they are invited with reverence. Julie was a very good interpreter, a good listener and an enthusiastic narrator, who also provided me with valuable information about various aspects of Krobo ways of life. One traditional priest from Plau division in Yilo, the late Tetteh Gaga, an educated man in his sixties, was particularly helpful in explaining about the performance of traditional practices and accompanying me to several functions. Although I talked to several *dipo* priests and priestesses, Julie's mother, priestess Lako Sakite, who I quoted earlier in this chapter, was my most valuable source of information about the history, performance and meaning of the *dipo* rites.

Fig. 1: Maa Lako and Marijke, Odumase, July 2000

Lako Sakite is the 'stool' priestess (*sɛ wǫyo*) for the *konǫ* of the (Manya) Krobo and the senior of all the priestesses serving the (*dipo*) deity Nana Klowɛki.[17] At the time of my research she must have been well over eighty years old. She also performs *dipo* every year and she said she would allow me 'to observe the rites from head to toe'. I call her 'maa' ('mother') Lako, as she is my Krobo (grand)mother, and she calls me '*I bi*' ('my child'). I always enjoyed just sitting in her little compound, watching her when she grinds tobacco on a large stone, mixing it with ashes out of plantain leaves and some strong Chinese 'rub'. Then she tears plastic bags into small pieces and makes little wraps with the tobacco that she sells. Occasionally she sniffs some of the stuff herself, which brings tears to her eyes, but then she looks very satisfied. At times I watched her thread beads, for which she wears the large pair of glasses her

---

[17] I will explain the meaning of a chiefly 'stool' in the next chapter.

daughter Julie once bought for her. She borrows her precious beads to people for a little fee. The whole day people walk in and out her door to the little inner courtyard. Some come to buy tobacco, or petty things like lemons and herbs. Others come to her for advice, since she is the senior woman in her family and the stool priestess. She never gets tired of talking. According to her daughter, this is because of her age. Moreover, she is always in the house, since she broke her hip in 1995 or so, and can hardly walk. The first time I met her was in 1994, when she still was a tall, strong looking woman. Now she looks much feebler and older. However, the look in her eyes shows that she is still the same intelligent and wise woman she has always been, even though she never attended school in her life. 'My head is my archive,' she once said to me.

Since I regard my research among the people in Odumase as a matter of interaction, in which not only my sex, age and skin colour influenced the research, but also the people I dealt with have influenced it and at times manipulated its outcome, it is important to make my own position clear in Krobo society during the research. As a person in Ghanaian society is a person through his/her relationship to others, especially through kinship relations, I also had to be made part of the family I lived with in Krobo-Odumase. During my initial stay in Krobo in 1994, I had at first unceremoniously been given the usual 'day-name': Adjo, for I was 'born on Monday', combined with 'Dede', indicating that I was the first daughter of my mother, thus 'Adjo Dede'. At the end of that stay I had been given a new name: 'manyɛ Okoryo Dale' and by this occasion was more or less adopted into the Sakite family. The title manyɛ was an honorary title given to me during an installation ceremony to install me as a 'deputy' or 'lesser' queen mother (manyɛ wayoo). A queen mother is the English title generally used in Ghana to designate a female 'traditional' leader. I was told that the name 'Okoryo Dale' refers to a song that goes: 'Coming from the sea. Dale was leading (them)' (Dale Okoyo sɛ' Wam).[18] The name 'Dale' or 'Dede' refers to the basic rule in Ga-Dangme societies that the name is determined by the order of birth. With this name everybody knew I am my (biological) mother's first born daughter. However, some names are specific for certain clans. While 'Dede' was general, people usually immediately knew that I was from Odumase 'proper' because of the name 'Dale'. My Krobo family in Odumase is part of the (very extended) royal family that occupies the paramount stool. The manyɛ title to me symbolised the reciprocal relationship I had involved myself in, and I tried to fulfil the expectations by raising some funds for the building of a kindergarten.

---

[18] Padi Odonkor further explained to me: " 'Oko' / Loko' / Noko'-- variants. There is what our people call 'wo no' loko', 'star of the sea'. 'Wo no' loko' served as a compass point for sea-farers / farmers. It was therefore like a guiding spirit at the sea. It is so bright but no one ever got to it. All sea-farers returning home to land had it as their guide and so their leader in the fore-front is called the 'wo no' loko'/ oko'/ noko'. Coming from the sea, 'Dale Okoyo sɛ' Wam'. The morpheme '-yo' is a gender marker. If you were a man Okoyo becomes Okono".

When I returned almost four years later in 1998, I was anxious about what more people would expect from me. Would this title hinder me in any way to do research? It turned out to be an advantage most of the time. I did not need to tell anybody I was a *manyε*. There always seemed to be somebody to say to another person: 'Hey, she is a *manyε* you know.' Or: 'Don't you know *manyε* Dale?' *Manyε* Dale on her moped became widely known and everywhere I went, people called out my name. My white skin made it impossible for me to go anywhere unnoticed anyway. So the 'name' *blεfono* (white 'man') was also shouted out loud everywhere I went, especially by little children.

Doing research is an interactive process indeed. Apart from being white in Africa, one's sex certainly influences fieldwork relationships. After the question where I was from, one of the first questions men, young or old, would ask me, was whether I had a husband. My status as an unmarried, childless woman, was hard to understand for many. As a single woman, who was about 27 or 28 years old at the time, I obviously was very attractive in the eyes of many men. People observed me just as intensively as I observed them. I was told I was beautiful by both men and women, because of my white skin, my broad hips and curved legs. Men even told me I looked 'appetising', and sometimes made sexual jokes about me. Not only was I in a stage of my life that people thought I should be married and at least start having children, men also saw in me a bridge to the Paradise called Europe. Many times men boldly stated that they wanted to marry me. I usually answered with a joke, for instance by saying that the man in question was too old for me, or that I needed a rich man. At the same time, my serious explanation for my single status that I still was a student was accepted for the meantime. I was sometimes even set as an example to other Krobo girls who dropped out of school because they were pregnant, and praised for my 'keeping away from men' and 'becoming somebody in life'.

In my view the study of 'culture' involves studying a dynamic process, which I tried to stress by investigating historical transformations. By giving people a name and quoting them and by positioning myself in the research, I also tried to show that this research was a matter of interaction between me and the people I studied. However, this is my account and I take full responsibility of its contents.

Outline of the study

This study is structured as follows. *Chapter two* introduces the research location and gives an overview of political, socio-economic and religious developments in Krobo, which forms the background to the chapters to follow. It shows the importance of Krobo-Odumase as a home-town and the site of 'custom'. *Chapter three* goes back in time and focuses on the origin of the friction between Christianity and *dipo*, on the way the Basel missionaries perceived *dipo* as an 'obstacle to the gospel', and the instrumental role the Basel missionaries paradoxically played in identifying 'Krobo tradition' and stigmatising Krobo women. The consequences of the created dilemma by the Basel Mission are still felt today and are sensed throughout this study. *Chapter four* deals with the implications of the interactions of the Krobo with the Basel missionaries and the British colonial administration at the end of the 19th century. After 1892, *dipo* was one of the main practices that were forbidden by the colonial government, because it was seen as an impediment to Christianity and development. However, *dipo* continued to be performed secretly under drastically changed circumstances.

Chapter five deals with the contemporary place of *dipo* on the ritual calendar and in local cosmology or what has been called 'traditional religion' since Christianity arrived. It shows that 'traditional religion' is very much alive, but its compartmentalisation has been the result of the colonial experience. That the symbols and ideology of Christianity have become internalised as reference points for all Krobo, including non-Christians, can on the one hand be explained by the variability and flexibility of Krobo religion, while on the other hand it shows that Christian discourse has become hegemonic in public life. *Chapter six* shows that without *dipo* it is impossible to perform other life cycle rituals, especially marriage, which, however, are either mediated by traditional religion or Christianity. People's performance of rites dealing with the ancestors or local deities and attendance of church service is seemingly contradictory. By taking a closer look at the complexity of Krobo personhood and life cycle rituals, presuppositions about the (invisible) world and notions of the person, and Krobo people's attempts to reconcile themselves to the, at times, competing demands, are highlighted. *Chapter seven* is devoted to the contemporary performance of *dipo* initiations. I focus on the multi-faceted meaning of its rituals, and on the ways in which its continued, but changing, practice by women (and some men) contributes to the reproduction of a Krobo ethnic identity. During the rites, the aspect of purification proves to be very central. *Chapter eight* deals with the debates on culture in Ghana, which focus on 'traditional practices'. The way the dichotomy 'Christianity-tradition' is upheld will be explored. It has received a renewed incentive with the increase of the Pentecostal influence and the question of how to relate (as Christians) to culture is hotly debated in Ghana. One of the issues that will also be addressed is how the objectification of sacred ritual relates to the state-sponsored discourse on 'culture'. *Dipo* is now increasingly performed for tourist audiences, and to some extent folklorised. How is the tension field between 'culture' and 'progress' experienced? Finally I will present a *conclusion* in *chapter nine*, in which I attempt to bring the various arguments together in a comprehensive discussion about the form and meaning of *dipo* and its implications for an understanding of the interplay of local and global aspects and the notion of culture.

2

Mountain dwellers in the plains

February 29, 1848. I could only sleep a little last night and had a severe headache, caused by too much exposure to the heat of the sun yesterday. Still I was able to make it on time to hit the road again to climb the Krobo, a round mountain, which rises lonely and majestically from the plain, giving the impression that it is coming towards us. It ascends very steeply, but on top of the mountain itself, where the houses are, it is even steeper, and it is more dangerous to go to some places. The stones are very smooth and slippery, and once I fell down very hard, but thank God, did not suffer any further damage. In some places I would not have been able to move if I had not taken off my shoes and a man had not guided me by the hand. It was, however, very unpleasant, because the stones were scorched by the sun. There are several villages on this mountain and the houses, mud-houses, many of which have two storeys, are positioned partly between and partly on top of large rocks that lie about. These rocks are very unique (the stone here is not quartz like in *Akvapim*, but gneiss). This mountain offers the most wonderful view. Unfortunately, I only met a few people at home, because many Krobo Negroes, who stand out in diligence from other tribes, are almost always at work at their plantations.

It could be a beautiful region for missionary activity. The people, as far as I can judge until now, are not unreceptive to the gospel. However, the location of the villages is very unsuitable, because the roads that lead to these villages and single houses are almost inaccessible to Europeans. Nevertheless, no place or person is out of reach for the word of God. (Missionary J.G. Widmann in his diary, February 1848; Original in German)[19]

Krobo Mountain, a steep solitary mountain rising out of the plain between the River Volta and the Akuapem-Akuamu mountain range, was the political and ritual centre of the Krobo until their expulsion in 1892 by the British colonial administration. The settlements on this *Inselberg*, with its flat top, constituted the 'hometowns', where most people did not live permanently, but where they usually only returned to for ceremonial events or as a place of refuge in times of war.[20] According to one particular oral tradition, Akro-Muase, a legendary

---

[19] BMA, D-1.2 Afrika 1842-48, Tagebuch, Akropong 1848, No. 22, J. G. Widmann, August 1848, Akropong.

[20] Twi (Akan) speaking Ghanaians refer to the English term 'hometown' when using the Twi word '*kurom*' and the complex set of meanings of that word (Middleton 1979: 256). The Krobo refer to 'hometown' ('*ma*' in Krobo) when they are using the word *Dǫm* ('in the plain below'). I will explain this further in this chapter.

hunter, first discovered Krobo Mountain (*Klo-yo* or *Klo-wem*) as a suitable dwelling place (Huber 1993: 15). The mountain is said to have been occupied 'from around the fourteenth century', and the name 'Crobbo' first appeared on a rough map of the region in 1701 (Wilson 1991: 33). This name follows the Akan spelling. Their Akan neighbours called the people living on Krobo Mountain *'Kro obo so fo'*: 'Kro-rock' or 'mountain dwellers' (Odonkor 1971: 1).[21] The people themselves usually prefer the name *Kloli* in the plural form and *Klono* (Klo-man) or *Kloyo* (Klo-woman) in the singular form when speaking their Dangme language. However, such is the dominance of the Akan (Twi) language in Ghana that even the *Kloli* themselves use the term 'Krobo' in English writing and in their contacts with outsiders.

The first Krobo probably immigrated into the present area in small groups consisting of various kinship groups, with their group leaders and religious leaders, and as part of larger Ga-Dangme groups that included Shai, Osudoku, Ada, Pram-pram, Ningo and Poni. Odonkor emphasises that each section already was a separate unit (1971: 5), but one should note that these separate 'units' were made up of different sections. Azu's account of 'Adangme history' (1927: 242) refers to the original home of these first Krobo as Sameh, situated either in present-day Benin or in Nigeria. They migrated through a place called Lolovo in the Accra plains to Krobo Mountain.[22] Odonkor (1971: 1) claims there were 'Mohammedan raids' behind the exodus from the east. The Akan peoples in the area, the Akuapem and the Akyem Abuakwa, had arrived in the region west of the River Volta before the Krobo. While groups of Akan people often fought Dangme groups, the latter's relationships with the Ewe who lived east of the River Volta have always been cordial: 'Indeed, Adangme traditions speak favourably about the migration through Ewe chiefdoms in present day Togo;

---

[21] The word 'Kro' is derived from the word 'Akro', which could refer to Akro-Muase. Huber (1993: 15) tells us that the origin of the name is uncertain, but it is always somehow linked with Krobo Mountain: 'Some maintain its derivation from *klo* with the meaning *tortoise*, thinking of their tortoise-shaped Mountain home. Others suggest the same root, but with the meaning *owl*, relating that the first settlers, when arriving on the Mountain, met with many of those night birds. Perhaps the most plausible explanation is the one which sees the name of the tribe connected with *Akro-Muase* that legendary hunter, who according to tradition, first discovered the Mountain as suitable dwelling place.' The same root *klo* is also found in the name of the main deity Nana Kloweki.

[22] The name Lolovo is derived from an Ewe term and means 'love ended' (Kropp-Dakubu 1973: 120). This place is significant in oral traditions, because the dispersal of the various Dangme and Ga groups is said to have taken place there (Azu 1927: 244-245; Obeng-Assamoa 1998: 11; Odonkor 1971: 2), and Wilson (1991: 13) calls this place the 'cradle of Adangme culture'. The Dangme may have reached this place in the Accra plains well before the fourteenth century (Obeng-Assamoa 1998: 7). Endemic warfare plagued the region around Lolovo and the different Dangme people looked for easily defensible or remote locations (Wilson 1991: 13-14), such as Krobo Mountain. The historian Wilks therefore warns that the story of the Dangme dispersion should mainly be regarded as a myth of common origin of the Dangme people in order to 'foster a sense of unity between themselves in the face of their common enemies' (Wilks 1956a: 86; 1956b).

30

moreover, the patrilineal Ewe contributed much to the religious structure of the Adangme' (Wilson 1991: 4).

The first series of settlements on Krobo Mountain, established roughly between the 14th and late 17th centuries, consisted of small groups of Dangme, and later of Ewe and a small number of Akan (Wilson 1991: 15-16, 29). These disparate groups of settlements became collectively known as 'Dose', and resided on the Eastern side of the mountain. Wilson suggests that the varied origins of the clans indicates the existence of a kind of policy in early Dose society of overcoming the disruptive potential of immigrants by incorporating them as groups into already established clans. The second settlement stage probably occurred between 1700 and the 1740s. Large numbers of people of Akan ancestry were then admitted to Krobo Mountain as refugees from the Akan wars. They settled on the western side of the mountain, and were called Bose. Now Krobo society was composed of the Dose, who remained predominantly Dangme, and the Bose who had an overwhelmingly Akan origin. As the name 'Krobo' is linked with the 'Kro-Mountain', the name 'Krobo' probably had already been in use for some time. In order to be accepted in society, newcomers on Krobo Mountain had to adhere to certain rules that were shared with other Dangme groups. These rules included the use of the Dangme language, patrilineal inheritance, male circumcision and the *dipo* initiation rites for girls. They also had to give Krobo names to their children (Azu 1927: 250).[23] In sum, the first Krobo were part of a very heterogeneous, dynamic and fluid society, with Krobo Mountain as their common home and united under general rules.

The expulsion from Krobo Mountain in 1892 has been a dramatic event for the Krobo, which was a result of the politics of both the Basel Mission and the British colonial government. While the Basel missionaries repeatedly praised the picturesque view from the mountain and its healthy climate, they also realised that they could not easily reach the people on this inaccessible mountain. Moreover, they saw the mountain as 'the Devils' bulwark', as it was the seat of the traditional priests. The British administration preferred its subjects to live in convenient surveyable and taxable towns in the plains. The colonial policy finally led to the expulsion in 1892, when the colonial government gave the Krobo only three days to collect their possessions, after which a British army of 100 Hausa soldiers occupied the mountain and destroyed all houses and shrines on the mountain top. (I will describe the causes and effects of this event in detail in chapter four).

The settlements in the plains not far from Krobo Mountain have developed into the new Krobo 'hometowns'. Since the year 2000 the eviction and the

---

[23] Finally, the rule mentioned by Azu that 'strangers' should also not send messengers anywhere without permission must have referred to the fact that the security of the Mountain and the secrecy of its access paths should be protected from potential spies (Azu 1927: 250).

flight from the mountaintop has been re-enacted in a cultural play at the foot of the mountain during the annual *Ngmayem* ('millet-eating') harvest festival of the Manya Krobo. This festival also includes a pilgrimage to the mountaintop to commemorate and honour their ancestors. The *Ngmayem* festival has existed since the 1940s and forms the public climax of the annual ritual cycle, which revolves around the cultivation of millet. The neighbouring Yilo Krobo festival, *Kloyosikplemi*, literally 'the descent from Krobo Mountain', was celebrated for the first time in 1992, therefore 100 years after the expulsion.[24] It is constructed specifically around the theme of the commemoration of the expulsion in 1892. One of the main events during the festival is also a pilgrimage to the ancient mountain home. However, the effects of colonial rule are hardly discussed during both festivals, and the role of the Basel Mission in the eviction remains unexposed. What is more important is that the historical links with the mountain are highlighted during the pilgrimage and the cultural play. In this way the festivals are part of a process whereby a Krobo identity, based on an association with the old 'hometowns' on the mountain, is reproduced.[25]

While being born and bred in the Krobo area is an aspect of contemporary Krobo ethnic identity to some extent, mere residence is not enough. Northern immigrants and spouses from other ethnic groups may never be regarded as 'real Krobo', even if they were born in Krobo area (cf. Middleton 1979: 253), while many Krobo people travel, work and raise their families outside the Krobo area.[26] Outside their own area they may emphasise a more broad ethnic identity, such as a regional, national, Ghanaian or even 'African' identity.[27] However, most Krobo people maintain a strong sense of Krobo identity and return 'home'

---

[24] On Easter Saturday April 2, 1972, the Yilo Krobo started to visit their ancestral home every year. The festival was observed as a centenary celebration, called *Kloyo sikplemi,* between 17-20 December, 2002. In subsequent years it was held in early November.

[25] In a working paper on changing forms of political legitimacy in the Krobo states, the historian Veit Arlt argues that the festivals provide an understanding of issues of competition and conflict over political authority in present day Yilo and Manya Krobo states. He notes that in the past, through the residence on the mountain, the dwellers distinguished themselves from their fellow Dangme speakers with whom they shared many characteristics, as well as from their other neighbours. Today, the link with the mountain functions to prove 'true Krobo identity', even though the mountain no longer serves its old purposes and has not been occupied for a long time now (Arlt 2002).

[26] Although the census 2000 does not make any further distinctions along ethnic lines, 613,025 of a total number of 748,014 Dangme people in Ghana are stated to live in the Greater Accra Region and in the Eastern Region, which are also the regions of the 'Dangme traditional states' (GSS 2002b: 'Table 4: Ethnic Grouping of Ghanaians by Birth by Region').

[27] As I stated above, the Krobo are one of the various Dangme speaking groups. Nii Quarcoopome invariably uses the term 'Dangme' to refer to 'Dangme art and culture' in his work (Quarcoopome 1991; 1993; 1994). However, I did not often hear Dangme speakers using this more general ethnic term to refer to themselves. Within Ghana Dangme, often taken together with 'Ga' as 'Ga-Dangme' mainly refers to language (see next chapter about this inheritance of the Basel Mission language politics). However, outside of Ghana, in Europe and America, Ghanaian migrants have formed 'Ga-Dangme associations' to represent themselves.

32

as often as possible, especially for feasts, funerals and ritual ceremonies. What makes one a 'real Krobo' is partly based on a shared history linked with the old mountain home. But most of all the 'hometowns' in the plains remain important in the lives of the people and continue to be places for the construction of a Krobo identity, whether they live there or not, because the hometowns remain the focus of 'custom' and ritual, clan and family life, as I will demonstrate.

In the following sections I will first try to give a general sense of the socio-economic set-up of the present day hometowns and the research setting, Krobo-Odumase. After this, I will focus on the situation of economic decline, before examining social and kinship structures and the religious context. Lastly, I will return to the mountain and the yearly festival.

'Under the Odum-tree': Odumase town and its setting

Today, a recently re-tarred road passes through Somanya and Odumase in the Eastern Region, the capital and hometowns of the Krobo. These towns lie about 80 kilometres north of the national capital Accra. If you have your own transport, it only takes about 45 minutes from the customs barrier at the outskirts of Accra to get to Odumase. If not, you have to exercise a little patience and take one of the mini-buses that ply this road many times a day. They are overloaded with passengers and goods, before taking off from the bus station where the 'mates' yell its destination: 'Somanya! Somanya!' The straight road takes you along a (distant) view of the Akuapem Mountain range on the left-hand side and along the plains filled with bushes and occasional farms and villages on the right-hand side. A few solitary mountains rising out of the plain are a sign that you are approaching Krobo area. One of the mountains that can be seen from afar is Krobo Mountain. First you reach Somanya, one of the capital towns of the Yilo Krobo.[28] These days it has surpassed Odumase in fame and fortune, at least economically. Many trading 'strangers', 'niboi' as the Krobo call the non-Krobo, mostly Akan and Hausa speaking people, make Somanya a busy and booming town.

Continuing through Kpemo and Sawer the road heads towards the Manya Krobo area. The contested boundary between Yilo and Manya, which mainly indicates a political division between the Krobo, lies, according to some, somewhere around the 'Universal Training College', a large building along the main road. The school was abandoned for a long time after its founder and owner died. Now it is used, amongst others, by a Christian organisation called the 'Full

---

[28] However, it is Srah, which is part of the same conglomeration, which forms the traditional capital with the seat of the paramount chief. Somanya has surpassed Srah in size and economic importance and therefore Somanya is usually mentioned as the capital. Somanya had 15,600 inhabitants in 2000, and Sra 4,733 (GSS 2002a: 32, 38).

Gospel Business Men's Fellowship International' who hold their weekly meetings there. After this you soon reach Atua, one of the towns adjacent to Odumase. Together the several Manya Krobo hometowns along the eleven kilometres road between Somanya and the River Volta at Kpong (the eastern border of the Krobo area) form one large conglomeration of almost 45,000 people.[29] For outsiders it seems as if one town merges almost invisibly into the next. Many of the names of the towns and their quarters refer to the geographical surroundings. Some areas have Akan names; other areas were named by those Krobo who came there first. *Odum-ase* for example is an Akan name and means 'under the *Odum* (tree)' (the Odum tree is also called the Iroko (*Chlorophora excelsa*)). Other names of towns are: *Kpongunor* ('steep area'), *Korletsom* ('where the eagle tree is'), *Hwekper* ('forest area' or 'between the forest'), *Kodunya* ('where banana trees are'), and *Salusi* ('under the baobab tree').

The first time I came to Odumase as a passenger in someone's private car in 1994 it was evening time. I remember quite well that I was anxious to visit 'the real field', and expected and hoped to see a quiet village after a week of acclimatisation in busy and noisy Accra. However, I was amazed to see the number of people and cars on the road. We had trouble driving through and had to blow the horn to urge people to move aside. Later I understood that the roadside is especially busy in the evening. Whilst enjoying the evening breeze, young people take a stroll and chat. Women go and sell prepared food on a table along the road, and men may go to drinking bars with loud music to take 'a shot' of *akpeteshie*, a strong liquor distilled from palm wine, also called 'local gin'. Especially youngsters attend late-night performances of locally produced Ghanaian (or Nigerian) video-films, or sometimes of Asian B-movies. The imitation of the karate scenes, complete with the sounds of blows and kicks, is a popular game for young boys. The many Pentecostal churches add to the evening cacophony with their prayer and singing sessions. The churches represent an important and respectable social outing for others. The distorted sounds from the microphones they use carry far into the night. In the weekend funeral ceremonies in the form of so-called wake-keepings that last the whole night, which are accompanied by loud music and sometimes drumming, can deprive you of your sleep.[30] The louder the sound system, the more people will be drawn and the more successful the funeral is considered to be. As many people have an extended network of

---

[29] According to the census 2000, Krobo-Odumase numbers 13,903 inhabitants; Agomanya 13,508; Manya-Kpongunor 6,276; Nuaso 5,751; Atua 3,358; Asite Mannwam 1,039; and Kojonya 759. Kpong is not considered a 'home-town', but as an economically thriving town along the River Volta nevertheless has the largest population of the Manya Krobo towns: 14,725.

[30] Due to complaints about wake-keepings having ill effects on the health and behaviour of people, they have been stopped now in some areas of southern Ghana. Funeral announcements explicitly state: 'no wake keeping'. However, in my experience, most people in Krobo area still performed wake keepings. Interestingly enough, the Basel Mission wanted to do away with such funerals from the very start.

family relations and friends, there is a funeral to attend almost every weekend. Usually, the wake will be kept on Friday evening. The thanksgiving service and burial will follow on Saturday and mourners will again attend church service on Sunday. Especially on Saturday many people, dressed in black and/or red mourning cloth, attend funerals all over town.

The main asphalt road divides Odumase in a 'top' and 'bottom' ('down' in local English).[31] Most other roads consist of beaten red earth. The 'bottom' part is a swampy area. In this area a public and a 'royal' cemetery, where men connected to the paramountcy are buried,[32] farms and many newly built houses can be found. Many Krobo who migrated for economic reasons but still strive to retire in their hometown, have purchased a plot at the 'bottom' part, as there is still land available, and are building a home. Many new churches are also being built, here and elsewhere in town. Sometimes only the foundations have been laid and services are held under roofs made up of bamboo poles or sticks and palm leaves or grass to protect people from the blazing sun. Such congregations are therefore called 'spear-grass churches'.

Towards the hills of the Akuapem range at the 'top' lies the older part of the town and the heart of so-called 'Odumase proper' (Odumase *tutuutu*), where I lived. One of the main buildings is the large 'Johannes Zimmermann church', named after the Basel missionary Zimmermann (1825-1876). Not far from there is the old, now too small, Presbyterian chapel that was constructed in 1869/70 by the Basel missionaries and had been in use for over a century.[33] Opposite the church lies the 'palace' of the paramount chief. Its architecture visibly bears the influences of the southern German style of the Basel missionaries. It is a two-storey stone building constructed by paramount chief (*konǫ*) Sakite in the 1880s, allegedly with the help of the Basel missionaries.[34] The residence faces a large courtyard where occasionally 'durbars' (public gatherings) are held. Up to this day Odumase is the seat of the Manya Krobo paramountcy and the capital of the Manya Krobo traditional state.

The many *trotros* and taxis on the road carry passengers all day anywhere from Somanya to Kpong, and even up to Akosombo (about 20 km from Kpong) and in between.[35] They stop whenever they spot a passenger standing at the

---

[31] This asphalted road actually does not correspond with the original main road, which ran further up along the slopes of the mountains right through the centre of the town.

[32] The word 'paramountcy' in Ghana refers to a chiefdom comprising several traditional rulers called 'chiefs' (male) and 'queen mothers' (female), which has a 'paramount chief' at the top of the hierarchy.

[33] Evangelisches Missions Magazin 1891, p.507.

[34] *Konǫ* is the Krobo title for a paramount chief and literally means 'he who is carried on the shoulders', referring to the olden days when a chief was not carried yet in a palanquin. A chief's addressing title is 'Nene' ('grandfather') or '*matse*' (literally 'father of the town').

[35] *Trotros* are small delivery vans or buses that take small fees for local transport and are private enterprises.

roadside, or when one of the passengers wants to 'be dropped', that is to say, get off. Very early in the morning a bus passes by the main road that also takes people straight to Kumasi (Asante Region's capital), a five-hour drive. For longer distances to nearby and more distant towns people usually have to go to a bus station or 'lorry park'. All stations have buses that go to Accra. The buses from Kpong also go to the Volta Region, and buses from Somanya drive to nearby Akuapem villages, such as Akropong and Aburi. The buses from the bus stations in Agomanya and Odumase go to Accra, but also to Koforidua, the regional capital, and for example, to the markets of Sekesua and Asesewa in Upper Manya. These markets have maintained their position as dominant upcountry markets since the most northerly extension of the Krobo frontier was reached by the 1930s. Between 1940 and 1970, the market of Asesewa was the largest wholesale food market in Ghana, but later it declined. This was due to the change in precipitation patterns and soil exhaustion as a result of an increased pressure on the land, both caused by the creation of Lake Volta, and the latter also by cocoa farming. However, it is still recognised as a market for quality palm oil and maize (Amanor 1994).

According to the Census Report of 2000, Krobo-Odumase alone numbers around 14,000 inhabitants.[36] The everyday population of Odumase differs and is smaller. The number of inhabitants is much larger during most weekends, when many Krobo who live elsewhere come 'home' for family, funeral and other gatherings. During the *Ngmayem* and *Kloyospikplemi* festivals in October and at Christmas, Easter and during the celebration of the *dipo* rites the numbers swell substantially, when people return to their hometown and every 'family-house' (see below) is filled by visiting kin, who usually live in 'the village' or elsewhere.[37] Many Krobo live all over Ghana's farming areas, while many others seek greener pastures abroad. I will come back to the question of migrations below.

Krobo-Odumase is reported to have 1,684 houses, while it had 3,319 households with an average size of 4.2 people in the year 2000 (GSS 2002b: 2). Most houses are one-storey buildings, varying in size and style, made out of a mixture of 'swish' or mud and plaster. The older houses that were built in the late 19th century still have the Southern German style copied from the Basel missionaries: painted black at the bottom, and white at the top. The newer ones are painted in bright blue, yellow or pink. The houses are square and most of them have a roofing of corrugated metal, which has replaced the grass roofing that used to be common. Metal sheets are considered modern, but they rust quickly, so most roofs appear reddish brown in colour. They make the heat in-

---

[36] To be exact: 13,903 inhabitants. For comparison, according to the Census Report of 1984, Odumase had a total population of 8,779 people.

[37] Cf. Middleton (1979: 248) who makes similar observations for Akropong, which serves as a hometown for people of the Akuapem traditional state.

side intolerable, especially when there is no electricity and therefore no ventilator. A great part of everyday life takes place outdoors anyway. Many houses, especially the typical 'family-houses', have an inner courtyard surrounded by various rooms. The doors face the inner yard. One room is usually referred to as the 'hall', where visitors are received. An inside veranda runs all around the courtyard to protect against the rain or the hot sun. Daily activities, such as the washing of clothes early in the morning, take place in the courtyard. Usually there is a separate building or a simple rough shed that is used as a kitchen and where the cooking utensils are kept. It is the domain of women. Most women use stoves with charcoal to cook on, while others use wood, which they usually collect themselves and which therefore helps in reducing costs. A few women also use gas cookers. Unlike some Ga people, however, (see e.g. Senah 1997: 78-79), the Krobo do not have separate compounds for women. Nevertheless, they often have their own room in the house. Young girls and boys help them in the kitchen and carry water. The town has water mains (since 1953). However, people still fetch water from the wells that have been sunk by *konọ*'s Emmanuel (especially in the 1920s) and Azzu Mate Kole (in the 1940s) and from streams, because of the irregular water provision and also for financial reasons. In addition, they have to pay per bucket for tapwater to people who own their own tap or to those in charge of the communal water pipes. Families that are more affluent also build a water tank in their yard or buy a tank, in order to be sure of a regular water supply.

A large number of functions and facilities make the Odumase conglomeration the centre of the Manya Krobo area. There are several health facilities. One government hospital is situated at Atua (built in 1971),[38] the other nearest hospital is a (Roman Catholic) mission hospital in Agomanya that has an AIDS clinic attached to it. There are also two maternity clinics (Kodjonya and Abanse). The much-criticised 'cash and carry' system prevents many people from seeking help in time. Everything, from a plaster to a needle, from food to an operation, has to be paid for in cash on the spot. This is one reason why people in need of medical help also frequently turn to herbalists who charge less than hospitals. Some of them have signboards outside their house. For example, on one signboard in my neighbourhood the person who had put it up advertised himself as a 'fracture specialist'. Others claim they can cure anything from diarrhoea to AIDS. Another strategy to avoid expensive hospitals is to use the knowledge of a pharmacist who sells many medicines without a prescription (see Senah 1997). Quite a number of popular pharmacies can be found in the neighbourhood.

---

[38] In addition, a government hospital is located in Asesewa in Upper-Manya, another one in Akuse along the River Volta. The larger River Volta Authority (VRA) hospital can be found in Akosombo.

Although the Krobo can boast of a large number of schools in the area, they are usually poorly equipped and lack books and other tools for learning. A number of names of primary schools testify to the continuing link between Christianity and education in Ghana. They are called: 'Kodjonya Presby(terian) Primary school', 'Odumase Presby(terian) Primary school', 'Anglican school', 'Agomanya Roman Catholic school', etcetera. Although the government assigns teachers to public schools, education is very much associated with Christianity, since European missionaries were the first to establish schools in Ghana. Most children use their English, 'Christian' names in school. Teachers are usually quite active in Sunday schools or prayer groups in churches and often tend to emphasise the superiority of Christianity above other religions. In Kpong, a multi-ethnic town along the River Volta under Krobo jurisdiction, a Muslim school has been set up, which is mostly attended by so-called 'northerners' or 'Hausa', as the Ghanaians in the south call a varied group of people who at one point migrated from the north. Each school requires their students to wear a uniform, a heritage from British colonial times. It has a brown and yellow colour for all primary school pupils, with the logo of the school in question sown on it.

The official language in Ghana is English, and it is also the language of school instruction. Only people who have attended school can speak and understand English. In Ghana there are about 75 other languages and dialects, each usually associated with an ethnic group. The government wants to promote local languages, and therefore the main vernacular languages are taught in school as well. For the Krobo this is Dangme, which is their principal language of communication in daily life. Many Krobo are fluent in Twi (the dominant Akan language in Ghana) and in Ga as well. The fact that many Krobo people speak Ga is mainly a heritage of the Basel Mission language politics, even though one strategy to realise their evangelical goal was to preach the Gospel in the local vernacular.[39] The Basel missionaries had started learning Ga when they stayed in Christiansborg (Accra) on the coast, they compiled a Ga dictionary and also translated biblical texts into Ga. They considered the Dangme language to be a dialect of Ga and therefore thought that the Ga language could even replace the Dangme language. As a result they used Ga in preaching and teaching, even though they soon noticed that they had to make use of interpreters to get their message across. They continued to use Ga all the same, so this was the language the Krobo had to learn in school and use in church. It was only in the early 1970s that schools began to teach the Dangme language and it was not until the year 2000 that the first Dangme bible translation was launched.

Some primary schools include a Junior Secondary School. In the capital towns in Manya Krobo there are twenty-six primary schools with nursery

---

[39] This strategy follows the belief, traceable to Luther, 'that an individual's mother tongue is the only medium for the insight that produces conversion and salvation' (Miller 1994: 14).

schools, and twenty-two of them include a Junior Secondary School (JSS). Most farming villages only have a primary school. There are five Senior Secondary Schools (SSS) in the area and two in Yilo Krobo, but not too many children manage to reach this level. There are many school dropouts. Often parents cannot afford to send their children to the more expensive secondary schools. Some girls get pregnant and therefore have to stop going to school.[40] High above Odumase on a hill overlooking the town, the Krobo Girl's School is located, which was founded by the (Presbyterian) missionaries from the Free Church of Scotland in 1927 (Odjidja 1977). The philosophy behind such a segregated girls' school on one of the hills surrounding Odumase goes back to the 1860s.[41] It consists of a primary, JSS and SSS. Students from all over Southern Ghana attend the latter two types. Another girls' school is the private 'St. Anne's Vocational Institute' in Nuaso, which is run by local Roman Catholic nuns. The 'Bana Hill Presbyterian Boys' Boarding School', founded by the Basel missionaries in 1905 and also situated on a hill, which once was the pride of Manya Krobo, has been abandoned now.[42] Many people in Odumase feel that the transfer of another school that was established by the Presbyterian missionaries in 1938, the 'Presbyterian Boys' Secondary School' (PRESEC), to Legon in 1968 contributed to the economic decline of the Manya Krobo area. Although it is hardly possible to trace a direct causal relationship between the transfer of PRESEC and the economic decline in Manya Krobo, for many people the loss of the schools became a major symbol of a sense of marginalisation. Another famous school, Mount Mary College, which was founded by the Catholic Mission in 1950 on land provided to them by *konọ* Azzu Mate Kole (Obeng-Assamoa 1998: 166), constituting a teacher training college for French language, is still in practice on the outskirts of Somanya.

There is only one major bank in the area. This independent 'Manya Krobo Rural Bank' is located in Agomanya. It has an agency in Kpong. The members of the 'Manya Krobo Women's Association' proudly told me that their lobbying had helped to convince the government to establish the bank in the Manya Krobo area at the end of the 1970s. Most members of this association are part of more affluent Krobo families that reside in Accra.[43] The bank has 'impoverished

---

[40] Pregnant girls are not allowed to attend school by law. Boys who get a girl pregnant do not have to leave school. The national literacy rate figures for 2000 were 45.7% for females, and 62.0% for males. For the Eastern Region these figures were 49.8% and 69.4% respectively. Census 2000, (GSS 2002c: 'Table 8: Selected Educational Characteristics of Population by Region and Sex'). The literacy rate of the northern regions is much lower than that of the southern regions in Ghana.

[41] BMA, D-1.20a Afrika 1868 1, Odumase 3, J. Zimmermann, 07.04.1868, Odumase.

[42] Bana Presbyterian Middle Boys' Boarding School used to be the 'Basel Mission Middle Boys' Boarding School' in Odumase. In 1903, it was moved to Bana Hill, about three and a half miles away from Odumase. For some time, it was the only 'Middle School' in the area and of very high standing (Odjidja 1973: 121-126). In the 1980s, it declined until it was finally closed. See Arlt (2003a).

[43] Attempts to inject new life into the association during my stay were not very successful.

persons, micro-entrepreneurs, young professionals, farmers and civil servants' as its clients.[44] It has some competition from a branch of the Ghana Commercial Bank in Somanya and its agency in Akuse. A tiny branch of the Barclays Bank at Somanya closed down around 1999.

The description of the general situation in Odumase and its surroundings shows that many Krobo have to deal with an economic decline, which I will further specify in the following section.

Politics and economic developments

'Poor in pocket, but happy in life' (Inscription on a house in a Krobo village)

On January 7, 2001, John Agyekum Kufuor from the New Patriotic Party (NPP) became the new president of Ghana. He succeeded Jerry Rawlings of the National Democratic Congress (NDC). Rawlings had come to power in 1981 after a military coup. He organised democratic elections for the first time in 1992, giving his Provisional National Defence Council (PNDC) a more democratic appearance, and won the elections. In 1996 he was re-elected. However, both elections and even the one of November 2000 were criticised by the opposition for a lack of fairness and for irregularities on the side of Rawlings and his NDC. According to the constitution, he could only rule for two periods and in 2000 Atta Mills was the leading man for the NDC. Rawlings has been criticised for his military past and the growing corruption in Ghana under his government. However, he has also been praised for maintaining peace and stability. After a socialist beginning, Rawlings increasingly embraced the policies of the IMF and the World Bank, and Ghana became the showpiece of their structural adjustment programmes.

In Ghana, PNDC Law 207 establishes the structure for the decentralisation of local government. The local governments are charged with carrying out 86 functions that include functions that came under the ministries of Health, Agriculture, Education, Water and Sewerage, Co-operation, the Ghana Highways Authority and the Post and Tele-communications Corporation:

> Local government is empowered to enact bye-laws in accordance with these functions;
> to form sub-committees which initiate and implement development plans and coordinate the activities of the various district sectors of the government ministries; and to raise local finances and organize communal labour (Amanor 1994: 50).

---

[44] Source: http://www.planetfinance/org.

40

However, district secretaries are not elected through popular franchise, but appointed by the government. Amanor is critical of these relatively recent policies of de-centralisation:

> (...) district assemblies frequently lack the funding to carry out such actions [mentioned above], and lack the competence to organize the various sectors of ministries to work within a coordinated plan. In reality, many of these committees have failed to develop into working bodies. The dominant concern of local government, given the lack of funding, is to raise rates and levies, and enact bye-laws as a means of gaining funds from licence fees and fines (Amanor 1994: 50).

The Krobo district has been divided according to 'traditional' political structures as established in colonial times: there is one District Assembly in Somanya for the Yilo Krobo, and one in Agomanya for the Manya Krobo. Local Councils were first established by the colonial central government in 1951. These were made up of elected local representatives. They were responsible for developmental projects such as markets, clinics, schools, etc, and for gathering human and material resources on a local level. This restricted the role of 'traditional' rulers, i.e. the paramount chief (Obeng-Assamoa 1998: 83). Besides the local government in the form of the District Assemblies and the national government, two paramount chiefs, the already mentioned *konos*, rule the 'Manya Krobo traditional state' and the 'Yilo Krobo traditional state'. This binary system of rule is typical for Ghana and in many ways it is a heritage of the colonial system of indirect rule and Kwame Nkrumah's efforts to reduce the power the chiefs had inherited under this system. I will return to the role of the chiefs in the next section and I will elaborate on the specific history of the Krobo chiefs in chapter three and four.

The Ghanaian economy in general relies on agriculture. Agriculture contributes 40 to 45 % to the GNP. Gold, timber and cocoa are the most important export products. The national percentage of the labour force employed in agriculture and related work is 49.1%. The major industrial activity in the Eastern Region comprises agriculture (including hunting, forestry and fishing), in which 54.3% of the labour force is employed, followed by 'wholesale and retail trade', with 13.2%. [45] For many Ghanaians agriculture is a life raft to which they cling in order to survive the hardships of structural adjustment policies. However, the economy is extremely vulnerable to droughts, other natural disasters, and international price fluctuations.[46] The Krobo district is a good example of a former centre of export crop production in decline. In the past, the Krobo farmers were great palm oil producers (from ca. 1815), which caused them to expand their plantations further and further to the north. They also cultivated maize (from the

---

[45] 'Table 11: Industry of Economically Active Population by Region and Sex' (GSS 2002c: 32).
[46] Source: http://www.buitenlandsezaken.nl/ : 'countries and regions'.

second half of the 18th century) and later cocoa (from the late 1880s onwards). The economic opportunities in Krobo in the late 19th and early 20th century brought about a massive influx of strangers into the area (Obeng-Assamoa 1998: 170). Whereas the Krobo area was once considered the best agricultural district in the colonial era and received much attention from government agricultural services, however with the decline of cocoa (partly due to the outbreak of 'swollen shoot' cocoa disease as well as WWII in the 1940s) the needs of the Krobo district have been forgotten.

The weakening and ongoing marginalisation of Krobo farmers after the decline of cocoa has been studied and described by Amanor in his book *The new frontier: farmer responses to land degradation* (1994). Amanor describes the complex effects of the crisis in the cocoa production after the 1940s and the lack of new available land in Manya Krobo on the social relationships of production and settlement patterns. At present, he writes, the young are, more often than not, doomed to a life of unemployment and life on the fringes of employment. The creation of the Volta Lake for hydro-electricity in the 1960s contributed to the decline. Over twenty percent of the semi-deciduous forest area of Manya Krobo was inundated. Consequently, there have been significant migrations to newer frontier farming areas and the urban sector within Ghana and other West African countries (such as Ivory Coast and Nigeria). The ideal of Ghanaians now in general, Krobo included, is to migrate to a Western country. A relatively large community of Krobo people can be found in Abidjan, Ivory Coast. The high migration rates have shown a correspondence with high HIV prevalence rates, as many women working in prostitution in Abidjan returned to their hometowns with the HIV virus. Within Manya Krobo there has also been a reallocation of population due to economic decline. The population of the lowland towns and the old palm oil belt grew significantly between 1960 and 2000 (the year of the last census), while the population of Upper Manya, the location of farming villages and plantations, hardly grew and in the end even declined. However, migration did not ease land pressures. It only made more land available for hiring and sharecropping and it consolidated absentee ownership. The commoditisation of the means of production in a declining agricultural economy, where degradation is a serious problem, and the resulting grave effects on the standards of living are further dealt with in Amanor's book.

Many people in Odumase are still involved in farming or (related) trading, but extended family labour no longer has any significant role like it had in the past. Men also work, for example, as drivers and mechanics, while men as well as women may work as artisans, hairdressers, dressmakers, teachers or pastors. Most people share a piece of land, or are absentee owners of land in 'the village' in Upper-Manya. Farming does not earn much cash, and wages in general are low.[47] Many women also carry out some additional trading. At different places in Odumase town, small markets can be found where the agricultural produce is sold. Mostly women put up small tables on which they lay out their merchandise: prepared or unprepared food stuffs such as fish, rice and *kenkey*, and in addition items such as sheabutter, chewing sticks and small bags of sugar or washing powder in small portions, bought by people who cannot afford to buy larger quantities at once.

Market trade is important. The main market is situated in Agomanya. Twice a week, on Wednesday and Saturday, the market takes place. Many traders and customers come from far and near to sell a large diversity of goods and foodstuffs, which show the Krobo's continuing skills and qualities as food producers. One can find staple foods such as maize, cassava, yam and palm oil, frequently used vegetables such as tomatoes and onions, but also the less common green peppers, carrots and salad leafs. Pineapple, mango, orange and coconut can be found in abundance, depending on the season. Fish, crab and shrimps from the nearby Volta, but also from the sea, are sold in steamed, salted, smoked, fried, dried and or unprocessed form. The roofed section of the market is where the cloth sellers (an all female affair) are located on a concrete floor, provided by the District Assembly. The colourful wax prints from Holland, England, Nigeria and Ghana are not cheap, but much desired by women. They let the dressmakers sew their '*kaba* and slit' (Ghanaian style top and skirt) from it. These 'traditional outfits' are usually worn to formal occasions or when travelling. Further down the market are the men and boys, both Akan and Krobo, who sell cheap, used clothes and shoes. People often asked me why white people throw away so much of their good stuff. *Ablotsi* (oversees/abroad) must be a rich place indeed![48] On a Krobo market you can also always find the locally produced glass beads and handmade clay pots. The Krobo are renowned bead makers, using the glass powder technology. Many bead-making workshops can be found in Krobo villages and towns. The glass beads (or 'Ghana beads') are also exported. At the same time you also have the treasured historical trade beads from Venice, the Netherlands etc., which are part of family treasures and are sold in times of bitter need, for example to cover medical expenses. These family beads are usually the property of the women in the family, who control them,

---

[47] However, the mostly subsistence-oriented farming reduces the cost of living and allows selling some of the produce to cover school fees etc. High-profit farming is mostly centred on cash crops such as Mango, Banana or Papaya, but the more easily exploited flat lands in the plains are expensive nowadays. Generally there is the wish to make fast money, which prevents people from making long-term investments that will yield higher profits over a longer period (much like their ancestors have taken up palm and cocoa farming). This is typical for the desperate economic situation in Ghana of nowadays.
[48] Also see Hansen (1999; 2000) about the trade in second-hand clothing in Zambia.

clean them and embellish their daughters of the house when they pass through *dipo* and other rites of passage (also see Sackey 1985).[49]

Much trading proceeds through extensive networks. This is also shown through the many wooden kiosk-like shops along the main road where not only 'provisions' (sugar, tea, matches and other smaller items) are sold, but also clothes, (wax print) cloths, bags, car parts, (second hand) bicycles and funeral items. Some garages and mechanics can be found here as well, while services such as signboard painting and sewing of dresses are offered. There are some undertakers and many hair saloons and seamstresses. They carry colourful names, often portraying a Christian affiliation, such as the 'God will provide' hair saloon, or the 'Jesus lives mechanics'. One undertaker in Somanya's advertises with the following text on a signboard: 'Whatever you do, death awaits you. Boast not. Sweet mother & Co. for your bereavements'. The image of a corpse 'laid in state' is painted on both sides.

Ghanaian newspapers, such as *The Daily Graphic* and *The Ghanaian Times* are sold in front of bus stations. Interestingly, a purchased item often is wrapped in an old Dutch or German newspaper. A mail van delivers and collects mail twice a week to the central post offices in Odumase and Somanya and to the small post office at Manyakpongunor. New 'communication centres' have sprung up in the last couple of years. These privately owned phone boots with air conditioning definitely cater for a pressing need, as they are often crowded. Especially in the evening time people are awaiting calls or try to get through.[50] The network is frequently down, as it depends on electricity. Ghana has to deal with an insufficient power supply. During my stay in 1998 this led to a crisis. As a result, households as well as the industry had been put on short rations. In Odumase we would have 'lights off' every other day.

Many people in the towns have electricity at home. Except for some houses with shrines where electricity is not allowed, everybody wants to be connected, however some cannot afford it. Electricity came to Odumase and the surrounding towns in the early 1970s. The market town of Asesewa, however, in Upper-Manya, was connected as late as in 1998, and most of the farming villages still do not have electricity. The availability of electricity has changed economic and social life. Some people in Odumase have a fridge or freezer that they use to produce and sell ice blocks and iced water or iced 'kenkey' (fermented maize). Others have a television set. They usually receive visitors in the evening time that come and watch the programmes. Especially films and plays performed and produced in Ghana are popular. During soccer games large

---

[49] For a recent study of beads in Ghana with a particular focus on bead-making in the Krobo area, see Wilson (2003).

[50] Mobile phone networks are now increasingly popular for obvious reasons, but because the Odumase conglomeration is situated at the foot of a mountain range and right in the middle between two transmitters (Accra and Akosombo) there is no good coverage (yet), except for some providers.

crowds of mainly men gather in front of a television that is placed outside a drinking bar or at a private home. Their cheering and loud comments can be heard all over town. Radio is popular too and more widespread, for obvious reasons. Especially 'Radio Ada', which broadcasts in the Dangme language and regularly has programs on Dangme culture and music, has many listeners.

Social and Kinship structures

Hometowns and divisions

A relative is more reliable than a friend (*Nyɛmi (hi) pe huɛ* - Krobo proverb)

The larger part of the Krobo population lives 'upcountry' (*yonọ* = 'on the mountain' or 'in the upcountry') in the farming areas in the western and northern areas on and beyond the Akuapem-Akwamu mountain range. Moreover, Krobo farmers live all over (Southern) Ghana in all the major cocoa growing areas. Especially in the 19th century Krobo farmers acquired land through the unique 'strip-farming' system, the so-called *huza* system (Field 1943; Hill 1970: 72-74). In this system land is purchased by co-operative groups under the guidance of a 'big man' who had enough importance and influence to deal successfully with the land-owning Akan and Akyem neighbours. Due to the characteristic pattern of purchased *huza* land, consisting of a valley with a stream and slopes up to the summit, Krobo farmers usually did not live in nucleated villages, but in linear ribbon settlements, which often consisted of only one single family with a man, his wife or wives and their children (Amanor 1994: 59-60). Nucleated settlements emerged around markets such as Asesewa, Bisa and Sekesua. Many of them are off the main road networks and lack piped water, electricity and other services. Although these village settlements in the 'upcountry' are physically separated from Odumase and the adjacent towns, they should be regarded as its satellites, with little independent viability (cf. Middleton 1979: 248).

The real 'home' is in *dọm*, ('in the valley', or 'in the plain below'), while *Klowɛm* (Krobo Mountain) literally is the 'Krobo house' or 'home'. *Dọm* refers to the capital towns in the plains, where the ancestral homes have been situated since the abolition of the settlement on Krobo Mountain. All people staying in *yonọ* have a compound ('family house') in the towns in the plain. People who live on the *huza* in *yonọ*, or those who migrated elsewhere, usually due to a lack of opportunity to acquire an income in the area, will only 'go home' a few times a year for *dipo*, funeral rites (cf. Ayi 1966: 13), or the annual festivals and sometimes Christmas, as these ceremonies will be celebrated or performed in the 'family house'. Therefore, these rituals can be characterised as 'home-coming' rituals. The *dipo* priests can in fact only perform the dipo rites in *dọm*, as the

45

dipo shrines are situated there and because they have to restrict their movements due to certain taboos, which I will discuss in another chapter.

Even though Kpong and Akuse along the River Volta, and Akosombo town near the Akosombo-dam site, are large settlements and economically more significant than Odumase, they are regarded as new satellite settlements of Odumase. People say they are 'nobody's towns', because they have no proper inhabitants, but only members of other 'home-towns' who happen to live and work in them. These people return to their 'home-town' whenever they can, and ultimately at their time of death (cf. Middleton 1979: 248, 255). These 'nobody's towns' are towns that have emerged on the margins of the Krobo territory as trading hubs and always consisted of a more 'cosmopolitan' population. Situated on the borders, on no-man's land as it were, their affiliation has always been contested.

Many people in Odumase where I lived, were in one way or another related to each other. *Odumase ngɛ kake*, Odumase is one, they would say. Not only because Odonkor Azu (†1867), one of the two founders of the town in the first half of the 19th century, had many wives and many children, but also because of many intermarriages between his offspring and cross-cousin marriages with the offspring of the other founder Nathanael Lawɛ. Most people in my surroundings in Odumase, including the members of the very extended family with whom I was staying, for example, can trace some lines of descent back to one of Odonkor Azu's sons. Their adult descendants are now usually of the fifth or sixth generation, and their children of the sixth or seventh, however a number of old people of the fourth generation are also even still alive. The web of the extended family reaches far, and there are always some traceable links between different families, lineages and clans. It happened more than once that my friend Julie and I would meet somebody we both did not know. But then she would start talking to him or her, they would ask each other where the other was from, from which area and which house, and it was not long before Julie happily exclaimed something like: 'Oh, s/he is a relative.' Then she would explain a relationship to me that seemed too complicated for me to comprehend, for example: 'This is my mother's uncle's in-law's son'.

As mentioned above, the Krobo are politically divided into two districts with local governments and two 'traditional states' with traditional rulers, which are organised along male-oriented power structures and largely based on an Akan model (see next chapter). The 'Manya Krobo traditional area' and the 'Yilo Krobo traditional area' are ruled by two different paramount chiefs, by *konọ* Sakite II, a descendant of Odonkor Azu, and *konọ* Kpetekple Narh Dawutey Ologo VI respectively, a descendent of Ologo Patu, another 'big man' and contemporary of Odonkor Azu. Each *konọ* has six so-called 'divisional chiefs' (*wɛtso mantsɛ*) under him for the six largest units of social grouping (*wɛtso*). All the main chiefs have a female ruler called a 'queen mother' (*manyɛ*) beside them.[51] *Wɛtso* means 'family tree', and patrilineal descent is, contrary to the Akan who are matrilineal, the base of social grouping among the Krobo. According to Huber *wɛtso* stands for:

> (…) an original patrilineal kinship group, which has grown to a large tree, or rather a plurality of such groups, united under one name. Thus ordinarily not all the members of a *wɛtso* claim descendency from one male ancestor. Whether the designation 'clan' should be adopted for it, is a matter of definition; it is perhaps too narrow, though these groups, to some extent, have developed as political units with a 'divisional' chief as their head, and though on the Mountain each formed a separate section or quarter within the two respective towns. (…) A more adequate description is 'sub-tribe', which expresses a social unit of a less strictly defined genealogical nature (Huber 1993: 25).

Instead of the colonial term 'sub-tribe', I shall call the *wɛtso* the main 'divisions', as the Krobo call their leaders 'divisional chiefs' and 'divisional queen mothers' in English. However, the Krobo also often call their divisions 'clans' in English. For the Manya Krobo these are: Djebiam, Dom, Akwɛno, Piɛngwa, Manya and Susui. The Yilo Krobo also recognise six major units: Plau, Bonya, Ogomɛ, Okpɛ, Bunase and Nyɛwɛ.

These major units are all sub-divided into smaller units called *kasi*, sub-divisions or clans, whose members reputedly descend from one common (unknown or mythical) ancestor or an immigrant kinship group. A *kasi* comprises all legitimate living offspring through the male line, also daughters who have married into another group and descendants of unmarried daughters. It also comprises all descendants of slaves who belonged to members of *kasi*, except the children of female slaves who married to another group and the offspring of possible other strangers who were permitted to join the group. Like the *wɛtso*, a *kasi* is not an exogamous unit, since marriages within it are rather common. Neither is it an exclusive cult group, although many of the original *kasi* have their principal deity with its sacred enclosure and grove. A *kasi* is headed by a so-called *asafoatsɛ*, or sometimes called sub-chief, who in the past also was the *kasi*'s military leader. The *kasi* are further sub-divided into secondary *kasi* or sub-clans. Huber makes a distinction between 'original *kasi*' and its split-off, a

---

[51] The term 'queen mother' was used by Rattray (1923) as a translation of the Akan 'ohemaa'. However, the term does not refer to the actual mother of the king or chief as in Europe. Female equivalents of male political leaders in the chieftaincy system have played a role in Krobo political affairs, at least since the 1930s. As with the whole chieftaincy system, the Krobo borrowed from the Akan here too. The study of Stoeltje shows the expansion of the Queen Mothers' position in matrilineal Akan society today and 'the trend for patrilineal societies to create Queen Mothers for the first time in their history' (Stoeltje 1995: 16). Now all chiefs want to have a queen mother by their side in order to 'mobilise women'.

'secondary *kasi*', but due to population growth and numerous split-offs, these distinctions are hard to make now. Etymologically *kasi* means 'people belonging to or eating from the same dish'. The names of *kasi* are usually derived from a geographical setting of the settlement, either on Krobo Mountain or on the farmlands, therefore not from the ancestral founder (Huber 1993: 28). The term *kasi* as such is not much used. However, people are able to indicate that they come, for example, from the Djebiam-Nam clan, or Djebiam-Agbom, or Susui-Adome, or Piengua-Lọm. The last extension usually indicates the geographical setting.

A *kasi* is divided into a large number of *wɛ* or *wɛku*. The term *wɛ* can mean 'home' or 'house', or 'people of a house', the lineage, i.e. 'house', conceived as a social unit. When referring to their lineage or extended family, people usually talk about their *wɛku*, the lineage. The leader of a *wɛ* is its most senior male member and is called *wɛ-nokotoma* (house elder). Whereas the *matsɛ* and the *asafoatsɛ* are elected, the *wɛ-nokotoma* is not. His position and responsibilities are especially prominent in his ritual obligations, such as organising the funerals. The members of a 'house' all descend from a particular male who is usually known by name. His name serves as a designation of the group in question. This is why my friend Julie told me, for instance: '*I je matsɛ Sakite wɛku*,' ('I am from *matsɔ* (chief) Sakite's 'house'). Marriages within the same house are not forbidden and sometimes even preferred. This was particularly the case in the past (as I will explain later). The growth of the population means that groups have split up into sub-groups and new 'houses' have been founded. This is an ongoing process (cf. Huber 1993: 29-31).

Each town in Lower Manya is divided into particular areas or quarters that only partly follow the pattern of social grouping. Before the expulsion from Krobo Mountain in 1892, the pattern of the habitations on this mountain corresponded with the divisional (*wɛtso*) grouping. These settlements then formed the 'home towns', as I mentioned in the introduction of this chapter. Already prior to the removal from the mountain, the farm settlements in the plains had developed into towns. Therefore, clans and 'houses' of different divisions can now be found in the same town. In addition, groups and individuals of Ewe, Akan, and 'Hausa' origin live between and within the original *wɛtso* and *kasi*. Huber places this in a historical context:

> While on Krobo Mountain each sub-tribe occupied as a group a particular portion, the land in the plains was rather first settled by individual farmers or smaller units, which naturally drew some of their relatives to their immediate neighbourhood, while other relatives acquired land, perhaps at another place. Thus in different localities new 'houses' of the same *kasi*, or new *kasis* of the same sub-tribe originated. Of secondary *kasi* splitting off from the original *kasi*, mention has already been made. As a result, most of the present towns comprise, apart from the strangers, sections of different sub-tribes (Huber 1993: 38).

This also explains why most of the towns have been named according to the geographical setting, and they are not called by the name of the social group, as used to be the case on Krobo Mountain.

The Family House (wɛku-wɛ)

> The *Asikọnabia* tree said: because they feel homesick for each other, that is why their fruits grow in bunches *(Asikọnabia kɛ: hɛ dja he nɛ awoọ kutuu ọ ne* – Krobo proverb)

The proverb above can be applied to the way of living of the Krobo in their hometowns, where family members live closely together. It refers to the closely packed housing of a Krobo extended family, which is not only caused by the lack of space in the towns, but also from their strong sense of common descent (Huber 1993: 71). The proverb was also explained to me in terms of 'unity stands'; if you are one, there will be no separation.

The primary unit of social organisation and identity in Krobo society is the patrilineal (extended) family or 'the house'. Middleton remarks that the 'house' provides its members with a sense of belonging (referring to the (Akan/Guan) town of Akropong, some 30 kilometres away from Odumase). The 'house' stands for a relevant factor in the continuing significance of the 'hometown':

> With the high degree of movement of their members throughout southern Ghana the persistence of 'houses' enables a sense of identity and cohesion to be maintained among their members, who would otherwise face ever-changing modern conditions as isolated individuals without effective support for their efforts being provided by sub clan kin (Middleton 1979: 253).

A 'house' is also appropriately a literal 'family house', where all-important ceremonies and rituals in the life of family members take place. So the term 'house' can refer to the extended patrilineal family, but also literally to the house built by a known ancestor. Ideally, settlement is virilocal, where a woman and her children live together with the husband and father in his own house, which is often built next to the old family house if there is sufficient space, on the same compound with the extended family. For example, the house opposite my 'mother' Lako Sakite's house, which was built by her great-grandfather Nene Sakite, was built by one of his grandsons called Ba. When there is not enough space, a man can build a house somewhere else, but will still contribute to the extension of the old family house. A man and his wife and children may also live in his old family house, together with relatives such as his parents (if alive), his brothers and unmarried sisters and their children. A woman who is not married or divorced can stay in her own family house or return to the family house. This situation is very common. Many women are either divorced or have children from different fathers without being (fully) married. In case a woman has divorced, her husband may claim any child. If he is not married to the mother, the child, even if the father is known, will be raised within the mother's family. Such children will inherit from the mother's father and are called *yo bi* (the woman's child) as opposed to *nyumu bi* (the man's child).

Some people prefer to stay in a rented place, usually consisting of one or two rooms in a larger house. They either cannot afford to build their own house, or maybe there was no space left in their family house. Some successful (business) women also build their own houses, but they cannot establish a 'family house'. Everybody prays for the day that he or she will have enough money to build a house. It is the ideal of parents to leave this to their children. One important reason why many people want to go abroad, is to earn money and send it to the family, so that they can set to build a house and ultimately retire there. If this is not possible, people strive to expand the old family house by building an additional block for themselves and their children. The more affluent people are, the greater the difference between the houses that are built separately for themselves and their immediate family. The inner veranda is often lacking, and sometimes even the inner yard. They usually have glass window shutters, bathroom facilities and a central door. Some of the people who returned from abroad have built this type of house. Many unfinished buildings are constructed bit by bit by people who live either in the city or abroad. The process can take years, depending on the flow of money. Due to a lack of funds or the death of the owner, it seems as if some buildings are never completed; the weed-grown walls in some places in town testify to this.

I lived in a newly built house during my fieldwork. My landlord's old mother (in her eighties), an unmarried sister, three orphaned grandchildren of his dead elder brother (one girl, two boys), the twins of a daughter (boy and girl) and occasional additional family members and tenants all shared the house with me. My landlord lived and worked in Tema (the main Ghanaian harbour and one of Nkrumah's planned towns) during the week, and often came to Odumase in the weekends. Opposite 'my' house, across the courtyard, a younger brother of my landlord had built the foundation for his own house. They also had a family house in Odumase, but in a different area. Although my landlord had built his own house, he also felt the obligation to extend his part of the family house. A poorer 'cousin' lived in his old mud-built house next door, and did chores for his 'big brother', my landlord.

Yo bi (a woman's child)

It was already mentioned before that some children live in their mother's father's house rather than in their father's house. The existence of a special social category named *yo bi* ('woman's child') seems to be a rather specific Krobo or

Dangme feature that is not found in kinship structures of neighbouring people. In order to be able to understand particular clashes with Christianity in this context and the relationship with *dipo*, we need to gain an understanding of this particular phenomenon, which has its roots in economic history. In the old days, at least until the 1940s (according to Field's report) and before the major economic decline, once the girls had passed their initiation rites (*dipo*), it was not uncommon for fathers and/or family heads to even encourage their daughters to have children before they were married, or not to marry at all, especially when there was a lack of sons in the family. The resultant children, the *yo bi*, belonged to the girl's father's family, her patrilineage, and not to her children's father. They would have equal rights of inheritance with the grandfather's own children. In this way he could continue to make use of the daughter's services on his own farm, and he had extra 'sons' without the expenses and obligations related to marrying additional wives (Field 1941a: 14). This ensured the future of the family and their wealth, as the children would form valuable labour forces on the ever expanding plantations.

Within the context of *yo bi* the late *kono* Azzu Mate Kole (1955) claimed in a published paper that there are no illegitimate children in Krobo society. He states that:

> Children born out of wedlock belong to the parents of the woman unless she later marries the man whose children they were. If the woman marries another man, her children before that marriage still belong to her parents, who have the powers and responsibilities of a father over the issue. In fact, they call him 'father' and inherit his property as his own children. (…) and, as in Krobo there is no illegitimate child, children born out of wedlock belong to the parents of the mother, so that it is not much of a problem for a woman who fails to get a husband bearing children (1955: 137-138).

According to Field and Azzu Mate Kole, a *yo bi* could be just as much appreciated as a *nyumu bi* (man's child), and the maternal grandfather would take care of him or her. This means that in case of a girl, he would also pay for her *dipo* ceremony. Azzu Mate Kole's quotation makes clear that having children was even more important for a Krobo woman than getting married.

Comfort Sikapa, an old lady of 72 who lives in Asitey, is the living example of a conscious choice for a *yo bi* in the old days. She is the youngest of her father's six children and the others died when they were children (also see Sikapa 1999). Two brothers of her mother's three children from a previous marriage had migrated and were dead now, and their children went to Europe and America. Her sister married off into other family. Gabriel Sikapa, her father, had foreseen that none of his (adopted) children would remain in his house and his property would be scattered. So he wanted Comfort to stay with him, bear children for him and inherit his property. Gabriel Sikapa, a colourful figure in his time, is mentioned in the records of the Basel missionaries, as he was among the first Krobo scholars and a member of the Basel Mission Church. His memoirs were recently recovered by his grandson, Comfort Sikapa's son, Evans Sikapa (1999).[52] Gabriel Sikapa invested in his last daughter. She went to the Krobo Girls' School. He presented a goat for her *dipo* when she must have been about eleven-years-old, as Comfort Sikapa remembers that her *dipo* had taken place just before 'the' earthquake (1939). For her outdooring ceremony her father gave her golden jewellery like a watch and a necklace. About five years later, Comfort Sikapa gave birth to her first child. Her four children have one father who hails from Osu, Accra, but they belong to their mother's father's house and carry his name, Sikapa. Today some fathers still do not allow their daughter to marry if she is his only child. Her children will then belong to his lineage.

So *yo bi* are ideally taken care of by their maternal grandfather. I observed the same thing in 'my' house. My landlord took care of the twins of his daughter and the three children of his dead brother's daughter like a father. All of the biological fathers of the children have never married their mothers. Therefore, they are all *yo bi* under my landlord's care, and belong to his family house. As the head of the household everybody calls him 'dada' (father). The father of the three orphans is said to have been a Nigerian. The twin's mother, my landlord's daughter, occasionally visited the twins, but lives elsewhere with the father of her younger children. My landlord's unmarried sister, who had no children of her own, took care of them like a mother. Their biological father is a 'northerner' and is said to live in Italy.

Tetteh Gaga, a traditional priest, gave another contemporary example. He told me that his father was a *yo bi*, and since he was dead, they could never 'go back' to his father's paternal relatives. One of Gaga's own daughters, who was a *yo bi* as well, and even already had children herself, would like to have the *la pomi* ceremony performed for her, a ceremony in which Gaga could reclaim his daughter as part of his family. At the time of her birth, he had just come out of school and was therefore not ready to take the responsibility. I asked why his daughter would want her father to do this after all this time. Are *yo bi* less respected than *nyumu bi* (the father's child)? Gaga answered wholeheartedly 'yes!', and told me that a *yo bi* has no say in family matters, in contrast with *nyumu bi*. He explained that in the old days *yo bi* would be the one who would be sent to war, while *nyumu bi* should stay within the house. Although a *yo bi* inherits from his or her maternal grandfather's side, he or she cannot also become the successor of a chief or queen mother. Only when the mother's side of the family

---

[52] See Arlt's unpublished paper (2003b) on the memoirs of Sikapa, whose life story is a fascinating account of the time of a cocoa revolution and increasing flows of ideas, fashions and migrants within Africa and between Africa and Europe at the end of the 19th century. 'Sikapa' means 'good money'. Sikapa was known as a big game hunter. He travelled to the Congo Free State as a carpenter and came back with a small fortune, took part in the British expedition against Asante (1900) and was made a chief over the town of Akuse.

(i.e., the mother's father) is wealthier, it is possible that they would prefer the mother's side, he said, as one can only inherit from one side of the family.

Today people often have an ambivalent attitude towards *yo bi*. In the past, *yo bi* ensured the future of the (farming) family and their wealth. It was often a conscious choice. However, the ideal is to be a *nyumu bi*. This idea may have been strengthened within the dominant Christian morale of today, where sexuality is (regarded as being) situated within marriage, within the nuclear family. As we will see in the next chapter, the Basel missionaries always resisted the idea of *dipo* as the prerequisite for sexual relationships.

La pomi ritual (re-claiming the child)

As I explained above, a father could encourage his (preferably first-born) daughter in the past to bear children for his family. This meant that the young woman would not be fully wedded to the father of her children. She stayed with her father and he took all responsibility over the children. Today many, especially young, women, or even teenage girls, experience unplanned pregnancies that are not supported as such by their relatives, and in which they also do not receive the support from their lovers. Sometimes the genitor of a child is not known. Sometimes a man is unwilling to marry the mother of his child because he is very young, or poor and not (yet) prepared to bear the responsibility for the upkeep of a child. The rule that a man who has not fulfilled the full marriage customs has no say over his child is still valid. Such a child has been named in his mother's father's house and therefore belongs to his house, even if the biological father contributes financially or otherwise to the upbringing of a child. However, a father can claim his child at a later stage. This is possible by performing the '*la pomi*' rite. Literally, *la pomi* means 'cutting of the *la*'. When the child concerned was born, a *la* string (a raffia fibre with a black and a white bead) was tied around the wrist and subsequently the paternal family of its mother gave him or her a name. In this rite this name will be ritually cancelled and the child will become part of his genitor's family after all and only inherit from him.

I witnessed the *la pomi* twice as a ceremony on its own and as far as I know, this ritual has not been described anywhere before as a ritual separate from the marriage performance. It may even be a relatively recently invented ceremony. Some people said it was introduced by the late *kono* Azzu Mate Kole. When I asked Hugo Huber about this, he told me he was not aware of any such ceremony. I think this ceremony must first be understood in the dominant Christian context where *yo bi* are seen as children born 'out of wedlock', and where the ideal is to be with the father's side of the family. Secondly, this ceremony has to be understood within the context of economic decline, the substantial costs of marriage ceremonies and the specific rule in Krobo that a man only has the right over his children when the full range of marriage customs has been performed. Fathers can claim their children or be urged to take their responsibility through the *la pomi*. Before explaining this in greater detail, I would like to remark that when the full marriage customs finally take place after a man and woman started to have children together, the *la pomi* can be part of this marriage ceremony. However, many times a man is not able to perform the full marriage customs, because of the high costs involved. One elder of the woman's family in a *la pomi* ritual I witnessed emphasised that the costs of a wedding should be reduced, so that a *la pomi* ritual would not be necessary. Then the man would have married the woman before children were born. Although the idea is that a man can take up the responsibility for his child without a marriage, another point of criticism is that this has no effect when the ceremony is performed for adult children. According to Julie, the *la pomi* has become a convenient ritual for some men, as they only claim the child 'when he or she has become somebody', and the costs in the upbringing are no longer necessary. Therefore, the mother's family sometimes does not agree with performing the rite. Usually however, in such a case the mother's family will ask for a much larger compensation.

In both cases that I was present at a *la pomi* ceremony it indeed involved adult children in their twenties, some of whom already had children themselves. During the simple ceremony, representatives of both families gathered in the mother's family house on a Sunday morning. In one case, the paternal family presented a big sheep, which may have cost about 40 USD, an amount of money and a bottle of schnapps. The maternal family then went to see the proverbial 'old lady' (*yomo'o*).[53] After mutual consultations, they returned and said that they would have to collect two more bottles of schnapps from the other family before they could deliver the message of 'the old lady'. After negotiations the demand was reduced to one bottle. The other side gave it to the head of the household (*sɛno hilo*). At this ceremony, the family head informed the other family that they were going to use the drink to pour a greeting libation. He poured a libation with the schnapps and then with water to inform the woman's father that the man who had children with his daughter when he, the woman's father, was still alive, was arriving today with schnapps and a sheep to perform the *la pomi* rite. He asked him to bless the ceremony and prayed for a long and fruitful life for the children. Then the sheep was slaughtered and its parts were divided. Arrangements were very similar in the other family where I witnessed the *la pomi*. However, no libations were poured (at least publicly), because the maternal family members were Pentecostals. Nevertheless, a bottle of schnapps

---

[53] In the Krobo context, 'the old lady' refers to the deity Nana Klowɛki as the prototype of a wise old woman. In Akan societies, the same expression is used, but it refers to a different context. In Akan cosmogony, women were said to be the founders of the various clans. As Boaten explains: 'They were repositories of knowledge and wisdom, therefore complicated issues were referred to them for counselling. Thus the concept of: *Yenkobrisa Abrewa* that is, "Let us seek counselling from the old lady" evolved and still persists up to today' (Boaten 1992: 90).

was still demanded (normally used for pouring a libation), and the agreement was still sealed with a drink. A bottle of *akpeteshie* went round. At both places, the ceremonies were finally concluded with Christian prayers.

Nowadays, Christianity is woven into the texture of many 'traditional' practices, as in the *la pomi* ceremony that I just described. As I shall show in the next section, Christianity plays a dominant role among the religions of the Krobo people.

Multiple religious spaces and practices

'Ghanaians by nature are religious' said the presenter of a local radio programme in Ghana, communicating a popular wisdom. This sentence caught my ears when listening to the radio in Accra in January 2003. It is true that religion literally seems to pervade every aspect of life in Ghana and likewise in Krobo, and the distinction between what is secular and what is spiritual is not very clear (cf. Senah 1997: 86). Every aspects of life therefore seem to be interwoven, although viewing religion in a 'totalist' fashion seems to be exaggerated.

Some elements that are characteristic of African religions also characterise Krobo religion, and account for its easy accumulation of foreign influences and elements and its scope for pluralism. Krobo religion is therefore variable and flexible religion. A variation in scale runs parallel to a variation in content: from magic, familial rites, lineage rituals to regional systems and regional and national churches. Religion here is often action-oriented. It means performing or doing something else. It means consulting a diviner, offering a sacrifice, praying or falling into a trance. It is often instrumental, a means to an end. People do things with a certain aim, for example, health, fertility and harmony. Although the actions are clustered and focused with regard to certain deities, therefore forming a system (although in constant change and adaptation), people are free to choose and can usually accumulate as many associations in their personal religious lives as they deem feasible (cf. Blakely, Beek, & Thompson 1994: 15, 17).

Specific religious expressions and practices of the Krobo revolving around the annual agricultural cycle in which the concepts of blessing and fertility and practices of purification and pacification are central, and in which *dipo* occupies a crucial place, will be discussed more elaborately in chapter five. In addition to this 'traditional religion', Christianity is also highly relevant in the majority of people's lives. In Krobo, most people now call themselves Christians. As conversion in the past meant access to education and materialistic progress and a step towards 'civilisation' and 'enlightenment', being a Christian today also has a certain status. Anybody in Odumase who has been baptised will say that he or she is a Christian and can use his or her Christian English name, especially at school or in church. However, the attitude of most people to indigenous religious practices and Christianity is very pragmatic as well and can be assessed in terms of 'worldly' benefits. For instance, they easily resort to traditional therapeutic systems in the event of illnesses whose etiologies are perceived as metaphysical. Most people in Odumase believe that their lives, health, success and happiness are affected in varying degrees by actions of many mystical forces. These forces already play a role at birth, when a child is given its character or temperament by its *sɛsee* ('parting word') from the 'other world', as I will describe in chapter six. During the lifetime of an individual, his or her health and success may suffer through actions of a multitude of forces. The means of identifying the identity of the mystical agents held to be responsible and discovering the means to remove their influence if they prove to be harmful, is part of the work of custodians of deity shrines and of Christian priests and prophets (cf. Middleton 1983: 7-8). Therefore people do not think and worship in terms of religious orthodoxy: their actions exhibit a pragmatic attitude toward different values, goods and institutions. They may switch from one religion to another in order to advance their own interest (cf. Beek 1998; Senah 1997: 88-89).

In this way, people may be 'shopping around' between religions in the 'religious market-place' (Peel 1978: 453). This is why I believe that statistics as the ones provided by the Ghana Statistical Service, which for example show that 8.5% of the total Ghanaian population reports a religious affiliation with 'traditional religion',[54] are not very informative. They may only indicate the number of people who act in one way or another as a traditional religious specialist or are involved in chieftaincy matters. It is more accurate to regard the situation as one with plural beliefs, in which people pragmatically use any of the religious means that can best help them to remove afflictions, than as a situation in which a person is defined as an adherent of one particular faith to the exclusion of others. However, a pluralist situation does not imply a situation of constant harmony and mutual respect. There are many conflicts concerning religious principles and practices between the various segments of the population (Middleton 1983: 8). Moreover, Christianity has definitely become the more dominant religion in public space in the last few decades.

Churches in Odumase

The first time I visited Ghana, in 1992, I was surprised by the variety of churches. In the past Dutch, German and other Protestant and Catholic missionaries had come to Africa on their civilising and converting missions. Now the roles seemed to be reversed and I was taken by surprise by questions such as: 'Did you take Jesus Christ as your personal Saviour?' On Sunday, like all over

---

[54] 'Table 7: Religious affiliation of Population by Region and Sex' (GSS 2002c: 26).

(Southern) Ghana, many people in Odumase go to church. All around music from different churches can be heard. Walking down the streets on Sunday, the 'Hallelujahs' and 'Amens' are omnipresent, encouraged by drums and jingling tambourines. People passing by on their way to a church service are all dressed in their Sunday best. Small girls wear cute, pink dresses with lace and white little socks, while small boys wear their best trousers and shirts. Men usually wear suits and ties that make them sweat in the hot tropical weather. They continuously wipe their faces with handkerchiefs. Women wear their finest '*kaba* and slit', while older men may also wear 'traditional' (wax print) cloth. Of course, their shoes have been polished and clothes neatly ironed. You do not have to look far to find a church. At the 'Jehovah Witness Hall' there is an activity going on every day, with apparently a lot of bible study. The wooden building of the Apostolic Church bulges out on Sunday. Benches are placed outside for people who cannot go inside. The Apostolic choir sounds very enthusiastic and is quite popular. The Roman Catholics and Anglicans stick to time and finish relatively early, but the other churches, including the Presbyterian church sometimes, can be busy until late afternoon. Church services often last at least three hours and sometimes, when there is a special programme, even half a day. People walk in and out to answer to 'nature's call', or eat or drink something. Young girls selling water and small food items can be seen hanging around, carrying their wares in a see-through box on their head.

I will only briefly mention Christianity and (the history of) conversion in the Krobo area to offer the necessary background information.[55] There are many denominations in Odumase and its surrounding towns. I counted at least twenty different ones, and I am sure there are many more. A rough distinction can be made along three lines. First, there are the mainline churches, the former mission churches of which the Presbyterian Church was the first and is still the most influential. Secondly, there are the so-called African Independent or 'Spiritual' Churches, which have become popular especially since the 1950s. The third group comprises the now very popular Pentecostal or Charismatic churches, whose influence has increased especially since the 1980s.

The Presbyterian Church has its origins in the Protestant missionaries of the Basel Mission Church and in the United Free Church of Scotland. As I stated in the introduction of this study, the Christianisation of the Krobo began approximately 150 years ago with the arrival of Basel missionaries from the Evangelical Missionary Society of Basel (*Evangelische Missionsgesellschaft zu Basel*), commonly known as the 'Basel Mission' (BM).[56] The first encounter between the Krobo and a representative of the BM took place as early as 1836 and

---

[55] For a recent example of an elaborate study on the history of Christianity in Eastern Ghana, see Meyer (1999).
[56] Recently the Basel Mission was reorganised as mission 21 (www.mission-21.org), with its headquarters still situated in Basel, Switzerland.

regular contacts have been maintained since 1848. The Basel missionaries be-friended Odonkor Azu, a 'big man' and owner of a large oil palm plantation in Odumase, who later came to be regarded as the first paramount chief of Manya Krobo. Through the possible conversion of Odonkor Azu and the education of his children, the missionaries believed they could gain a strong foothold in Krobo society. With his help, the missionaries obtained land in Odumase on which they established a chapel and a mission house.[57] From 1857, a few Afri-can mission workers, including Thomas Kwatei, Carl Reindorf and Christian Obobi, stayed in Odumase, followed by the Basel missionaries Carl Aldinger and Johannes Zimmermann in 1859. After this the establishment of the Odu-mase mission post was considered a fact.

The Basel missionaries created the Christian quarters in Odumase in 1877 and other Krobo towns followed. The formation of segregated Christian villages within the towns called Salem (from 'Jeru-Salem'), was a practice followed eve-rywhere by the Basel missionaries on the Gold Coast. The BM would buy the land and then a piece of the land was leased to the head of a Christian family. The rationale was that if the Christians were separated from 'the heathen', the latter could not influence them so much and a feeling of unity among the Chris-tians would be created. Therefore a convert would have to break with his or her old ties and live according to the rules of the Christian congregation, e.g. live in a nuclear family and abstain from 'heathen' rites. Becoming a Christian meant a total separation from the 'heathen' world in every respect. In Odumase these Christian quarters were called *lebo*.[58]

Nowadays there is no immediate visible distinction anymore between the old *lebo* and the rest of the town. However, people are aware of its existence. It is near the old chapel and the new Presbyterian Church. The descendents of the first Christians form a small minority, belonging to the old elite. They claim they do not perform *dipo* in their house in the former Christian quarters. How-ever, this does not mean that these people are free from their obligations towards the old family house. Many people living in the former Christian quarters have even (secretly) performed *dipo* for their daughters.

The Basel missionaries were forced to leave the Gold Coast in December 1917 as a result of the outcome of World War I. Because many of the Basel mis-sionaries were German nationals, they were held to pose a threat to the British Colonial position. The Mission's entire institutional infrastructure of Churches, schools, book stores and workshops and the lands it owned were (reluctantly)

---

[57] The missionaries did not, however, obtain legal rights over the land in the first one or two decades. By 1872 they still did not own a contract to prove ownership over the land (BMA, D-1.24 Afrika 1872, Odumase 183).

[58] Nobody I asked was able to explain the etymology of the term to me, but my guess that there could be an analogy with the word 'labour', referring to the Protestant working ethos, was confirmed in a booklet of the Somanya Presbyterian centenary celebration of 1980 (Appertey 1988 13, 22).

transferred to the Presbyterians of the United Free Church of Scotland (Lamin 1983: 115; Miller 1994: 14). And the properties of the Basel Trading Company, which had developed from the former Basel Mission Trading Company but had become an independent Swiss enterprise by 1917, were confiscated and transferred to the Commonwealth Thrust. The period of this church between the two world wars:

> was marked by a widening of the educational facilities, an increased emphasis on literary as distinct from the vocational and industrial training that had been so important in the Basel Mission's programme, and a lessening of the earlier missionaries' sense of opposition to local society (Middleton 1983: 6).

Under the direction of the Scots, the Presbyterian Church of Ghana grew to institutional independence out of the structures and communities established by the BM. The Basel missionaries were not allowed to return to the Gold Coast in any significant role until 1926. Since then they have been involved in a 'partnership' with the autonomous Presbyterian Church of Ghana, 'which, not incidentally, identifies its own foundation with the arrival in 1828 of the first Baslers' (Miller 1994: 14). Basel missionaries from then on were active in new mission fields (Agogo, Pamu, the North) and at times at the Akropong teacher training college, but not in Krobo.

The Roman Catholics (who only established a church after 1941) and the Anglicans followed the Basel missionaries to Krobo land much later in time.[59] Their churches all have different branches around. The Methodists, who had been present much longer, and the Anglicans form relatively small congregations.[60] The Presbyterian and Roman Catholic churches have the largest congregations and most impressive church buildings. A Presbyterian school compound lies adjacent to the large, white building of the Presbyterian 'Johannes

---

[59] The first missionaries of the Divine Word congregation (SVD) were sent to the Gold Coast in 1938. The first Mass at Agomanya was held by Fr. A. J. Elsbernd on the occasion of his first visit in Krobo in 1938. He was invited by a group of Ewe Catholics from Lomé who had come to live at Agomanya. _Kono_ Azzu Mate Kole granted full permission to establish the RC Church at Agomanya in 1941, and two years later (1943), the first resident priest was Fr. J. O. Bowers. Several missionary out-stations were opened in the upcountry (Besease, Oloahai Osonson, Dzomua, Akrusu etc.) from 1942ff (personal communication with H. Huber, October '03 and also see the 'Burial service of Nene Azzu Mate Kole'-pamphlet (1990)). I have no data for the Anglican Church, which, however, was active before the RC Church.

[60] The Methodists and the Basel missionaries had been rivals when they became active in the area around the same time (1848). For example, missionary Widmann of the BM mentioned that he urged 'big man' Ologo Patu, who I mentioned above, to bring his children to the Basel missionaries for education, but that Ologo Patu had already sent three of his children to the school of the Methodists in Accra (BMA, D-1.2 Afrika 1842-48, Akropong 1848, No. 5, J.G. Widmann, 02.03 1848, Akropong, ' Copie eines Briefes an die Konferenz der Missionare in Akvapim & Akra - wegen Krobo'). At that time the Methodists lacked the means and personnel to develop a substantial Christian community in the Krobo region. At least by 1884, the Methodists had a congregation of their own in the trading town Akuse (BMA, D-1.40 Afrika 1884, Odumase 114).

Zimmermann' church in Odumase.[61] Behind the church is the Presbyterian cemetery. In front lies a small cemetery where only a number of German missionaries and some highly distinguished Krobo clergymen are buried. The Presbyterian Church still enjoys considerable prestige, as it provided the first schools and therefore the first Krobo scholars. Old Krobo people still call the Presbyterian Church *Basli*, and refer to the Basel missionaries as 'the Germans', who are still fondly remembered. The Presbyterian Church in Odumase has about 1,200 adult members, and additional branches in Kodjonya, Atua, Agomanya, Asitey and Ayermesu.

The Roman Catholic Church also gained considerable popularity, possibly due to its liberal attitude towards 'tradition' and 'culture'.[62] Including all local branches in Krobo and children, this church claims to have over 7,000 members.[63] A green lawn surrounds the Catholic Church in Agomanya, with shady palm trees along the access road. The two (Ghanaian) priests live in a pretty house opposite the church building. Behind there is a building where the (Ghanaian) nuns stay. On the same terrain, there is a Roman Catholic primary school and Junior Secondary School, plus the above-mentioned hospital and AIDS clinic.

The so-called African Independent or 'Spiritual' Churches became popular, especially since the 1950s. Examples in and around Odumase are the 'Prayer Deliverance Church of Christ' (Odumase), the 'Isaiah Roman Faith Church' (Asitey), the 'Divine Healers Church' and the 'Twelve Apostles Church' (Nuaso). Their members are mostly women. Individuals founded them at different times. Some have other branches in other regions, or even countries. The other churches accuse this type of church of being syncretistic, mixing Christianity and 'traditional religion'. In their healing rituals, they make use of remedies such as incense, candles, olive oil and 'florida water'. Because the Presbyterian Church started to lose members to these churches, it started to 'Africanise' its services, for example by allowing drumming and dancing in the church.

However, class differences still play a role to a certain extent, which is especially linked with education. Many prominent members of Krobo society were trained in the schools and colleges of the Presbyterian Church. A burial in the

---

[61] The Presbyterian 'Johannes Zimmermann Church' was completed in the 1970s with the help of the people of Gerlingen, the place of birth of Johannes Zimmermann (1825-1876) in the south of Germany. The mayor of Gerlingen and his wife visited Krobo-Odumase in 1972 and presented a statue of Zimmermann on this occasion (Odjidja 1973).

[62] Another reason for its increased popularity may have been the late *Kono*'s switch to the Catholic Church. Azzu Mate Kole withdrew his membership from the Presbyterian Church in protest against the apparent insensitivity of the Presbyterians to the educational needs of his state when they transferred the boys' secondary school in Odumase (PRESEC) to Accra in 1968 (see above) (Obeng-Assamoa 1998: 166-167).

[63] This estimation is based on what the Catholic priest in Agomanya (he left for a different post in 2001), Paul Lawe, told me.

Presbyterian cemetery still has a high status. The worldly success of the deceased when alive is then reflected in the prestige this will bring to the person's kin (cf. Middleton 1983: 13). Those people who do not attend the Presbyterian Church in Odumase (or any of its branches in the area), but go to the newer churches and to deity shrines, even if they have been educated at Presbyterian schools or were baptised in the Presbyterian Church, mostly include those who cannot afford dues, fees and the required standards of clothing, or people who are illiterate and generally occupy a low position in society. But things are changing. Some of the prestigious schools have ceased to exist (for example the former BM boarding school for boys, Bana Hill, which was mentioned before). In addition, the Pentecostal Churches now form serious rivals to the mainline churches.

Pentecostal churches have become popular in Ghana since the 1960s. Pentecostalism is a brand of revivalist Christianity with profound roots in African-American communities. The churches that are part of the so-called 'second Pentecostal wave' (Van Dijk 2001: 37) were founded by Ghanaians, especially after the mid-1980s. These are the so-called 'charismatic churches', with many different, small-sized denominations. They proliferated at the time of the great economic crisis in Ghana in the 1980s, when people were seeking protection within these churches (Ghana-Evangelism-Committee 1993; Gifford 1994; Meyer 1994; 1995b). Pentecostalism is characterised by a charismatic inspiration through the Holy Spirit, through which ecstasy, speaking in tongues and various forms of faith healing become available to the believer. Pentecostalism is also distinguished by its emphasis on strict moral codes and its ideologies relating to the material well-being of its members, sometimes called the 'prosperity gospel'. Particularly in the urban centres many young people are fascinated by the Pentecostals, who are highly visible and audible in the public domain (Van Dijk 2002: 94).[64] The larger charismatic Pentecostal churches, emphasising reading and study, preaching in English and underscoring the need for intellectual reflection, especially appeal to the middle classes of society in urban environments, to those who have been to school or have been able to attend university. The university in fact became the natural 'habitat' for the expansion of charismatic Pentecostalism (Van Dijk 2001: 38). Out of a total of over 13 million (13,014,779) reported Christians in Ghana in 2000, over 4½ million (4,551,597) people declared they were affiliated with a Pentecostal/Charismatic church (GSS 2002b: 26), which makes them the largest group of Christians in Ghana.[65]

---

[64] For the study of Pentecostalism in Africa see e.g. Gifford (1994), Meyer (1992b; 1994; 1998; 1999), and Van Dijk (2000).

[65] The number of people who reported an affiliation with Protestantism in general was 3,513,060; with Catholicism 2,864,387; and with 'other Christian' groups 2,085,735 (GSS 2002c: 'Table 7: Religious affiliation of Population by Region and Sex'). One should note that the number of people reporting an

In a still predominantly rural area such as the Krobo district however, the Roman Catholic and the Presbyterian churches still seem to have the largest numbers of steady members. The Coastland Assemblies of God, the Divine Apostolic church, the Christ Apostolic church, plus the church of Pentecost, are among the older and largest, usually mission-based, Pentecostal churches established in Ghana (even since the mid 1930s) that can also be found in Odumase and surrounding towns. Some of the many small-sized 'second-wave' denominations that can be found in and around Odumase are for example: the Christian Outreach Missions (Odumase), the Living Praise Bible Church (Odumase), the Christ City Church (Odumase), the World-Wide Evangelical Healing Charter (Odumase), and the Christ Anointed Church (Agomanya). Other churches around are: Deeper Life Bible Church; United Church of Christ (UCC) and Church of Christ. There are many more. Some have a handful of members, others attract hundreds of people to their services and prayer meetings.

The new Pentecostal churches and their often charismatic leaders attract young people in particular in Odumase. In addition, older and often uneducated women are drawn to their promises of (material) welfare and the often exciting services. Although old churches in particular have steady members, many people also rotate. Some people also attend two churches. They may, for example, formally belong to the Presbyterian Church, having been baptised there, but also attend a charismatic church. People within one nuclear family may attend different churches. Finally, the Jehovah Witnesses and Baptists constitute other Christian denominations in and around Odumase. The Ewe people living in Krobo usually attend the separate Evangelical Presbyterian Church (see Meyer 1999 about the EPC among the Ewe).

In Agomanya, a small Muslim community and a small mosque can be found. Somanya and Kpong also have mosques and larger Muslim areas (the so-called *zongo*'s). They usually consist of people who migrated recently or longer ago to the south from northern or eastern areas. There are already regular references to Muslims 'from the north and from Lagos', trading at the markets in Kpong and Somanya, in Basel Mission reports after the 1880s.[66] Their numbers grew rapidly, especially as a result of the cocoa boom, which sparked off an important labour migration. The *zongo*'s are religiously and ethnically distinct quarters, and the Krobo do not mingle much with their people.

---

affiliation with a certain church does not nearly coincide with the number of steady members of that particular church.
[66] E.g. BMA/ D-1.40 Afrika 1884, Odumase 112, Weiss, 30.09.1884, Quartalbericht.

Back to the mountain

Finally, in this last section I would like to return to the annual festival to which I referred in the introduction of this chapter, when the expulsion of the Krobo from their mountain home is commemorated, and to the role the festival plays in the reproduction of a Krobo identity, partly based on an association with the old 'home-towns' on the mountain.

Upon the advice of his chief counsellor, _kono_ Azzu Mate Kole is said to have instituted the annual yearly _Ngmayem_ festival in 1944. According to historian Obeng-Assamoa: 'The _Kono_ used this occasion to take stock of the previous year and to urge his people to greater progress' (Obeng-Assamoa 1998: 161).[67] From its very beginning it therefore was a political forum, an annual occasion for the _kono_ to address his people. However, it was more than that. The _Ngmayem_ festival can be called an 'invention of tradition' by the late _kono_, whose father's earlier attempts to constitute a 'yam festival' after the example of neighbouring Akan chiefdoms' (for example, the Akuapem _Odwira_ festival), in a time when the Krobo paramountcy still was in a forming phase (see next chapter), were rather unsuccessful. The introduction of a public _Ngmayem_ festival at the end of the already existing _Ngmayem_ rites, which was celebrated more or less in private by the traditional priests and chiefs (see chapter five), proved to be more successful. It stimulated people to return to the towns and as such, the festival filled a certain void after the expulsion from Krobo Mountain, when the towns in the plains had become the new 'hometowns'. As a 'home-coming' event, a political forum and a tourist attraction, it displays different important elements of 'Krobo culture', even though the festival is clearly Akan-inspired.

I witnessed the festival at the end of October 1998. Months in advance, the festival committee had started to prepare for the festivities. At the queen mothers' association meetings, which I attended regularly from July onwards, the design and price of the special _Ngmayem_ cloth that was to be printed was debated and songs were practised. The cloth that was finally presented was yellow ('gold') with the portrait of _kono_ Nene Sakite II on it, obviously a political statement (see below). In the last few weeks prior to the _Ngmayem_ festival, families came together as usual to complete funeral rites before the end of the ceremonial year. There were several installations (I witnessed about six of them) of new sub-chiefs (_asafoatsɛ_) and queen mothers to fill up vacancies before the festival. The weeks before the festival the towns were therefore very busy and the air was filled with excitation, especially because this was the first grand public festival after a pause of ten years and the first great public introduction of the

---

[67] The exact date of the introduction of the festival is not clear. It probably did not take place regularly in the beginning (Arlt 2002: 7).

new, still disputed, *kono*.[68] The *kono*'s function had been vacant since the famous *kono* Azzu Mate Kole died in 1990 after a reign of over fifty years.

The *Ngmayem* festival for the Manya Krobo lasted from Sunday to Sunday in the last week of October. On the first Sunday (*klutu*-day) and on Monday the customary black sheep had been slaughtered at the different ancestral house-shrines (*klutu*) of the divisional chiefs to pacify the ancestors and remove any threats of danger. For the *kono*'s Djebiam-Nam division it was slaughtered at the shrine just next to the old Presbyterian Church on Monday. On Tuesday, the 'stool day' for the people of the Djebiam-Nam division, the chiefs and (main) queen mothers symbolically 'wash', that is purify, their ceremonial stool (other divisions may do this at different times in the year).[69] On the same Tuesday, the Piengua and Manya divisions had their own particular celebrations. For the paramountcy, the Djebiam-Nam lineage, special rituals took place at the special stool room in the 'palace' (*wenguam*). As I was told, the stools of the last three *konos*, (Sakite, Emmanuel Mate Kole and Azzu Mate Kole) are kept here. Only men are allowed to enter. However, I was permitted to peek out of a window that looked into a little courtyard in front of the stool room. I saw heaps of feathers of sacrificed fowl to pacify the deities and ancestors and many empty cartons for (foreign) schnapps bottles that had been used to pour libations to them. The men that came outside had a white cross drawn on their chest with clay as a sign of their cleansing. The stool priestess sat in front of the door that led to the courtyard of the stool room with a calabash in front of her. The calabash was filled with a purifying emulsion of water with special leaves, and everybody who wanted to, could bathe with it, especially those who entered the stool room. The upper body and arms of the priestess were decorated with white clay. Many other traditional priestesses sat beside her. They kept on singing and dancing and having fun. Some of the women evoked laughter when they modelled their cloth in the form of something representing a penis and moved it in a suggestive way towards other women, just for the fun of it. In a different part of the large courtyard of *wenguam*, the queen mothers, the female 'traditional' rulers, had assembled under the blazing sun. They were waiting until a ritually slaughtered sheep was cooked, after which everybody was given a portion to eat.

---

[68] His installation was disputed in court by the Azu family and the Dom division (also see chapter four). The case is still pending. On the history of the disputed Manya Krobo paramountcy, see Arlt (1996; 1997), Henige (1974) and Obeng-Assamoa (1998). During the festival, the headlines in *The Ghanaian Times* stated 'Tension in Manya Krobo' (Noonoo 1998). It was rumoured in Odumase that rivalling factions were behind this story to frighten visitors and stop them from attending the festival.

[69] A 'stool' symbolises power and authority similar to a 'throne' in Europe, it is however not displayed in public (cf. Quarcoopome 1993). A stool also refers to the powers of the ancestors and can be used as a medium to interact with them (Sarpong 1971).

The stool carrier and other men sprinkled some yam around the palace to feed the ancestors.[70]

Wednesday, the day of remembrance of the ancestors (*akleme*), most people went dressed in mourning clothes, usually black and red cloth. Some people had tied a red scarf around their heads. Many women had assembled at the junction down the main road in Odumase that led to the 'royal cemetery'. The women were singing and waived with branches they had broken off trees. The queen mothers sat aside and were almost fully dressed in red. All women were in an an elated mood. Some women were dressed like men going to war in a *batakari*, a Northern type of dress. Ako, a woman belonging to the royal family, was dressed in her dead father's cloth, and wore his hat and carried his walking stick in his memory. In the meantime, men had been passing by on their way to the cemetery, where women were not allowed, since the crack of dawn. Only men are said to be buried there. This cemetery was instituted by the late *kono* Emmanuel Mate Kole, when he was not allowed by the Christians to bury his father Peter Nyarko (who had been expelled from the Presbyterian Church as a 'back-slider') at the Presbyterian cemetery. My colleague Veit Arlt, who as a man was allowed to enter the cemetery in the company of one *asafoatsε*, witnessed the libations that were poured there. When it was announced that the men were coming back, all the other queen mothers and I hastened to the palace. From a privileged place on the veranda on the first floor, I could see the chiefs coming in a huge crowd. The *asafoatsε* were carried on other men's shoulders, while the divisional chiefs and the *kono* were carried in their palanquins. Men were wildly shooting in the air with their shotguns. Women waved with branches. The crowd was boisterous and the noise was deafening. I was glad I stood safely high up the veranda, from where I had a wonderful view. Under the big shady tree at the palace courtyard people were pushing for a place outside the sun. Others were dancing round the tree. When the kono came outside the palace, everybody cheered. Different queen mothers and *asafoatsε* danced in turn, in front of where he was seated.

Thursday is the day of the pilgrimage to Krobo Mountain, the ancient Krobo home. On this day, the Akweno, Suisi, and Dom divisions also had some celebrations of their own. After the rough climb up the steep mountain, I was taken to a section where the Djebiam people had formerly resided. The men that were present there had slaughtered a sheep in the early morning. They wore a red band around their head, in order to commemorate their ancestors. However, serious matters had been taken care of and a large crowd, consisting especially of rowdy young men, had gathered on the mountaintop by noon. I was amazed to see young men selling 'Fan ice' (ice-cream) from heavy cool boxes that they

---

[70] Note that in this ritual yam is used rather than millet, even though the festival is referred to as 'millet eating'. This is a indication of the Akan roots of the Krobo chieftaincy.

had carried all the way up there. Young women also sold lemonade and iced water. At the foot of the mountain, a 'mini durbar' (public gathering with chiefs and queens sitting 'in state')[71] had been staged. Many of the queen mothers who had climbed the mountain were dressed in *batakari* or another male dress, as if they went to war. Loud music was coming from big stereo sets to which people were dancing. There was a traffic jam, caused by all the vehicles travelling between the mountain and the towns. Cars were hooting and the atmosphere was wild and boisterous. There was no re-enactment of the expulsion when I was there in 1998. A queen mother friend told me that this had taken place in 2000 for the first time, and the queen mothers' association had an active role in staging the drama performed.

On Friday, the durbar of chiefs and queen mothers, which lasts a long time, was held at Laasi in Odumase, on a large open field. The chiefs and paramount queen mother were gorgeously dressed and carried in palanquins to the durbar field. The lesser queen mothers and chiefs walked behind them, surrounded by assistants who protected them from the sun by holding huge umbrellas, which are also part of the royal paraphernalia. Along the sides of the road, the crowd was cheering and waving. On this day of the festival I finally saw some other *blɛfoɲo*, white people, around, who were either attracted by the impressive sight of the chiefs and queen mothers, or were invited guests. It is the intention to attract more tourists to these events, but usually there are just a handful, as tourism in Ghana is still in its infancy. Moreover, this festival has to compete with dozens of similar festivals in Ghana. President Rawlings had been invited, but unfortunately, he did not show up. Instead, he had sent a representative. Different local politicians were present, as well as some newspaper reporters. First, the traditional priests connected to the Klowɛki shrine performed the ritual invocations on behalf of the whole community gathered at this large public celebration and sprinkled the millet. People tried to catch the millet seeds and told me that they meant 'blessing'. Then the politicians, including the paramount chief, addressed the audience with long speeches, which were hardly audible due to the poor sound system. After this there was some time for cultural play in the form of girls of a cultural troupe, who were dressed like *dipo* girls and performed *dipo* dancing. I noticed that they had tied a brown skin-coloured scarf around their breasts, which would be uncovered during the common *dipo* performance.

On Saturday, a 'fund-raising bazaar to support development projects' took place in the morning. That day I was not feeling well, so I also missed the 'state

---

[71] 'Durbars' developed during the British colonial period on the basis of the Akan concept of a reunion, where the chief or king 'sits in state' surrounded by his attendants in a horse-shoe pattern. According to Arlt (2002: 3): 'The British compared these colourful gatherings in which state regalia are displayed, chiefly authority is enacted and popular allegiance is demonstrated with what they had seen in India and therefore referred to it as a 'durbar', a name which is still in use today.'

dance' and the election and crowning of 'Miss Ngmayem Festival '98' at the site of a hotel in the neighbourhood in the evening. The *Ngmayem* festival always ends with a interdenominational thanksgiving service on Sunday, held at the Laasi field in which the *konǫ* and the paramount queen mother take part (also see Obeng-Assamoa 1998: 159). Here the church and state meet and the occasion brings the cordial relationship between *konǫ* Odonkor Azu and the Basel Mission back to mind, as the Basel Mission Church's successor, the Presbyterian Church, is the one dominantly present. Finally, a meeting of the traditional council was held on the following Monday.

The *Ngmayem* festival is therefore a relatively recent invention by the late *konǫ* and partly is borrowed from the Akan. The advertisement for the festival in 1998, sponsored by 'Club beer' in *The Daily Graphic* (a national daily newspaper) welcomed people 'home to Manya Krobo Ngmayem '98', and portrayed a photo of a dancing and richly dressed *dipo* girl as the symbol of 'Krobo culture'. It used a slogan that made clear that the festival should not be missed: 'Be Home!!! Don't Be Told About Ngmayem '98'. During the festival, the 'homecoming' aspect is important as people make use of the occasion to arrange family matters. A sense of unity is felt in performing the chiefly rituals, the remembering of the ancestors and the general festivities. However, conflicts within Krobo society also become apparent. By not taking part or occupying a prominent place during the durbar for example, different factions can make political statements.[72] During the durbar 'Krobo culture', in the sense of a kind of folklore, is displayed in the form of the *dipo* dancing. The whole festival is concluded with a Christian gathering. However, behind the scenes traditional priests were the ones to determine the time of the festival, as it can only take place after they have celebrated their millet-eating (*ngma-yemi*) ceremonies.

In recent years, the homecoming aspect has been discovered as a more central theme by marking the expulsion in 1892 from *Klo-wɛm*, the Krobo Mountain, during a cultural display.[73] A common Krobo identity is provoked by the link with the ancestral mountain home as the place of common descent and with the shared history of the expulsion. However, the importance of the mountain in the past was based on it being the seat of 'custom', which role has been successfully taken over by the towns in the plains. Part of this success lies in the

---

[72] During the festival in 1998 the Dǫm division had not been present at the general durbar, neither was the Azu family (see above). Last year divisional chief Angmortey Zogri stayed away out of protest. Likewise, during the Yilo festival in 1998, traditional priests were upset by not having been accorded enough space at the durbar, while one particular chief of a lower ranking order boldly challenged the *konǫ* in his display of chiefly regalia. Arlt (2002) particularly sees the *Ngmayem* and the *Kloyosik-plemi* festivals as occasions where rivalry and competing claims for political legitimacy between and within the Manya and Yilo Krobo states come to the fore.

[73] Although it has to be said that the Yilo-Krobo were the first to do this during their festival and thus the competition between the two Krobo states may have triggered the cultural dramatisation of the expulsion on the Manya Krobo site.

continued symbolic link with the mountain, shown for example by the power of a new kind of shrine named *klutu*, which was introduced after 1892. It is partly based on the secret matter that lies buried beneath the shrine. This secret matter often contains a particle of a rock or another object from Krobo Mountain (cf. Arlt 2002: 22; Quarcoopome 1994).[74] As the new seat of 'custom', where all rituals take place, the towns in the plains have become the hometowns now, but the symbolic link with the mountain is maintained.

Conclusion

In this chapter, it became obvious that Krobo-Odumase is not an isolated community, but is incorporated in wider political and socio-economic processes and networks. These networks have broadened in the course of history, especially through colonisation and missionisation, as will become clearer in the next two chapters. However, contrary to the prevailing ideas of globalisation and modernisation, which are theories assuming that a process of homogenisation of cultures is taking place in the world, people are conscious of differences and boundaries. In Krobo society, the 'hometowns' are significant places of Krobo identity construction, as they are the scene of 'home-coming' events and rituals during which a sense of belonging is created. Odumase and the adjacent towns in the plains are therefore important as hometowns for the Krobo. The Krobo share a communal identity, based on their association with these home-towns. The Krobo Mountain has been a determining factor in distinguishing the Krobo geographically from other Dangme speakers. However, the really important aspect is that this mountain was the 'home' of the Krobo and the seat of 'custom', which is nowadays more consciously commemorated during the yearly festivals, for which people also come 'home' to the 'home-towns' in the plains.

There are different factors that are relevant in the importance of Odumase and its adjacent towns as hometowns. First, Odumase was the place where Christianity had been established in the mid-19th century as represented by the Basel Mission, which had a lasting impact on its population, as it brought education and was accompanied by other socio-economic changes. This will become even clearer in the following chapters. Nowadays Christianity is the dominant religion in the public sphere in Krobo and there are churches everywhere. People return 'home' for their Christmas and Easter holidays. The dominance of Christianity clearly has (had) repercussions on the performance of *dipo* as we will see. However, although the 'traditional' shrines are constructed out of sight,

---

[74] Quarcoopome explains that power (*hewam*) in the various Dangme states is based on secret knowledge (*agbaa*).

they remain in function. In practice, most people display a pragmatic attitude towards religion.

Secondly, the function of the old hometowns on Krobo Mountain, the ritual and political centre and place of 'custom', had been taken over by the Odumase conglomeration after 1892. What is most essential is that Odumase and the other hometowns have become the place of 'custom' (*kusumi*) and the focus of the still important clan and family life. Odumase is the seat of the paramountcy, and all important rituals related to chieftaincy take place in the hometowns. The shrines of the main deities and accompanying ceremonies and rituals can also be found here, including the *dipo* initiation rites for girls. People who consider themselves as 'real Krobo' retain their ties with relatives in their hometown. They return 'home' to their 'family houses' for the annual Krobo festivals, for funerals and the *dipo* rites, whereby family ties are renewed and 'custom' is observed.

Therefore the homecoming visits are part of a process whereby a Krobo consciousness and identity, based on an association with the hometowns as the seat of 'custom', is continually constructed and reproduced. As I will demonstrate, the significance of *dipo* and its transformations can only be understood within this context. The 'hometown' continues to be important in the lives of people, as it above all gives them a sense of tradition, loyalty and cohesion. The essential factor in being regarded 'a real Krobo' is a willing acceptance of a particular body of 'custom'. In a place where the same language, forms of leadership, appearance and religion (in the form of Christianity) can be found among other Dangme speaking groups and all over Southern Ghana, allegiance to this 'custom', of which the *dipo* rites form an essential part, is the most obvious and effective means of defining individual and group identity (cf. Middleton 1979: 246, 252-253), as will become more evident in the remainder of this study.

In order to gain a deeper understanding of how Krobo identity is constructed and reproduced and the role of ritual and 'custom' in this identity, in particular the *dipo* rites, it is necessary to explore some of the major themes in Krobo history. The interactions of the Krobo with the Basel Mission and the confrontation with colonial rule have been decisive periods. They will be discussed in the next two chapters. History will lead us back from Krobo Mountain to the plains once again.

3

"A mighty obstacle to the gospel":
Basel missionaries and paganising dipo[75]

As I mentioned in the previous chapter, the Christianisation of the Krobo in Ghana began with the arrival of Protestant missionaries of the 'Basel Mission' (BM), and the first extensive written accounts we have from the Krobo area were written by the Basel missionaries. Characteristic is the following description from 1877 in the *Deutsches Kollekte Blatt*, one of the Basel missionary periodicals, on the '*otufo*' or '*dipo* custom':[76]

> It is an old national custom among the tribe of the Krobo Negroes that girls are sent away from their home and family to the holy Krobo Mountain, when they are about twelve years old. This mountain, which rises firmly up from the plains, is the national sanctuary of the Krobo. Up here, they celebrate their feasts and bury the deceased. This is also the site where they seek refuge in case of war. And finally it is up here that their daughters have to spend their Otufo year and perform customs (that is, festive tradition). In groups they are placed under the supervision of old women, mostly priestesses, and spend their time with processions, singing and dancing, learning the old anthems and customs. In this way, the young Krobo women are initiated into heathendom with all its sinful traditions and immoral terrors. That is the way the Krobo want it; and every girl who does not take part in the Otufo custom, will surely be banned from her home and family and country. Since they have started to evangelise among the Krobo in 1856, our missionaries have to a great extent experienced the mighty obstacle to the introduction of the gospel that resides in this pagan custom. They have had so many girls in their Christian care and education! But then came the time for the Otufo custom. Nobody dared to miss it. And when girls came back from the mountain, they once again became a prey to heathendom. (*Deutsches Kollekte Blatt*, August 1877). (Original in German, my translation)

The Basel Mission made it compulsory for their missionaries to send quarterly reports to Basel. These reports, together with letters, diaries and photographs,

---

[75] Parts of this chapter are taken from Steegstra (2002).

[76] As the Basel missionaries in general used the Ga language in Dangme societies, they used the Ga word '*otufo*', the name for comparable initiation rites for Ga girls, more frequently than the common Dangme term '*dipo*' for these rites. Field calls them *otofu* (see Field 1961: Ch. 5). In Dangme '*otufo*' literally refers to a cloth or cushion which women used to tie to their back to support their child or to let their child sit on. Only initiated women who had started to have children would wear such a cushion. Today, during a traditional festivity women may use big cushions to make their buttocks exaggeratedly big for fun.

were kept and archived in the BM's headquarters in Basel. They offer a wealth of early descriptions of the Krobo and information with regard to Krobo history. Publications by the BM in their journals and periodicals, such as the above ones, were mostly directed to the mission's supporters in local congregations in Switzerland and Germany. In order to raise funds they had to inform them of the good work done by the missionaries, and at the same time they had to assure them of the persisting need to convert the 'heathen', stressing the task still ahead.

The Basel missionaries' writings covered the progress of the mission, but also included descriptions of the life and character of the people, their beliefs and the obstacles to conversion under headings such as 'About the Land and the People' (*Über Land und Leute*) and 'Customs and Traditions' (*Sitten und Gebräuche*). During the pioneer stages, there were many travel reports; later on most reports were accounts from the mission posts. These early reports described the many travels made into the interior of the country to explore whether or not the population of town X was open to Christianity and, for example, whether or not the chiefs were co-operative. Not only did the missionaries believe the climate inland to be far healthier than along the coast, they also felt the people were 'more receptive to Christianity'.[77] From their mission posts they reported on the results of their work: the construction of church buildings, the number and content of services held, the progress of school pupils, how many churchgoers there were, how many baptisms and how many Christians had to be excluded from taking Holy Communion or were excommunicated. The latter category concerned people who had contravened to some of the rules of the congregation. In that case they were considered to have 'slid back' into 'heathendom' and were labelled 'backsliders' in the missionary reports.[78]

---

[77] European missionary activity on the Gold Coast began as early as the 15th century with the arrival of the Portuguese, but was limited to the coast and only served the needs of the Europeans and children of African and European parents. The 19th century saw a new era of missionary activity in which the three pioneering missionary societies were the Wesleyans of Britain, the Bremen Missionary Society from North Germany and the Basel Mission with mostly German and some Swiss personnel (Debrunner 1967; Miller 1994: 13; Wilson 1991: 135-136). People along the coast were often considered as 'spoiled' by the Basel missionaries in contrast with the 'pure', less hybridised inland people they could still mould to their image. In addition, Andreas Riis, who was among the first team of four Basel missionaries who arrived in the colonial fort at Christiansborg in December 1828 (and was the only one who survived), wanted to avoid difficulties with the Danish local government on the coast and founded a mission post in Akropong, which was outside the Danish zone of control (Debrunner 1967: 99). Also see abstracts from letters and diaries from Andreas Riis in *Missionsmagazin* 1837, pp. 540-1, 551.

[78] The expression 'back-sliding into heathendom' emphasised the spatial and temporal difference constructed to distinguish Christianity and 'heathendom' (cf. Meyer 1999: 104). Many cases of 'back-sliding' had to do with the strict Christian sexual morals and at the same time the exigencies of Krobo social life, which the missionaries saw as 'sins of the flesh', for example, young unmarried catechists and teachers who had 'fornicated', or people who engaged in polygamy or had committed 'adultery'.

Reports assembled under the section 'Odumase' from the Krobo area are available from 1857, the time of the founding of a permanent mission post in Odumase-Krobo, until 1917, when, as I mentioned in the previous chapter, the Basel missionaries were forced to leave the Gold Coast as a result of World War I. However, the first report in which the Krobo are mentioned already dates from 1836, when the pioneer missionary Andreas Riis visited the Krobo with a Danish delegation.[79] In July 1838, he paid them another visit and described the 'Crobbo' and their dwellings on Krobo Mountain. To Riis they seemed 'calm and diligent', but also 'timid, malicious and vindictive'. In the past no white people, fearing for their life, had dared to approach them, he said. But Riis was convinced that a missionary could find friendly admission here.[80] From 1848 onwards, when the missionary Johann Widmann undertook an exploratory trip to the Krobo area,[81] there were regular contacts between the Krobo and the Basel missionaries.

What needs to be pointed out is that the subsequent missionaries prepared for their work by reading the reports of predecessors, since similar words and phrases can often be found in the writings of different missionaries (cf. Arlt 1995: 18). So although there were differences in outlook among individual missionaries,[82] what was described as characteristically Krobo was frequently reiterated by successive missionaries, reproducing biases of predecessors. The description above from the *Deutsches Kollekte Blatt*, which was written by an editor in Basel who culled his information from various reports, is therefore exemplary for the way in which *dipo* was usually described and replicates typical images in an even more condensed way than the original texts. The text depicts the Krobo people as a 'tribe' (*Stamm*) that sent its girls to its holy Krobo Mountain, the 'national centre', to spend a year in something called *dipo* ('*otufo*') in order to be initiated into heathendom. What is striking in this description is the experienced tenacity of the 'custom'. The missionaries seemed to be somewhat powerless, because it was 'the way the Krobo want it'. The description starts by saying that this 'is an old national custom', emphasizing for the reader that we are dealing here with something ancient and persistent. *Dipo* was experienced as an obstacle to the gospel because, from the missionaries' point of view, it was the reason why all attempts to educate and convert the Krobo girls failed.

Other cases concerned 'relapses into heathendom' by, for example, participating in *dipo* and non-Christian funeral ceremonies.

[79] *Evangelische Heidenbote* 12.01.836, Andreas Riss, 'Akropong auf der Goldküste. Aus einem Briefe von Misionar A. Riis daselbst vom 10. Febr. 1836'.

[80] BMA, D-1.1 Afrika 1829-39, Akropong 1838, no. 6, Andreas Riis, 06.07.1838, Akropong.

[81] BMA, D-1.2 Afrika 1842-48, Akropong 1848, no. 5, J.G. Widmann, 02.03.1848, Akropong, 'Copie eines Briefes an die Konferenz der Missionare in Akvapim & Akra - wegen Krobo'.

[82] For an extensive account of the lives and social and professional background of the different missionaries who worked in the Krobo area, see for example Miller's (1994) study of the organisational structure of the Basel Mission.

In the eyes of the Basel missionaries, conversion to Christianity in Africa meant the advancement of European 'civilisation' and 'enlightenment' (Halldén 1968; cf. Hefner 1993: 6; cf. Van der Veer 1996).[83] In this view, the only way to bring about conversion was for the new converts to abandon all contact with 'African traditional religion and culture' (Kirby 1994: 61). But it was the missionaries who talked about 'religion' and asked themselves which practices of the 'pagan' Krobo constituted their 'religion', and therefore needed to be abandoned after conversion (cf. Peel 1978: 443). In this chapter I want to show that, although the Basel missionaries did not succeed in abolishing the *dipo* rites, they were very successful in shaping a discourse in which 'Krobo religion', i.e. customary practices such as *dipo*, was identified and defined as 'pagan' and backward. Whereas *dipo* was part of this 'outmoded heathenism', Christianity was to become associated with 'modernity' and 'progress'. Examining the response of the Basel Mission to *dipo* will contribute to a better understanding of why *dipo* became a special focus of attention, as well as why the tensions between Christianity and *dipo* still exist today.

I will start this chapter by briefly outlining the necessary historical context, which will show that the Basel missionaries (and colonial agents) arrived when the Krobo were in the process of radical internal political and economic changes, while at the same time some of these developments in Krobo society, such as the evolution of power of the paramount chiefs (*kono̱s*), starting with Odonkor Azu and Ologo Patu, and the weakening of the ruling priests, can only be understood as a result of increased contact with both Akan and European strangers (such as missionaries). Describing the way *dipo* was celebrated on Krobo Mountain will help to explain the importance of *dipo* in Krobo society in the 19th century. After that, I will describe the missionaries' encounters with *dipo* and make clear why and how the missionaries experienced *dipo* as an obstacle to conversion. Finally, I will come back to the dualist discourse of the missionaries and its consequences for Christianity in Krobo today.

Priestly rule and chieftaincy

The first publications on Krobo history are written by members of the first generation of Krobo converts, e.g. Noa Azu and Thomas Odonkor.[84] In addition,

---

[83] However, the relationship of the Basel missionaries with European 'civilisation' and 'enlightenment' was ambivalent in matters of materiality and consumption (see e.g. Meyer 1997).

[84] Due to the Basel Mission language policy, they were written in Ga (see previous chapter). Noa Akunor Aguae Azu was a son of Odonkor Azu. He was trained by the Basel missionaries in Odumase and Akropong as a catechist and teacher. He was probably born in 1832 and died on June 28, 1917. His son Enoch Azu translated his Ga writings into English and published them in the *Gold Coast Review* (1927; 1928); Odonkor's *The Rise of the Krobos* was transcribed from an original Ga text as well. Thomas Harrison Odonkor was a relative of Odonkor Azu, but hailed from Yilo Krobo. He was made

some unpublished (and unedited) writings exist, such as those of Gabriel Si-kapa.[85] These scholars were descendants of Odonkor Azu (†1867), who is said to have been the first recognised paramount chief (*kono*) of Manya Krobo. He was the one who received the Basel missionaries warmly and through whose children's education they hoped to gain a strong foothold in Krobo society. Using them as sources of history one first of all has to be aware that the authors show a tendency to speak in favour of their particular families, supporting their respective claims to authority and seniority in Krobo. Literacy and especially written history has been successfully used by the present ruling 'house' in Manya Krobo in order to gain access and secure its line of succession to the para-mountcy. Secondly, all authors were educated in mission schools, which also causes a certain bias. Krobo history therefore favours the Manya Krobo over the Yilo Krobo,[86] and more data are available for Odumase (the site of the main BM post) than any of the other towns. By the very fact of introducing a written re-cord, Christianity has therefore played an important role in shaping Krobo his-tory and historiography.

The work of the mission-educated Ghanaian historians (also e.g. Reindorf 1889) is still used as a basis for writings on Krobo history today. The only more or less comprehensive published historical work on the Krobo so far, *The Krobo People of Ghana to 1892. A political and Social History*, and a number of earlier articles by the same author, were written by the American historian Louis E. Wilson (1986; 1990; 1991). Although Wilson claims to give a general political and social history of the whole of Krobo, he also makes (uncritical) use of the sources mentioned above, and therefore puts more emphasis on the Manya Krobo and explains the former (political) rule of priests as a 'theocracy'.[87] As Arlt (2002: 10-11) points out, Wilson's idea of an evolutionary process, from priestly to secular rule, is problematic, because one has to be aware of its Chris-tian connotations, based on a biblical model: from prophet, to priest, to king-stage. Still, Wilson's work is important all the same, because it directs our atten-tion to the generally neglected Dangme-societies of Southern Ghana. It has also

---

chief of Kpong by Odonkor Azu's son and successor Sakite in 1871, as it was believed that his educa-tion would ease the interaction there with European and other strangers. The text is not dated. Thomas Odonkor was probably born in 1857 and died in 1940. His son Rev. Samuel Saki Odonkor, ex-moderator of the Presbyterian Church of Ghana, translated the text into English (1971).

[85] The memoirs of Gabriel T. Sikapa (1874 – 1958) were written in Ga between 1937 and 1943, and translated by his grandson Evans Sikapa Madjitey (who was raised by Gabriel), upon the request of Veit Arlt (1999). Gabriel Sikapa was a grandson of Odonkor Azu, and another nephew of Sakite I; he was made chief of Akuse in 1912.

[86] An exception is Johnson's unpublished thesis in African Studies (1997). Hailing partly from Yilo Bunase, Odonkor (1971) puts more emphasis on the Yilo Krobo than the other above-mentioned au-thors who also describe Krobo history. Still, it shows that he grew up and lived within the family of the paramount chief of Manya Krobo and within that set-up gained access to political authority.

[87] That he falls prey to his sources, especially when it comes to the Manya Krobo paramount chiefs, is shown when he praises them in the same language as his sources.

collected rich material on the Krobo from various fields, thereby illuminating the significant changes in 19th century Krobo history relating to the agricultural and the political system of the Krobo. Therefore I will use some of his findings in the brief historical context I will sketch.[88]

Priestly rule

As I mentioned in the introduction to the previous chapter, in order to be accepted into the Krobo society, newcomers on Krobo Mountain (roughly between the 14th and early 18th centuries), had to adhere to certain rules that were shared with other Dangme groups. These rules included the use of the Dangme language, patrilineal inheritance, male circumcision and the *dipo* initiation rites for girls. The latter two rules adhered to the veneration of the female deity Nana (a title showing respect, also meaning 'grandmother', therefore expressing seniority) Kloweki. By contrast to the neighbouring Akan speaking peoples to their West, the Krobo did not have a hierarchical military structure of rule, but rather were led by a council of priests, the *djemeli*, who had both ritual and politico-judicial functions.[89] One of their duties was to watch the seasons in order to be able to announce or proclaim the time for sowing wheat to the public in general (Azu 1927: 254). They also were in charge of controlling public order and of ritually re-establishing it in cases of violation (Huber 1993: 242).[90] These priestly officials were attached to the worship of Nana Kloweki:

> It is said that the repertoire of Krobo rituals was greatly enriched by the addition of the cult of Nana Kloweki; not only were the millet-planting and millet-'eating' ceremonies introduced, but the *dipo* initiation was also reorganized as a much more magnificent performance. Many of the other deities have, through their priests, adopted the ritual practices of Nana Kloweki (Huber 1993: 243).

Early Krobo history should be seen as a composite of different family and clan traditions. Although some migration stories of the Krobo ascribe a special role

---

[88] I would like to add that, as mentioned above, a wealth of information about Krobo history can obviously be found in the Basel Mission Archives (BMA), a source which, besides by mission scholars, remains largely unexploited (but see Arlt forthcoming; Haenger 1997). As it was not my aim to write a Krobo history, I have not made extensive use of these records for this purpose, but nevertheless I made myself familiar with them in my search for specific information and I have used them whenever appropriate.

[89] This does not mean that the metaphysical and spirituality were not important in Akan concepts of power and authority (Akyeampong & Obeng 1995).

[90] In one of his last unpublished papers, Norbert Elias interpreted Krobo priestly rule as an early stage in the development of sedentary society (Elias 1987). The same caution should be applied as in Wilson's case: an evolutionary process seems too ethnocentric, because it is based on a biblical or Western model.

to the mythical figure of Nana Klowɛki in clearing many obstacles during their trek (Odonkor 1971: 1-2; Teyegaga 1985: 13), these must be interpreted as particular clan (Susui and Akweno) traditions and Huber's account makes clear that Klowɛki's cult was not among the 'first comers', but among the 'very early comers'. We are not given a clue in any of the historical accounts about the exact dates of events, but Wilson places the arrival of the clans associated with the *djemeli* (Manya, Bonya, Susui and Akweno) in the first series of settlements between the 14th and the late 17th centuries. He claims that Nana Klowɛki's rise to importance from a family to a clan and group deity must have been well-established before the 16th and 17th century settlements of Djebiam, Piengua and Dom clans (Wilson 1991: 21-24). It makes sense that some kind of *dipo* performance already existed, as other Dangme speaking groups (in particular the Shai and Osudoku) also perform similar initiation rites they call *dipo*, while the Klowɛki cult is unique to the Krobo.

A deity's worship was under the authority of a family ('house') elder and the deity's priest. Most female deities in addition to a male priest, demanded the services of a priestess and some other female assistants (cf. Huber 1993: 241-243). No other deity affected the politico-religious authority of the Krobo priesthood as did the female deity Nana Klowɛki, but her senior priestess could not act as ruler, because she was prohibited from interacting personally with strangers and was confined to the shrines associated with the deity. All important matters on Krobo Mountain were decided by the *djemeli* council, which consisted of four male priests (*Okumo, Asa, Adjime* and the male Klowɛki priest) and the Klowɛki priestess, and which met on a large flat rock named Anikaka that served as a high-court. On the Anikaka rock were four smaller stones on which the four chief priests sat. Each priest represented a different group around a god, namely Klowɛki, (Klo-) Nako, Nause and Hiono. All four groups were a composite of different subdivisions (Field 1942; Huber 1993: 17). The matter was only referred to 'the old lady', the priestess of Nana Klowɛki, when the court had reached a total deadlock, or an individual wished to contest the court or council's decision. Her decisions were irrevocable (Huber 1993: 242; Wilson 1991: 22-25). Wilson (1991: 26) states that the control over Klowɛki and the *dipo* ceremony lay at the core of the 'theocratic oligarchy', as he called the council. Considering the great importance of the deity Klowɛki for the Krobo priesthood and Krobo society, the historical information in written sources is very scarce. One early account comes from Odonkor. The most elaborate early description, however, is provided by the Basel missionary Christian Kölle in an unpublished fiction on three generations of a Krobo family written in 1936.[91] The story can be

---

[91] Through the life stories of the different generations in his story, *Der Kopfjäger und sein Sohn. Eine Erzählung aus Kroboland* ('The headhunter and his son. A tale from Krobo land'), Kölle tries to give his readers an insight into the most common life cycle rituals, agricultural customs, folk stories and the

called remarkable, because the Basel missionaries hardly paid any attention to the female priests. Although Kölle's story clearly is written from a Christian point of view, his version coincides with Odonkor's and it provides some additional clues to the importance of the Kloweki deity and her priestess. Odonkor's description makes clear that a woman who was (as usual 'called' by the deity) to become her priestess, had to dedicate her life to the priesthood and start her training at a young age:

> The post of a Kroweki fetish-woman demanded a very high moral standard. The would-be priestess began her training at a very tender age, and she had to dedicate her maidenhood and her whole life to the fetish. She was forbidden to salute, touch or shake hands with a man. She could not marry or be a concubine. She rarely went out, and when she went out a young girl served as a forerunner announcing her approach, so that all men might get out of her way. She never stepped aside if she met anyone in her path. However, she was not a soothsayer, but a priestess and she alone could cap an *otufo-girl* and order to the performance of particular rites and customs (Odonkor 1971: 53).

From the two descriptions, it turns out that Kloweki was primarily associated with *dipo*. Kölle's sentence that states that Kloweki was the 'head fetish' in Krobo and had "the control over the full religious, national, civilian, and economic life of the tribe", indicates the wider importance of Kloweki, but does not provide us with any details.[92] Kölle does give us some insights into the taboos surrounding the priestess, which must have attributed to her status. He said this 'holy' woman was to be 'embodied by the originally virgin, fetish mother' and should be an 'irreproachable woman', which may mean she was to remain celibate (as Odonkor suggests) and/or had passed the menopausal life stage. This status was emphasised by the prohibition to speak out her name, she was referred to as 'the old lady' (*yo mo'o*), and by her seclusion:

> She always lived on the [Krobo] Mountain in her hut. Only once a year would she step into the limelight. When this happened, somebody would lead the way and drive men, women, and children out of the street, through whose sight she could have become unclean (Kölle 1936: 9-10) (Original in German, my translation)

---

development of 'civilisation' (as represented by the mission and its schools) in Krobo. He himself expressed his goal in slightly different words and wrote that he wanted to give an insight into the way 'the fetish' in Africa 'rules the life of the Negro from his birth to the grave'. Christian Kölle was on the Gold Coast between 1889 and 1914. He was posted in Odumase in 1891 and between 1896 and 1900. He worked as a teacher at Bana Hill, the Krobo Boys' Boarding school founded by the BM, during the final years of his stay on the Gold Coast between 1908 and 1914. He based his story on: 'my own observations for many years, as well as oral and written reports from reliable locals' (Kölle 1936: 1). Kölle also made widely use of essays on customs and traditions written by his pupils.
[92] Where Wilson also mentions Nana Kloweki as the highest authority in Krobo (Wilson 1991), he seems to rely mainly on Hugo Huber (1988; 1993), and they both do not elaborate on the statement.

Like the deity, her priests had to stay ritually clean as well:

> In order not to be defiled, her priests always wear their own drinking bottles under their high edge-less straw hat. They do not touch firearms, spears or arrows; do not work with cutlasses and pickaxes either, because blood could be shed through them (ibid.). (Original in German, my translation)

It was therefore very important for the priests attached to her cult to be careful about potentially dangerous, powerful fluids, i.e. water and blood, that were also used in ritual affairs (cf. Akyeampong 1996). Other sources confirm that, in order not to become defiled, the priestess and the priests were not to mix with uncircumcised, i.e. unclean and usually Akan, people, were not to participate in warfare and that their movements were therefore limited to the mountain and adjacent farmlands (Huber 1993: 242; Wilson 1991: 25).

However, due to the demands of warfare in the area and the need for the Krobo to enlarge their territory due to population growth, the *djemeli* tried to maintain their authority by expanding it more to the realm of the secular. Therefore, they selected a member of their own ranks from the Akwɛnɔ or Susui clans as their agent. This official was known as the *Okumo*, who was perceived as the head-assistant and the spokesperson for Nana Klowɛki and the *djemeli*, exercised considerable authority over the towns and served as the main executioner in murder cases.[93] However, like all priests of Nana Klowɛki, he was also restricted in his movements and forbidden to interact personally with, especially uncircumcised, 'strangers', or interact in bloodshed or warfare (Wilson 1991: 25-26).

In short, on Krobo Mountain a joint council of priests had judicial and ritual power. The female deity Nana Klowɛki was represented by both a male and a female priest, of whom the priestess had the highest moral authority. The most significant religious ceremonies were centred on Klowɛki, who introduced the ceremonies for the cultivation of millet and whose cult enhanced the female initiation rites (*dipo*). Initiation for girls and circumcision for boys were among the most important rules that made it possible for migrants to settle on Krobo Mountain. Although the ritual expertise and celibacy of the priestess contributed to the prestige of the Klowɛki shrine,[94] the ritual taboos to which she and the other priests were restricted, limited their movements and contact with 'strangers'.

---

[93] Up to this very day the *Okumo* priest is not 'called by the gods', but is selected by the elders of his clan. The Asa priest's main function was to perform expiation and purification rituals. The Adjime priest's responsibility was to perform certain rites related to the cultivation of millet (cf. Huber 1993: 241-243).

[94] It is not uncommon for women who act as sacred professionals in different societies to be either celibate or to have passed the menopausal life stage (Hoch-Smith & Spring 1978: 14; Sinclair 1986: 115).

As the role of the priests was too limited as a result of ritual restrictions, a different type of leadership became necessary to deal with continuing slave raids and wars with the Akan states of Akwamu and Asante in the second half of the 18th century. Refugees, who joined the Krobo settlers on the mountain, were to introduce Akan forms of chieftaincy. Huber asserts that among them, tradition identifies a number of 'Denkyera' groups, who are believed to have been part of the army that was defeated and dispersed by the Asante around 1700 (Huber 1993: 19),[95] and which therefore was part of the second major wave of immigrants identified by Wilson (1991: 29). The population must have increased drastically, as after 1700 the number of sub-groups or divisions (*wɛtso*) was raised from the original seven to twelve.[96] According to Field (1942), the Denkyera refugees set up the first and most important Krobo war stool with Late Odue as first *konɔ,* but without any rulership attached to the stool. During the late 18th century, due to raging war within the forest districts of Akyem, a large number of Akyem people had also sought refuge on Krobo Mountain and were ritually admitted into Dangme societies (Wilson 1991: 38). They are said to have been the ones who introduced more elaborate forms of chieftaincy into Krobo society.

According to Wilson, the emergence of rival factions of politico-military organisation, both involved in transforming Krobo society, led to the emergence of two distinct Krobo polities since the middle of the 18th century: Manya and Yilo, with distinct leaders, and their separate capital towns on Krobo Mountain, called Manya and Yilo. This split can be traced back to the basic ethnic and cultural differences between the two main settlements on Krobo Mountain, respectively Dose (Manya) and Bose (Yilo) (Wilson 1991: 16).[97] However, the Bose divisions Bonya and Ogome continued their political-religious ties with the Dose Krobo through their membership in the *djemeli*; and their chief (*matsɛ*) and priest (*wonɔ*) continued to be installed by the *Okumo wonɔ*:

> The subtribes of Ogome and Bonya are now the only Yilo who have priests among the *djemeli.* It is important to note that the continued importance of Nana Klowɛki and the *dipo* ceremony and the presence of *djemeli* within the Yilo chiefdom insured the con-

---

[95] During the seventeenth century, the Denkyira had tributary control over the entire central and southern region of Ghana. In a series of wars that began in the late 1690s, the Asante defeated the Denkyira. The Akwamu formed the major political force under the Denkyira in the southeastern region. They managed to hold on to their power until the mid-1730s, while the Asante were extending their authority throughout central, western, and southern Ghana (Wilson 1991: 34).

[96] They comprised: Manya, Susui, Akweno, Dom, Bonya, Piengua, Djebiam, Nyewe, Okpe, Plau, Bunase and Ogome.

[97] However, Field (1941a) maintains that the Krobo were "one people until the evacuation of the Krobo Hill" in 1892.

tinued influence of the *Okumo* over the Yilo Krobo. The Yilo were therefore not completely politically independent of the old Dose Krobo theocracy (Wilson 1991: 54).

Wilson adds that the Yilo divisions were more receptive to Akan chieftaincy traditions because they had integrated more clans with Akan ancestry than the Manya Krobo. Even though the Ogome division in Yilo Krobo based its claims to the paramountcy on its descent from a priestly ruler, the chieftaincy in the line of Ologo Patu (see below) was a separate institution from the oldtime rulership by priestly kings (Wilson 1991: 53-54).

The above-mentioned Akyem refugees came to Krobo Mountain after they had been defeated by the Asante in the late 18th century. By the 1750s the Asante were the most powerful empire in the hinterlands, whose zone of political control at its zenith almost corresponded with present-day Ghana (Arhin 1967; Wilks 1975). By 1770, the Krobo eventually came under Asante domination, but, according to Odonkor (1971: 4), the Asante only had an indirect interest in the Krobo, and sporadic rebellions and skirmishes with neighbouring Akan people continued. The important markets in the proximity of Krobo Hill, such as Kokutsonya near present day Somanya or Kpong on the Volta River, were also part of the Asante's elaborate trading network. Throughout the late 18th century and the first two decades of the 19th century, the Krobo, however, were able to withstand several attacks of the Asante on their Mountain. Therefore they gained respect as formidable warriors (Wilson 1991: 39, 43).[98]

At first the Krobo farmland was concentrated around Krobo Mountain and the farmers retreated to their hill fortress at night (Odonkor 1971: 4). As the population grew rapidly, the Krobo expanded their economic base by spreading out into the plains. The expansion into lands between Krobo Mountain and the Akuapem foothills had already started in the aftermath of the defeat of the Akwamu around 1730 (see above). The Akwamu and their allies vacated large parcels of land that were subsequently purchased or simply annexed by the Krobo. The cheap cultivable land, the absence of oppressive (Akwamu) political authority and the introduction of new food crops led to a natural population increase and territorial expansion (Wilson 1991: 35-37). By the second half of the 18th century, maize had ousted millet as a staple food. The Akyem, although challenged by the Asante who were the hegemonic power, filled the power vacuum in the forests to the West of the Akuapem-Togo range created by the Akwamu's defeat and exodus (Wilson 1991: 38). The Akyem Abuakwa, who used these lands very extensively, co-operated commercially and politically with the Krobo:

---

[98] Arlt (2002: 10) also states: "The Krobo are fond of their ancestors' prowess in war and on the knowledge of 'guerrilla' tactics adapted to fighting in the bush."

[T]he Krobo had learned to form strategic alliances with competing and often hostile neighbors. The Krobo's general support of the Akyem Abuakwa against the Asante, and their alliances in the region, may also help to explain why the Krobo were able to acquire hundreds of acres of land from the Akyem Abuakwa in the late 18th and 19th centuries (Wilson 1991: 40).

The introduction of palm oil as a cash crop (ca. 1815) and increasing demand by Europeans for palm oil further stimulated the Krobo expansion. Palm oil, which after the 1820s was in high demand in Europe as a lubricant and ingredient for soap making, became an important export item in the legitimate trade. Therefore the Danes, at that time competing with the British, were interested in extending their authority over the Krobo, who were great palm oil producers (Wilson 1991: 45). The large-scale production of palm oil was facilitated by the fact that this oil was, unlike the later introduced cocoa, an indigenous West African food and a staple in the Krobo diet with a wide range of uses (Wilson 1991: 57).

Although the expansion of the farmlands continued at a rapid pace to the fertile North,[99] the *djemeli* still did not allow permanent settlement on the plains. As the distance between the plantations and the hometowns on Krobo Mountain grew larger, and the Mountain had become crammed with houses, this policy seems to have changed at least by 1845, after which the Krobo established permanent houses on their plantations instead of the simple huts (*gba tsu*) sanctioned by the priests (Arlt 1996). These settlements gradually turned into villages consisting of farm owners with their families and slaves, and later became the towns known today as Agomanya, Manyakpongunor, Somanya, Sra and Odumase. The latter two towns were the most prominent. They formed the land estates of the two greatest farmers and slave owners Ologo Patu from Yilo, and Odonkor Azu from Manya.

As I already mentioned in the previous chapter, the Krobo acquired land through the unique 'strip-farming', the so-called *huza* system (Field 1943; Hill 1970: 72-74), which is the purchasing of land by co-operative groups under the guidance of a 'big man'. Ologo Patu and Odonkor Azu both were good examples of such big men. Field (1943: 54) referred to this process as 'the bloodless conquest', and she argued that the *huza* system changed Krobo social life and Krobo politics radically. The fact that the Krobo farmers moved further and further away to their expanding plantations beyond *Okumo*'s spheres of influence, and his inability to interact with strangers, contributed to a decrease in his influence and the rise of 'big men' Odonkor Azu and Ologo Patu.[100]

---

[99] According to Odonkor, this further expansion started after the 'Katamanso war' of 1826, when combined forces of Krobo, Ga, Akwamu, Peki, and other Dangme groups defeated the Asante in a battle at Dodowa (Odonkor 1971: 9), in which the British had a leading role (Wilson 1991: 44).

[100] By 1860 the river Ponpon was reached. In the land up to this river farmers observed Thursday, the day of worship of Nana Klowɛki, as the day of rest: 'In their prayers for blessing the Krobo priests called upon the deities of all the streams and hills up to the Popo [Ponpon] but not beyond' (Field

The Krobo area, which belonged to the Danish Gold Coast protectorate, was taken over by the British in 1849. Colonisation changed the social order of the Krobo, as it started to support 'secular leadership' among the 'big men', the large oil palm plantation holders:

> Because all the Krobo's neighbors had paramount chiefs, the Danes, and later the British, incorrectly assumed that both Krobo chiefdoms had the same political and religious structure and the same history. If in the 1830s Ologo Patu was the *konor* of the Western Krobo, then Odonkor Azu, the most prominent Manya Krobo *matse*, must be the *konor* of the Eastern Krobo.[101] Thus, British and Danish assumptions bolstered the authority of both men, especially Odonkor Azu (Wilson 1991: 62).[102]

But not only the British and the Danish assumed that these two men were the leaders of Yilo and Manya Krobo, early encounters with Basel missionaries also created the impression that they were both the richest and most powerful men.[103] Hardly any reference was made to the priests. This was due to the fact that the priests did not interact with strangers and the missionaries did not associate the priests with politics.

When the British government introduced a poll tax in 1852, this led to serious conflicts and eventually to the Krobo Saturday War of 1858 (also called 'Krobo rebellion'). Hereafter both Ologo Patu and Odonkor Azu as the supposed leaders of the Krobo were arrested and taken to Accra, and ordered to pay a war indemnity in the form of palm oil to the British colonial government (Odonkor 1971: 16-17), which then was subcontracted to some merchants on the coast, who were interested in establishing a monopoly on the export of the Krobo's palm oil production. The Krobo rebellion and its consequences have been described elaborately by Wilson (1991).[104] He concludes that the Krobo came out

---

1941a: 4). According to Field this means that earlier owners did not have a residual interest in the land. But above the Ponpon River, Krobo farmers still observed the Akan taboos and days of rest. For the Krobo priests this land was 'unclean' and they did not go there. They avoided contact with the 'unclean', uncircumcised Akan, and attributed their uncleanness to the land as well. Up to this day, the main priests are not allowed to go beyond the Ponpon River, and the sacred millet may not be planted beyond this boundary. It would not have adapted to the conditions in the semi-deciduous forest anyway.

[101] In the 19th century Europeans referred to the two chiefdoms in geographical terms: Eastern (Manya) and Western (Yilo) Krobo (Wilson 1991: 62).

[102] Field maintains that around 1830 Odonkor Azu became the new occupant of the war stool first introduced by the Denkyera. By his own people he probably was considered more as a *primus inter pares* among the chiefs until the early 1860s.

[103] Examples are numerous. See e.g. BMA, D-1.4a, Afrika 1851-1853, no. 56, J. Chr. Dieterle, 31.05.1852, Akropong; BMA, D-1.6 Afrika 1855, Christiansborg, no. 2/II 39, n.d., Chr. W. Locher, Christiansborg, '3. Vierteljahrsbericht'.

[104] Chapter 6: 'The Krobo rebellion and boycott 1858-1866'. Whereas Wilson's account is widely based on the fascinating research by Freda Wolfson on the economic aspects of the rebellion, Veit Arlt has added interesting details in his MA thesis (1995) on the political turmoil within Krobo during the rebellion, making use of a diary written by a Dangme catechist of the Basel Mission.

of the war more unified socially, while at the same time it marked a turning point in their relationships with Europeans as it linked them more deeply to the wider world economy.

The expansion of the farm lands encouraged a rapid population growth to provide sufficient labour. Until the 1880s, the needs were partially met by buying slave labour. The slaves included women who were brought into the family to increase its fecundity. According to Sikapa (1999), Odonkor Azu had sixteen wives, with whom he had more than twenty sons (he does not mention the number of daughters), and he also had many slaves (also see Odonkor 1971: 24).[105] Ologo Patu also was said to have ten to twelve wives.[106] Krobo families were highly mobile and managed to farm lands in different locations (Amanor 1994: 59-60). While young men worked in the new frontier districts bringing new land into cultivation and tending to food crop cultivation, and old men inhabited the old plantation districts where labour requirements were least (Amanor 1994: 61),[107] women maintained the palm-farms, weeding them and gardening both for subsistence and the market. A (rich) man with several wives would have one wife and her children on each of his plantations.

The processing of the palm oil and especially the labour-intensive pounding of the palm nuts was a task for the extended family or even community. Hereby, according to Wilson (1991: 93), "palm oil profits belonged to men, and the profits from the oil extracted from the inner hard kernel belonged to women". The division of the fruits of the oil palm tree probably dates from the early years of the commercialisation of the palm oil.[108] The palm oil was traded to the coast (to Prampram and later by boat over the Volta River to Ada). Groups of Krobo could then be seen returning with bags of salt, tobacco, fish, cloth and other goods (Huber 1993: 57). Women generally controlled the non-export trade. They were excluded from land ownership, except where there were no male children in a deceased husband's nearer kin group, or where a wife or

---

[105] According to Odonkor (1971) slaves were largely used as agricultural labourers to facilitate frontier expansion. Amanor (1994: 56) points out that they were not reproduced as slaves, but incorporated as household dependants who provided a portion of their farm product to their masters as rent in kind and rendered them services (also see Haenger 1997). This is confirmed in the manuscripts of Gabriel Sikapa (1999). Slaves married among each other, but also with Krobo people. They owned land and used Krobo names. Female slaves however, were excluded from (full) participation in the *dipo* ceremony and slaves in general could not be buried on Krobo Mountain. This prevented them from becoming full members of Krobo society (Wilson 1991: 95). However, it seems slaves have had considerable opportunity for upward mobility, and gradually almost completely integrated into Krobo society. The Krobo, after all, had integrated newcomers into their society before. Nevertheless, to this very day, people who are descendants from slaves are excluded from chiefly functions, and in many chieftaincy disputes the slave ancestry of a candidate is used as the final 'knock-out' argument.

[106] BMA, D-1.4a, Afrika 1851-1853, no. 56, J. Chr. Dieterle, 31.05.1852, Akropong.

[107] From the 1880s onwards, plantations included both palm oil and cocoa plantations.

[108] According to Sikapa (1999) and a number of Basel missionaries, it was a taboo in the past for women to crack palm nuts, 'because Nana Kroweki hates or abhors it'. The palm tree was not indigenous to Krobo Mountain.

daughter was given land by her husband or father (Wilson 1991: 92). According to Amanor (1994: 62), it was the ambition of most propertied men to acquire lands for all sons and to have many sons. A large part of the proceeds from the land the son worked on would accrue to the father, the landowner. However, the sons would eventually inherit the land they cultivated.

When there was a lack of sons in the family, it was not uncommon for a father and/or family head to encourage his daughter, once she had passed her *dipo* initiation rites, to have children before she was married, or not to marry at all. As I explained in the previous chapter, the resulting *yo bi* then belonged to his patrilineage. In this way the daughter's services were retained on his own farm and he had additional 'sons' without the expenses and obligations attached to marrying additional wives (Field 1941a: 14). It ensured the future of the family and their wealth, as the children would provide a valuable labour force on the ever-expanding plantations. Population growth and consolidation of the family thus were, besides by polygyny, also fostered by the social institution of *dipo*, especially after access to family labour became more important after the abolition of slavery in 1874.

When Odonkor Azu died in 1867, his son Sakite succeeded him as the new *kono* of Manya Krobo. Sakite would reign until his death in 1892: "Inside Manya Krobo it was Odonkor Azu's son and successor Sakite who consolidated his father's political gains and permanently established the office of *kono*" (Wilson 1991: 63). Through his important and consistent service to the British colonial government during the Asante War of 1873-4, Sakite strengthened his position as *kono*: "Sakite's military exploits and loyalty to [governor] Glover led directly to closer relations with colonial officials, at a crucial time in the expansion of British rule over south-eastern Ghana" (Wilson 1991: 132). After the Asante war, the Asante's supremacy over the southern half of Ghana had ended forever. Although their defeat in 1874 established the British as political rulers over southern Ghana, "a position that they systematically exploited after 1874" (Wilson 1991: 121), British rule remained disputed, as several subsequent clashes with the Asante show (e.g. Asante War 1895-1896 and the Yaa Asantewaa uprising in 1900).

By the mid-19th century, the time the Basel missionaries came to settle in Krobo area, the Krobo district produced about 60 per cent of total Gold Coast exports of palm oil (Amanor 1994). The Krobo had become an important participant in the Volta and international trade. The rise in importance of the *huza* had further challenged the authority of the *Okumo* priest and empowered 'big men' (*huzatse*). Polygyny and *dipo* fostered land expansion and population growth, and the *huza* and the commercialisation of food crops also enhanced economic opportunities for both men and women. The Basel missionaries were confronted with a highly mobile population, eager to enhance economic prosperity, which only returned 'home' to the mountain for funerals, ceremonies, festivals and the *dipo* rites.

Krobo history shows a past of continuous struggles with their Akan neighbours. While the evolution of the position of (war) chiefs is associated with the tensions of the 18th century, the history of the evolution of power of the paramount chiefs – *konos*- starting with Ologo Patu and Odonkor Azu, is associated with the growth and development of the palm-oil industry, and increased contact with Akan and European strangers (Wilson 1991: 61). Big men such as Odonkor Azu were eager to expand and consolidate their relationships with Europeans. The Swiss-based, but generally German-staffed, Basel Mission arrived during this time of tension between a secular leadership that was strengthening its position and a priesthood that was losing influence.

Dipo on Krobo Mountain

To understand how the Krobo reacted to the missionaries' attempts to abolish *dipo*, it is necessary to have some idea first of the Krobo starting-point: the importance of *dipo* to the Krobo themselves and the way it was performed. I have already mentioned the close relationship of Nana Klowɛki with *dipo*, the initial importance of *dipo* as one of the conditions for strangers to become accepted on Krobo Mountain, and its entanglement as a social institution with population growth and economic prosperity. In this section I will present an outline of the basic features of *dipo* as it was celebrated on Krobo Mountain in the second half of the 19th century, whereby I do not intend to present an essentialist picture of an 'authentic' *dipo*. Although missionaries and colonial administration as agents of social change had a strong impact on the changing performance of *dipo*, the practice was not static in pre-colonial times. Without any written historical sources, it is hardly possible to reconstruct the *dipo* rites in pre-missionary times. The first written documents about *dipo* were produced by those who intended to replace and destroy it, i.e. the Basel missionaries, which also makes its reconstruction in the 19th century difficult, as the bias of the missionaries influenced their perception of Krobo (religious) practices. Still, the writings contain some detailed descriptions from which certain characteristics can be deduced. British colonial agents provide alternative, and hardly more objective descriptions, that should be read with the same caution. Hesketh J. Bell for example, who as a customs officer had been charged to write a report on the economic conditions in the Volta River District, 'exoticised' his report findings in the form of a novel (Bell 1911 [1893]). His writings were clearly intended for a European audience, as they reflect racial ideas of the time as well as ideas of romantic love. The same goes for Adams, probably another British colonial agent, who also published his findings on *dipo* in the form of a short story ('The Tail Girl of Krobo Hill', Adams 1908). However, it is possible to generate a tentative picture from both these colonial agents' reports and writings, accounts by Krobo historians and Huber's references to the historical practice of *dipo*, for which he made use of interviews with informants who were born before 1892.[109]

Whereas the farm villages and lowland towns represented the economic centre of society, the mountain settlements remained the spiritual centre where the population gathered for religious festivals and funerals until 1892. Besides the priests and the old and feeble people, young girls passing through the obligatory *dipo* rites resided on Krobo Mountain. The elders had a great deal of authority over the young people in matters of sexuality and marriage. It was a father's responsibility in particular to let his daughter pass through *dipo*. No Krobo girl could marry until she had resided on Krobo Mountain and passed the custom. Krobo farming families moved back and forth a lot between Krobo Mountain, the hometowns on the plains (*dǫm*), and the upcountry farming settlements (*yonǫ*).[110] During this time girls were under the authority of elderly women, mostly priestesses and ultimately the Klowɛki priestess. Initially they were not supposed to work hard in order to become well fed and beautiful. Their brothers, close relatives, or fiancés would provide them with food, water and firewood. However, all 'foreign' (i.e. 'Akan') or imported food, such as maize and plantain, was taboo for them. This was one of the features that the girls' initiation had in common with the induction ceremony of a priest. One task of the *Okumo* priest was to teach the *dipo* girls to be careful to not have any wounds during *dipo*. He also used to assist the Klowɛki priestess in the burial of any deceased *dipo* girl.[111] Therefore, like the priestess, girls had to be as pure and clean as possible and avoid any contact with blood.

In case there was a fiancé, it usually meant that the girl had been promised for marriage by her father when she still was an infant. Basel missionary reports show that in this way many strategic alliances were made between families. The fiancé had specific customary obligations toward his bride during the period of the *dipo* ceremonies. For example, when his future father-in-law started creating the millet farm (the crops of which were used in preparing the 'beer' for the rituals), he came himself or sent some of his friends to clear the place for the plantation. Although there was no physical coercion on the part of the parents in the choice of a marriage partner, the social and moral pressure was so strong that

---

[109] I was told that this generation that has died away by now was called *Klo yom 'tsɛmɛ* in Krobo, meaning 'Krobo Mountain bred'. This designation must most likely be seen as a traditional indicator of time periods, as probably most of them were born in the upcountry and had hardly spent a substantial amount of time on Krobo Mountain.

[110] This becomes particularly clear from a court case brought before DC Williams, in which different members from one family were involved. (GNA/ADM 31/4/23, DC Williams, 09.01.1891, Akuse, 'Regina vs. Maku').

[111] GNA/ADM 11/1115, The District Commissioner, 07.11.1892, Odumasie, 'Notes of enquiry into the complaints of Christian Tei Azzu and others against the conduct of Peter Nyako and King Mate Kole in connection with the fetish worshippers and as to the alleged restoration of the *dipo* custom'.

respectful children would have found it difficult to choose their own partner against the will of their parents. A fiancé was allowed to visit his future wife from time to time when she was still 'under custom'. Sexual play between them was condoned, but full intercourse was strictly forbidden (Huber 1993: 98-100).

Girls who were not yet initiated, and therefore not yet allowed to enter into sexual relationships, could easily be recognised. Uninitiated girls would only wear a loincloth, wrapped around their hips, exposing the upper part of their body. It enabled social control, as in this way, the elderly women were also able to detect a possible pregnancy. Girls going through the *dipo* custom could also be distinguished easily by their particular way of dressing and hairstyle. In the initial stages the heads of girls would be shaved around the neck and the rest of their hair would be plaited. They would not wear any waist beads, but a simple string with a long, red loincloth, hanging down back and front, tied to it. Adams (1908: 518) described it as a 'dark blue cloth'. According to Hesketh Bell, girls wore:

> a handsome silk cloth, velvet, or even brocade. This cloth, rather short in front, would be very long and narrow behind, sometimes seven or eight feet in length, so long, in fact, as to necessitate its being tucked or tied up. (…) No expense is spared by the Kroboes on the adornment of their girls while on the Fetish-Mountain, and the materials which form the tail are often of a very costly description (Bell 1911 [1893]: 69).

It is not clear however, whether Bell was talking about the loincloth here, or rather about the cloths used for the final dressing up of girls. Elsewhere Bell also called the loincloth 'a bright red cloth' (Bell 1911 [1893]: 145), as is still worn today. He also described the anklets that girls wore. The sound would make it difficult for them to conceal their whereabouts (ibid.: 70).

The rituals that initiated girls into *dipo* lasted about ten days, while the whole initiation could take up to one year or more. Girls had to dance every day "with their friends, lovers and acquaintances watching them".[112] Acting governor Hodgson described a dancing ground for the *dipo* girls at the end of *konọ* Sakite's villages in his report on 'Krobo customs' in 1891. It was a natural platform of granite, flat at one end sufficiently large for the dance, and then sloping gradually upwards where the spectators sat to watch the dance. According to Hesketh J. Bell, reporting on Krobo matters in the (late) 1880s and who witnessed the climax of the *dipo* celebrations during his visit to Krobo Mountain, girls who were made ready for going to the '*dipo*-rock' (*tɛgbɛtɛ* or *totroku ayimanọ*) were aged between nine and fifteen years. He observed that some girls wore no less than five or six of the 'fatty linings of goats' stomachs', and he explained that the number of these 'head-dresses' indicated the wealth of the girls' families, as they represented the number of sheep and goats slaughtered to cele-

---

[112] GNA/ADM 11/1115/CO 96/219, J.M. Hodgson, 09.11.1891, 'Krobo customs'.

brate the ceremony (Bell 1911 [1893]: 61). This 'killing of the goat' (*to-gbemi*) ritual had been performed at an earlier stage and must have referred to a purification ceremony. Girls also held a leaf between their lips. He further described the scene as follows:

> Dozens of tom-toms, brass pans, and iron bells made an overpowering din, considerably increased by the blowing of elephant-tusk horns and the never-ceasing song yelled with the greatest enthusiasm by the thousands of natives. The candidates alone were perfectly silent and motionless; the leaves were still between their lips, and each girl hung her head in evident timidity. It seemed as if they were dreading some part of the ceremony, which was apparently close at hand, and we looked forward with curiosity to what was coming (Bell 1911 [1893]: 64).

Bell (ibid.: 63) described the *tɛgbɛtɛ* as "a curiously shaped rock of considerable size. It rose out of the ground like a large regular mound, its sides fairly steep and perfectly smooth". Girls stood in a circle around the rock, and five or six priests were said to walk and dance around it. He continues his description:

> Girls were then arranged in a single file, and they were each to climb up and down the rock in turn. It was explained to us that this was the test by which it could be decided whether each maiden was a fit candidate to be admitted to a residence on the Mountain as an *Otufo*.[113] Each girl was, in her turn, to ascend the smooth sides of the rock and descend with the sole assistance of her wand.[114] If she performed this task without slipping or falling, she was considered of unimpeachable virtue; but if any unfortunate should slip, tumble, or fall on her knees, such accident was to be taken as an unmistakable token of her unfitness to be received as an *Otufo*. The summit of the rock was not more than eighteen or twenty feet from the ground, and, though the sides were steep and slippery, the task was by no means difficult, especially to hardy little black maidens accustomed to run about over hill and crag all day. The knowledge or consciousness of being unworthy was probably relied on to point out the truth, and the effect of guilty unsteadiness would be attributed to the unmistakable action of the great Fetish in causing the girl to stumble and fall (Bell 1911 [1893]: 65-66).

Azu (1928) simply said that a girl would be set on the *tɛgbɛtɛ* three times and he also called it the 'entrance ceremony'.

It was believed that the *tɛgbɛtɛ* rock could reveal a pregnancy. According to several descriptions, an uninitiated pregnant girl would face life-long banishment from her home, or even death (e.g. Azu 1927: 265). We do not know how often this punishment had to be applied, but the taboo was so strong that it probably did not occur frequently. In some accounts, we are also told that 'unchaste' women sometimes were 'sold' into marriage to neighbouring groups.

---

[113] Like the Basel missionaries, the British used the Ga term *otufo*, but different reports show that they were also familiar with the term *dipo*. The usage of the Ga term was most probably due to the interpreters of the visitors, who were mostly Ga.
[114] With wand he must have referred to the tall walking stick the *dipo* candidates are sporting.

They may also have ended up in prostitution. This prospect, and probably the shame, even sometimes caused suicide.[115] The 'selling' of Krobo girls to the surrounding Ga and Akan areas was probably not as extensive as the import of women from outside to marry. The importance of female economic production and biological reproduction bolstered polygyny (Akyeampong 1997: 150). According to Haenger (1997: 199-201), this 'exchange of women' could be found all over the southern Gold Coast.[116] However, the 'selling' of Krobo girls was special, because it was religiously legitimised and connected to the *dipo* rites. Haenger argues that the Krobo, dominated by the neighbouring and numerically superior Akwamus and Akuapems, had developed a pronounced sense of society that was incompatible with marrying out their own women to neighbouring areas. Therefore the 'selling' only concerned girls who were found to be pregnant before passing through the rites. Odonkor also tells us that:

> The lot of a defaulting girl who had not yet been initiated into the *Otufo*-cult was most pathetic. The girl was banished from the land and the male offender was fined heavily. The maximum fine was 15.00 cedis or about 150 shillings (150 head-loads of cowries), which went to the parents of the girl. The parents, in turn, gave the Jemeli [*djemeli*] (thirty-two shillings), 3.20 cedis, sheep and other articles for purification ceremonies. Very often, these fines proved too heavy for some families and thus many people found their way into domestic slavery (Odonkor 1971: 55).[117]

So in sum, the lot of 'a defaulting girl' not only fell on herself and her lover, but also on the whole family. The family was held responsible. As was common in those days, in the case where people were unable to pay their debts, a family member would be pawned to pay off those debts.[118]

After the *tɛgbɛtɛ* ritual, the girls' heads would be completely shaved and they wore tall straw hats: "On their heads they wore long conical hats three feet high, shaped like an old strawberry pottle" (Adams 1908: 518). As they remained out of sight of the strangers, we have no description of the appearance of the senior Klowɛki priests, but from later descriptions it becomes clear that these hats were similar to those worn by them (and they still wear them today). After the shaving, the girl was brought to a round hut (*dipo tsu*). She would be con-

---

[115] GNA, Christian Akutei Azzu, 01.09.1890.

[116] After the abolition of slavery by the British in 1874, the missionary Schönefeld wrote to the missionary Mader: "The only comment I have heard about the emancipation is that it will be unfortunate that the Krobos will no longer be able to buy women and girls for marriage from outside the tribe" (Jenkins BMS Abstracts, 8 July 1875, Odumase, 'Schönefeld to Mader').

[117] T.T. Ashie also mentions a fine of fifty head bags of cowries for the priests and another hundred for the costs of purification (Ashie n.d.).

[118] The system of pawning was very common. In case a man took a loan from somebody, he would have to pawn a relative as security. That person would work on the other man's farm until the debtor paid back the amount (cf. Haenger 1997). Gabriel Sikapa drew up a list of thirty-five people that were 'pawned' to him in 1938. He noted down that these people came from Manya, Yilo, Accra, Prampram, but also from Akyem and Akwapim (Sikapa 1999).

fined for one week, but was allowed to sleep at her parents' house during the night. After this, the girl was allowed to work again, but she could not go beyond the foot of the mountain until the hair on her shaven head was fully-grown again. When the hair had grown, it was dressed with a mixture of kernel oil and a black substance, and tied into several locks. Then another girl would put on her hat again and she was allowed to move around, but she had to spend every night on the mountain. During this time, plantain and coco-yam were still prohibited food, but it was allowed to eat yams and cereals. Such a girl was not allowed to go near the Volta River and she had to avoid the uncircumcised (Odonkor 1971: 56). This phase could last for a long time. According to Odonkor, it lasted one year. Bell even thought it was four to five years (1911 [1893]: 70). The longer the relatives of a girl were able to afford her upkeep on Krobo Mountain, the greater their status. If a *dipo* initiate was found pregnant during this phase, this caused a great scandal, but the girl would no longer be banished from the mountain. The Asa priest would just take away the girl's *dipo* hat at the foot of the mountain and put a handful of corn into her mouth, which was repeated three times. Meanwhile the other *dipo* girls would dance around her, teasing her with songs of disgrace, and striking her with light scourges they carried in their hands. According to Odonkor (1971: 57), the girl's mother would be fined to pay 1.60 cedis (sixteen shillings) and the male culprit 3.20 cedis (thirty-two shillings).

According to Azu (1928: 28-29), the initiands received some training during their stay on the mountain. After they had successfully proved their sweeping skills, they were rewarded with: "some cuts on the back of both thumbs, and the scars are left there as an everlasting certificate." They also learned how to dance and sing the historical songs called *klama*, and those who proved to be talented were chosen for the priesthood. Finally, Azu describes, the initiands would receive "some cuts on their stomachs and waist to show that they have passed under this training". Other than that these cuts were proof of their initiation, Azu does not explain the purpose. His remark that it was applied to "all candidates who have emerged from their teens", suggests that these marks had something to do with sexual maturity. This is confirmed by Omenyo (2001) and Ashie (n.d.).

At the end of the *dipo* time of girls, the black hair dressing would be washed out of the hair on Saturday (Azu 1928: 29), and there was a large gathering for a dance on Sunday. Girls would show their dancing skills and receive presents from relatives and friends. The larger the family, the more presents they would get. At this final stage girls were dressed with expensive cloths. Valuable beads were then draped around their neck, ankles, hips, knees and arms. This stage was called 'dressing up' (*bo-bumi*) and after this girls were declared marriageable.

According to Huber, female slaves who had never been pregnant before, could also undergo the *dipo* rites in order to become 'children of the tribe'. Female slaves who already came to Krobo with children only went through part of the ceremonies, namely 'killing of the goat' (*to-gbemi*) and 'dressing up' (*bobumi* or *bobum*) (Huber 1993: 94). The Basel missionary Christian Kölle however, describes *bobum* as the only initiation rite possible for what he calls 'serf girls' (*'leibeigen Mädchen'* or in Krobo *'nyongnei'*).[119] According to him, the reason for this ceremony was to offer a substitute to those who were not allowed to undergo *dipo*.[120] As with *dipo*, family members would gather in one of the mountain towns on a Sunday. There would be much meat and maize porridge (*'Maisbrei'* in Kölle's description) to eat, of which part was given to the ancestors. The main drink was maize beer, but palm wine and schnapps were also available. After the meals, the women decorated the girl with beads around their neck, arms and legs. Her father would then put a white linen or cotton cloth on her. After this, other people gave her more cloths and gifts. In contrast with the regulations of *dipo*, a girl who became pregnant before her *bobum* would not be excluded from society. However, she would undergo the ceremony on Monday instead of Sunday, which would make it clear to everyone that she was not a virgin anymore. The main purpose of the abbreviated celebration of the initiation rites for slave girls therefore seems to have been to declare them marriageable.

The number of girls and the amount of money involved in *dipo* can only be guessed at. However, from different reports we can conclude that *dipo* must have been very significant in both Krobo social and economic life. According to (acting governor) Hodgson's report on 'Krobo customs', families banded together to be able to afford the expensive *dipo* custom. Sometimes there would be eighty to hundred girls on the mountain at one time.[121] Other estimations were much higher than that. In a letter, probably from chief Odonkor of Kpong to the Gold Coast government a year before, it was stated that there were over 300 girls staying on top of Krobo Mountain at the time.[122] Bell even thought he observed between 700 and 800 girls gathered for the *tɛgbɛtɛ* rite. District Commissioner (DC) Williams of Akuse stated in February 1891 that *dipo* had started in November and that no less than 2000 girls were taken up the mountain for the purpose, who would remain up there for about two years. Williams thought that the

---

[119] BMA, D-10.2, 10C, C. Kölle, 'Sitten und Gebräuche II'. The different 'customs' ('Sitten') described in these files were school essays (from Bana Hill, the BM boys' boarding school), collected between 1908-1914 and, like Kölle's novel 'Der Kopfjäger und sein Sohn', written down by the author in the 1930s.

[120] According to Kölle's essay, the *bobum* ceremony was also meant for girls who served in certain shrines. Maybe these girls were not of Krobo origin. He calls them *woyokwabii*, and describes a similar system to what is known as *trokosi* in the Volta Region in Ghana, where young virgins are compelled to become betrothed to deities to 'atone' or serve for the transgressions of a family member. Priestess Lako Sakite used the term *woyokwɛ* in an interview with me to refer to such girls.

[121] GNA/ADM 11/1115/CO 96/219, J.M. Hodgson, 09.11.1891, 'Krobo customs'.

[122] GNA, 17.09.1890, 'letter attached to C. A. Azu's letter'.

total amount of money spent on one girl during her *dipo* time would even amount to £20,000. During the preparations for the custom the trade in Akuse and Kpong flourished, he said, as Krobo people bought the necessary items for the upkeep of girls. In the latter part of November and the whole of December, however, business had slowed down considerably: "and the falling off was caused by an entire abandonment of the Croboes to everything and devoting their energies to the celebrations of the virginal custom otofu – I apprehend however, a revival during the ensuing quarter".[123] The same year he reported in July that: "The greater part of the Croboe girls in the 'Otofu' or Virginal custom having been taken out, the markets of Akuse and Kpong were overflowed with the supply of palm oil and palm kernels during the quarter".[124] The relatives of girls who came from the upcountry villages to celebrate their daughter's coming out of *dipo*, apparently took the opportunity to sell the palm oil and palm kernels from their plantations on these markets.

In sum, the *dipo* rites first of all formed an intrinsic component of the veneration of the female deity Nana Klowɛki on Krobo Mountain. Like her priests, girls were to be ritually clean, were not allowed to eat non-indigenous food and wore priestly hats. Girls were closely guided by priestesses and elderly women. Even though maize had already ousted millet as a staple food during the second half of the 18th century, millet remained significant for ceremonial use, and both the father and the fiancé of a *dipo* girl had a special plot to grow millet to prepare for the rites. Different stages indicating a girl's maturity before, during and after the rites were clearly marked by her bodily adornment. One of the most important ceremonies during the rites was 'the climbing of the *tɛgbɛtɛ*', in order to test a girl's virginity. If she failed the test, it would make her a social outcast. *Dipo* also was a family affair. A girl was often already betrothed before the rites. However, after the main initiation rites, a girl could remain on the mountain up to one year or more to be beautified, to be prepared for a future life as an adult woman and add to the prestige of the family before she married. The people in the farm villages and the lowland towns regularly returned to Krobo Mountain to visit their daughters, and the final coming out of many girls at the same time was a homecoming ritual for all Krobo. In the past, the *dipo* rites were among the most important rules that made it possible for 'strangers' to be admitted into Krobo society. Female slaves and descendants from slaves, however, could probably only undergo the final stage of *dipo*, the *bobum* ceremony, as a substi-

---

[123] PRO/CO 96/217 Gold Coast 1891, Governor Griffith, 25.06.1891, Christiansborg Castle, 'Gold Coast, no. 210 to Lord Knutsford'; Governor W.B. Griffith/Act. Gov., 21.02.1891, Akuse, 'forwarding DC William's report'.
[124] PRO/CO 96/218 Gold Coast 1891, Act. Gov. Hodgson, 28.07.1891, Akuse, 'forwarding D.C. Williams' report'; Governor Hodgson, Victoriaborg, 12.09.1891, Accra, 'Gold Coast, no. 304 to Lord Knutsford'.

tute, and therefore did not become full members of Krobo society, but were declared marriageable. 'Defiled' girls, girls who became pregnant before having passed through the rites, would face life-long banishment from Krobo society and were 'sold' to surrounding, mostly Akan, peoples. Normally Krobo women were not likely to marry outside their own society, especially not to Akan people who were regarded unclean.

'A swamp of immorality and wickedness': Missionaries encounter dipo [125]

The Basel Mission is identified with a version of the Pietist movement, which was influential in Southern Germany and Switzerland in the late 18th and early 19th centuries, called Württemberg Pietism, after the region in which it found its strongest expression. Miller (1994: 12) defines Pietism as: "an emotionally intense set of beliefs and practices that placed especially strong emphasis on spiritual rebirth, close individual reading of scripture, personal asceticism, discipline, and – apart from occasional expressions of millenarianism- social conservatism". The German Society for Christianity that founded the BM in 1815 as a seminary for the education of overseas evangelists wanted to express its religious beliefs to the outside world. The founding of the BM had also been influenced by contemporary journeys of discovery and a related aroused interest in exotic peoples, the decline in the Atlantic slave trade, an increased interest in encouraging legitimate trade and a desire to establish mission stations in the inland regions.[126]

The BM considered itself a bearer of the ideal of civilisation and culture. Although, after having lived in Africa for some time, some Basel missionaries came to disagree with the viewpoint that Africans were 'uncivilised', their aim was not to credit, preserve or restore native societies, but they intended to create an entirely new social structure around which stable communities built on a European model could be organized (Miller 1994: 116):

> Missionaries sent to Africa typically believed that their special calling was to guide the natives to salvation by teaching them a way of living radically different from what they had previously known. The new life would be centered on the villages, churches, and schools attached to the Mission's stations and outstations. Converts were required to accept European names, dress, customs, and family forms and to assume positions in their new lives that were subordinate to the missionaries in the Christian community (Miller 1994: 131-132).

---

[125] '… a swamp of immorality..', translated from: '…ein Sumpf von Sittenlosigkeit und Lasterhaftigkeit.' *Der evangelische Heidenbote*, March 1852 (3), p. 19.
[126] See e.g. Debrunner (1967: Ch. 6) and Miller (1994: 116, 135-136) on the BM and the abolition movement.

The word 'culture' was mostly used in connection with the material side, such as agriculture, trade, handicrafts and school activities. Where Africans cultivated their land intensively, missionaries tended to ascribe them a certain cultural level (Halldén 1968: 43, 47-48). It is in this regard that the Krobo were described positively by Basel missionaries as industrious and hardworking with their oil palm plantations planted 'in beautiful order'.[127] The missionaries usually had a strong rural background themselves.[128] The general assumption, however, was that the Africans were at a low stage of the evolutionary scale. It was thought that, through the presence of the whites, Africans could be brought to a higher stage of culture. The general character of 'the Negro' was described as bad and with erroneous moral valuations. This view was based on the biblical fundamentalism of the mission. However, missionary thinking was ambivalent. On the one hand it was believed that 'the Negro' was still under the influence of the Curse of Ham and suffered from several inherited weaknesses of character.[129] On the other hand people believed that there were only differences of degree between the potential for development of different people. The missionaries believed that the great task of the mission was to create a morality in primitive peoples, so that moral values could be enhanced (cf. Halldén 1968: 81-82).

In describing 'Krobo religion', the missionaries underplayed the importance of religious practices and emphasised 'belief' instead.[130] Whereas religion was essentially a matter of the mind to them, for the Krobo it was also a matter of outward action and instrumental in achieving certain goals. For example, the priests were the ones to determine the planting season and perform certain rites in order to assure success. And to persons like Odonkor Azu, Christianity must

---

[127] See for example: BMA, D-1.2 Afrika 1842-48, Ussu u. Akropong 1845, no. 16, H.N. Riis, 05.06.1845, Akropong.

[128] Most of the missionaries had backgrounds as artisans or were sons of farmers (Miller 1994).

[129] Ham, Sem and Jafet were the sons of Noah who survived the Flood on Noah's ark. One day Noah became drunk after drinking wine from his vineyard. He fell asleep in his tent while being naked. Ham looked at his father's nakedness and told his brothers about it. The latter two took a coat and walked backwards without looking at their father to cover him. When Noah woke up and heard what his youngest son Ham had done, he cursed him and his descendants to always remain servants to Ham's brothers and their offspring (Genesis 9: 8-17). According to then current 19th-century Protestant missionary discourse, the African peoples were descended from Ham's progeny and formed 'the lost tribes of Israel'. See e.g. BMA, D-1,7 Afrika 1856, Akropong, no. 21/IV 219, J. A. Mader, 01.09.1856, Akropong, 'Reisebericht nach Akwam'. Also see Braude (1997) on how the Curse of Ham has influenced the complex European attitude toward the Other. The idea that the Krobo also descended from people who once migrated from Israel, is still replicated in writings of Christian Krobo scholars today. They believe, for example, that the practice of male circumcision was adopted from the Jews (Ashie n.d.: 45-46; Odonkor 1971; Ofoe 1979: 2).

[130] The view of religion in terms of belief is not merely confined to Protestant missions, but is part of a general and dominant Western tradition in the study of religion. This tradition is based on a post-Enlightenment Christian definition of religion as 'belief' at the expense of religious practices, and is mistakenly assumed to be universal (Asad 1993: 27-54). Also see Meyer (1999: 103-104) with regard to the Bremen Mission among the Ewe in Ghana.

have seemed to be one of a variety of new cults that were spreading at the time (cf. Middleton 1983: 8), as he tried to use the mission as an alternative system of religious power to the system of the old priests. Because Christianity went together with education, it was the perfect religion for trading on the Southern Gold Coast (cf. Arlt 2002: 15). He therefore showed a great interest in 'European ways'.[131]

In portraying Krobo culture and religion, the missionaries tried to create an antithesis with Christianity. In order to legitimate and depict the need for salvation and conversion of the Krobo to their homebase, the missionaries painted an image of a primitive, heathen Krobo society (cf. Meyer 1999: 83-84; Van den Bersselaar 1998: 153). The darkness of 'heathendom' was often contrasted with the light of Christianity. 'Darkness' is a recurring trope in the missionary image of Africa, mostly referring to 'heathendom' and the realm of the devil, the 'Prince of Darkness'. However, a great variety of meanings can be found. In Christian symbolism 'white' is good, 'black' is bad. Africans were characterised by their 'black' skins. Some missionaries believed that the Africans belonged to the race of Ham and as a consequence fell under the biblical 'curse' of Canaan. This line of thought also points to the Western linkage of skin colour and moral state (Braude 1997; Hastings 1994: 299-300), and the then current view of an analogy between race and gender degeneration (McClintock 1995). A very common means of describing the darkness of the 'heathen world' was therefore the depiction of the sexual immorality and degeneration of the 'heathen'. Out of the descriptions of the Gold Coast by the missionary Johannes Zimmerman (to whom I will return at a later stage) the following picture was composed in 'The Heathen Messenger' (Der evangelische Heidenbote):

> Oh what a pitiful life is such a Negro life. And could a healthy moral life be able to unfold here? Where the soul has no living, holy and merciful God to hold on to, she has to perish in the abyss of sin. That is how it is with the Negro race. It is a swamp of immorality and wickedness into which the Negro peoples are immersed. The devil of animal lust in particular holds them captured, and not just men and women, young men and young women, but children between the age of six and eight suffer in these chains.[132] (Original in German, my translation)

---

[131] Odonkor Azu was said to be dressed in European suits when interacting with Europeans and to have European furniture in his house on the mountain. Much to the frustration of the missionaries he was never baptised. (BMA, D-1.9 Afrika 1858, Akropong, no. 39, G. Auer, 29.10.1858, Akropong, 'Quartalsbericht'; BMA, D-1.7, Afrika 1856, Abokobi, no. 8/III 89, A. Steinhauser, September 1856, Abokobi) (also Odonkor 1971: 23-24).

[132] Der evangelische Heidenbote, March 1852, No. 3, p. 19

In the many, very detailed descriptions, the large number of references to *dipo* may not be surprising.[133] Whereas polygyny and sexual behaviour were the grounds on which frequent decisions were made to prevent the baptism of applicants or exclude church members, *dipo* was seen as a main cause of immorality and the primary obstacle to the conversion of Krobo women. The characteristics of *dipo* served as exemplary proof of the necessary moral education of the 'heathen'.

The then current notion that the 'primitive religion' of the Africans was in a state of decay and consisted of nothing but devil-worshipping, frequently recurs in the reports of the Basel missionaries. For example, the missionary Stanger remarked after a first acquaintance with the Krobo in 1851:

> They worship the fetish, like all Negroes in this area. However, the outstanding feature here is that they always maintain a number of harlots on this mountain, who may not marry. The fetish, they say, has dedicated them into this sinful life. The religion of these people truly is nothing else but a devil's institution, a cover of all evil and sin and it takes different forms at the various places […]. (Original in German, my translation)

Stanger noticed here that in serving the 'fetish' or 'idols', the Krobo distinguished themselves by maintaining 'cheap whores' on their 'native home', Krobo Mountain.[134] He was referring either to the virgin girls serving in some shrines (see above) or the *dipo* girls for the first time. He claims that they could not marry. He implies that this was because they were connected to a 'fetish', meaning a shrine or a god. Apparently, he imagined that these women also had sexual relations in 'serving the fetish', as he also calls them 'whores'. This first impression was repeated in subsequent descriptions, where the same 'whores' or 'harlots', apparently because of their 'nakedness', were taken to be the *dipo* girls, who were also compared to a kind of nuns. In this context the missionary Auer wrote in his quarterly report, for example: "A number of girls devote themselves to the fetish for some years",[135] which in the published story in the *Evangelische Heidenbote* was interpreted as: "[G]irls that lead a kind of convent life. They are engaged or devoted to the idols for some years and live on the mountain walking around almost naked".[136] In this way girls 'devoted to the fetish' were portrayed

---

[133] Other examples are references to polygyny, adultery and fornication, and liquor consumption. For example, see Kanogo (1993), who describes the same attitude of missionaries towards cultural practices of the Kikuyu in Kenya.

[134] The word 'fetish' is supposed to have derived from the Portuguese word *feitiço*, and was originally used to refer to charms and amulets. Later it became a denoting word in French and English used for any indigenous religious expression in West Africa (Parrinder 1976: 15-16). Today, Ghanaians still talk about 'fetish priests' and call 'traditional' religious expressions 'fetish'.

[135] BMA, D-1.9 Afrika 1858, Akropong no. 39G, Auer, 29.10.1858, Akropong; original in German, my translation.

[136] *Der Evangelische Heidenbote* 1859 (5 & 6), 'Ein Ausflug von Akropong nach Odumase'; original in German, my translation.

according to the biblical image of temple prostitutes in the published version for a European audience.

The dubious morality of the Africans and of the Krobo was related to the idea that wizardry and superstition had replaced the original folk religion (cf. Meyer 1999: 57-58). It is on the basis of this viewpoint that we must also understand the following example in the first elaborate description of *dipo* in 1858, when the author, the missionary Heck, remarks: "At first these customs did not have anything to do with the fetish, but now the fetish priests interfere and say: any girl that has not undergone *otufo* [*dipo*] either has to die or be banned from Krobo country".[137] Heck and the other missionaries believed that the 'fetish priests' were originally not involved in the *dipo* practice. He saw the proof in a story about the creation of *dipo*, in which the traditional priests were not mentioned. The summary of this myth tells us: 'the origin of the custom lies with a mother whose twelve children, except for one girl, died. She now wanted to do something special for that girl and took her to a mountain town where the girl did not have to take care of anything but her beauty. After some years, the mother prepared a meal and invited all friends and relatives and they came with gifts. Afterwards, the girl got married'. Similar stories still circulate between the Krobo and other Dangme-speaking groups today.[138] Another myth of origin refers to the mythical figure of Nana Klowɛki as the instigator of *dipo*. However, the missionaries ignored the importance of traditional priests in Krobo society in general and in *dipo* in particular. Especially female priests are hardly mentioned. The missionaries were unable to see the function of these women in traditional religion (cf. Meyer 1999: 62).

The missionaries saw the exposure of the body of the *dipo* girls as evidence of the sensuality of 'the Negro'. In one of his early reports Johannes Zimmermann described the Shai and Krobo *dipo* girls he saw in a market as "almost naked but for the many glass beads and other jewellery they were wearing". He calls them "a kind of female Nazarenes, whose nakedness, however, doesn't match with their oaths of chastity".[139] Therefore, to him the specific

---

[137] 'Reisebericht', J. Heck, Abokobi, 25.5.1858 (BMA, D-1.9 Afrika 1858, Abokobi no. 13); original in German, my translation.

[138] Usually the story goes that a man had two wives, of whom only one had sons and the other only had daughters. The one with the daughters was jealous of the gifts the other's sons received after their circumcision. In order to compensate her, the *dipo* custom was instituted as a celebration for her daughters.

[139] *Missions Magazin* 1856 (II), p. 74, (Zimmermann, October 1855, Abokobi); original in German, my translation.
'Nazarenes' are referred to as an early Christian sect: "(…) the earliest reference to a sect of Nazarenes occurs in Acts 24:5, when it is used by Tertullus, Paul's 'prosecutor.' While it can be argued that the lawyer Tertullus invented the name for the occasion, there is a tradition as early as Tertullian that an early name for Christians was Nazarenes, and his claim is borne out by the earliest name in the various Semitic languages. The name of the sect obviously came from the title 'Nazoraios/Nazarenos'"(*Nazarene Jewish Christianity--from the End of the New Testament Period until*

dress of girls was in contrast with the chastity they had to adhere to during their *dipo* time. As these girls were seen off the mountain and were extensively adorned, they must have passed their 'outdooring' stage and therefore already been initiated. At the same time, the 'nakedness' of young girls for the Krobo could also rather mean they were not yet ready for sexual relationships.

Although some of the missionaries were able to see that the *dipo* rites regulated sexual behaviour, the 'immoral' content of the rites dominated their negative opinion. Heck also wrote:

> [S]ins that are more secret take place, especially onanism. In general, this custom consists of an enormous, sinful fleshliness - such an immoral life prevails among the black youths of both sexes on this mountain, that my feelings do not permit me to describe it in more detail. (…) When I looked at this in every respect unbelievable misery of the poor black youth, I sighed by myself: Lord, have mercy on these poor people! This custom is a mighty obstacle to the gospel.[140] (Original in German, my translation)

Heck's reports and those of his successors in later years claim that they cannot go into detail, because of the immorality of the rites. It is more likely, however, that the rites were a complete mystery to the missionaries. In mentioning 'both sexes', Heck may be referring to the fiancés visiting their future brides. Although, as we saw before, sexual play probably was condoned to a certain degree, however only under strict regulations. Nonetheless, any reference to sexuality was an abomination to the missionaries and confirmed their assumptions. The missionary Carl Schönfeld provides us with another typical example:

> A five-year-old girl is aware of all the mess of sins and shame of her mother. Living in the same rooms of immorality with the adults, she hears everything, imitates the mother. My report would become filthy in its expressions if I were to go into details. When the girl-child, already with a spoiled mind and in most cases already defiled, enters her twelfth year, she is taken to the mountain then. There she is carefully instructed in all filthy sexual secrets (as we would say in Europe; here people don't know secrets in this respect), initiated, seduced, shown how to disturb the fruit of the sin, and above all the Krobo woman becomes the bearer of the fetish veneration and spoilt customs. When the girl, who in the meanwhile has grown up, comes from the mountain, she is fully uncommitted in all her movements.[141] (Original in German, my translation)

A related aspect of *dipo* that is mentioned time and time again in the missionary descriptions was the fact that *dipo*, not marriage, served as the prerequi-

---

its Disappearance in the Fourth Century, Ray Pritz, Magnes Press, (1988: 11), retrieved from http://www.christian-thinktank.com).

[140] BMA, D-1.9 Afrika 1858, Abokobi, no. 13, J. Heck, 25.5.1858, Abokobi, 'Reisebericht'; original in German, my translation.

[141] BMA, D-1.25 Afrika 1873, Odumase 14, C. Schönfeld, 31.12.1873, Odumase, '15. Jahresbericht'; original in German, my translation.

site for girls to enter into sexual relationships and conceive. If a Krobo woman was not yet married, any children she bore would belong to her father's family and not to her children's father. As mentioned before, they would be called *yo bi*. Zimmermann understood that a father, lacking a large number of sons, tried to maintain the strength of his family by not allowing his daughter to marry into another one, but he felt the practice led to promiscuity, venereal diseases and a general deprivation.[142] The missionaries considered children born out of wedlock as illegitimate children. However, as outlined earlier in this chapter, these children were rather welcomed as an important labour force by the Krobo, and became full family members.

We are not provided with very detailed descriptions of the actual content of the *dipo* rites. The nakedness of girls and the association with the 'fetish priests' were enough for the missionaries to conclude that 'immoral' things went on. Their contempt of Krobo religious practices and their approach of religion in terms of individual 'belief' prevented them from investigating the details of ritual performances (cf. Meyer 1999: 62). The missionary Kölle, for example, talked about the 'hocus-pocus' the male chief priest for Klowɛki performed for the *dipo* girls on Krobo Mountain.[143] Another reason why the missionaries were in the dark about what actually happened, was because *dipo* was a female affair, and girls stayed in seclusion during a longer period of *dipo* to protect their purity. It is also likely that the particular content of certain rites was secret knowledge (*agbaa*) that was only known to priests and women, as Dangme ideology equates secrecy with power (Quarcoopome 1993). Furthermore the early informants of the missionaries were male Ga and Akan catechists, who already had a certain bias towards the Krobo. Neither did the missionaries link the importance of procreation and fertility, which was expressed in the *dipo* rites, to the agricultural life of the Krobo, which they admired so much.

Many missionaries produced or simply replicated a very negative image of the Krobo, their 'heathen world' and *dipo*. The only true exception to this was the missionary Johannes Zimmermann (1825-1876). This was partly due to his long stay in Africa, between 1850 and 1876, with only one leave to Europe in 1872. Many others did not survive long enough and died of tropical fevers. He also held a different position due to his marriage to a black woman, Catherine Mulgrave. Another decisive factor was his knowledge of the local languages. Zimmermann was a linguist and an ethnographer. His views grew milder over the years, and he increasingly became an insider in Krobo society. Zimmermann disagreed with the mission's view of a natural hierarchy that scaled Africans in the lowest position and strongly discouraged socialising between Europeans and Africans in any form that suggested equality (Miller 1994: 132-133). Although

---

[142] BMA, D-1.23 Afrika 1871, Odumase, no. 13, J. Zimmermann, 01.07.1871, Odumase, '2. Quartalbericht'; original in German, my translation.
[143] BMA, D-1.54, Station Odumase, C. Kölle, 25.9.1891.

he also wrote critically about immoral practices, he was able to make sympathetic anthropological interpretations of *dipo*, stating that:

> Young unmarried brothers have written many foolish things about this custom in the past. Girls are not 'temple harlots', nor are they 'devoted to the fetish', but they are, when they grow to maturity, gathered on the mountain and secluded until the wedding, that most of the time forms the end of the customs.[144] (Original in German, my translation)

Zimmermann almost seems to suggest that the fact that these 'brothers' were young and not married explains their obsession with the sexuality of young girls. At the same time Zimmermann was also convinced that *dipo* eventually had to be replaced by Christian education, because the practice supposedly led to immorality.[145]

'A mighty obstacle to the gospel': dipo and the problems of conversion

The missionaries saw the education of girls as crucial, and as a replacement of 'the pagan way'. In the Krobo context, this meant the eradication of *dipo*. In this context Zimmermann noted:

---

[144] BMA, D-1.18B Afrika 1866, Teil 2, Odumase, no. 3, J. Zimmermann, 06.06.1866, Odumase.

[145] Johannes Zimmermann arrived on the Gold Coast in 1850. He married Catherine Mulgrave in 1851. She was a Christian school teacher who had come to the Gold Coast with the West Indian settlers recruited by Andreas Riis. This marriage was against BM policy. Only when a missionary had lived and worked for two years in his mission field, he could ask the highest BM authority, the so-called 'Committee' permission to marry (Konrad 2001). The bride for a missionary was often recruited in Europe by the BM and then sent to Ghana. The Mission also prohibited interracial sexual contact and marriage. In contrast to the Church Missionary Society in London who believed that marriage had a steadying influence on missionaries, because it enabled them to live normal family lives and kept them from being tempted into sexual improprieties in the field, the Basel Mission Committee thought that missionaries should, ideally, be single, because it was convinced that celibacy would allow all of their loyalty and emotional energy to be focused on the evangelical task. Practically as well, it was less expensive to support single missionaries in the field and easier to move them from one station to another at the Committee's discretion. Unmarried male missionaries were to have male servants in Africa and elsewhere. Marriage was permitted only under carefully supervised conditions (Konrad 2001: 235-251; Miller 1994: 55-56). If it had been any other person he would have been dismissed because of this marriage, but Johannes Zimmermann was considered to be too useful to the Basel Mission. The person of Catherine Mulgrave herself contributed to the unusual tolerance of her marriage. She was not a local convert or a local African woman, but considered more 'cultured' because of her upbringing as a Christian in the household of the British governor of the West Indies. She also was considered an irreplaceable person in the mission community because of her work. She had considered joining a rival Methodist mission and by marrying her, Zimmermann kept her talent at the disposal of the mission. Against all odds Zimmermann was therefore not excluded, but he was stipulated to no longer consider himself a European citizen and never expect to bring his wife or children to Europe (Konrad 2001: 190; Miller 1994: 133-5).

[*Dipo*] is incompatible with Christianity and has to end because of its horrible influence, customs and rules. Both Christians and heathens here are of the same conviction. It was not demanded from our few Christian girls until now, however it stops them from being baptised, Christian family education or a girls' school in our tribe will be the means to uplift the female population and overcome the pagan customs.[146] (Original in German, my translation)

According to the mission, women therefore had to be liberated from ignorance and pagan beliefs through education. Freeing girls from 'the chains of heathendom' only meant a basic teaching of reading, writing and calculating. The raising of their moral standards was considered especially important.[147]

The work among women in general was deemed crucial to the success of Christianising African society as a whole. Women were regarded as central in creating a family environment in which African Christianity could grow. After becoming Christian housewives, women were supposed to support their husbands and raise their children in discipline and fear of God.[148] However, the BM's regulations concerning contact between male missionaries and women made it difficult to approach girls. For example: "In the outdoors, men walking near where native women might rest or bathe must always call out before approaching, in order to avoid unexpected contact with women who were by European standards less than fully clothed" (Miller 1994: 55). The education of girls therefore was the task of the wives of missionaries and catechists, and a few single female missionaries (for more details see Miller 1994; Prodolliet 1987). The director of the girls' school, however, was a male missionary.

In spite of the hopes and expectations of missionaries, progress in general and with the female Krobo population in particular remained very slow in the 19th century. In their reports, the missionaries continuously blamed *dipo* for their difficulties. The Krobo did not want to give up this practise as demanded by the missionaries. The missionaries must have proclaimed from the beginning that a person must renounce *dipo* in order to become a Christian. *Kono* Odonkor Azu had been aware of the consequent dilemma right away. Although the education and first conversions of the Krobo had started with his children (in 1856 the first two of Odonkor Azu's sons had been baptised), he refused to allow one of his daughters to be educated, when Johannes Zimmermann asked him to do so.

---

[146] BMA, D-1.18b Afrika 1866, Teil 2, Odumas, no. 4, M. Röss/ J. Zimmermann, 13.06.1866, Odumase, 'Beantwortung einiger Paragraphen an Briefen der Geehrten Committee dat. 8. u. 11. Jan. 1866. No. 74 Fol. 93.97'; original in German, my translation.
[147] They were not marked for the courses they took in school for example. Apparently only moral testimony was important (Prodolliet 1987: 49).
[148] See e.g. *Evangelisches Missions Magazin* 1893, pp. 403-411, 'Die Mission unter dem weiblichen geschlecht Afrikas. 1. Die heidnische Frauenwelt im Krobo-Land. Nach Mitteilungen von Miss. J. Kopp'.

Fig. 2: Original caption: 'Learning to make clothes, Odumase' ('École de couture Odumasé'). Source: BMA, QD-30.043.0024. The picture shows miss Spahn and school girls in 'proper' dress, and was taken by Friedrich August Louis Ramseyer, between 01.011888 and 25.08.1891.

He said he would wait until a missionary was permanently stationed in Odumase, so that his daughters could be taught at home. (The boys were taken to Christiansborg (Accra)).[149] This indicates that daughters were more closely supervised than sons. When the request had been repeated several times after the founding of the mission post, Odonkor Azu admitted that he could not have any of his girls attending school because of a 'certain custom'. According to the missionaries, he argued that if they went to school, they would no longer perform this 'custom' and would not be tolerated in the community anymore.[150] The custom referred to was, of course, *dipo*.

Because of *dipo*, the Krobo girls did not attend school at all or left prematurely in order to pass through the rites. Parents or other relatives would come for the girls, or even, from the point of view of missionaries, 'abduct' them when

---

[149] The first two sons were baptised with the names 'Nyako Petro' and 'Agwai Noa' (later referred to as Noa Aguae Azu).

[150] BMA, D-1.7 Afrika 1856, Abokobi, no. 8/III 89, 'Vierteljahrsbericht', A. Steinhauser, September 1856, Abokobi; BMA, D-1.8 Afrika 1857, Akropong, no. 28J, J. Zimmermann, Juli 1857, Akropong, 'Vierteljahrsbericht'.

it was time for them to pass the *dipo* rites. After this, girls were considered mature and were often married, therefore they usually did not return to school. They began to work on the farms of their parents or husbands, and started their own families. What probably attracted people to the school to some extent was the fact that missionaries at first gave a fee to the parents of their pupils, and provided free food and free clothing to their pupils. This was a policy which was also common in other mission societies like the Bremen Mission (cf. Meyer 1997). However, it also meant that Krobo parents regarded the time spent at school by their children as employment. Although the school children were not yet ready for employment by local standards, they 'worked' for the missionaries and brought in money until they could work on their own farms. The children, boys and girls, actually performed some physical labour, for example on school farms, of which the produce helped the missionaries to support pupils. Pupils also carried stones for the construction of new buildings, picked coffee, produced oil and soap, etc., thereby learning about crops and crafts.

The missionaries also felt that women generally were more devoted to the gods and superstition than men were. Among the Krobo, the devotion to *dipo* was a sign of the women's proximity to 'heathendom'. According to Zimmermann, young Christian men were forced to marry 'pagan' girls, because of a consequent lack of Christian girls. However, the decisive factor will rather have been the fact that these girls had already been betrothed to them, as Zimmermann mentioned himself. Young men and women would not easily go against the will of their parents. Zimmermann reported in 1864:

> Only three Christian women and a few little girls among the Krobo have been baptised so far, not a single adult girl. The outward reason in the first place is the puberty custom, which girls do not want to miss to such an extent that we are deprived of all means for female education and that until now girls do not want to attend the distant [girls'] institutes. Then there is also the stronger devotion of the female population to idolatry and superstition. This is the reason why our Christian young men until now had to take, and will have to take, pagan girls, who were promised to them already before the baptism. Two of these girls have let themselves be baptised since then, while three others have not been baptised yet.[151] (Original in German, my translation)

The story of one Krobo girl in particular, named Maria Koryo, exemplifies the problems the missionaries experienced with regard to the Christian education of Krobo women.[152] In 1868, Koryo, then eight years old and 'still a heathen', came to stay with the missionaries, probably as a housemaid. When Mr. and Mrs. Schönfeld took over the post from Johannes Zimmermann and Catherine Mul-

---

[151] *Jahresberichte* 1864, 'II. Adangme Gebiet, I. Station Odumase, A. Die Gemeinde in Odumase, Bericht von Missionar Zimmermann vom Juli 1864'; original in German, my translation.
[152] Her case is also mentioned briefly in Debrunner's account of 'Christianity in Ghana' (Debrunner 1967: 189).

grave in 1872,[153] they also took care of Koryo and let her take part in the lessons at the girls' school. By then, the children were still taught in the premises of the mission house. Although boys and girls were educated separately, the schools were not physically separated yet (a separate girls' boarding school was opened in 1880). Like their predecessors, the Schönfelds experienced the problems of educating and baptising girls, which they attributed to *dipo*. In the year before (1871), only one Krobo boy had been baptised, a six-fingered child.[154] The other fifteen people were all 'strangers', i.e. mostly Ada, Ga and Ewe. Like the other girls, Koryo had been prepared for her 'natural job' as (house) wife and mother by receiving lessons in personal hygiene and domestic science. She learnt how to sew clothes, to knit and crochet. Koryo was described as an industrious and joyful girl, who was 'receptive to the Christian message'.

However, the missionaries thought that a dark cloud was hanging over Koryo's head. It was clear that the 'spell' of *dipo* would also strike Koryo. Moreover, like most other girls she probably would not return afterwards, as from then on she would be initiated into paganism, as according to the missionaries. Carl Schönfeld reported that Krobo girls were gathered to start the *dipo* rites in August 1873. Apparently, it was also Koryo's turn, because he wrote that Koryo was determined not to go, even though this meant that she - as an uninitiated girl - would not be able to stay in Odumase.[155] Although the missionaries had tried to convince the other girls of the evils of *dipo*, they went to Krobo Mountain without much ado. One day, Mrs. Schönfeld sent Koryo and an older girl to a market that was a two-hour walk from Odumase. As the Schönfelds may have suggested to Koryo, she seized the opportunity to escape from *dipo* and the Krobo area and flee to Abokobi, which was a fifteen-hour walk from Odumase. There she stayed with the residing missionaries.

Koryo's flight did not go by unnoticed. Tabitha Schönfeld reported to the Basel Mission Committee in Basel:

> Now a storm broke out over us. The fetish priests were enraged, and not only Odumase, but also the whole of Krobo were angry. More than once our house was besieged up to the doors by an angry and fuming mob. Maria's [= Koryo's] mother filled our house with her screaming for days on end. She danced on the veranda as if she was possessed, and threw whatever she could get hold of out on the street. Dark schemes were plotted against us, there were rumours that the mission house would be invaded and set alight. The Lord has guarded us and has not allowed His Kingdom's enemies to harm us in any way.[156] (Original in German, my translation)

---

[153] This was the end of the Zimmermanns' work in Krobo.

[154] Six-finger children used to be seen as a bad omen and therefore were killed at birth. Some were saved by the missionaries.

[155] BMA, D-1.25, Afrika 1873, Odumase 14, C. Schönfeld, 31.12.1873, Odumase, '15. Jahresbericht'.

[156] BMA, D-1.25 Afrika 1873, Odumase 13, Tabitha Schönfeld, 31.12.1873, Odumase, 'Jahresbericht der Mädchenanstalt'; original in German, my translation.

In the meantime, Koryo had been baptised and given the name Maria. This happened immediately on the day after her arrival in Abokobi, where she continued her education. In the spring time of 1876, however, she fell ill and would not stop coughing as a result of pneumonia. Some members of her family came to take her back to Odumase in July of that same year. Apparently, her whereabouts were not unknown to them by that time, and since she was still young and had not become pregnant yet, she still could come back. Maria Koryo went to stay with the Schönfelds again. They were hoping that she would recover so that she could take over the nursery. However, her illness became worse and it became clear that the end was near. According to the Schönfelds, the mother and a brother did not leave the side of the girl in the end, prayed with the missionaries, and took care of Maria Koryo until she died.

Maria Koryo's case must have seemed a perfect example for the mission of the eventual victory of Christianity over paganism, because what stands out most in the story is her martyr's death. Maria Koryo lived on in the mission's memory as a pure and pious Christian girl. After her death, her story was printed in the *Deutsches Kollekte Blatt* (1877) under the title: 'Power of mercy upon the West African heathendom'.[157] In addition, her flight urged the few Krobo converts at hand to take a stronger stand against *dipo* and the 'fetish priests', and declare their solidarity with Koryo. As a result, four wives of Christians, three of whom were Krobo (and had gone through *dipo*), were finally baptised in the following year. This was remarkable, because since 1868 no adult Krobo woman had been baptised. From the accounts it becomes clear that the BM believed it was only a matter of time and perseverance before *dipo* would cease to exist. Maria Koryo's 'act of faith' was proof that in the end 'Krobo-heathendom' would be conquered by the gospel. In future, she could serve as an example for other girls to resist to the call of *dipo*.

However, from a report the missionary Carl Weiss wrote a year after Maria Koryo's death we can infer that most of the Krobo must have linked her illness to the *dipo* rites. From other accounts, we know that they would attribute her misfortune to her disregard of the obligation to take part in *dipo*. If Maria Koryo had stayed in Krobo and passed through *dipo*, she would not have died. Weiss concluded: "And to talk this nonsense out of the heathens' head is not as easy as one might believe".[158] The missionaries reported that, after the flight of Maria Koryo, all other 'pagan' girls were taken out of the school. A few Christian children and 'pagan' girls from other 'tribes' remained. These were mainly from the coastal town of Ada. When a girls' school was built in Ada in 1877, the number of girls in Krobo dropped again. The missionary Weiss then remarked

---

[157] The original title was: 'Macht der Gnade gegenüber Westafrikanischem Heidenthum', in: *Deutsches Kollekte Blatt,* August 1877.
[158] BMA, D-1.29, Weiss, 18.2.1878, Odumase, 'Jahresbericht der Mädchenanstalt pro 1877 (als Beibericht zum Jahresbericht der Station Odumase)'; original in German, my translation.

that, if the school had to rely on Krobo girls alone, it would take a long time before an appropriate number could be reached, unless *dipo* declined.[159]

If we want to fully understand the commotion brought about by Koryo, we have to consider that this incident happened in a period of unrest and change. The impact of colonial rule and Christianity was felt more strongly after the 1870s. In 1873, the year that Maria Koryo ran away from *dipo*, the *dipo* performance had just started again after an interruption of three years.[160] Likewise, in the year after her death, 1877, missionary Weiss reported that the *dipo* had begun with larger pomp than before, because it had been interrupted for some time. In each case the priest who was going to lead the ceremony died before it could begin. As, according to local beliefs, deaths like that would never happen without a cause, people must have established a connection between the deaths of the priests and Christians trying to prevent the *dipo* rites (Koryo's own death was considered a powerful sign). The same year also saw the start of a so-called 'Salem', a segregated Christian ward within the town, which was called *lebo* in Odumase. At the same time a changing political environment had an impact on *dipo*. In the aftermath of the Asante or Sagrenti war (1873-74), in which the Krobo fought alongside the British, and which had put an end to the Asante's dominance, the British established their Gold Coast Crown Colony in the area to the south of metropolitan Asante (Wilson 1991: 121). Krobo became part of the Volta River District and was placed under the supervision of a British District Commissioner. This presence and more active policy of the British was to be felt in Odumase and people seemed to believe that the governor might soon prohibit the *dipo* practice. Therefore, all girls should go through *dipo* before it was 'too late'. According to Weiss in 1877, not only mature girls therefore went through the rites on Krobo Mountain, but also girls of six or seven years old.[161]

In his compilation of oral traditions Odjidja (1973: 69) confirms that not only Europeans, but also Krobo Christians were challenging the laws of traditional priests connected to the veneration of the Klowɛki goddess and the laws that ensured the control of these priests over the people. For example, Christians had started to rear goats, which was the animal used as the customary sacrifice for Nana Klowɛki and therefore also used during the *dipo* rites. Before this, it had been taboo to rear goats as domestic animals in private homes. In order to meet the challenge resulting from the new and alternative system of belief, i.e. Chris-

---

[159] BMA, D-1.29, Weiss, 18.2.1878, Odumase, 'Jahresbericht der Mädchenanstalt pro 1877 (als Beibericht zum Jahresbericht der Station Odumase'.
As a matter of fact, even the later prestigious Krobo Girls' School (1927) had difficulties in recruiting pupils from Krobo and right from the beginning had to rely on girls from all over Southern Ghana.
[160] BMA, D-1.25, T. Schönfeld, 31.12.1873, 'Mädchenanstalts-Bericht der Station Odumase bis 31. Dezember 1873'.
[161] BMA, D-1.29, Weiss, 18.2.1878, Odumase, 'Jahresbericht der Mädchenanstalt pro 1877 (als Beibericht zum Jahresbericht der Station Odumase)'.

tianity, the priests had regulated that girls should not be baptised or sent to school. Converts were therefore given a hard time. Reading some of the life histories collected by Odjidja (1977: 39 and 61), we can see that the early converts became outcasts on the fringe of society. They were often declared ritually dead by their families and buried symbolically. Many of the earliest generation of converts - often (former) slaves or old women - had been on the margin of society anyway (cf. Hastings 1993: 112; Middleton 1983), or they were 'strangers' trading in Krobo.

One important group of early converts and marginalized individuals in Krobo society were women who had become pregnant before passing through *dipo*. For these women Christianity offered a way out and they could be 'saved' from their marginalization through conversion. In particular the Christian congregation in the outpost of the town of Sra consisted of several women who had become pregnant before performing *dipo* and therefore sought protection with the church. For these women the mission provided a safe haven where they could escape the punishment of traditional priests. However, their salvation only led to another and even twofold marginalization: They became Christians with a past, while the wider community regarded the mission as an asylum for girls who had broken the social mores of Krobo society by disobeying the priests and elders. Therefore such Christian women hardly enjoyed any respect.

In one report by Johannes Zimmermann from 1871, two years before Koryo's flight, we find an example of the contempt such 'fallen women' experienced in Krobo society.[162] During a smallpox epidemic, the traditional priests attacked a Christian couple from Sra when the two fell ill. The priests accused the Christians of bringing the illness upon them, because the woman was uninitiated and therefore to bring about misfortune. The priests also blamed the missionaries and *konọ* Sakite in particular for the sickness, because the latter two neglected *dipo*. Missionary Zimmermann wrote that women were the first to seek help from the 'fetish priests' in this time of crisis, and their seats in the church remained vacant during the epidemic. Only a few persons turned to the missionaries for help instead. A similar telling event, mentioned by the missionary Furrer, occurred in Sra, some ten years later, in 1881.[163] A Christian woman named Salome Amedi was on her way home from the stream where she had drawn water. A 'fetish woman' stopped her on the road and threw Salome's water jar on the ground. Then she beat her with a stick and kicked her in the belly "even though she knew", Furrer wrote, "that Salome was pregnant". Yet, the pregnancy was the very reason why the woman was beating Salome. Brought before the Yilo *konọ* Akrobetto, the 'fetish woman' claimed that Salome was responsible for the drought the Krobo area was suffering at the time, because she

---

[162] BMA, D-1.23 Afrika 1871, Odumase 17, J. Zimmermann, 30.09.1871, Odumase, '3. Quartalbericht'.
[163] BMA, D-1, 33 Afrika 1881, Odumase 129, Furrer, n.d. 1882, Odumase, 'Jahresbericht 1881'.

108

had offended the 'fetishes' by being pregnant without having passed through the *dipo* rites before.

These women had lost all respect and status as adult marriageable women in their own society. Even though the missionaries strongly opposed *dipo*, they recognised the bad influence 'fallen women', who had converted for obvious reasons, had on the congregation. Josenhans considered the poor state of the Sra congregation to be the reason for the influence of these 'unchaste' women when he wrote: "Sra has borne the seed of the ruin already for a long time through the admittance of fallen *otufo* [*dipo*] girls, whom the local Christians have married eventually".[164] The local Christian men did not have much choice if they wanted a Christian wife. Apart from these 'fallen *dipo* girls', not many young women converted to Christianity. This again kept the men from converting.

Heathendom versus Christianity

The Basel missionaries created contradictions they were unable to resolve. On the one hand the missionaries identified the work among women as crucial to the success of Christianising the Krobo as a whole. On the other hand women were part of the problem of spreading Christianity, as they were not willing to dissociate themselves from *dipo*, which was a precondition for conversion. Whereas the Basel Mission wanted to turn Krobo women into good wives and mothers according to Christian standards, of course without letting them pass through *dipo*, matters of sexuality and reproduction were not limited to marriage according to the Krobo. Moreover, *dipo* was rather the precondition for pregnancy and marriage, because it was also linked to kinship ties, economic prosperity, the worship of Nana Kloweki and the integrative aspect of the rituals that constructed Krobo identity. The costs of conversion were too high for Krobo women if it meant giving up *dipo*.

The Basel Mission experienced a very slow progress during the 19th century. Small successes were followed by failure. *Dipo* was thereby perceived as a main obstacle. Evaluating fifty years of missionary work among the Krobo in 1909, the missionary Steiner, who collected information from reports by other missionaries on the subject of *dipo*, stated: "In particular this national heathen institution, which the Krobo people adheres to with unbelievable persistence and which is a breeding ground for the old Heathendom, proved itself as one of the strongest and almost inconvincible bulwarks of darkness."[165]

---

[164] BMA, D-1.52 Goldküste 1890 Ga, Odumase 204, Josenhans, 07.04.1891, Odumase, 'Beilage zum Jahresbericht'; original in German, my translation.
[165] *Der evangelische Heidenbote* vol. 82 (12), 1909, 'Fünfzig Jahre Missionsarbeit in Krobo. Ein Rückblick von Missionar B. Steiner', pp. 90-91; (Original in German, my translation).

The long process of socialisation, cultural identification and personal maturation surrounding *dipo* could not easily be replaced by Christian education. Parents withdrew their children from school rather than give up *dipo*. Girls who were not initiated were met with contempt. Maria Koryo's rejection of *dipo* jeopardised an age-old paradigm of societal organisation. She betrayed traditional values. In traditional Krobo society, an uninitiated female never graduated to the status of a woman. Men would not consider marrying such a woman and even converts preferred a proper, i.e. 'heathen', Krobo woman. Christian girls were considered inadequate and unclean. Mission interference also threatened established local authority structures, those of the elders and those of the priests.

The missionaries themselves recognised that their cultural policy had resulted in undesired effects. It was quite paradoxical, for example, that they had 'saved' unmarried pregnant women and hence had made Christianity a way out for 'unchaste' women who would normally have been banned from society. So whereas the Mission wanted to create 'Christian wives', the result was non-initiated women unfit for marriage in Krobo eyes. And whereas they advocated strict Christian sexual morals, they promoted illegitimate sexual relations and child birth in terms of Krobo society. In the past Krobo women who were 'outcasts' were probably already engaged in prostitution outside Krobo area. Now uninitiated 'Christian' women contributed to a negative image of Krobo women as 'loose'. The enforcement of 'proper dressing' contributed to such a message. Now the initiated and therefore socially adult girls could no longer be distinguished from the uninitiated ones.

Although the Basel missionaries were quite unsuccessful in banishing the *dipo* rites, they were eventually very successful in another important respect. While most Krobo did not see initially the necessity to convert, they did perceive the missionaries as the holders of immense and new external power. It is hardly surprising then, as Middleton argues, "that Christ and God have appeared to be part of a wider and European-controlled world" (Middleton 1983: 10), and therefore the key to worldly success. The Krobo were already involved in interacting with Europeans. Paradoxically, they formed a very dynamic and entrepreneuring society in the 19th century, to which their social institutions had contributed. Nevertheless, the missionaries managed to draw the line between what they defined as 'heathendom', which was perceived as 'something of the past', 'immoral', 'uncivilised', and 'devilish' or 'diabolical' on the one hand, and 'Christianity', which was regarded as 'enlightened', 'modern' and 'civilised' on the other hand. *Dipo* was perceived as belonging to Krobo religion and therefore as part of 'heathendom'. In other words, *dipo* was 'paganised' and its socio-economic importance to the Krobo was ignored. For the missionaries *dipo* was representative of everything they saw as appalling and heathen and it therefore should be eradicated. After conversion, *dipo* should be left behind as a relic of the past. Christianity was presented as the guiding light and part of civilisation, and the Krobo increasingly associated it with prosperity and progress.

Although *dipo* did *not* form an obstacle for many Krobo to convert to Christianity in the long run, the ambivalence towards *dipo* is still part and parcel of contemporary Christian discourse, as will become clear in this study. I will investigate how Krobo Christians today deal with the dissociation from Krobo religion, and *dipo* in particular. However, first of all I will examine in the next chapter why the BM thought that their prayers would be answered through the help of British colonial government: they hoped that the instalment of a Christian *konọ* and a ban on all 'fetish customs' would cause the downfall of *dipo* and the breakthrough of Christianity.

4

A break with 'the past'?:
The eviction from the mountain home
and criminalizing dipo

'1892 was an outstanding signpost in Krobo history – a break from the old Krobo and a change to the modern age' (Odonkor 1971: 45).

In the last chapter, I studied the encounter of Basel missionaries with the Krobo as a determining factor in Krobo history. I argued that, although the Basel missionaries had been unsuccessful in abolishing *dipo* until the end of the 19th century, the boundary they drew between what they perceived as 'heathen' and 'backward' on the one hand, and Christianity and 'civilised' on the other, was to have a lasting impact on Krobo society, as I will show in this study. *Dipo* was one of the main practices that became 'paganised'.

In order to be able to analyse the form *dipo* takes today, another decisive period in Krobo history needs to be studied first. From the late 19th century onwards, Basel missionaries, the British colonial administration and local actors engaged in a combined action towards 'heathendom' and 'barbarism', which finally led to the expulsion of the traditional priests from Krobo Mountain and the destruction of their shrines in 1892. In this chapter I investigate the circumstances that led to the eviction from the mountain, the events of 1892 and the effects of the institution of the colonial 'Native Customs Ordinance' that forbade all 'fetish worship'. The contested nature of the *dipo* rites thus has to be examined within the context of interrelated processes of Christianisation, colonisation and the rise of Krobo chiefs.

Dipo and other obstacles to 'civilisation'

There were significant differences between British colonial and missionary discourses on Krobo culture. While the missionaries were concerned with the differences between Christianity and 'traditional culture', the colonial administration was more interested in determining the mechanisms of traditional power and authority. British policy was often based on the assumption that in principle the best guarantee of assent to colonial rule was the preservation of traditional institutions of subject peoples (Kuklick 1991: 194). This principle of 'indirect rule' required a careful documentation of the 'traditional' institutions of indigenous rule that was established in several ways: first by the enquiries of European administrators with varying degrees of anthropological training, and later by the employment of official government anthropologists. As Van den Bersselaar (1998: 174) argues, the knowledge created was much more than merely knowledge to assist the administration, as it emerged in the context of an imperialist world view that justified the subjection of large parts of the world on the basis of racial stereotypes and notions of colonial European influence.

Even though the Basel missionaries wanted their converts to leave most of their 'traditions' behind, in the promotion of the institution of 'traditional' chieftaincy, the missionaries and the colonial administration found a common ground. Although the BM continued to have an ambivalent attitude towards chieftaincy and its links with 'tradition', they hoped to gain a strong foothold in Krobo society through the (paramount) chiefs who they called 'kings', while the colonial administration wanted to apply the principle of 'indirect rule' to the 'Krobo chiefdom', as they assumed the Krobo had paramount chiefs or kings like their Akan neighbours (as I explained in the previous chapter). Both the Basel missionaries and the British colonial administration perceived *dipo* and other 'Krobo customs' as an impediment to civilisation and development and sought ways to get rid of them.

Tales of 'tail girls'

British colonial agents and travellers provide us with some more or less detailed reports on *dipo*, but as acting governor Hodgson admitted: "The Fetish practices are veiled in such mystery as to render it difficult to obtain reliable information about them".[166] Still he felt *dipo* was more important than the veneration of the war-gods *Nadu* and *Kotoklo* in Krobo society.[167]

Well-acquainted with the ruling ideology of the late 19th century, Hesketh J. Bell, one of the British colonial agents who I mentioned in the previous chapter, wrote about the Gold Coast:

> To those interested in folklore and ethnography the Gold Coast offers a grand field for investigation, the inhabitants having remained for the most part in the same condition of primitive simplicity in which they were found by the first European visitors to the coast four or five centuries ago (Bell 1911 [1893]: 45).

---

[166] GNA/ADM 11/1/1115/CO 96/219, J.M. Hodgson, 09.11.1891, 'Krobo customs'.
[167] I will explain the term 'war-gods' below.

In Bell's view the people in the Gold Coast had not changed much over the centuries, and therefore studying them would offer insight into 'ancient' customs and traditions. In his opinion the presence of Europeans only had little impact:

> Despite a tolerable supply of missionaries of all denominations, Fetishism flourishes almost as vigorously as ever; and if its horrible rites have been rigorously suppressed in those territories which recognise British authority, there are still numbers of curious customs and ceremonies practised which are extremely interesting as illustrating the peculiar ideas of the people (Bell 1911 [1893]: 45).

One of the 'curious customs' Bell was interested in seeing, was *dipo*:

> I was particularly anxious to visit the Krobo Mountain, having been told that it was, at certain times of the year, the scene of many curious customs, which might be well worth observing. One of the most interesting of all, the *Otufo*, or "Tail-girl" custom, was about to be celebrated (...) (Bell 1911 [1893]: 45).

In line with the Basel missionaries, the British colonials also called *dipo* '*otufo*', but they knew the word '*dipo*' too, and at times referred to the *dipo* girls as 'tail girls':

> (...) from the fact that until the custom is passed every Krobo girl has to wear a cloth which is passed between the legs and through the strings of beads which all native women wear round the waist, so that the ends hang down in front and behind in a sort of 'tail'.[168]

According to Bell (1911 [1893]: 69), the Krobo girls and women were famous for their 'tail' 'on the West Coast of Africa'.

Bell called *dipo* a practice that had been carried out by the Krobo 'from time immemorial', and although he felt it was a 'fetish' custom, he praised the way the Krobo were careful about the virtuous conduct of their daughters, as they, he wrote, segregated their daughters as soon as they approached the marriageable age (ibid.: 52). However, Bell felt that different rituals such as the placing of goat fat and intestines on the girls' heads and around their necks, were 'barbarous' (ibid. : 61). Acting governor Hodgson was informed by Bell that 'no indecency took place at the scene', apparently referring to sexual 'indecency'. However, as it was also reported that there were vast amounts of rum and palm wine consumed during *dipo*, and girls were bare-breasted, the governor drew his own conclusions: "[T]his can hardly be so in view of the fact that the girls are clothed in the manner I have stated and all the spectators and priests are more or

---

[168] GNA/ADM 11/1/1115/CO 96/219, J.M. Hodgson, 09.11.1891, 'Krobo customs'. Also for example: GNA/ADM 11/1/1115/COnf. M.P. 286/90, 04.10.1890, Akuse, 'Letter from Mr. S. A. Williams, D.C in reply to the C. S. Conf. No 263/90 of 13.09.1890'; and Adams (1908: 518).

less under the influence of drink".[169] D.C. Williams reported earlier in February 1891 from Akuse that:

> During the [*dipo*] procession there were incessant gun firing. I took the opportunity to visit the Hill on two occasions and warned kings Sackitey [Manya] and Akrobetto [Yilo] against any riot occurring, as I am informed is always the case when this custom is being held, and I am glad that during the whole time of the custom there was no disturbance.[170]

Where the *dipo* ceremony was considered fairly innocent, apart from the sexual connotations, its 'barbarous-ness' and apparent occasional commotion, the descriptions of the so-called 'fetish priests' performing *dipo* were extremely negative. According to Hesketh Bell, male 'fetish priests' could be distinguished by their white garments and they "wore expressions of ill-will and malevolence but thinly disguised" (Bell 1911 [1893]: 57). The Basel missionaries totally ignored the priests, except when one of them converted to Christianity. Otherwise there are no descriptions during this time. However, Bell gave a vivid description of 'fetish priestesses' during the *dipo* rites:

> Tom-toms were beaten incessantly, and a ring of the most hideous old black women circled round and round the girls, uttering strange cries and waving their lean withered arms. (...) One of these ancient females was the most unearthly specimen of humanity I had ever seen. Her age must have been very great, for her small wizened body was so shrunk and bent that it looked like the remains of a smoke-dried mummy; the bones of her legs and arms were as clearly defined as in any anatomical specimen, and the wrinkled black skin hung in gristly knots round the gnarled joints. Her sole garment consisted of a tattered cloth tied below her breast, and a string of cowries dangled from her palsied neck. Her head had been cleanly shaved with the exception of a circle at the top of her scalp, where the snow-white woolly hairs were drawn up tight together and tied with a piece of red cotton, forming a ghastly sort of plume. The prominent cheekbones, which seemed to be almost piercing the skin, the dim sunken eyes, and the toothless jaws which tremblingly murmured a weird incantation, completed the portrait of this Mother of the Tribe (Bell 1911 [1893]: 57).

Bell thus described one of the old priestesses as a complete 'Other' and the priests in general as people who should be feared.

The British were aware however, that the performance of the *dipo* rites provided the priestess of the Klowɛki deity ('the Great Fetish') and the priests and priestesses involved in the worship of the deity with a source of power over their people. As Adams remarked:

---

[169] GNA/ADM 11/1/1115/CO 96/219, J.M. Hodgson, 09.11.1891, 'Krobo customs'.
[170] PRO/CO 96/217 Gold Coast 1891 Governor W.B. Griffith/Act. Gov, 21.02.1891, Akuse, 'forwarding D.C. William's report'; Governor Griffith, 25.06.1891, Christiansborg Castle, 'Gold Coast No. 210 to Lord Knutsford'.

By securing the custody of the girls the Great Fetish gained full control of the rest of the people. Of the older men and men of importance, because no one would take for wife a girl that had not the 'cachet' of Krobo Hill. Of the young men, because any one of them who had offended it was forbidden to attend the Custom and got no wife at all. Of the girls themselves and of their parents, because she who had not been through the ceremonies was ostracised and looked down upon as being no better than a slave (Adams 1908: 519).

The priests, and elders in general, indeed played key roles in rites of passage such as *dipo*, because they were the ones to communicate with the deities and the ancestors, for example by pouring libation to secure the blessings of the ancestors during the rites (cf. Akyeampong 1996: 30). The British and the missionaries knew that the mountain was in the hands of the 'fetish priests', and that the 'kings' as they called them, did not enjoy overall authority. Hodgson wrote that the priests: "have far more power over the Krobos than the kings". Bell similarly reported that the 'fetish priests' exercised more influence than the two 'kings'.[171]

In his report about a visit to Krobo Mountain to find out, according to governor Hodgson himself, how the 'heathen customs' were carried out and to see how the dead were buried, he described how he also tried to investigate the practice of the rites of the priests, as he obviously wanted to know more about the functioning of traditional power and authority. He therefore summoned the priests. But they were unwilling to talk to him as he concluded from the information he received that 'the priests had gone down to the plains'. He still tried to find some of them and he located four priests, "of who", according to Hodgson, "only one was sober". These priests cannot have been any men of great importance, as it was a taboo for the main (*djeméli*) priests to interact with strangers. Hodgson was not able to obtain any information, nor were the priests willing to show him their shrines, "their whole demeanour being truculent to a degree and independent". Hodgson felt that people seemed to mock him while he was descending from the mountain and in a final remark he grudged: "There were several girls in the villages [on the mountain] graduating for the *dipo* custom and the whole place, I should say, is one vast orgy ground."[172]

Hence the 'fetish' priests performing the rites were regarded as 'too independent' and 'truculent', and they hindered the political control of the British and the chiefs. The British government was looking for an opportunity to get a

---

[171] GNA/ADM 11/1/1115, M.P. 309/91, 19.01.1891, 'Report of Mr. Bell, D.S.V.R. on the Krobo Customs'.
[172] GNA/ADM 11/1/1115/CO 96/219, J. M. Hodgson, acting governor, 09.11.1891, Aburi House, 'Krobo customs'. Also: CO 96/219, J.M. Hodgson, 09.11.1891, Aburi House, 'Letter to governor Knutsford'.

firmer grip on the political structures of the Krobo and their rather inaccessible mountain.

'War' deities

Among the Krobo and their neighbours the success of Akan military organisation in the 17th, 18th and 19th centuries promoted a perception of chieftaincy as a 'war-medicine', and *abosom-brafo* (Akan gods that often originated as 'hunting-medicines') as 'war gods' (Akyeampong 1996: 22-23). The adoption and veneration of 'war-gods' *Nadu* and *Kotoklo* among the Krobo implied male initiation, which in essence consisted of circumcision, and provided a mechanism for mobilising men for military purposes, protecting them at the same time. Whereas it seems that circumcision was the sufficient condition for a young man to be considered a Krobo, in order to earn prestige and recognition he had to be initiated into the cults of one of the war deities, the most prominent of which were Nadu and Kotoklo. With the establishment of British authority over the whole of the Gold Coast at the close of the 19th century, inter-ethnic wars had virtually ceased and as a result the importance of war-gods declined. Today only a few traditionalists seem to make reference to the war deities when they circumcise their male children. But in most cases circumcision is free of any ritual connotation (see chapter six).

However, the end of the 19th century was also a period that saw the introduction of many new gods and a renewed incentive of the *Nadu* and *Kotoklo* cults, especially in the upcountry farming areas. Young pioneer farmers in particular were adherents of new gods such as *Koko-Nadu*, as they needed protection from wild animals and in land disputes in the frontier farming areas (Arlt 2002: 18). In addition, colonial law paradoxically encouraged the adherents of the war gods. The missionary reports state that before 1883, when the colonial Native Jurisdiction Ordinance was introduced, neighbouring peoples of the Krobo who discovered that one of their members had been slayed as a sacrifice for one of the Krobo war gods would demand the extradition of the murderers under the threat of war. However, this had become impossible under the new colonial law that demanded such cases to be brought before a court, while at the same time the Krobo were said to show little respect for the British laws that required the presence of eyewitnesses. They would not easily testify against each other, as the cults of war deities took place in secret societies and promoted secrecy among their members (cf. Arlt 2002: 19).

Both the colonial administration and the Basel missionaries deemed the war gods to be an impediment to peace and 'civilisation'. The Basel missionaries wrote the first reports about these deities. The missionary Andreas Riis had reported in the past that strangers were afraid to approach the Krobo out of fear for their lives. He witnessed a 'yearly feast' on Krobo Mountain in 1838, during which the women danced their 'fetish dance' and the men held 'murder weapons', and he was told that every year people were killed for this celebration.[173] The missionary Dieterle gave us the following account in 1852:

> The Krobo people still sacrifice, as I was told, a human being every year, however not one of their own, but instead they try to catch a victim. They go out in the country, and when they have found someone who does not respond to their greeting in their language, they cut off his head, take the killed person home, where a part of his flesh is eaten and the skull is used to make a drinking cup for one of the elders; because every man should have such a cup in his possession.[174] (Original in German, my translation)

Der Heidenbote called the practice "a strange characteristic of the pitiful darkness that still covers the poor Negro world".[175] Every now and then a case was detected. In 1862 for example, Johannes Zimmermann reported that two young men had murdered an Ada and an Akwamu man, cut off their head and took them to the 'main fetish' in Manya on Krobo Mountain, Odonkor Azu's hometown.[176] In the years hereafter, there were more, similar rumours. The missionary Röss also witnessed the annual feast on the mountain in 1864, whereby he described: "Never before had I seen Heathendom performed in such a horrible wild way." He saw people dancing and jumping to the rhythm of the drums and drinking from human skulls. This all happened under the authority of a 'fetish priest' and his helpers. Only the men participated. The women were said to stand aside and just sway their upper bodies. In disbelief he wrote: "Are these people our dear Krobo, I thought, whom we have preached the gospel for many years now, who received us so friendly under their shady palms and in their houses and listened to us so often with clear interest when we visited them in their towns, villages and farms?"[177]

Later on, the missionaries learned that these yearly celebrations were held for *Nadu* and *Kotoklo*, gods of respectively Manya and Yilo Krobo factions. Although *Nadu* and *Kotoklo* were described as the 'main fetishes' of the Krobo in some accounts, the missionary reports do not provide many detailed descriptions of the character of these cults.[178] One obvious reason is that a person had to be

---

[173] BMA, D-1.1 Afrika 1829-39, Akropong 1838, No. 6, Riis, Andreas, 06.07.1838, Akropong.

[174] BMA, D-1.4a Afrika 1851-1853, No. 56J, Chr. Dieterle, 31.05.1852, Akropong.

[175] *Der evangelische Heidenbote* 1853, No. 1, 'Die Opfer der Neger auf der Goldküste'; Quote originally in German, my translation.

[176] BMA, D-1.13b Afrika 1862, Teil 2, Odumase No. 10a, J. Zimmermann, 06.05.1862, Odumase, 'Vierteljahrsbericht'.

[177] *Der evangelische Heidenbote* 1864, 'Aus der Mission unter den Krobo-Negern. 1. Das Volksfest auf dem Berge'. Quote originally in German, my translation.

[178] However, the Basel missionary Mischlisch described in some detail how in the *Nadu* cult human victims that were sacrificed (usually strangers or enemies), had their heart ripped out and their head cut off, because it was believed that the soul resides in the heart. The heart was burnt with leaves and the ashes were drunk, mixed with palm wine, from the skull of the victim. By drinking this concoction, it was believed that the killer was freed from being hunted by his 'soul' or 'spirit'. He would now

initiated into the cult in order to witness the rituals fully. Even in the moderate form in which they are performed today, the rituals feature dangerous liminal moments and to join the celebration is not evident. As the cult works like a secret society it is no wonder that the missionaries were kept in the dark about the nature of the rituals. These cults were said to deal with human sacrifice.[179] Another reason is that they were not celebrated by everyone, because they were not compulsive, as was the case with the *dipo* rites. But the missionaries did not show much awareness of differences between various clans and 'houses'. They seemed to assume that every Krobo man had to be initiated by killing somebody: "No Krobo is seen as a proper man who has not killed a human being yet!"[180] One thing was clear to the missionaries however: these rites were part of 'Krobo Heathendom' and blocked the way to Christianity.

The circulating rumours and sometimes the actual proof of murders in connection with the worship of *Kotoklo* and *Nadu* among the Krobo also reached the colonial administration. They were one reason why Hodgson recommended the suppression of the 'customs' and subsequent action to be taken in the form of the destruction of the 'fetishes' and the closing of Krobo Mountain in his report on 'Krobo customs' of November 1891. Together with his colleagues he was only thinking about a way to do it without a major disturbance or a popular outbreak. Hodgson did not expect much resistance:

> I do not anticipate that there will be any active resistance on the part of the people. They are for the most part weary of the tyranny and greed of the priests and although they would undoubtedly regret the abolition of the *Otofu* [*dipo*] custom, they would not, as a body, have any regret for the loss of the fetishes *Kotoklo* and *Nadu*.[181]

Hodgson was probably right that the war gods did not serve the needs of the whole population. In fact, *kono̱* Sakite and his (partly Basel Mission educated)

---

even gain strength. Still, afterwards, the priest had to perform a purification ritual in which he used hairs or other parts from the dead person to brew a mixture with certain leaves, with which the man had to wash himself in order to prevent him from becoming mad (*der evangelische Heidenbote* 1892, no. 11, 'Wichtige Tage für das Krobo-land. Nach einem Bericht des Bruders Misschlich in Odumase (Goldküste)').

[179] The essence of the cult is to protect the one who has killed somebody from being haunted by his victim's spirit and to spiritually and bodily strengthen him, as Misschlisch's description above also made clear (*der evangelische Heidenbote* 1892, no. 11, 'Wichtige Tage für das Krobo-land. Nach einem Bericht des Bruders Misschlich in Odumase (Goldküste)'). Today a sheep is killed in the performance of the ritual and, like the sheep killed in Odwira (Gilbert 1994), it may be a replacement of a human being which was killed in former days. What is certain, however, is that in order to be initiated one had to have killed somebody and therefore travelling through the Krobo region was dangerous for any stranger. Therefore colonial and missionary reports invariably referred to human sacrifices, although no colonial agent or missionary will have ever witnessed the ritual.

[180] BMA, D-1.52, J. Kopp, 25.2.1891, Odumase, 'Jahresbericht der Station Odumase pro 1890'.

[181] GNA/ADM 11/1/1115/CO 96/219, J.M. Hodgson, 09.11.1891, 'Krobo customs'.

entourage sought to use the support of Europeans to increase their authority over their people at the expense of the traditional priests.

This becomes clear, for example, from a petition which *konọ* Sakite and some of his headmen and councillors (notably his Basel Mission educated brother Peter Nyarko)[182] had already signed to the governor in 1884. In this petition they complained about *Koko-Nadu*, Krobo farmers neglecting their houses in the towns and the lack of children in the Basel Mission school.[183] As the petitioners state, there were about 600 villages in the upcountry farm plantations, and their inhabitants only returned to the towns for funerals.[184] Especially the people of *Akwenọ*, *Dom* and *Djebiam* divisions were said to live on the plantations, neglecting their houses in the towns that 'are in decay'. These people were also accused of worshipping *Koko-Nadu*, which was said to involve the stealing of sheep, goats and palm wine. At the same time, the fact that the BM was not able to attract enough children to their school in Odumase was attributed by the petitioners to: "the amount of children kept at the Crobo plantations by their parents and brought up in heathen practices, some of the parents themselves have no idea whatever as to whether there is any place built for the worshipping of the true God having left their village long, long ago." Therefore the petitioners asked for the help of the governor in abolishing *Koko-Nadu* and strengthening the towns. Making use of the missionary and colonial discourse, the petitioners ended their message with the words:

> Should your Excellency accede to our wishes, the promulgation of the Gospel of Christ will be increased, Civilization be extended and the rising generations will in a few years be a blessing to our country and 'Koko Nadu' be entirely abolished; for we wish many improvements in this country which would allow Christianity to have a firm rooting, and this cannot be easily effected by ourselves alone, but by the aid of the Government, who is only to command, and we shall see all commands carried effectually. And your Excellency's Petitioners as in duty bound will ever pray.

This petition clearly anticipates indirect rule and has to be understood in the context of political and socio-economic developments at the time. *Konọ* Sakite like his father Odonkor Azu, was eager to expand and consolidate his relationships with Europeans, and there was a tension between the strengthening of his leadership and the loss in influence of the class of priestly leaders. Even though Odumase and the other towns, the seat of Sakite and his chiefs, had gained in

---

[182] Peter Nyarko was among the first Krobo converts as his father Odonkor Azu sent him to be trained by the Basel missionaries. Although he was to become a catechist, he was excluded from the congregation for his royalist and therefore traditionalist ambitions (cf. Arlt 2002: 16). He played a crucial intermediary role in the installation of his son as the new *konọ* in 1892.

[183] GNA/ADM 11/1/1115/ MP 2677A/84, 28.11.1884, 'To his Excellency William A.G. Young'.

[184] As I explained in chapter three, Krobo farmers did not live in nucleated villages, but in single family compounds. So among the 600 'villages' many small settlements may have been counted.

importance since the Gold Coast Crown Colony was established, people did not spend much time there. They only made a stopover when they had to attend a funeral on Krobo Mountain or to see to the upkeep of their daughters who were passing through the *dipo* rites. On the mountain the priests still controlled the important ceremonies that held the people together. Moreover, Krobo people were engaged in frontier farming, moving further and further to the northwest (see previous chapter), and therefore lived on their plantations for most of the time out of reach of both the chiefs and the missionaries. As Arlt (2002: 17) writing about the same petition explains:

> Not only did the chiefs have difficulties in enforcing their authority over their people and in creating income through their courts (...), living in those settlements [the towns in the plains] had also become more and more difficult. The decay of the houses that is lamented in the petition is a sign of the shifting of the Krobo frontier. There was only a limited [food] supply, as every bit of land had been planted with oil palms. (...) If not in some home-gardens, surplus food crops were only produced on the frontier, where new forest lands were cleared.

It was therefore expensive to live in the hometowns, as food had to be brought down from the upcountry as afar as six to eight hours walking distance. The chiefs nevertheless were seeking means to bring people to their towns and place them regularly under their authority.

Despite the petition and earlier attempts of the colonial government to suppress 'undesirable cults', it was not until 1892 that the *Native Customs Ordinance* was drawn up. Actual proof of the killing of human beings in relation with the war deities provided the immediate cause for action. The English D.C. of Akuse had reported the murder of three Juaben people in 1890, supposedly for the celebration of the *Kotoklo* rituals (the mighty war deity venerated by the Yilo Krobo).[185] The next year, the missionary Adam Mischlisch reported the murder of a runaway slave by four young men,[186] who, according to Azu (1928: 16), belonged to the Dom division. The slave had been cut to pieces, his heart had been ripped out and his head had been cut off. At least the beheading was said to be typical for a victim killed in connection with the cults of the *Nadu* and *Kotoklo* deities, as the skull and yaw bones were to be brought before the deity's priest by the candidate for initiation, to prove his having killed somebody. According to Hodgson's report, the victim was from Kwahu and was murdered for *Kotoklo*. When the paramount chief of Kwahu got to know this, Hodgson wrote, he sent one of his chiefs with an army of 200 men to Odumase to demand satisfaction. However, the D.C. in Akuse also got wind of the case and wanted to put

---

[185] GNA/ADM 11/1/1115/COnf. M. P. 286/90, 04.10.1890, Akuse, 'Letter from Mr. S. A. Williams, D. C. in reply to the C. S. Conf. No 263/90 of 13.09.1890'.

[186] *Der evangelische Heidenbote* 1892, no. 11, 'Wichtige Tage für das Krobo-land. Nach einem Bericht des Bruders Mischlisch in Odumase (Goldküste)'.

the four on trial. The British government officials assured the Kwahu chief that justice would be done, so the chief withdrew his army. Hodgson himself expressed his regret to *konọ* Sakite that the latter had failed to report the murder to the D.C. Although he also spoke to Akrobetto of Yilo Krobo, it seems he related the murder to Sakite's responsibility, like the Kwahu did when they came to Odumase to demand satisfaction. Since the case took place within *konọ* Sakite's jurisdiction, he was made responsible for it (Azu 1928: 16).

Funeral rites

Another 'custom' that was to contribute to the governor's actions in 1892, was the continued burial of the deceased on Krobo Mountain, which contravened to the *Native Cemeteries Ordinance* that was already proclaimed in 1888. This ordinance provided for interments in cemeteries and prohibited intramural sepulture. However, the Krobo took all their deceased to Krobo Mountain and buried them in their houses. The missionary Heck, for example, complained in the 1860s that: "Almost every day there is a custom for the dead in these mountain cities and there is a lot of sinning going on. Boozing, gorging, playing, dancing etc. is the principal occupation there."[187] Many accounts speak of the enormous amount of alcohol consumed during funeral rites, which to the missionaries was an abomination. They saw this drinking, drumming and dancing as another obstacle to the conversion of the Krobo. However, alcohol was an intricate part of ritual action for the Krobo, as the pouring of a libation with alcohol for the ancestors and/or the deities preceded any ritual or ceremony. Moreover, as Akyeampong states: "In the observation of funeral rites, the intimate relationship with the world of ancestors – into which the deceased was about to enter – necessitated an extensive use of alcohol." Drinking also numbed the feeling of grief, while at the same time it expressed grief and solidarity among the living (1996: 37, 39).

The British government instructed the paramount chiefs to establish cemeteries in the neighbourhood of the towns. The government argued that the number of graves on Krobo Mountain had reached a maximum capacity, and this created unsanitary conditions. Moreover, the Krobo mode of burial was found to be 'very primitive'. Hodgson related upon hearsay:

> Throughout the table land on the top of the Mountain there are deep rents or chasms, and after the burial party has performed the usual custom in one of the villages – the principal element of which is the consumption of rum and palm wine – the body wrapped up in cloths and enclosed in a basket coffin made to fit closely by cords

---

[187] BMA, D-1.13b Afrika 1862, Teil 2, Odumase No. 18, J. Heck, 01.11.1862, Odumase, 'Reisebericht'.

passed round it, is taken to one of these chasms (...), and pitched over the edge there to lie exposed, but out of sight, with many hundreds of other bodies dealt with in a similar manner. It is not difficult therefore to account for the unsanitary condition of the Mountain.[188]

This practice differs from Heck's description that people were rather buried under their houses, but it is possible that exceptional deaths were dealt with differently. The corpses of those who were believed to have suffered abominable deaths, for example caused by accidents, a murder, suicide and, in the case of a woman, death in pregnancy or childbirth, are known to have been disposed of at special places (Huber 1993: 220). Still, the 'many hundreds of bodies' seem to give an exaggerated picture. Several reports confirm that the deceased were buried within the house. It was difficult to persuade the people to bury them at the cemeteries, and they were sometimes fined for it: "(...) it is to be regretted that after all the troubles which had been taken by the two kings [of Yilo and Manya] in erecting cemeteries to find that some of the Croboes are stealthily carrying their corpses to the Hill for interment in their dwelling houses".[189] This was one area where it became clear that the 'kings' did not enjoy the overall authority ascribed to them.[190] Their lack of power also shows from the difficulties they experienced in persuading young men in particular to obey their orders to clean the roads.[191]

The destruction of 'Satan's bulwarks'

The Native Customs Ordinance

When *kono* Sakite died on January 28, 1892, the British governor at the time, Sir Brandford Griffith, forbade the Manya Krobo to select a successor until he himself would arrive in Odumase in mid-July that very year. Because the Krobo feared military action against them, they complied. Peter Nyarko, Sakite's half-brother, informed the D.C. of Akuse that *kono* Sakite was buried in the basement of his palace. However, rumours claimed that he was buried on Krobo Mountain

---

[188] GNA/ADM 11/1/1115/CO 96/219, J.M. Hodgson, 09.11.1891, 'Krobo customs'.
[189] PRO/CO 96/217 Gold Coast 1891, 'Gov. W. B. Griffith/Act. Gov: (forwarding D.C. Williams' report, Akuse, 30.04.1891)'; Governor Griffith, 26. 06.1891, Victoriaborg, Accra, 'Gold Coast no. 211 to Lord Knutsford'.
[190] Also see GNA/ADM 11/1/1115, 21.05.1891, Odumase, 'letter to the district commissioner's office by clerks Harding (for Sakite) and Meyer (for Akrobetto)'.
[191] CO 96/218 Gold Coast 1891 Act. Gov. Hodgson, 12.09.1891, Victoriaborg, Accra, 'Gold Coast No. 304 to lord Knutsford'.

like his father before him.[192] When the D.C. came to Odumase and tried to persuade Peter Nyarko to have his brother buried at a cemetery, he was pursued by an angry mob and had to seek refuge in the Basel Mission house. Apparently his action had aroused the suspicion that he had intended to open the *kono*'s grave to verify the burial. Thereupon one detachment of twenty-five and a second detachment of fifty 'Hausa' soldiers was despatched to Odumase.[193] Later on, the D.C. became convinced that the *kono* had been buried in Odumase and not on the mountain, as all his widows were still in his residence in Odumase and an old aunt had descended from the mountain on account of his death. He was told that it was customary that the widows would stay where the husband was buried until all the rituals were performed.[194]

At meetings of the executive council of the Gold Coast in January 1891, and again on July 1, 1892, the question of the 'native customs and fetish practices' on 'Krobo Hill' and their abolishment were discussed. Apart from putting an end to 'the most barbarous practices', therefore promoting 'civilisation', the governor hoped that the abolishment would also promote trade in the area, as traders from other regions feared to pass Krobo territory.[195] When the governor, in a letter to his D.C. at Akuse dated February 15, 1892, enquired whether all 'fetish' customs and practices in Krobo should be made penal and Krobo Mountain closed and what the effect of this would be, D.C. Williams replied in detail. In his letter dated March 2, 1892, he wrote that the only 'fetishes' that demanded human sacrifices were *Nadu*, *Kotoklo* and *Koko-Nadu*. Other minor 'fetishes' belonged to particular families and did not require human sacrifices. He declared that *otufo* and *dipo* were one and the same ('tail girl') custom and that it was the source of 'clandestine slave dealing' of a girl found pregnant before *dipo*. In October 1890 he had therefore advised on its abolishment.[196] Maybe this was in reaction to the letters sent in September 1890 by Basel Mission educated Krobo scholars Christian Akutei Azu (son of Odonkor Azu) and Thomas Odonkor (a

---

[192] GNA/ADM 11/1/1115, Conf. 14/92, 30.01.1892, 'Telegram from D.C. [Akuse] at Odumase to Hon. C'; To this very day, important people such as chiefs and priests, are not buried at a cemetery, but in their residence. It is a public secret that the *kono's* have a special place in the palace built by Sakite in Odumase.

[193] Disease, mortality and cost ruled out the extensive use of European troops in West Africa. Instead the British recruited Africans for their military campaigns along ethnic lines. The ethnonym 'Hausa', however, was applied in a highly anachronistic fashion (Killingray 2000).

[194] GNA/ADM 11/1/1115/Conf. 14/92, 16.02.1892, 'Reply from D.C. Akuse to Colonial Secretary's letter of 09.02.1892'; By being buried in the basement of his palace in Odumase instead of on the mountain, *kono* Sakite was accorded a pioneering role in the establishment of the towns in the plains as hometowns with ancestral homes, i.e. family houses (cf. Arlt 2002: 21).

[195] CO 98/7 Gold Coast Minutes and Executive Council 1884 to 1893, 22.01.1891 and 01.07.1892, Christiansborg Castle, Accra, 'Minutes of a meeting of the executive council of the Gold Coast Colony held at Government House'.

[196] GNA/ADM 11/1/1115/Conf. M.P.286/90, 04.10.1990, 'Letter from Mr. S.A. Williams, D.C. Akuse'.

son of a sister of Odonkor Azu), who had probably wanted to familiarise the government with their names as they had an interest in the succession of the then aged _konọ_ Sakite (cf. Arlt 2002: 19). In their letters they addressed the government asking for the abolishment of 'native customs', thereby drawing special attention to _dipo_. Christian Azu painted a picture of 'fetish' priests as money-grubbers, and according to him, a woman could be sold if she did not comply with the _dipo_ rites and her parents would have to pay the _dipo_ priest a large sum of money. Odonkor mentioned in typical missionary idiom that the girls on the mountain are "doing nothing but sitting idle from six months to a year".[197] However, in his letter of 1892, D.C. Williams declared that _dipo_ was harmless and served as a check on the morals of the girls, and that the _dipo_ season meant a brisk trading season in the area. He recommended that it could be celebrated in the plains in case Krobo Mountain would be closed down. However, no custom should be celebrated without his own permission and presence. In the letter he included some pictures of _dipo_ girls in different stages of the ceremony,[198] possibly to serve as proof of its innocence. In his letter, the D.C. also mentioned a possible heir to the stool of Sakite: according to Williams, Sakite's half-brother Peter Nyarko would be the rightful heir, but because of his age would relinquish his right in favour of his son, a Basel Mission trained school master at Ada, named Emmanuel Mate Kole.

As he had announced, Governor Griffith arrived in Odumase with an army of hundred 'Hausa' on July 19, 1892 and on the next day held a grand and colourful meeting with the chiefs and the people of Krobo to which he had also invited representatives of the chiefs of Accra, Akropong, and other places. He did not only want to arrange the succession of _konọ_ Sakite, but also take the opportunity to put a stop to the 'barbarous killings' related to the notorious war gods. The governor therefore decreed the new _Native Customs Ordinance_ that forbade the worshipping of all 'fetishes' and the burials on Krobo Mountain. The ordinance was not meant exclusively for 'Krobo customs', but was to deal with 'undesirable cults and customs' all over the colony.[199]

---

[197] GNA/ADM 11/1/1115/Conf.263/90, 01.09.1890 and 17.09.1990, 'Letter from Christian Akutei Azzu, Odumase with an attached letter by chief Odonkor'.

[198] GNA/ADM 11/1/1115, Conf. 10/92 (attached to 428/92 and Conf. 14/92), 02.03.1892, 'Letter from D.C. at Akuse to the governor'; These pictures do not seem to have been preserved as Williams wrote that the pictures were already fading at the time.

[199] The specific law banning 'Krobo custom' stated: 'The celebration of the Krobo custom is hereby prohibited and any person who joins or is concerned or takes any part in such celebration shall be liable to imprisonment with or without hard labour for a term not exceeding one year or to a fine not exceeding hundred pounds. (...) Any chief who directly or indirectly permits, encourages, abets or is concerned in the celebration in his division of the Krobo custom or who knowing of any celebration or intended celebration does not with all reasonable dispatch report the same to the district commissioner shall be liable to a fine which may extend to five hundred pounds.' (Ordinance to amend law relating to native customs. _Gold Coast Laws_, Faculty of Law, UG, p. 196, cited in: Obeng-Asamoa (1998: 85)).

The governor argued that the 'customs' referred to in Odumase were not originally Krobo and not universally applied on the Gold Coast. Moreover, as he stated later, his impression was that: "unless these Krobo customs are dealt with root and branch, they will not be destroyed out of the land, a matter which it is my settled determination to effect to the fullest extent".[200] The shrines would be destroyed and the priests would have to move down to the towns in the plains. One of the customs that was forbidden from now on was *dipo*. At the gathering the governor lamented the expense caused by the ritual and the nakedness of the girls, while the Basel missionaries were appreciative bystanders. The missionary Mischlisch later described in his report: "It is very laudable that he also condemned the bad, immoral clothing of the female population and included a related paragraph in the (...) law, whereby everybody is obliged to dress decently".[201] The very reference to the Krobo women's 'indecent dressing' is said to have been so horrifying to the missionary wives Eckhardt and Mischlisch, that it caused them to leave the scene.[202]

On a second gathering three days later, on July 23, the British governor, to the great joy of the missionaries, installed the first Christian chief in Krobo. The governor unveiled a portrait of the late Sakite wrapped in an English flag at this occasion. The new chief was the mission-trained former catechist and teacher Emmanuel Mate Kole, son of Peter Nyarko and thus *kono* Sakite's nephew, whom the D.C. had also recommended after. Peter Nyarko had successfully managed to use his position as a middleman in the contact with the colonial officials and Basel missionaries to push his son, Emmanuel Mate Kole, forward. He convinced the British government that Emmanuel would support a ban on the 'pagan Krobo practices' as well as the abandonment of Krobo Mountain (cf. Obeng-Assamoa 1998: 47). Whereas the British expected that the new laws would restore peace and therefore promote commerce in the area that would benefit the whole colony, the missionaries obviously felt that this was an answer to their prayers and that it meant the breakthrough of Christianity. They had proclaimed 'the downfall of paganism in Krobo land' before,[203] but now they exclaimed: "The land has a Christian monarch, the main bastions of the Enemy [Satan] have fallen and the gospel has a free way!"[204]

---

[200] GNA/ADM 11/1/1115, 04.08.1892, 'Minute by Governor Sir W. B. Griffith'.
[201] BMA, D-1.56 Goldküste 1892 Ga, Odumase 128, A. Mischlisch, 30.07 and 03.08.1892, Odumase, 'Quartalbericht: Verbot der nationalen Kostüme und Einsetzung des ersten christlichen Königs in Krobo'.
[202] GNA/NP 13/1/The Gold Coast Chronicle Vol. III, No. 87, 01.08.1892, 'Mr. Brew, shorthand writer to the governor'.
[203] For example, see: *Jahresberichte* 1888, 'Der Niedergang des Heidentums im Krobolande. Aus dem Jahresbericht der Station Odumase von Br. Kopp.'
[204] *Evangelische Missions Magazin* 1893, 'Die Mission unter dem weiblichen geschlecht Afrikas. 1. Die heidnische Frauenwelt im Krobo-Land. Nach Mitteilungen von Miss. J. Kopp', pp. 403-411.

However, what the Basel missionaries did not mention in their reports was that there had been a lot of political scheming regarding the stool by the different factions around *kono* Sakite, as some of the letters mentioned above already indicated. A Krobo historian, Obeng-Assamoa, arguing in favour of the current ruling 'house', states that Emmanuel Mate Kole's nomination shows that the king-makers deemed him, as an educated person, to be the most suitable person to steer the state towards 'modernism' (Obeng-Assamoa 1998: 49). But most Krobo, including the priests, regarded Akute, a brother of the late Sakite, as the most likely successor, while Akute himself favoured his, also educated, younger brother Christian Akutei Azu.[205]

The new *kono* was taken through a series of vows by the governor, through which he recognised the supremacy of the British government and the ultimate authority of the governor. After his installation a gun salute was fired and music was played by a band provided by the British government (Obeng-Assamoa 1998: 51). The newly elected king sent two of his photographs to the D.C., in one of which he posed with a sword and a medal, probably a particular medal and the silver sword awarded to *kono* Sakite in 1888 by Queen Victoria as a reward for his military service.[206] The photographs therefore carried the visible emblems of British imperial influence, while it is likely that the photographs were taken by the Basel missionaries who also had an interest in endorsing the image of this ruler, through whose relationships they wanted to promote Christianity.[207]

On July 24, 1892 it was announced that the Krobo were given three days to gather their possessions from the mountain. The old and feeble people living up there were carried down the mountain by their relatives in hammocks to their respective homes in the plains (Azu 1928: 18). After these three days, the Union Jack was hoisted on the mountain and the army of 100 Hausa man under the authority of a British officer destroyed all shrines and plundered the houses. The

---

[205] The descendants of Akute Azu and Christian Akutei Azu have been fighting the legitimacy of the succession to the stool to this very day (see Arlt 1996; 1997; Henige 1974). The case has been taken to the Eastern Regional House of Chiefs in Koforidua and the Supreme Court in Accra (for example, for a description about ongoing chieftaincy disputes in Krobo, see the articles in *The Ghanaian Times* (Noonoo 1998) and *The Ghanaian Chronicle* ("Absentee chiefs banned at Krobo" 2002)).

[206] GNA/ADM 11/1/1115, CO 96/225, despatch no. 179, 01.08.1892, 'Abolition of Krobo Customs', letter from governor Brandford Griffith to Lord Knutsford'; It is most likely that a copy of one of these pictures is preserved at the picture archive of mission 21, Basel Mission holdings (www.bmpix.org) under the reference number QD-30.016.0013.

[207] One of the earliest missionary portraits, probably dating to the late 1870s, shows Emmanuel Mate Kole's predecessor and uncle, *kono* Sakite, surrounded by Akan symbols of chieftaincy (BMA D-30.06.039). He further accumulated some royal regalia awarded by the British in recognition of his support (e.g. in the Asante war). Sakite's father Odonkor Azu already had shown a great likening of Akan and Western regalia. Emmanuel Mate Kole continued using the British regalia. Later on he was knighted as a reward for his support and henceforth he was known among the Krobo as 'Sir' Emmanuel. On the use of photography by the Manya Krobo paramount chiefs see Nii O. Quarcoopome (n.d.).

officer in command stated in detail, probably to prove the 'barbarous and hideous' customs of the Krobo but without further explanation, that 133 'fetish haunts' had been destroyed, 65 on the West-eastern side of the mountain and 68 on the South-western side. Furthermore 47 drums were destroyed and 18 kept, 37 skulls buried and again 16 were kept, perhaps to send some of these off to a museum. Another two thighbones and four other bones attached to a drum were found, and several jaw bones. The officer further reported that one of the Hausas found a basket hidden under a rock containing four sticks each about 2 ½ feet long, to each of which the jaw bones of twelve supposed victims were tied. One of these would be sent to the colonial office in Liverpool, where they were to a museum, of which no name was given.[208]

The two Krobo paramount chiefs were said to have voluntarily called on their people to bring their 'fetishes' to be burnt. Peter Nyarko's role as an intermediary between the chiefs and elders of Odumase and the British government was proven once more by the fact that he was given the contract to feed the Hausa troops on the mountain. The large trees on Krobo Mountain forming part of the various 'fetish' groves had all been cut down to the stumps. Still the governor wanted them to be blown up with dynamite.[209] Finally, the four men convicted of the murder of a slave a month earlier, were publicly executed as a warning to other people. In the meantime, Griffith wrote a letter to inform the chiefs of neighbouring Dangme speaking peoples that the same thing would happen to them and that they should announce to their people that the worship of *Nadu*, *Koko-Nadu*, *Kotoklo* and the practice of *dipo* was abolished. It was peculiar again how he referred to the apparently offensive dressing in *dipo*:

> The girls who wear tails to their dresses must also be informed that the wearing of such tails will be part and parcel of the fetish practices which have been rendered illegal, and the police will be instructed to inform against the girls wearing such tails to their clothes and they will be summoned before the District Commissioner and fined as often as they do it, and the fine will be increased in any fresh case.[210]

At first there seemed to be remarkably little reaction from among the Krobo. There was no apparent resistance or uproar and people came down from the mountain. Governor Griffith triumphantly reported on the speech he held in Odumase:

> Several native gentlemen have expressed to me their astonishment at the total absence of disturbance when I stated to the assembled chiefs and multitude that not only was it

---

[208] PRO/CO 96/225/No. 229, 25.08.1892, Christiansborg Castle, Accra, ' 'Krobo customs', letter from governor Griffith to Lord Knutsford from the government house'.
[209] GNA/ADM 11/1/1115, M.P. 3906/92, 21.10.1892.
[210] GNA/ADM 1/9/4, No. 31-35, 25.07.1892, Odumase, 'Governor Griffith to Kings/chiefs of Shai, Osudoku, Prampram, Ningo and Ada'.

the wish of Her Majesty's government that their barbarous, revolting and murderous practices should cease then and forever, but that all access to Krobo Mountain would cease on and after the 26th of July. Although immediately surrounded by hundreds of people – closely packed together and increasing in numbers as the mass went back - they were most attentive to catch every word I uttered, and were silent orderly, and very well behaved. This exemplary conduct was the general remark of my staff.[211]

This seemed nothing like the 'savage and warlike character' of the people on the mountain that Hesketh Bell had described after his visit in the late 1880s (Bell 1911 [1893]: 49). Only the traditional priests were said to have set up some booby-traps. Gunpowder was found hidden in the thatched roof of the Okumo's hut, which would have exploded when the hut was set on fire.[212] The missionary Mischlisch thought that the relative peace was clearly due to the Christian influence:

> The governor could not have acted so strict and tough, have forbidden by law, old, enfleshed, heathen customs and traditions, and have chased the Krobo from their national sanctuary without experiencing serious resistance, if not, thanks to the Mission, Christian notions, Christian customs and traditions had entered the whole country and found an entrance there and then.[213] (Original in German, my translation)

The remarks of Odonkor however, set the lack of resistance in a slightly different light:

> The governor came along with a large force armed with heavy artillery to bombard the Mountain should the Krobos put up a fight. (...) The governor ordered the formal installation of the new chief at once. A few rounds of machine-gun fired in jubilation assured the Krobos of the prowess of the white man; there was a general stampede, and they found it useless to offer any opposition (Odonkor 1971: 45).

Obeng-Asamoa (1998: 52) even thinks there were "rockets fired into the mountain home". It is also very likely, considering the timing of the descent (one day after Emmanuel's installation) and the lack of any organised resistance, that the *kono* had foreknowledge of the event. He secretly agreed with the British, as a condition for government support, to carry out the order to descend immediately after he was enstooled (Obeng-Assamoa 1998: 53). However, it should not be forgotten that usually only old people, especially old women, priests and *dipo*

---

[211] GNA/ADM 11/1/1115, CO 96/225, despatch no. 179, 01.08.1892, ''Abolition of Krobo Customs', letter from governor Brandford Griffith to Lord Knutsford'; The 'native gentlemen' will have referred to the principal Krobo scholars at the time, among them were Peter Nyarko, Emmanuel Mate Kole, Thomas Odonkor, Solomon Kodjiku, Noa Agwae Azu and Christian Tei.

[212] GNA/ADM 1/9/4, 09.08.1892, 'Governor Griffith to D.C'; It was common to store valuable things under the roof.

[213] BMA, D-1.56 Goldküste 1892 Ga, Odumase 128', A. Mischlisch, 30.7 / 3.8.1892, Odumase, 'Quartalbericht: Verbot der nationalen Kostüme und Einsetzung des ersten christlichen Königs in Krobo'.

girls stayed permanently on the mountain. Obeng-Asamoa writes that the 1891 census suggests that about 2,268 people left the mountain: 1,115 Manya and 1,153 Yilo Krobo (Obeng-Assamoa 1998: 54), while the total Krobo population was estimated to be about 35,000 at the time.[214] The majority of the Krobo people by then was living in the upcountry on their farms.

It was part of the general British colonial policy to 'pacify' the people in their colony by bringing them down from their mountains in surveyable and taxable towns and settled villages, so that trade and commerce would be promoted and a united colony created. The death of *kono* Sakite had provided the British with the occasion to strengthen their control over the Krobo states. The forced abandonment of the mountain finally appeared to break the authority of the priests and favour the rise of the chiefs. The events of 1892 would indeed have severe results for the priests and the performance of *dipo*, as will be described in the next sections.

The defilement of Nana Kloweki

Several reports written after the closure of Krobo Mountain in July 1892 confirm that especially widows and old women, some of whom were priestesses, used to stay on top of Krobo Mountain, where they were the exclusive manufacturers of clay pots (men were forbidden to make pottery),[215] supervised the young women during *dipo* and accordingly looked after the Kloweki priestess. After the closure of Krobo Mountain, it was announced to the Shai, who occupied several hills rather than one mountain, that their hills would be next in line.[216] The accounts on the Shai women also shed light on the Krobo case and showed that some of the Krobo Mountain inhabitants sought refuge on the Shai Hills where a much larger pottery industry existed,[217] and that some Krobo from

---

[214] GNA/ADM 11/1/115, M.P.309/91, 19.01.1891, 'Report of Mr. Bell, D.S.V.R. on the Krobo Customs'.

[215] From a statement by Emmanuel Mate Kole it becomes clear that there must have been a taboo on manufacturing pots and dishes on the plains. He said that the priestesses and the clay pot manufacturers believed they might die if they did not make the pots out of the mountain clay; GNA/ADM 11/1/1115, 07.11.1892, Odumasie, 'Notes of enquiry into the complaints of Christian Tei Azzu and others against the conduct of Peter Nyako and King Mate Kole in connection with the fetish worshippers and as to the alleged restoration of the *Dipo* custom'.

[216] The Dangme speaking Osudoku people's mountain, the 'Osudoku Hill', also was to be occupied later on, on September 14, 1892; GNA/ADM 11/1/1115, 3593/92, 01.10.1892, 'letter from D.C. Williams at Akuse';

[217] Part of the earthenware was manufactured for ritual use, which partly explains the importance of Krobo mountain and the Shai Hills as the ritual centres of production. Huber tells us that only very few Krobo women were involved in pot-making during the time of his research in the 1950s, and that it used to be more important on Krobo Mountain. But even then production did not cover the needs, and part of the supply came from the Shai Hills and also from the Ewe villages near the river Volta. Today there is only one pot-making centre within the Krobo area. This is a small village between

Odumase had placed their daughters in the *dipo* celebrations there.[218] So Krobo *dipo* girls had found a shelter with their neighbours. But the governor gave the Shai fifteen days to remove their property from their hills. In several requests the Shai begged the governor to allow the old women to stay on the hills to obtain the necessary gneiss as an ingredient for their pots. The Colonial Secretary replied that, according to him, the women in question were not manufacturers of native pots, but 'fetish women' who desired to remain on the hills to continue to perform *dipo*.[219] However, for the women who left the mountain under protest, making pottery involved serious ritual taboos.[220]

Whereas most male Krobo priests, even the *djeméli*, had already been visiting the towns in the plains before 1892, and continued to administer their shrines at new hidden locations, the eviction from the mountain severely affected the position of the high or principal priestess of Nana Klowεki. There are only a few written accounts of what happened to the priestess after her removal from the mountain. The earliest elaborate description I found comes from the daily newspaper *The Gold Coast Chronicle* of 1893:

> The lady-superior holds herself quite aloof from the sterner sex. It is said that she was dedicated to the work in her infancy and at no time of her life has she so much as touched a male. Indeed, until the soldiers in carrying out the Governor's orders conducted the old lady out of her house, no man had dared to darken her doorway. The pagans quite expected to see the soldiers fall down dead at their daring act. The house, nevertheless, was doomed, and shortly afterwards was in ruins.[221]

Here we are told that the main priestess of Klowεki lived in seclusion and was celibate. According to local beliefs, it was a taboo to approach her, at the danger of even being killed instantly. The missionary Kölle also described the effect of the priestess' contact with the soldiers:

Akuse and Somanya called Okwenya. Its inhabitants are mostly Ningo and Ewe immigrants (Huber 1993: 63).

[218] GNA/ADM 11/1/1115, M.P. 2761/92, 'Letter from king Awah to the governor, 27.07.1892; letter from D.C. Williams, 16.08.1982; letter from the governor, 23.08.1892'. See also GNA/NP 13/1/ The Gold Coast Chronicle, 05.09.1892; The Shai women would not be allowed anymore to obtain the clay and other materials for their pots on their hills. Their paramount chief Awah of Agomeda then sent a request to the governor to plea that those women should be allowed to remain on the Shai Hills. But when the D.C. at Akuse was asked for advice in the matter, he replied that the clay could be found on the Shai plains as well and there was no need to grant the request.

[219] GNA/ADM 11/1/1115, M.P. 3748/92, 07.09.1892.

[220] Quarcoo and Kilson's study of Shai pottery (1968) shows that, although the clay was dug in river valleys below, there was an absolute prohibition on the making of pots in the farm villages until 1892. The clay also had to be mixed with ground-up gneiss from the hills, or else it would crack. The clay-pits were under the control of priestesses, and the digging of the clay was hedged about with ritual prohibitions. Only Shai women who had passed through the *dipo* rites were allowed to dig and carry the clay. All clay was carried up the hill and the pots were made in the hill villages.

[221] GNA/NP 13/1, The Gold Coast Chronicle, 07.01.1893.

The Krobo Mountain was cleared later on instigation of the colonial government to break the power of the murder fetishes (that had their seat there). The *Otufo* [*dipo*] priestess was evacuated as well. When she refused to leave her sanctuary, the soldiers gently forced her out. This touch made her unclean, therefore the *Otufo*-custom has been desecrated from that day on (Kölle 1936: 15).

Maybe because she had been in hiding, the Klowɛki priestess was only removed from her mountain home a few weeks after the actual abolition of the mountain settlements.[222] According to Kölle's story, this removal from the mountain caused the desecration of the priestess. Her house was destroyed. We are not told what happened to the priestess after this, but Odonkor (1971: 46) narrates that: "They destroyed the fetish-houses, even Krowɛki – the priestess – who had grown to be part of the mountain was carried down in a hammock to the village of the Okumo [priest]." So, according to Odonkor, the priestess moved to the towns in the plains.[223]

After the closure of the mountains and the descent of the priests to the plains, the colonial government wanted to keep track of the residences and movements of the 'fetish' priests. Therefore the paramount chiefs Emmanuel Mate Kole of Manya, Akrobetto of Yilo and Awah of Shai were requested to furnish the British with the name and rank of all priests as well as the name of the town or village they were staying now.[224] *Kono* Akrobetto responded that the head of the 'fetishes' was called 'Kroweke', which was under supervision of a woman who was considered to be a queen and was called 'yomoh'. All priests of both Yilo and Manya Krobo paid her very great respect and 'adored her from time immemorial'. After she had been driven from Krobo Mountain, she stayed at Korletsom, near Odumase, he wrote.[225]

So how was the Klowɛki cult reorganised in the plains? On the mountain the requirement that its priests should be in a perpetual state of ritual cleanliness had initially restrained them from leaving the mountain home, dealing with blood or having contact with strangers. These ritual restrictions had already largely undermined their power before the forced descent from the mountain and had facilitated the rise of the (paramount) chiefs, especially during the reign of Odonkor Azu as from 1835. It should be emphasised, however, that the changes in the political structure did not mean an elimination of spiritual power, but a

---

[222] GNA/ADM 1/9/4, No. 36, 01.08.1892, Christiansborg Castle, 'Griffith to DC Williams'.
[223] Apparently some of the priests tried to seek refuge on hills in the vicinity. One British colonial official reported from Krobo Mountain that smoke could be seen coming from a small hill nearby. Two 'fetish people', an old man and an old woman were said to have fled there after the forced abandonment of Krobo Mountain. They had taken their 'fetish' belongings with them and were said to be living in a cave; GNA, H.C. Franks Lieut. Asst. Inspector, 02.08.1892, Krobo Hill.
[224] GNA/ADM 11/1/1115, M.P. 3535/92, 'letter to the D.C. at Akuse dated 30.09.1892'.
[225] GNA/ADM 11/1/1115, M.P. 3535/92, 17.10.1892, 'letter from king Akrobetto in reply to the D.C.'s enquiries'.

separation of powers (cf. Obeng-Assamoa 1998: 22, 30). The power of the kono was, and in fact is, sanctified by the (Okumo) priest who installs him. But even though the rise of the chiefs was probably unavoidable, it is peculiar that in the long run the colonial exercise of power affected the senior Kloweki priestess more than the senior male priests. There are several reasons for this. First, the priests were compelled to change their sphere of influence when they were forced from the mountain, which in the long run actually benefited the continuation of their influence. As I pointed out above, the male priests had already begun visiting the towns in the plains before 1892. The power of the Kloweki priestess, however, was undermined when strangers forcefully removed her from the mountain. Whereas the male priests were also prohibited to interact with strangers, but by then could move about in an area restricted to the old Krobo boundaries and were allowed to marry, the priestess still used to be a woman who lived a celibate life, totally secluded on the mountain. Kölle's remark that her contacts with male strangers forever desecrated her position and discontinued her power, seems to be correct. Furthermore, female ritual and political powers were ignored both by the British colonials and the Basel missionaries. Their support of the kono was to the advantage of the male Kloweki priests who were still needed to sanctify the kono 's power behind the scenes.

The first Christian chief

The new kono, Emmanuel Mate Kole, did what the British government expected him to do. He had announced in a letter to the D.C. at Akuse that he would introduce himself to the Krobo people 'according to Krobo custom', on April 28, 1893. This meant he would formally be introduced to the general public. He said he would take the opportunity to impress upon his people the advisability of improving their villages and settling down in a 'proper town'. He would also announce the celebration of a yearly yam festival (*yereyeli*, 'eating of yam'), apparently modelled after the Odwira festivals of neighbouring Akan (Akuapem) people,[226] which should replace the public celebration of the old cults and the *dipo* ceremonies. Recalling the occasion of this formal outdooring he wrote in 1895:

> I said in the meeting that the *dipo* and other customs are dead and that, when they [the Krobo] were up the hill, they were barbarious and it is the will of God that the customs be abolished so that they may be civilized by degrees and that they may not have the least thought that it will be restored.[227]

---

[226] Different Ewe peoples also celebrate 'yam-eating' festivals. For a description of the Odwira festival of the Akuapem, see Gilbert (1994).
[227] GNA/ADM 11/1/1115, 14.10.1895, 'Mate Kole to the C.S.'.

According to the D.C., the meeting in April 1893 was a great success. The *kono* also advised his people to send their children to school and to pay proper attention to the morals of their daughters in the light of the *dipo* rites having been abolished. The latter part of August should from now on be reserved each year for the annual yam custom that should come in place of the old celebrations on the mountain.[228] The Hausa soldiers were withdrawn from Krobo Mountain in August 1893. Due to heavy rains, the remaining houses there had become unsuitable for habitation. Still, patrols were visiting the mountain at regular intervals and informants received financial rewards when they reported people who visited the hills. These hills had now been declared government property. *Kono* Emmanuel Mate Kole promised to report attempts of the Krobo to reinstate any of the customs.[229]

Emmanuel Mate Kole maintained cordial relationships with the British colonial government but, like his predecessor Sakite at the end of his reign, he experienced difficulties in exerting influence on his people during the first years of his governance. One reason was his liaison with the British that had caused the forced abandonment of the mountain. Another continued reason was that most Krobo people lived dispersed on their village farms, but now that they were no more allowed to return to the old mountain-home, there was no need for them to come down to the towns at all. To be able to assert his authority, *kono* Emmanuel Mate Kole tried to create new ties between his dispersed people and his town Odumase and the other towns in the plains that had to become the new hometowns. The above-mentioned yam festival was an attempt to constitute a new homecoming event. One reason why yam was chosen instead of the traditional millet may have been the fact that eating of millet was part of most ceremonies on the ritual calendar and therefore had a 'fetish' connotation. Introducing the yam may have been another attempt to de-emphasise the power of the priests (cf. Obeng-Assamoa 1998: 157). Elderly people today remember the 'yam eating' (*yereyeli*) festival from their youth. This festival, according to Obeng-Asamoa (ibid.), was only celebrated once every five years. The first time was probably in December 1896.[230]

Another reason for the new *kono*'s difficulties, was his controversial election. In order to discredit Mate Kole with the colonial government, his political adversaries pointed at his father Peter Nyarko as the source of rumours circulating among the Krobo in 1892. These rumours said that the British Queen Victoria had disapproved of the Ordinance prohibiting the Krobo customs, and as a result not only had the government authorised the revival of *dipo*, but it was also

---

[228] GNA/ADM 11/1/1115 ?789/93
[229] GNA/ADM 11/1/1115, M.P. 3448/93, 01.08.1893; 13.09.1893, 'Native officer Akkere reporting'.
[230] BMA, D-1.64 Goldküste 1896 Ga, Odumase 169, W.A. Quartey, Undated yearly report, most probably for the year 1896 and written in January 1897, Odumase.

willing to pay £50 as a compensation to those traditional priests whose means of living had been interfered with.[231] It was said that Peter Nyarko had his private reasons to seek a restoration of *dipo*. One of his wives, whose daughter had not passed *dipo* yet, was said to 'trouble him'. Emmanuel Mate Kole and his father protested against the accusations, and the D.C., who had organised a hearing on the matter, believed charges against them had been made up out of hatred by Christian Akutei Azu and his followers, who had objected to Mate Kole being made *kono*. Peter Nyarko declared that none of his daughters had gone through *dipo* before. He also recalled that no man was to touch the *dipo* priestess, but since the Hausa had desecrated her, not any *dipo* would be celebrated for perhaps five to ten years.[232] The Okumo priest also claimed that he had received a message from Mate Kole and his father Peter Nyarko. The message allegedly said that the British queen would send £14 to the Kloweki priestess for her upkeep, and that the priests would soon be allowed to return to Krobo Mountain.[233] What is clear from the accusations is that Christian Akutei Azu and the Okumo priest were challenging the position of Emmanuel Mate Kole. The roles of Peter Nyarko and his son in the whole affair, however, are difficult to assess.

Other accusations in subsequent years suggest that Mate Kole and his councillors, despite their denial, tried to meet the Krobo people's wishes to restore *dipo*. Basel Mission catechist Emmanuel B. Odonkor accused Mate Kole and his father Peter Nyarko of having ordered for the *tɛgbɛtɛ* (the sacred *dipo* stone) to be brought down from Krobo Mountain. All the men who were involved, except one, supposedly died, the remaining one became insane.[234] These remarks referred to beliefs surrounding the spiritual powers of the *tɛgbɛtɛ*, which made it very dangerous to handle. In another letter the same E.B. Odonkor reported that the sacred stone was brought to the market at Laasi. He accused Emmanuel Mate Kole and his father of allowing *dipo* to be performed,

---

[231] The priests made a living out of the performance of the rituals, and therefore, after the abolishment from Krobo Mountain, the executive council of the Gold Coast discussed a possible compensation for their loss of income; CO 98/7 Gold Coast Minutes and Executive Council 1884 to 1893, 22.01.1891 and 01.07.1892, Christiansborg Castle, Accra, 'Minutes of a meeting of the executive council of the Gold Coast Colony held at Government House'.

[232] It is unclear why he mentions this period. Maybe he felt *dipo* could only be celebrated when a new priestess had replaced the desecrated one, which could take time.

[233] GNA/ADM 11/1/1115, Conf. 191/92 (M.P. 3924/92), 20.10.1892, 'Letter of Christian Akutei Azzu'; and 07.11.1892, Odumasie, 'Notes of enquiry into the complaints of Christian Tei Azzu and others against the conduct of Peter Nyako and King Mate Kole in connection with the fetish worshippers and as to the alleged restoration of the *dipo* custom'.

[234] GNA/ADM 11/1/1115, 09.10.1893. Emmanuel B. Odonkor was a catechist until at least 1885 (Odjidja 1973: 72). Later he was a clerk at Swanzy's store in Kpong. As another brother of the late *kono* Sakite I, he may have been on the other stool claimants' side, i.e., Akute and Christian Akutei Azu. Otherwise, except for his Christian convictions, his reasons for the allegations are not clear.

apparently in the town.[235] The D.C. later also reported that one of the three men supposedly involved in bringing down the stone (*tɛgbɛtɛ*), had killed himself. Killing oneself was seen as an abomination to the Krobo, and the event may have proved to them once more that dealing with the *tɛgbɛtɛ* was very hazardous and could cause even death. The D.C. must have partly believed the accusations as he apparently tried to protect the British government's protégé, by stating that Peter Nyarko alone was responsible for the order, but not his son Emmanuel.[236] In the same year (1895) however, Mate Kole ordered some elders to be arrested and taken to Accra, when they tried to clear the path leading to Krobo Mountain. The *kono* allegedly also fined some men for impregnating girls who had not been initiated yet. This shows that people still adhered to 'the old ways' and also that the *kono* could not fully withdraw himself from 'customary affairs'.[237]

Whereas the educated political adversaries of *kono* Mate Kole and his father accused him of secretly continuing *dipo*, his other political adversaries, the 'fetish' priests, in particular their leader Okumo, and people in general, rather attacked him because of his refusal to fully restore *dipo*. The new D.C. at Akuse, J. N. Coy, reported in July 1896 that still many of the people in 'Eastern Krobo' (Manya Krobo) opposed Emmanuel Mate Kole:

> [T]he one reason so far as I can find out being that he will not assist them in getting back the old Krobo's customs and also is opposed to fetish practices and fetish priests having a very strong hold in his district are doing all they can to estrange his subjects from him. The old customs die so hard that very few of the girls now marry properly, as many of them are driven away from the towns if they become enceinte before they have passed the custom.[238]

The last remark is very important. Even though *dipo* was abolished, girls who got pregnant without passing through the rites were still considered unclean and driven away, possibly ending up in prostitution.[239] Therefore behind the scenes women especially tried to assert their influence, as the story about Peter Nyarko's wife above also showed, and urged husbands to re-institute *dipo*, as

---

[235] GNA/ADM 11/1/1115, 05.07.1895, Akuse, 'letter of E. B. Odonkor to the colonial secretary Hodgson'.

[236] GNA/ADM 11/1/1115, 12.08.1895, Akuse, 'letter of the district commissioner to the colonial secretary'.

[237] GNA/ADM 11/1/1115, 05.07.1895, Akuse, 'letter of E. B. Odonkor to the colonial secretary Hodgson'.

[238] GNA/ ADM 11/1/1115 (M.P. 4997A/96?), J.N. Coy, D.C. Akuse, 14.07.1896, Akuse, 'Extract from a report from the District Commissioner Akuse to the Colonial Secretary dated 14th July 1896'.

[239] Prostitutes in colonial (and post-colonial) Africa were often outsiders with no kinship ties in the communities where they practised their profession (Akyeampong 1997: 157). It is tempting to see a link between 'the preponderance of Krobo prostitutes in colonial Asante towns' (ibid. 1997: 159) and the Krobo women that were driven away from their society, although this 'preponderance' may also be of a later date.

their daughters would not become proper, marriageable women without *dipo* and would be banned from their home.

Obeng-Assamoa (1998: 88) argues that the continuing allegations of a revival of *dipo* were meant to hide the political motives of the reporters, implying that those critics did not have a real interest in *dipo* itself. Although it is true that *dipo* now became a political instrument in asserting influence, it is no coincidence that the *dipo* rites were the centre of concern, as the rites themselves were a source of spiritual, moral and therefore political power as I pointed out above. With the ban on *dipo*, the power of the priests had been eroded even more. The Okumo and related priests of the Klowɛki cult therefore had a real interest in restoring *dipo*. The desire to restore *Nadu* and *Kotoklo*, and the other cults, seemed, at least publicly, less strong.[240] The fact that *dipo*, and not any of the other now forbidden practices, was one of the main issues in the dispute around the election of Emmanuel Mate Kole as *kono*, and that the *dipo* ceremony was one of the first practices to re-emerge, as I will show in the next sections, shows the central importance of its rituals in Krobo society.

The use of *dipo* as a political instrument and at the same time its central importance is also evident from a petition that Emmanuel Mate Kole, his father Peter Nyarko and a number of Manya Krobo linguists, chiefs and elders wrote to the British governor in 1899 in order to claim authority over 'Western Krobo' (= Yilo Krobo). It is not within the scope of this chapter to elaborate on the split-up between Manya and Yilo Krobo that probably already occurred in the 18th century (see Henige (1974)). What is of concern in the following petition, is that the petitioners claim overall political authority and thereby allocate a major role to Klowɛki and the *dipo* rites in proving a common identity for all Krobo. The 'king' of Manya Krobo is presented in the petition as being equal to the 'chief priestess' (Klowɛki). The 'proof' for the claim of authority over all Krobo was given on the basis of: "The following customs existing until our removal from the Krobo Hill", that "confirm the above traditional facts which prove that there was until lately only one king from the family of the present king 'Mate Kole' who rules over the whole Kroboes". The following 'customs' were mentioned in particular:

---

[240] However, there are clues that the veneration of the war gods also continued and not only in the upcountry as I mentioned earlier. Even though *kono* Emmanuel Mate Kole upheld the ban on the war god *Nadu*, his choice of warriors from the *tegble* sub-cult of *Nadu* for the British invasion of Asante in 1896 was remarkable in this respect. (In the Asante War of 1895-1896 the Krobo fought on the side of the British under the command of major Robert, later Lord Baden-Powell. This war resulted in the capture and exile of Asantehene Prempeh I to the Seychelles Islands (Obeng-Assamoa 1998: 177-178)). And later, during the First World War, Mate Kole again relied on the *Nadu* warriors for his choice of men to fight for the British against the Germans in Togoland. So the *kono* was not able to oust neither the dipo nor the *Nadu* cult, and even made use of the latter's adherents. He also did not remove the human skulls that hung on the royal drums as symbols of the war cult, as this would have enraged many people (Obeng-Assamoa 1998: 156).

- The girls of Eastern and Western Kroboes, after finishing their terms of confinement in accordance with the *dipo* customs, had to undergo the rites of consecration
  in Manya, which was the residence of the king and chief priestess.
- Should a *dipo* girl fail to keep her vows, she was to be brought before the king and
  chief priestess in Manya to be declared guilty and consequently banished for life
  from the country.
- The remains of a *dipo* girl who is dead are not to be interred, unless by order of the
  king and chief priestess.
- Ceremonies in connection with marriage and delivery of twins are to be performed
  nowhere but in Manya by the chief priestess by order of the king.
- Death punishments were to be performed nowhere but in Manya in the presence of
  the king of Krobo.
- The first day of every annual custom is celebrated by the four tribes in Manya, during which time presents of provisions and drinkables are offered to the king and
  the chief priestess.[241]

With this petition Emmanuel Mate Kole, who still did not have full control over
his own Manya Krobo state at the time, apparently tried to usurp the overall control the priests had had, as in fact the senior priesthood had always continued to
have influence in both Yilo and Manya, despite the split-up. However, the petition to gain control over Yilo Krobo was not granted by the British government.
Still, Emmanuel Mate Kole slowly strengthened his position in Manya Krobo as
he appropriated the 'tradition' of chieftaincy, adopted a more pragmatic attitude
towards particular Krobo (ritual) practices and made strategic economic moves,
which strengthened his position.[242]
    However, the price Mate Kole had to pay for his turn to 'tradition' was
that his relationship with the Basel Mission became ambiguous. The high hopes
the missionaries had had of the Christian chief faded within a few years. Paradoxically, the Christian chief soon had to become a 'backslider' in order to
strengthen his position as a chief among the whole of Manya Krobo, not just
among the still relatively small group of Christians. In order to establish his authority and increase his status, he could no longer withdraw himself from customary laws. For example, according to his status as a chief, he eventually had
concubines and had to agree to a polygamous marriage (he married five additional non-Christian wives). For this reason he was excluded from the Lord's

---

[241] GNA/ ADM 11/1/1115, 28.08.1899, The Palace, Odumase, 'Petition (signed by E. Mate Kole c.s.)'.
(Also see Obeng-Assamoa 1998: 56-57).
[242] For example, he managed to survive the 'Dom riots' of 1903. (See Obeng-Asamoa's account for a
detailed description of the events in which the Dom division rioted against Emmanuel Mate Kole
(1998: 97-101)). With the back-up of the British government he also won the first 'market war' in
1906, whereby a new market was established in Agomanya, a suburb of Odumase, and the old market
of Manyakpongunor lost importance at the expense of chief Odonkor of Kpong and chief Amitei of
the Dom division. In the late 1930s, the *konọ* also erected a new market at Asesewa in Djebiam territory in Upper-Manya, and as a result the Bisa market went down. Therefore the markets became important sources of revenue for the *konọ* (Obeng-Assamoa 1998: 90-97).

Supper in 1894,[243] and again in 1895.[244] In the expression of status, Mate Kole and other Christian converts in general still needed respect and acceptance within mainstream Krobo society rather than the approval of their still quite marginal fellow Christians.[245]

'An upsurge of Heathendom': expectations of missionaries fading away

The Basel Mission had been disappointed with the effects of the eviction from Krobo Mountain in general. In his yearly report for 1893, the African Basel Mission pastor Quartey (a Ga) wrote that:

> I thought the heathens would - after they had plainly seen that their fetishes have neither power to save nor might to help on a day of disappointment, and affliction - flock into the Church of Christ, but things had not been so smooth as I thought, and the heathens around us are still kept in fetters of intoxication, superstition, polygamy, fornication, adultery and many other Satanical powers.[246]

The number of exclusions from the church was rising again. According to Quartey, moral standards were 'even lower' since the abolition. Many Christian girls 'fell', that is, they were excluded for becoming pregnant before they married. Again and again the missionaries complained about the moral weakness of the heathens and the adherence of the female population to 'fetishes'.

Of course it took time before the forced changes would be accepted. In the first years people still secretly buried their dead inside the house or even up Krobo Mountain, and tried to fool the authorities by putting stones inside the coffins that they buried at the cemetery. More importantly, as I pointed out above, after the loss of their ritual centre, the Krobo farmers had no reason to return to the towns in the plains, and remained on their plantations, still moving further to the northwest. The missionaries were therefore left somewhat isolated and frustrated in Odumase, which was centred around the *kono*'s palace and their main mission post, schools and church, as it was difficult to reach the peo-

---

[243] BMA, D-1.60 Goldküste 1894 Ga, Odumase 180, Josenhans, 16.01.1895, Odumase, 'Jahresbericht'.

[244] BMA, D-1.62, Goldküste 1895 Ga, Odumase 138, W.A. Quartey, 13.02.1896, Odumase, 'Jahresbericht'; Obeng-Asamoa claims that he went to church every Sunday and that all of his 31 children were baptised and educated (Obeng-Assamoa 1998: 151). The compilation of Christian pioneers in Krobo in *Mustard Seed. The Growth of the Church in Kroboland* (Odjidja 1973), simply declares that: 'He lived as a Christian until his death in 1939'. Obeng-Assamoa further states that he 'had a reputation for being a strict disciplinarian' (1998: 151). In the eyes of the local population this was equal to being a Christian, as mission Christianity became renowned for its strong emphasis on discipline.

[245] See also Van den Bersselaar (1998: 158), who describes a similar situation among Igbo converts in Nigeria in the 19th century.

[246] BMA, D-1.58, W. Quartey, 20.2.1894, Odumase, 'Yearly report for 1893'.

ple in their remote and dispersed farm households in the upcountry. Only old and feeble people were staying in the towns (cf. Arlt 2002: 20).

The missionaries thought that the yam festival that was introduced by Mate Kole also had a detrimental effect, even though it was supposed to bring people 'home' to the towns and in this sense was therefore beneficial for the missionaries. It was already called 'heathen' at its introduction at the end of 1896. The missionary Erhardt described what he called an upsurge of the festival, in 1909:

> We experience more and more that a modern heathenism is spreading. About four weeks after we celebrated our jubilee (26.09.1909), the king and his subjects celebrated a huge yam feast, as we had never experienced before. Until now these festivities had only been performed in a quiet way in a private house. However, this time the whole population participated and the whole town was filled with dancing and singing people. There were mighty rifle volleys. One might think, now that the Christians had celebrated their jubilee, that the heathens should also have their share. The whole thing had the character of one big, heathen popular feast. It is an upsurge of Heathendom as we had never expected.[247] (Original in German, my translation)

Erhardt calls the yam feast 'modern heathenism', as in the missionary view, 'Heathendom' was something of the past and would eventually disappear. Contrarily to what the missionaries expected, new forms of what they called 'Heathendom' rather were introduced, and existing feasts and ceremonies continued in a changed form.[248] The traditional priests re-established themselves in the towns in the plains, and secretly visited Krobo Mountain to bring down bits of the 'original' sacred rocks to install new tɛgbɛtɛs at the outskirts of the towns. The main centres for the *dipo* rites were the Klowɛki shrine in Kodjonya and the Nako shrine in Somanya, where *dipo* was performed secretly under the guise of the night.

Therefore the towns in the plains by and by became the new 'hometowns', the new ancestral homes, as people now started to patronise the new and/or revised festivals and ceremonies, and were compelled to bury their dead at the cemeteries at *dom*. Priests and chiefs however, whose position still demanded intra-mural interment, were secretly buried within their houses. The *dipo* rites went underground after 1892, but partly re-emerged in a revised form, as will become clear in the next section.

---

[247] BMA, D-1.93 Goldküste 1909, Odumase 15, W. Erhardt, 14.02.1910, Odumase, 'Jahresbericht'.

[248] Apparently the implementation of the yam-feast was not an absolute success, as the first mention of it again in a missionary report dates from 1917, when the missionary Renz claimed it was rather introduced only that very same year (BMA, D-3.9 Quartalsberichte 1915-17, Friedrich Renz, 'Züge des Heidenthums im Krobolande'). In 1944 the yam-festival *yereyeli* was re-invented as the *Ngmayem* ('millet eating') festival to be celebrated yearly in public. It took up an ancient and central rite of the Krobo and in fact re-acknowledged the role of the priests, binding them into the chieftaincy institution (see chapter two and five).

Dressing dipo girls: 'bobum'

Emmanuel Mate Kole denied the allegations of his adversaries that he tried to restore *dipo*. However, in order to meet his people's wishes, he tried to introduce an alternative, the so-called *bobum* ceremony. Interestingly, *bobum* had already existed before as a separate ceremony for newcomers and slaves in Krobo society who were not allowed to pass through *dipo*, while it also was the name for the final stage (the 'outdooring') of *dipo* (see previous chapter). This stage announced to the general public that the girls had been initiated and were ready for marriage. Emmanuel Mate Kole tried to explain 'the difference between the *dipo* and *bobum* customs', and the innocence of *bobum* in a letter to the D.C. He explained that '*bo*' meant 'cloth' and '*bum(i)*'' meant 'dressing', so *bobum* simply meant 'dressing up'. '*Bobum*' was indeed not a new custom, he wrote, but it used to be a custom for 'slaves and strangers', who:

> are not real Krobo and are not all to pass the dipo customs. The father simply makes a bobum custom for her. She is to be dressed and friends are to be called for chopping and drinking. After that, the girl parades in the town and visits her father's relations and friends. Anyone who has something to dash her dashes them. She is to go to her husband.[249]

By stating that *dipo* had been 'a big custom for Croboes from time immemorial' and was 'a pure fetish custom' because a 'fetish priestess and priest' presided over it, Mate Kole claimed that *bobum* was nothing like that and denied any relationship of *bobum* with *dipo*. The *kono* therefore tried to present *bobum* as an innocent alternative to *dipo*, and at the same time defended himself against accusations of personally reviving something similar to *dipo* by stating that *bobum* had already existed as a separate ceremony long before his installation. Still, his presentation of *bobum* was obviously nothing less than an attempt to transform *dipo* into a similar ceremony without the 'fetish' parts.

Bobum indeed looked like a perfect substitute that could both partly meet the wishes of the Krobo people to restore *dipo*, and at the same time give in to Basel missionaries' objections to *dipo*. The missionaries and colonials chiefly disapproved of the nakedness of the *dipo* girls and the immorality they associated with this. This 'new' ceremony literally was a cover-up, dressing the girls and doing away with the 'fetish' rituals. However, D.C. Coy wrote in 1896 that Mate Kole's efforts to introduce 'an alternative custom' (*bobum*), which was performed for his own sister in order to set an example, had failed so far, be-

---

[249] With 'dashing', Mate Kole meant that people were expected to give the girls a gift as a sign of appreciation. Source: GNA/ADM 11/1/1115, 23.10.1895, 'Forwarding a letter from King Mate Kole in explanation of the difference between the *dipo* and *bobum* customs'.

cause the priests rejected it.[250] Their rejection is hardly surprising, as the priests played a key role in performing the omitted rituals and derived status and power from their tasks, while to most Krobo, these rituals were essential for protecting girls from ritual danger and pollution and for proving 'Krobo-ness'.

Fig. 3: 'Original caption: 'Frauen mit europäischen Schirmen und Zahnhölzern'. Source : BMA, QD-30.019.0005. Photographer unknown.

I found one photo in the Basel Mission Archives with the title 'Women with European umbrellas and tooth-sticks'. It is unknown when the photo was taken, but it probably dates from between 1.01.1900 and 31.12.1917. The photograph shows a group of about twenty girls. The majority of the girls seems to be between twelve and sixteen years old; three girls may perhaps be six or seven years old. From what is visible on the photograph, two of the girls wear wax print cloths and the others wear a woven *kente* cloth wrapped around them. Their waist is big, so they probably wear beads underneath the cloth, as is customary in the original *bobum* celebration during *dipo*. Around the neck they

[250] GNA/ ADM 11/1/1115 (M.P. 4997A/96?), J.N. Coy, D.C. Akuse, 14.07.1896, Akuse, 'Extract from a report from the District Commissioner Akuse to the Colonial Secretary dated 14th July 1896'.

143

wear several strings of beads, and they all wear a headgear. Some are holding an opened umbrella above them. I asked two old ladies in Kodjonya (a suburb of Odumase, and the place of the Klowɛki shrine), who were both probably in their eighties and experts in *dipo*: Tɛko-*tsu* ('red', or 'fair' Tɛko), and her slightly younger niece, *dipo* priestess Tɛko-*yumu* ('dark' Tɛko), about the nature of the photo. According to them, the photo showed *bobum*. They could see it from the way the girls had tied a scarf around their heads, which meant their heads had been shaved. From the fact that most of the girls had a chewing stick in their mouth, they also concluded that the photo had been taken just after the *yo-sami* ritual. This ritual used to be performed during the confinement stage of *dipo*, just before the final outdooring.[251] *Dipo* priestess Lako Sakite, who I asked about the photo as well, confirmed this. She also noticed the chewing sticks, and also detected one boy among the girls in the right corner of the photo. The boy is the only one without a headgear. During *yo-sami*, a young virgin boy, gorgeously dressed, would come inside the room where the *dipo* girls were confined, with a chewing stick in his mouth to prevent him from talking. He sat on the girls' buttocks three times, to symbolise that the 'door to sex' was open to them. This boy was called the 'husband of *dipoyi*' (*dipoyi a huno*). What I derived from Lako Sakite's explanation about the chewing stick was that it symbolised married life, which however may be a Christianised explanation. She said that one of the first things a wife would do after waking up with her husband was to take a chewing stick to brush her teeth. Then she would continue with her normal household chores.[252]

It is not likely that the Basel missionaries were aware of the *yo-sami* ritual, as the priestesses performed it in a secluded room at night. The description with the photograph shows that the Basel missionaries were probably also not aware that this represented a *bobum* scene either, but the missionaries had mentioned *bobum* in their writings at least since 1897. Moreover, the person at Basel who had pasted the picture into an album and added the caption may have misunderstood or corrupted the information that came with the picture. It was the missionary Josenhans who referred to a new ritual called *bobum* in his yearly report in 1897 as a feast for dressing up girls. He wrote that Emmanuel Mate Kole had instigated or at least approved of the ritual. Josenhans was sceptical about this 'new custom'. Although *bobum* may not be as bad as *dipo*, he thought it might again lead to 'sexual indulgence' because, as he wrote: "The Krobo are the most immoral and fleshly nation of the whole coast."[253] He suspected that in reality, the new so-called *bobum* rites were actually the same as the old *dipo* rites. In the published account of his report the reaction to the introduction of

---

[251] Interview with Tɛko-jumu and Tɛko-tsu, 12.06.2000, Kodjonya.
[252] Interview with Lako Sakite, 22.04.1999, Odumase.
[253] BMA, D-1.66 Goldküste 1897 Ga, Odumase 195, Josenhans, 24.01.1898, Odumase, 'Jahresbericht'; quotation translated from German.

bobum was that on the whole Gold Coast paganism presented the greatest challenge in the Odumase congregation in Krobo land.[254]

There are several signs that *bobum* indeed became the cover-up for *dipo*. As was the case with the missionaries, the Krobo people also considered *bobum* to be 'heathen' and part of what the missionaries constructed as 'the past'. This is evident in their postponing of baptism until they had let their daughters or sisters pass '*bobum*'.[255] Most likely the 'fetish' rituals had gone underground and preceded the final *bobum* ceremony. Three years after his first reference to *bobum*, Josenhans stated that *bobum* had become common in the whole of Krobo. The ceremony was said to last for at least eight days. Because of *bobum* it was difficult to get girls attending school, and now it was *bobum*'s turn to be called 'a big obstacle to the mission'.[256] Once the girls had passed through the rites, they were considered as 'real Krobo' and grown-up women, which meant that they were allowed to enter into sexual relationships. Josenhans reported that eighty percent of the Christian women between the age of 18 and 24 'fell' as a result, that is to say, had sexual relations outside marriage and/or became pregnant after *bobum*, and all women had to be expelled from the church as backsliders at least once before they were married, usually because of 'indecency'.[257] Again we can see that it was not marriage that traditionally was the condition for women to engage in sexual relationships, but their initiation. In the view of the missionaries the women who lived with a partner without being legally married were nothing more than concubines and their offspring were considered illegitimate. In addition it was very important for Krobo women to have children, and the Christian women complained that they had to wait too long for a marriage and hence were growing too old before they could have children. The African pastor Quartey complained that many of these women became what he called 'concubine'. He wrote: "Now in the Krobo country one meets swarms of these destructive unmarried girls and women who are daily and nightly roaming about in search of money and children, who could be had for a 3d. or a 6d, sometimes for nothing."[258]

---

[254] *Jahresberichte* 1898, 'Goldküste', p. 23.

[255] BMA, D-1.72, W. Quartey, 4.2.1901, Odumase, 'Yearly Report pro 1900'.

[256] BMA, D-1.72 Afrika 1900, Odumase 121, Josenhans, 19.02.1901, Odumase, 'Jahresbericht'.

[257] BMA, D-1.80 Afrika 1904, Odumase 133, Josenhans, 24.01.1905, Odumase, 'Jahresbericht'

[258] BMA, D-1.80 Afrika 1904, Odumase 137, W. A. Quartey, 10.03.1905, Odumase, 'Jahresbericht'.

Fig. 4: Original caption: 'Mädchen in Brautracht im Kroboland (Goldküste)' ('Girls in bridal cloth in Krobo land (Gold Coast)'). Source: BMA, QQ-30.011.0040. Probbaly taken by Dr. Vortisch between 1903-1905. Notice the sacred antelope skin in front of the girls (see chapter seven).

By the time the Basel missionaries were forced to leave the Gold Coast in 1917, nothing seemed to have changed with *dipo*, in the sense that the institution was still very much alive. Basel Mission photos taken by the missionaries Vortisch between 1903-06[259] and Kölle between 1889-1908,[260] show (studio) portraits of *Otufo Bräute* ('Otufo brides'). Just over ten years after the ban, *dipo* was apparently already celebrated more or less in the open again, at least outside the Salems in Odumase and elsewhere. In a report on the final years of the Basel Mission, before they were expelled, the missionary Friedrich Renz, for example, stated that the ties of the 'old heathendom' still entangled the women in particular, and withheld them from Christianity. The worst, he wrote, was "the puberty feast for the maidens", that all the non-baptised girls had to go through.[261]

---

[259] BMA, QW-30.011.0039 and QW-30.011.0040; It is not sure that the picture was taken by Vortisch, but it was used in an article he wrote.
[260] BMA D-30.08.043, D-30.08.044 and D-30.08.045.
[261] BMA, D-3.9 Quartalsberichte 1915-17, Friedrich Renz, 'Züge des Heidenthums im Krobolande'.

146

Dipo after 1917

From 1917 until the period of the 1940s and 1950s, when Field and Huber conducted their fieldwork, information on the Krobo is relatively scarce. When the Basel missionaries left, their African pastors and clerks took over their work, and the few mission workers sent out by the Free Church of Scotland could never rely on such a large European staff as their predecessors. Therefore it is not surprising that they were more concerned with extending educational facilities than with opposing local cultural practices and traditions. At the same time, with colonial rule fully established, British suspicions of the Krobo decreased and as a result they did not directly interfere anymore. This is the reason that we find relatively few references to Krobo in the archives.

Although elsewhere in Africa Europeans began to be more interested in and sympathetic towards the 'irrational' and ritualistic aspects of 'tradition' after the first World War, which resulted in the policy of missionary 'adaptation' (Ranger 1983: 252), and although the Basel missionaries were no longer present after 1917 as a result of the war, their cultural policies persisted in the regulations of the Presbyterian Church of the Gold Coast and later Ghana. As with the Basel Mission, the church's new converts had to forsake the 'dipo custom' in order to be baptised as a Presbyterian Christian. African pastors continued their strong opposition to this 'tradition'. Dipo continued to be an issue in local power politics.

The number of Christians slowly started to grow from the early twentieth century onwards. This was largely due to the greater need for education because of increasing economic possibilities and the political and economic ramifications it entailed. In the eyes of the people, schooling was associated with Christianity.[262] They even called Christians 'school people' (sukuufo), products of the mission boarding and day schools (Wilson 1991: 156 and 159). Educated, and therefore Christian, people experienced a shift in status from a marginal to a more mainstream position, and in colonial society they obviously were the ones who could accede to elite positions. Although, as Meyer (1999: 14) points out for the Ewe, the reason to convert cannot be reduced to purely economic considerations, Christian religion was attractive because it offered the means to achieve a prosperous and relatively high position in colonial society, especially for men, but increasingly also for women. For girls education could give access to new avenues of revenue and financial independence. With colonialism, the proliferation of towns and the extension of the market economy, women found more room within the emerging social order to assert their autonomy, accumulate

---

[262] BMA, D-11.1, Berichte 1889-1924, W. Erhardt, 10.06.1918, Abschluss-Bericht über das Gebiet der Station Odumase'; Erhardt wrote for example that the people in Odumase often did not understand the difference between schooling and conversion and mixed them up.

wealth on their own, and define marriage and what they expected of it (Akyeampong 1997: 177). However, Christian marriages in Krobo were still rare. Rather, young Christian women were frequently excluded from the church in the early twentieth century because they married in the customary way. Many of them refused to enter into a monogamous marriage with a Christian farmer, and were said to prefer 'heathen' farmers. Most likely this was because of the (economic) advantage of polygynous marriages on the plantations, where family labour was badly needed,[263] as the palm oil industry and in particular the cocoa industry (in the first two to three decades) was booming.

As the late 19th century until the cocoa crisis of the late 1930s was a time of great economic prosperity for the Krobo, when fathers could afford European umbrellas, expensive *kente* and wax print cloths, beads and sheep for the *bobum* of their daughters to show off their welfare, *bobum* was an even larger celebration than *dipo*.[264] The missionary Renz had already observed in 1917 that, according to him, the availability of the necessary funds was more important than the girls' age in determining the time required for the rites.[265] The Krobo secretly continued to perform the ritual aspects of *dipo* at the dead of night, and carried out the parade through the streets during the day under the guise of *bobum*.[266] Despite attempts of the *kono* to make *bobum* more respectable as a ceremony on its own by first performing it for his sister in 1896 (see above), and later by performing it in grand style for one of his own daughters, Beatrice Ata Mate-Kole in September 1925 (Obeng-Assamoa 1998: 155), the secret rituals continued. Despite his formal disapproval, Emmanuel Mate Kole was forced to adopt a more tolerant attitude to *dipo* and give it his tacit approval, as most Krobo were not willing to give it up.[267] This situation continued until the end of *kono* Emmanuel Mate Kole's reign, when he died in 1939.

Interviews I conducted with elderly women who were born in the first quarter of the twentieth century confirmed that *dipo* continued to be celebrated during Emmanuel Mate Kole's reign. Tɛko-tsu for example, who was probably born before 1920, recalled that she was among those for whom *dipo* was performed secretly, about two years before 'Sir Emmanuel', as she called him, had

---

[263] The missionaries complained about the increasing independence of educated women, as their aim was to make Christian housewives out of their pupils. They complained about the more successful male converts as well, who turned their missionary education to good account, by, for example, working with one of the trading companies or with the colonial administration as clerks instead of becoming teachers and catechists. As their social status in society rose, they often were tempted to marry a second wife. Many men were consequently expelled from the Basel Mission and later the Presbyterian Church for their polygynous relationships.

[264] This was confirmed in an interview with Lako Sakite, 28.06.2000, Odumase.

[265] BMA, D-3.9 Quartalsberichte 1915-17, Friedrich Renz, 'Züge des Heidenthums im Krobolande'.

[266] In the suburbs of Odumase and more out of sight of the *kono* and the church, things may have been less hidden.

[267] Government anthropologist Margaret Field ascribed Emmanuel Mate Kole's tacit approval to 'the mellow wisdom' he acquired in middle and later life (Field 1941b: 2).

died (see note 42). She told me that local policemen from the traditional council came to arrest the girls and, in cooperation with the responsible priestess, sent them to the *kono*. She was one of the six 'big girls' in the group, and the priestess pointed them out to the *kono* and asked him whether he wanted these grown-up girls 'to spoil', i.e. be pregnant without being initiated, and therefore become social outcasts. He then said they were allowed to continue. Tɛko-tsu's niece, *dipo* priestess Tɛko-yumu, who is just slightly younger, said that her *dipo* performance was two years later, just before Sir Emmanuel's death (1939). She remembered how she and the other girls went to the Klowɛki shrine at early dawn so that nobody would see them. Her *dipo* performance lasted for three weeks, she said, then she had the public outdooring.[268] Lako Sakite, great-granddaughter of *kono* Sakite, remembered her own *dipo* proudly, which must have taken place around the same time in the mid 1930s, because she too most likely was born around or before 1920. She recalled that: 'My elder sister [probably a cousin] Korlenyɛ' and her age group could not undergo the *dipo* ritual. The *dipo* was banned at Korlenyɛ's time. It was during our time that *dipo* was reintroduced. (...) We were forty who were in confinement, all [great-]grandchildren of King Sakite.'[269] Her story confirms that after the eviction from the mountain there was a period when girls officially went uninitiated and only did the *bobum*. But since her cousin was not banished from the town, her initiation must have been performed (more) secretly.[270] She also confirms that most of the girls from the 'royal' family of the Sakite's and Mate Kole's were still initiated.

The story of Janet Otuwa Opata ('maa' Adjoka), the mother of my landlord, a woman in her early eighties, shows that *dipo* was a homecoming event again in those days for those Krobo who lived in the upcountry.[271] She remembered how she, together with her elder half-sisters and other relatives, left her native village Dawazutsumi in *yonno* to go to *dom* for her *dipo* performance. '*I wa*', she said, 'I was grown'. It must have been somewhere in the mid 1930s, because she remembered that she was already married and had had her first child at the time of the last earthquake, which occurred in 1939. She narrated how before leaving for *dom*, she prepared this by buying a large enamel bowl with a handle. Her relatives wrapped the beads and other things she would use and put them inside the bowl. She carried a very large mirror on top. When they left, somebody carried a stool for her to sit on during the rites. They passed through Bisa market, which was a thriving upcountry market at the time, where they waited for everybody to assemble. Then together with many other girls and relatives they were driven in a lorry to *dom* and stopped at an outskirt of Odumase

---

[268] Interview 12.06.2000 at Kodjonya, translated from Dangme.
[269] Interview 05.08.1998 at Odumase, translated from Dangme.
[270] Lako Sakite confirmed this in a later interview, 28.06.2000, Odumase.
[271] Interview with 'maa' Adjoka, 20.06.2000 and 03.07.2000, Odumase, translated from Dangme.

called Adome. From there people came to meet them with traditional (*klama*) songs and brought them to their respective homes. In her family house in Salosi (a part of town) there was also music and dancing. After the actual rites were performed, the girls received some donations and went back to the village. There they had to help their parents to save money before the *bobum* rites could be performed. 'Maa' said that some people did not return to the village, but remained in confinement in *dom*, until their parents came. She said that "the whole thing was something like a competition". Those girls whose parents had money would be joined by many friends and relatives from the village, and this added to their status and prestige. So *dipo* and *bobum* could be performed separately, but *dipo* remained the necessary ritual requirement for initiation, while *bobum* was the public part.

For the outside world, all was quiet on the *dipo* front for some time. The colonial administration did not seem to interfere much with Krobo internal affairs. In February 1935, however, some articles appeared in *The African Morning Post*, reporting the pending expulsion of a pregnant girl in Yilo Krobo who had not undergone the *dipo* rites. This was called 'a form of slavery', because it supposedly offered an opportunity for parents to make money out of the misconduct of their daughters.[272] Again on March 23, 1935, *The African Morning Post* opened with a big headline saying: "Writer says slavery exists in Krobo. Yilo Krobo state still deals in slave trade. Sale of three girls occurred this year, 1935, at cheapest price of £15 - £26 each." The anonymous writer claimed to hail from Somanya. The immediate cause to write the piece was said to be the banishment of the writer's maternal cousin who became pregnant without having passed the rites. He, however, stated that girls had been banished from the Krobo state since about 1898 at an average rate of two per year.[273]

The articles triggered reactions from the Yilo Krobo state council and questions from the British colonial government in Accra.[274] The *konọ* of Yilo-Krobo at the time, Nuer Ologo V, denied that the *dipo* custom had taken place since 1892, and replied in a letter to the colonial secretary that it was substituted by a ceremony, which he did not define, but he probably referred to *bobum*. Any person who wanted to marry a girl who had become pregnant before she had passed the undefined 'custom' could marry her and pay the parents a compensation.[275] On May 20, 1936, another short article appeared in the *African Morning*

---

[272] The dowry paid for such a girl would be higher in case the male culprit did not come forward, because the parents wanted it to cover the costs involved in the purification ceremonies to avert evil from the family, for which they had to buy a sheep and other items.

[273] GNA, *The African Morning Post*, Vol. 1, No. 76, 23.03.1935, 'Yilo Krobo state still deals in slave-trade'.

[274] GNA, *The African Morning Post*, Kwasivi, 25.03.1935, 'Slavery in Yilo Krobo'; GNA/96/37, 1935?, 'Notorious "*dipo*" custom assumes malignant nature'; GNA/96/37, 1945?, 'The "*dipo*" custom'.

[275] GNA/C.S.O. 21/50/8, 14.05.1935, 'letter from *Konor* Nuer Ologo V to the Colonial Secretary'.

Post, with the headline 'Kotokro festival celebrated', stating that the festival "was one of the grandest ever witnessed for some time".[276] The acting D.C. at Akuse then informed the Commissioner of the Eastern Region that the celebration of *Kotoklo*, *Nadu* and *dipo* had been taking place yearly "for at least the last ten years without any objection from the District Commissioner or police (…)".[277] And the new D.C. at Akuse, Norton Jones, wrote to the commissioner in May 1937 that: "I have been informed that the [*dipo*] custom was resuscitated about three years ago at the request of the women in the state". He witnessed a *dipo* ceremony in Asité near Odumase. According to him, non-initiated girls who became pregnant would be 'bought' by men from the neighbouring Akyem states, Akuapem and elsewhere. Apart from objecting to this 'slavery', he objected to the early age at which some girls went through the rites and the supposedly related promiscuity:

> Once the girls have been initiated and have undergone their training, they are free to select a husband or a lover. If they choose a lover, no penalty is imposed, as in Akan States, upon the man who has intercourse with them before they are given in marriage. The danger which attends this freedom from liabilities is the undoubted promiscuity which prevails especially in the case of young girls.[278]

The D.C., however, acknowledged that in Krobo, men who seduced non-initiated girls were fined, but he still saw the young ages of initiates linked with sex outside of marriage as a problem. Again in 1940, another D.C. and his assistant asked the *kono*'s of Yilo and Manya Krobo and the Gold Coast Police at Akuse to assist them to: "suppress the customs, particularly *dipo*".[279] Margaret Field, however, rather advocated a restoration of *dipo*, and wrote in 1941:

> It must be admitted that even at the present day the heathen '*Dipo* families' do continue to regard unchastity in young girls as a disgrace, whereas school-girls have the reputation of being always willing to earn a few shillings by casual prostitution – almost the only form of earning they regard as ladylike (Field 1941b: 4).

---

[276] Apparently a sheep instead of a human being was slaughtered at the celebration. In 1942 however, it was reported that a 'fetish murder' had been committed again in Yilo Krobo in connection with *Kotoklo*. The police then raided the *Kotoklo* shrine in May 1942; GNA/ADM 11/1/1679/Conf. 226/39, 21.02.1942, 'R. Tottenham, superintendent Eastern Province, Gold Coast Police in Koforidua to the Commissioner of the Police headquarters in Accra'; GNA/ADM 11/1/1679, no. 89, 22.05.1942, 'D.C. at Akuse to the Commissioner in Koforidua'.

[277] GNA/ADM 111/1629, no. 641/7/1910, 28.05.1936, Akuse, 'the acting D.C. to the Commissioner of Eastern Province, Koforidua'.

[278] GNA/C.S.O 21/10/8, No. 512/7/1910, 03.05.1937, Akuse, 'Letter from D.C. Norton Jones to the Commissioner of the Eastern Province, Koforidua'.

[279] GNA 11/1/1679, no. 374/18/1910, 08.03.1940, 'Asst. D.C. to the inspector of Gold Coast Police Akuse'; no. 375/18/1910, 08.03.1940, 'D.C. to Yilo and Manya *kono*'.

She supported her plea by giving the example of a man in Sra who seduced a young, non-initiated girl. The parents summoned him to the court of the *konọ*, complaining that he had no right to do such a thing, as the girl had not passed through *dipo*. But he retorted that the parents had no right to perform *dipo* anyway. The man pleaded his case with the D.C. and referred to the clause in the Native Customs Ordinance. The D.C. had no choice but to stand by the Ordinance. Therefore the man went free (Field 1941b: 5).

The D.C.'s writings and Field's example and plea make clear that both the colonial and Christian prohibition and condemnation of *dipo* had undesired effects. The Basel Mission had forbidden their converts to be initiated. However, as Krobo women were not willing to give up on *dipo*, paradoxically the first converted girls were 'fallen girls' who became pregnant before *dipo*, and therefore were social outcasts and unfit for marriage in the eyes of the Krobo, as I pointed out in the previous chapter. The dubious moral status of Christian girls persisted, as the writings of Field and others (e.g. Tettey 1977) show. Schoolgirls, i.e. Christian girls, now had a reputation of engaging in prostitution. Instead of enhancing morality, colonial law also achieved opposite effects. Because it was prohibited, girls often seemed to have been initiated at a younger age. Yet, sexual relations were still permitted after *dipo*. While at the same time men who engaged in sexual relationships with non-initiated girls violated local rules, but could call upon colonial law. After all, *dipo* was forbidden, so they could not be prosecuted for violating moral laws.

But Field's view that, since no one respected the prohibition of *dipo*, it was 'a farce' and "an anachronism out of harmony with the broader-minded attitude now taken by enlightened Governments" (Field 1941b: 2), was not shared by other representatives of the colonial administration. Her remarks about the prohibition as "an intolerant persecution and a short-sighted policy" were not taken lightly. Correspondence between government officials alluded to 'those anthropologists!' They felt that Field should have read the reports of Bell about 'the real thing' on the mountain, which was of a 'vicious nature', 'indecent', 'barbarous' and 'disgusting', and that the prohibition was rather responsible for the 'harmless form' of *dipo* at this time.[280]

The last documents I found about *dipo* in the Ghana National Archives during colonial times date from 1948 and 1949, when the *konọ* of Yilo Krobo asked for permission to fix a fee payable to the market collectors from girls passing the *bobum* ceremony. Such girls normally came to parade in full dress

---

[280] GNA/CSO 21/10/16, no. 2367, 17.04.1941, 'governor to Secretary of Native Affairs' (with supplementary hand-written notes); no. 2367/11, 23.05.1941, 'H.W. Thomas, Secretary for Native Affairs to Margaret Field'.

on the market to present themselves to the public as marriageable girls.[281] These documents suggest that the situation had persisted the way it was. *Bobum* was the official event, *dipo* remained underground.

During Azzu Mate Kole's reign (1939-1990), Emmanuel Mate Kole's son and successor, *dipo* gradually re-emerged. The decrease in the British suspicion of Krobo, the appreciative attitude of *kono* Azzu Mate Kole and the spread of new (independent) churches contributed to the renewed celebration of Krobo ceremonies, *dipo* in particular. This was especially the case after the 1950s and mainly after independence (1957), to which I will come back in chapter eight. However, the Presbyterian Church remained influential and continued its harsh stance towards *dipo*, as the writings of Krobo pastors, for example Odjidja (1973; 1977) and Teyegaga (1974; 1985), demonstrate. The continued Christian opposition in the second half of the twentieth century shows that *dipo* persisted, but the rites had changed considerably: they had been reduced in time and space. *Dipo* now longer took place on Krobo Mountain, but in more or less hidden shrines at the outskirts of the towns. Whereas the girls used to stay on the mountain for up to one year, the subsequent initiation period was reduced from about three weeks to about one week. The increased attendance of schools contributed to this reduction in time. As many girls went to school now, they no longer left the school after *dipo*, as they used to, but instead they were initiated during school vacations (cf. Quarcoo & Johnson 1968: 72).

In conclusion we can state that the Basel Mission encouraged the British government in their endeavour to close down the mountain as a bulwark of the priests and promote the rise of the chiefs. Both the mission and the British had an interest in eliminating the power of the priests, because in their opinion they hindered the development of peaceful trade and 'civilisation', that is, Christianity. The dramatic events of 1892 had changed Krobo society forever and in some ways they meant a true break with the past. The eviction from Krobo Mountain involved a brutal colonial interference: the execution of *Kotoklo* adherents, the military occupation of the mountain, the destruction of the shrines and houses, the forced removal of old people and priests from their mountain home and the hoisting of the Union Jack as a sign of victory. The action desecrated the Kloweki priestess forever. Although some sources state that such a priestess existed until the 1940s (Field n.d.; Huber 1988),[282] she never fully recovered her

---

[281] For example: GNA/ADM/KD31/6/111, 18.11.1948, 'Bobum custom – fee resolution. D.C. Kerr at Akuse to the Chief Commissioner of the Colony at Cape Coast'; 20.07.1949 , 'D.C. Kerr to the Chief Commissioner of the Colony at Cape Coast'.

[282] Field claims that there was an important priestess for Nana Kloweki who lived in seclusion, and died in the early 1940s (Field n.d.: 71). Huber writes that the exact date when the last priestess was in office is unclear. He received information through a letter from one of his informants, claiming that the last priestess was in function for less than ten years, and died in 1945 or 1946. Her name was said to be Abla Dedu. Huber doubted whether the information of his informant referred to a unanimously

original position, and nowadays only a male priest represents the goddess. The first Christian, Basel Mission trained _kono_ was installed with the strong support of the British. This direct interference was a radical departure from the past policies of the colonial administration. It was sparked off in part by the continuing demand of the Basel missionaries to end traditional religious practices, and in part by the needs of the administration of the colony after 1874 because of the system of indirect rule. The general British policy aimed at a 'pacification' of the people in the colony. Removing them from their mountain homes to surveyable and taxable towns was to promote commerce and create a colony of united traditional states.

On the mountain, _dipo_ used to be an integrative ceremony by preparing girls for womanhood, proclaiming them to be 'real Krobo' and providing a homecoming event for all Krobo, whereby the priests played an important role as ritual specialists. After the Basel Mission had 'paganised' it, the colonial administration 'criminalised' _dipo_. Whereas the missionaries and colonial agents had always emphasised the nakedness of the _dipo_ girls, and therefore the 'primitive' and immoral aspects of _dipo_, its substitute _bobum_ literally was a 'dressing up' ritual. In public the girls were covered and 'decent'. Although the new Christian _kono_ was therefore successful in 'civilising' _dipo_ by re-defining its _bobum_ stage as a ritual that in itself replaced _dipo_, the missionaries and the British correctly suspected that in practice _bobum_ was a cover-up for the abolished _dipo_. Against the expectations of the missionaries, the priests did not lose their power entirely, but rather continued to exert their influence behind the scenes. Now that their shrines had been brought down to the plains, they were in touch with their people again. All the necessary so-called 'fetish' rituals were still performed in secret, but away from Krobo Mountain and in a drastically reduced way. The intended break with 'the past' did not materialise. _Dipo_ became an instrument in the struggle for power. The contest over Krobo rituals reveals a struggle over political power, whereby the gap between chiefly and priestly power widened in the public domain. The main effect of the Native Customs Ordinance was a more extreme separation between what happened in public and what went on behind the scenes.

Finally, what already became clear from the description of historical developments in the previous chapter is that the eviction from Krobo Mountain rather accommodated major social, economic and political changes that were already taking place in Krobo society prior to the advent of the BM and on the Gold Coast in general. The eviction worked as a catalyst in further reforming Krobo society. Christianity slowly got a steadier grip on the people, but it did not have an encompassing ritual force to hold society together. The old rituals

---

recognised representative of the supreme post, because during the period of his research in the 1950s nobody had been able to give him clear clues about the last priestess (Huber 1988: 82).

that had integrated a heterogeneous society could not just be dismissed. Rituals also provided male elders and priests with a source of social control over young men and women. They partly lost control, and for some young people, in particular girls who had become pregnant before *dipo*, Christianity offered a way out. At the same time, many young men and women stayed out of reach of both the mission and traditional elders on the plantations at *yono* (upcountry). So even the first Christian chief needed to create new rituals in order to enforce control over his supposed subjects, while the priests and elders continued their rituals in secret. As a result deities and their rituals as well as new festivals soon either re-emerged, appeared in a new form or for the first time, whereby the towns in the plains (*dom*) around Odumase became the new ancestral Krobo home.

The successor of the Basel mission church, the Presbyterian Church, continued the harsh stance of the mission towards 'traditional customs'. It still opposes *dipo*, until this very day. But new, independent African churches, which did not impede non-Christian rites, have become serious competitors in the Christian field. Moreover, the Roman Catholic Church has also adopted a liberal attitude towards *dipo* (I will discuss these churches in chapter eight). Christianity became part and parcel of people's lives, both of educated and non-educated persons, both of Christians and non-Christians. However, the deep ambiguous feelings towards *dipo* and the negative reputation of Krobo women concerning sexuality persisted, as we will see in the next chapters. In this respect 'tradition' and 'culture' are nowadays hotly debated issues in Ghana and in Krobo.

The next chapter will show that priests and their supporting circle of ritual specialists have, despite the political shift, continued to operate and organise the *dipo* rites, amongst others, to this very day.

5

"Every year around Easter":
The dynamics of Krobo religion

In his booklet *Dipo custom and the Christian faith*, reverend Teyegaga,[283] gives his version of a vision the mythical figure of Nana Klowɛki is said to have had:

> She [Klowɛki] entered into trance and saw a man with a symbol in the form of a cross standing before her. The man raised the cross before her and said: 'This is the symbol of purification that is coming.' The man ordered her to see both sides, and behold, she saw very many girls playing on a vast plain. The man raised the cross before her again and said: 'The purification of these souls will be upon you. The cross, the symbol then assured the meaning of purification.' Suddenly, the man vanished from her sight. She became conscious, she was pondering over her vision, and had intuition that her time to stay with the Krobos had ended. She than quickly went to her grove and began preparation for departure: she looked into water, moulded a clay bust of herself and placed it on a stand. Then she made a cross out of sticks, using raffia to tie and placed it against the bust. She then summoned her chief priest, Asikpe, and narrated to him what she saw and the message she got from the man. (...) Some few weeks later, Klowɛki vanished. The Krobos in commemoration of Nana Klowɛki began to worship the image (the bust), using the cross 'Gazo we s<u>o</u>mi' in the ritual of *dipo* custom. This was about 1820 A.D (Teyegaga 1985: 31-32).

A cross as mentioned above is indeed used nowadays during the *dipo* rites as a symbol of Nana Klowɛki. A cross-like stick with a particular palm fibre, *soni* (*Borrasus aethiopicum*), is carried along by priestesses and female relatives on the way to the sacred stone (*tɛgbɛtɛ*). According to Huber (1993: 176), it is a sign of protection. Teyegaga, however, interprets the manifestation of the cross in a Christianised way. He places the story around 1820, a few years before the Basel missionaries arrived on the Gold Coast in 1828. He implies that Klowɛki, knowing that 'the new light' was coming, disappeared, and the cross really was 'the cross of Christ' (Teyegaga 1985: 32). Adjaye also calls the cross 'an obvious Christian influence' (Adjaye 1999: 20; cf. Ashie n.d.: 10). Whether this is 'obvious' is hard to assess. It can only be said for certain that, because of its

---

[283] Rev. Benjamin Didymus Teyegaga was born in a Manya Krobo village. He received his education amongst others at Bana Hill. He was ordained as a Presbyterian reverend minister on February 19, 1956, at Krobo-Odumase, and retired in 1976. He died at the age of 88 on March 12, 1994 (Anonymous 1994).

mystical meaning due to ancestral connotations, the particular palm fibre is used in several *dipo* and other rites, which rather indicates a continuity in the ritual format of *dipo*.

Current popular historiography either christianises the story of Klowɛki after Teyegaga's example or implies that the priestess mysteriously disappeared. However, the words: 'We all rely on/'are supported by Nana Klowɛki', a variation on a Krobo saying,[284] is one example revealing that the presence of the deity is still felt. Nana Klowɛki is often referred to as a 'mother' and the Krobo people are her 'children'. Even though the function of her main priestess ceased to exist, the deity Nana Klowɛki and her senior priest are still important for the Krobo community,[285] because the deity dictates the *dipo* rites, and takes a central place on the ritual Krobo calendar that even now revolves around millet, the old staple food of the Krobo. The principal male priests, who, as in the past, are always named Okumo, Asa, Adjime etc, are still there. 'Traditional religion', as it was called since Christianity was introduced, has not simply disappeared, neither has it become 'outmoded', as Christian representatives would like to think.

Although there hardly exist any systematic written accounts of any specific 'Krobo' or umbrella 'Dangme traditional religion', as is the case for 'Ashanti' or 'Akan traditional religion' (e.g. Rattray 1927; Sarpong 1976), and even seemingly general descriptions of 'traditional religion' in Ghana or West-Africa often only address Akan religion,[286] the dualist discourse introduced by the Basel Mission has been very influential in Krobo religious experience. Krobo Christians often use the missionary category of 'heathenism' to designate 'traditional religion', and label it as 'pagan' or 'fetish'. Teyegaga (1985), for example, describing 'what makes Dipo custom a pagan custom', literally said that there have been two divisions in Krobo society since the opening of a Basel Mission post in 1859, 'the traditional community' and 'the Christian community', and juxtaposed the first's 'beliefs' to the latter's 'faith'. Krobo people place *dipo* within 'traditional religion' or 'custom' (*kusumi*), and it is celebrated without any Christian or christianised rituals. At the same time, it takes place 'every year around Easter', as will become clear in this chapter. After more than 150 years of Christianity in Krobo, the symbols and ideology of Christianity

---

[284] This particular statement *'Wa ngɛ Maa Klowɛki tufo o nɔ'* was made by the priest *Asa* when he poured a libation on August 24, 1998. As I explained in chapter three, *'a tufo'* literally means a cloth or cushion, which women used to tie to their back to support their child or to let their child sit on. The word could also mean 'backbone' in other contexts. For example: *Piengwa ma a, mɛji atufo kɛ ha Odoko Azu sɛ ɔ nɛ* 'The Piengwa division is the backbone of Odonkor Azu's stool'.

[285] However, the last male priest died in the late 1980s. One of his sons is currently acting as his regent (*seyelɔ*) until a new priest will be installed, who it is believed, will be pointed out by the goddess herself.

[286] This is mainly due to the Akan's dominance in size, in politics and in culture in Ghana. However, see Kudadjie (1976; 1997) and Quarcoopome (1993b), who treat some particular aspects of Dangme religion.

158

have become internalised as reference points for all Krobo, including non-Christians.

This chapter then deals with the contemporary place of *dipo* on the ritual calendar, therefore in ´traditional religion´. In the existing situation of 'religious pluralism', referring to "the co-existence of a diversity of ideologies, faiths and world-views within one society", (Platvoet & Toorn 1995: 349), it is clear that there is no dialogue between equals. Christianity is the dominant religion, at least in the public sphere. At the same time, because they have access to secret knowledge, the traditional priests as ritual specialists maintain power behind the scenes, as they always did. Here the concept of *agbaa*, in the meaning of a 'communal secret', is important. It denotes religious and political matters that are vital to the community's survival, and encompasses old ritual practices, oaths, certain forms of knowledge and secrets about ancestral emblems. Because power (*hewam*) is correlated with secret knowledge, it must be hidden from public view (Quarcoopome 1993a: 114-116). A related important concept is *kusumi*, which refers to 'customs': "practices, chiefly ritual performances prescribed within *agbaa*, which ultimately demonstrate the ancestral way of life" (Quarcoopome 1991: 57; 1994: 341). *Kusumi* therefore denotes a body of (often secret) ancestral lore.[287]

In order to understand the importance of *dipo* as *kusumi*, we have to understand the realm of 'traditional religion' in which it is placed and what this comprises today. Before describing the calendrical rites, I will start with outlining the organisation of worship, with an emphasis on Nana Klowɛki and her priests, by whom *dipo* is performed. Then *dipo* is placed within the agricultural cycle that revolves around millet cultivation.

Performing religion

'Krobo religion' is whatever religion(s) the Krobo choose to practise, not necessarily what is supposedly of distinctive Krobo origin and character. Moreover, there is no set of static, unchanging beliefs, or a separate 'religion'. Although Huber (1993) describes general Krobo ideas based on his research in the 1950s, he mentions that people do not pretend to have a clear perception of these ideas, and he calls the ruling concepts 'somewhat obscure'. He points to some notable Ewe and Akan influences. And Field wrote in her (unpublished) field notes in the early 1940s about Dangme religious ideas that different concepts are linked with several different systems of thought, and therefore 'various inconsistencies'

---

[287] Elsewhere Quarcoopome defines *kusumi* as "the reenactment of long-held traditional practices" (1991: 57). The word 'kusum' (kùsúm`, kùsúmì) is defined as "custom, ceremony, rites, tradition" in Kropp-Dakubu's 'Ga-English dictionary' and is derived from the Portuguese word 'costume' (Kropp-Dakubu 1999).

have developed (Field n.d.: 20).[288] Huber and Field seem to perceive the 'obscurity' and 'inconsistencies' as effects of outside influences on 'the' Krobo. I think that it is one area which rather demonstrates the hybrid and dynamic character of the Krobo group of people, and that 'the Krobo' and their 'religious beliefs' are the product of both (historical) local and trans-local forces.

My approach in studying religion is similar to that of Blakely, Beek and Thompson (1994: 2), who as a (working) definition of religion propose an approach of: "religion as human interaction with a culturally postulated non-falsifiable reality". They stress the importance in their approach of the cultural angle: "religion is expressed and experienced in ways and forms offered by culture or constituted as culture" (ibid. 1994: 2). I want to stress that 'traditional religion' cannot be studied 'as if Christianity has never been present'. The compartmentalisation of traditional religion has largely been a result of the influence of Christianity. I would also like to emphasise the importance of 'praxis' and 'action' where there has often been a greater focus on 'belief' and 'cosmology' as a result of the scriptural definition of religion dominant in many religious studies (cf. Shaw 1990: 346). With this in mind, I will provide a brief outline of Krobo cosmology, before examining the performance of religious practices.

In contemporary Odumase, the outward signs of traditional religion are not immediately visible to the outsider, while the many church signboards along the roads can hardly be overlooked. A shrine or a sacred grove, the place of worship of a deity (*piɛmi*), is preferably situated on the outskirts of towns. Most of the important Krobo deities have a shrine that is even more hidden in the 'bush', usually a few hundred yards from the main sacred grove. However, a shrine can sometimes be recognised by a high bamboo pole with a small white stripe of cloth attached to the top, which is placed by the roadside or just outside the house of a deity's priest. A shrine is further marked off by a fence of *buna* trees, which are also used to demarcate farms. These trees are said to be very strong and almost impossible to uproot, which means that they are very durable. Usually a few bushes of which the leaves have medicinal power have been planted inside a grove.[289] As Coplan explains:

> Sacred herbs play an essential role in the ritual effectiveness of purification and pacification rites for towns, houses and shrines, and in the curing of physical illnesses caused by mystical agents. It is the gods who manifest their power through herbs and instruct the people through priestly agents what herbs are needed to affect the various ritual purposes and cures to which they may be applied. (...) The clan priests play a key role in this practice, an many are skilled 'gbal̲o̲i' (diviners) (Coplan 1972: 82).

---

[288] These notes were probably written between 1938-1944, when Field was working as a government anthropologist on the British colonial Gold Coast.

[289] These medicinal herbs, particularly *gbo̲* and *nerɛyu*, are the two indispensable ingredients of most 'medicines' (Huber 1993: 239).

160

So-called medicine-shrines, that is to say, pots containing water and medicinal leaves, are often placed in this grove. The water is used for ritual washing. A circle of empty bottles attests to former libations with alcoholic drinks and therefore to the active serving of the deity. Some disks of white clay (*nguo̱*) may lie around, which are used in rituals as well. Inside Klowɛki's grove and that of other indigenous gods you can find a round one-room clay hut covered with a straw roof (*wo̱tsum*).[290] The interior of the hut will be hidden from view by a white curtain.

The sacred stone called *tɛgbɛtɛ*, on which *dipo* girls have to sit during the rites, is hidden likewise, and the priests claim that every *tɛgbɛtɛ* contains at least a particle of the original sacred rock on Krobo Mountain. The *tɛgbɛtɛs* of seven main *dipo* priests are said to be the oldest and 'most original' ones. I was told these are the ones of: Klowɛki, Okumo, Adjase, Adjime, Hio̱no̱, Nause and Mɛtɛ. These seven represent the original seven divisions on Krobo Mountain, and the number seven is of metaphysical importance (Quarcoopome 1993b: 136). It is said that when the priests were driven from Krobo Mountain, they carried the original sacred receptacles and symbols of their gods to these hidden places in the 'bush', so that "they could hold their undisturbed meetings here", as Huber said without further explanation (Huber 1993: 239). As became clear in the previous chapter, priests secretly returned to the mountain after their eviction in 1892, and retrieved some sacred items. One old *dipo* priestess, referring to the fact that the British government forbade the veneration of the important gods, told me that during this time, "the bold and daring ones took their things along with them [sacred objects], the cowards left their things behind".

Currently, there are supposedly about 38 *tɛgbɛtɛs* in Manya Krobo, and 24 in Yilo Krobo, each of which is used by different 'houses' where *dipo* is performed. Most presiding priests will have two, three or sometimes even four consequent groups of *dipo* girls in one season, which may amount to over one hundred girls per priest. If I take a low average of around fifty girls per shrine per season, my estimation is that some 3,000 girls are initiated in the whole of Krobo per year, which is a large majority that could reach up to roughly 97%.[291]

The *dipo* rites can only be performed in *do̱m* (the capital towns in the plains) by the priests who are authorised to do so. Those Krobo who migrated to

---

[290] War deities' shrines look different. Deities which are seen as 'imported', also have different types of shrines. Mami Wata's altar for example, is indicated with the colours red, black and white.

[291] According to 'Table 22: Population by district by sex and locality of enumeration, Eastern Region' (GSS 2002c), the Yilo and Manya Krobo District together had a total female population of 123,292 in the year 2000, of which an estimated 49.65 % (61,215) is under the age of 20 (based on figures for the whole Eastern Region, 'Table 2: age structure of population by region' (GSS 2002c). Assuming that the age structure of the population has not changed too much in the last two decades, and that girls will be initiated before the age of 20, rough estimations then are that over 3,000 girls per year are potentially initiated. Of course not everybody living in Krobo District is of Krobo origin, however, many Krobo living outside their District will come home to have their daughters initiated.

far-away farming areas in for example the Western or Ashanti Region, or live outside the country, in Abidjan, or even in Europe, return to their hometown at the time of the ceremonies to initiate their children. Girls from the same town or village in *yono* (upcountry), from different families, but often from the same 'house' and at least the same clan, will come together to do *dipo* in their family house in *dom*, in the 'hometown'. They will have the main rituals performed at a particular traditional house of a priest or priestess who usually comes from the same clan. People who want to 'hide' at the scene, can go to another town. People from Odumase may, for example, go to Somanya and vice versa. A woman I knew from Manya-Kpongunor (one of the adjacent hometowns of Odumase) took her granddaughter of six years old to Plau (Somanya) in Yilo Krobo to perform *dipo* for her, because as a member of the Women's Fellowship in the Presbyterian Church she wanted to avoid comments from her surroundings.[292]

Although Krobo priestly authority has always been based on secrecy and taboos (as became clear in the previous chapters), this does not imply that objects that embody secret meanings have to be hidden (cf. Quarcoopome 1994) or that people should 'hide' performing certain rites. And although 'the bush' is not an accidental place for worship, as it is an African metaphor for a domain of dangerous powers and of vital energies (Jackson & Karp 1990: 20), the hidden and secretive character of the Krobo shrines, ancestral symbols and some of the performed rituals has been influenced by the removal from the mountain in 1892 and the prominent presence of the Basel Mission in Odumase. The clay and wooden figures as described by Field (n.d.) and Quarcoopome (1994) for other Dangme speaking groups, which were used in ritual ceremonies, cannot easily be found in Odumase today.[293] However, there is evidence that they were more common here as well before the twentieth century. Johannes Zimmermann reported in 1871 that clay images (which he called '*Schandbilder*', 'shameful images') in pairs, representing a naked male and female, were placed at the entrance of every Krobo village, except for Odumase, to ward off illness. Apparently the missionaries had already banned these images in their surroundings in Odumase at that time.[294] The Basel missionary Josenhans reported in 1910 that these 'immoral figures' as he called them, had generally disappeared from the public eye, and could only be found inside huts.[295]

The hidden character of the shrines may be a reverse effect of what art historian Quarcoopome, in his article on *the morphology and symbolism of*

---

[292] Her son, who was the father of her granddaughter, had died, and the girl was under her care.

[293] Field (n.d.: 27-34), for example, described the 'cult of the *dzangbii*'. The *dzangbii* were the playmates a child had left behind in the other world. They could sometimes come to try and entice a child to leave this world and come back 'home' again. In such a case a ritual was performed to prevent this, in which the *dzangbii* were represented by clay dolls.

[294] BMA, D-1.23 Afrika 1871, Odumase 17, J. Zimmermann, 30.09.1871, Odumase, '3. Quartalsbericht'.

[295] BMA, D-1.95 Goldküste 1910, Odumase 12, G. Josenhans, 11.03.1911, Odumase, 'Jahresbericht'.

Dangme public altars (1994), describes in general for (other) Dangme towns. Whereas early Dangme public altars only consisted of undecorated rocks or stones,[296] Quarcoopome states that contemporary elaborate architectural forms of Dangme altars and their ubiquity in Dangme towns may simply be a recent development dating back no earlier than to the turn of the twentieth century as a result of the increasing influence of Christianity:

> If Dangme altar complexes, in their present forms, are indeed phenomena of the last one hundred years, then they represent an attempt to add new dimensions to the efficacy and durability of Dangme religious concepts at a time of intense proselytization by European missionaries (Quarcoopome 1994: 345).

The elaborate architectural forms of Dangme altars he describes, are nearly absent in Krobo area, or at least are more hidden from public view. When I once visited the coastal town called Prampram of the Dangme-speaking Prampram people, I was therefore surprised to see a large shrine enclosed by a white-washed mud wall at a prominent place in the centre of town.

The only shrine in Odumase town that is not situated behind or inside a house or off the road and in the 'bush', is the *klutu* at the site of the 'royal palace' (*wenguam*), to which a black sheep is sacrificed every year for the *konọ*'s stool during the *ngmayem* festival. It is situated next to the old Basel Mission chapel, as *konọ* Sakite built his palace opposite the church in the 1880s and the shrine also possibly dates from this time. This shrine must therefore rather be related to the proliferation of chiefly rituals. The particular shrine was an eyesore to the Basel missionaries. Missionary Erhardt reported in 1917 that, although there were hardly anymore 'fetishes' in the streets and houses of Odumase: "Only the pagan town elders have the doubtful honour to possess a fetish in the form of a stack of stones and bones in front of the palaver hall, unfortunately right next to the church."[297]

The shrines I encountered most, usually in a smaller form, were these protective shrines called *klutu*, often situated in the inner courtyard of an ancestral 'family house'. The outside looks very inconspicuous: usually a rough stone

---

[296] Indeed, as was described in chapter three, on Krobo Mountain one such rock was called *Anikaka*, a large flat rock with a circle of four arranged flat stones dedicated to the 'high court' of the priestess of the deity Klowɛki (cf. Teyegaga 1985: 19). Another such rock was the *tɛgbɛtɛ*, which is still used during the *dipo* rites. The *tɛgbɛtɛ* is also called *Totroku*. This is also the name of its deity still worshipped at Atua in the Djebiam-Ogomɛ and Manya-Kpongunọ sub-divisions. The worship of sacred rocks probably existed prior to the advent of the Klowɛki deity, which the *Totroku* priestess at Atua also insisted on in an interview with me (Interview September 29, 1998, Atua). The worship of the *Totroku* deity at a certain point in time probably merged with the worship of the Klowɛki deity. Sacred stones and related pregnancy tests can be found elsewhere in West-Africa. Not only among the neighbouring Osu, but also among the Kabre people in Northern Togo (Huber 1993: 192).

[297] BMA, D-3.9, Quartalsberichte 1915-1917, VII, 5, W. Erhardt, 10.07.1917, Odumase, 'Krobo einst und jetzt'; quotation originally in German, my translation.

cemented into the floor. What is important is what may be buried underneath that gives it its power, for instance a piece of rock from Krobo Mountain.[298] As Arlt (2002: 22) also points out, an important constituent of the *klutu*'s power is therefore the link with the ancestral home and the whole related body of history. Some people told me that the burial of items with spiritual potency or (live) animals (such as chickens) underneath an altar or building is also practiced by churches, usually indigenous churches. Other types of shrines are the sanctuaries for the *abǫdǫi* (*abǫdǫi piɛmi*), mysterious little creatures that are held to be children or messengers of the gods, which can sometimes be found in between the houses.[299] They are marked by a surrounding fence of bamboo poles. Apart from the priests, other people often reacted very evasive when I tried to find out about the particular character of what obviously was a shrine, mostly for a family deity, inside their house. As Christians they wanted to avoid that I had the impression that they were involved in 'traditional' practices.

In non-Christian Krobo cosmology the ghosts of the dead, spirits of nature and ancestors play an important role. However, the actual cults and customary religious performances centre on important deities, the *djemawǫi*. '*Djemi*' means 'in the world', and '*wǫ*' (plural '*wǫi*') means something like 'guardian', (but also refers to 'deity'), therefore *djemawoi* could be translated as 'guardians in the world'. They are generally conceived as personal or personified but invisible beings. They can either be male of female, endowed with supernatural powers of blessing and killing. Normally they will not kill, unless their ritually sanctioned laws and prohibitions have been violated, or when they have been invoked to do so by means of ritual oaths against an offender. Some of the deities are mystically attached to a sacred animal. The ball-python (*Nako*) for example, is the sacred animal of the deities *Nako* and Klowɛki. It is a taboo to kill it. Some gods are associated with sacred rocks or streams. The spirits of the dead (*kpade*) are distinguished from the *djemawoi*, but some of the latter, of whom Nana Klowɛki is a good example, seem to come close to mythified ancestors (Huber 1993: 235-236).

The cult around the *djemawǫi* is mainly organised on a clan level, yet the gods may choose devotees from other clans and sub-divisions. As the Krobo have a history of migration, and different waves of immigrants arrived at different points in time, it is likely that the various parties brought with them the worship of their own particular deities, as I also explained in chapter three. Some clan gods became important to the whole group at a later stage, in particular the

---

[298] This is an example of the correlation of power with secret knowledge. Therefore such a visual expression of power must be either understated or disguised. Dangme objects are often manufactured from perishable and non-precious materials, or are kept to their simplest forms without bright colours. The result is that emblems of power may pass unnoticed in public (Quarcoopome 1993a: 115-116).
[299] See Huber (1993: 276-279) for more details about the *abǫdǫi*.

164

Kloweki deity. Some also remained significant in places from which they are said to originate. *Nause* (Manya division) and *Nako* (Bonya division) are considered among the senior Krobo gods, and the first ones who arrived. After this Nana Kloweki and *Hiono* (both *Susui* division) came soon, as well as *Leete-Na* (*Djebiam*). Other important gods arrived after these, for instance the war gods *Nadu* and *Kotoklo* that were mentioned in the previous chapter, the gods *Likpotsu* (*Djebiam-Agbom*) and *Mɛɛtɛ* (*Djebiam-Yokwenya*), and war gods of Akan origin such as *Kofi-Dade* (*Okpɛ*). Some gods are said to have been accidentally found in the 'bush' (Huber 1993: 236).

Although religious actions are clustered and mainly focused on the clan deities, additional deities can be accumulated by individual people. The goddess Mammy Water is an example of a god whose shrines can be found with some Krobo priests, while she is worshipped along the West-African coast (cf. Jell-Bahlsen 1997). When a god is not served well, it can also 'go back to where it came from.' For example, a priestess from the Plau division told me that the Plau god Oboyima, a war god, went back to Ada (along the coast) because it was not served well, which means that there is no shrine anymore for this deity in Plau. Therefore she regularly went to Ada to bring him offerings on behalf of the Plau division, in order to keep the deity satisfied.

The Krobo recognise a high god or supreme being who is called *Mawu*. *Mawu* (also spelled *Mãu*) does not have a special shrine and is not worshipped directly. However, many libation texts start by invoking this high god with the words: *'Tsatse Mawu kɛ e Yo Zugba Zu'*: 'God the father and his wife, the earth.' The indirect use of the pronoun 'his' is a way of showing deference. The same name is used by the Ewe neighbours. The concept of a supreme being is most likely influenced by Christian ideas.[300] Originally *Mawu* was not a generic term for 'God', but the personal name of a distant deity already known in pre-Christian times (Meyer 1999: 65). In Christian churches the same name *Mawu* is used as a translation for the Christian God. As Huber (1993: 234) also points out, the Christian conception of *Mawu* may have modified the beliefs and idioms of speech during the past hundred and fifty years.

The serving of the gods is jointly organised by priests, priestesses, their male and female representatives and assistants, and the seniors of the clan or 'house' to which a particular shrine is attached. A male priest is called a *wono* and a female priest *woyo*. The designations simply express 'a man or a woman dedicated to a god (*wo*)'. Most of the gods demand the services of both a priest and a priestess, especially the female deities. A priest and priestess worshipping the

---

[300] Huber's idea that "the name and concept of a Supreme Being go back to the days before Christian missionaries arrived among the Krobo" (Huber 1993: 234) seems to build on Schmidt's notion of 'primitive monotheism' (Schmidt 1931).

same god are not actually married to each other, but espoused to the deity in some mystical way. Priests and priestesses are allowed to marry, however, some priestesses attribute their failed marriage or lack of a partner to the deity they worship. One elderly *dipo* priestess told me that: "The gods forbid me to marry. If I get a new man today he will leave me tomorrow. I was married before for fifteen years, but we had no children. The gods want me to stay at home to cook for them and myself. This time I feel fit." Her colleague, the stool priestess for the war god Mɛtɛ, a woman in her mid-fifties, added: "We are beautiful, but the gods hate to behold a rival."[301] Priests guard a shrine of the deity they are serving. In the name of the community or sometimes of individuals, they pour libations or make sacrifices to inform the deity about occasions and ask for blessings. There are certain priests for installing the ('secular') chiefs.

The priests make a living from the offerings of the people for the ceremonies they perform and from the heavy fines or ransom sums in ritual oath cases. A male priest then settles cases especially when his deity's sanction has been invoked for the killing of an opponent or of members of the latter's family (Huber 1993: 240-241). The swearing of oaths is forbidden by law, but still takes place, and I witnessed the settling of cases by the priests a few times. The priests give an apportioned share of the fines and offerings to each of their assistants. The performance of the *dipo* rites also generates an income, and this is one reason why several *dipo* rites are not performed anymore in individual houses as in the olden days, but in the premises of the priests. Although male priests can supervise the *dipo* rites, female priests in particular play an important role in performing the rituals for girls. Assistants to the priests usually act as messengers and also have a number of minor duties with regard to the sanctuary and its upkeep. Most priests do some (subsistence) farming, and some priestesses are involved in trading.

A priest can be recognised by the white calico (*klala*) he wears like a toga, covering one shoulder. The colour white symbolises purity and blessing. The priestesses usually wear a single large piece of white calico as a waist-cloth, and often another cloth which they tie above their breasts, plus a third piece as headgear. The men also tie a piece of calico around their head when they have not been fully ordained yet as priests, or when they are assistants to priests. The first time I met the Okumo priest in 1994, he wore a piece of white cloth fastened around the head. The second time, in 1998, he wore a conical hat, like the other head priests Asa, Ajase and Klemesi. This hat (*komi pee*), which is woven from either of two particular palm fibres, s<u>o</u>ni (*Borrasus aethiopicum*) or raffia, *komi* (*Raphia ruffia*) (Quarcoopome 1993b: 128),[302] is reserved for these senior priests, while priestesses are not allowed to wear them. The priestly hat is im-

---

[301] Interview December 24, 1998, Agomanya.

[302] According to Huber, the use of raffia, dried grass, refers to a grassland's custom, thus to the East where the first Krobo migrated from (Huber 1993: 191).

bued with immense religious significance, and therefore one has to be ritually clean to wear it. It is kept in a special room set aside for the *dipo* rites. A priest is installed by undergoing rites that are similar to *dipo*. He must cleanse himself spiritually before he can wear the hat (Huber 1993: 228; Quarcoopome 1991: 63). Straw hats and beads belong to the core of indigenous artistic symbols of power (Quarcoopome 1993b: 468).[303] Around their right wrist male as well as female priests wear a characteristic bracelet, which consists of a combination of simple strings with beads, called the *la*. The *la* consists of a raffia fibre with a white *nyoli* bead (of foreign origin, according to one priestess from Ewe land and very precious), the black *tovi* bead (fruit of a liana plant), and a fibre with the blue *koli* bead. These priestly beads are regarded as a symbol of ancient cultural and ritual traditions. Sometimes they are also said to refer to traditional concepts regarding personhood, which I will discuss in the next chapter. Tetteh Gaga, a *wono* from Yilo Krobo, mockingly explained to me that the three beads represent the (Christian) holy trinity, and he crossed himself to underline his words. The priests usually consider black and white as belonging together, like good and evil, and believe that the blue *koli* bead represents one's ancestry. During ceremonies priestesses in particular wear additional necklaces with black and white beads, bracelets and anklets. Some of them told me that each bracelet represents the dedication to a different deity.

Priests and their assistants are usually experts in the singing of *klama*. *Klama* songs are part of the old oral tradition, which texts are often proverbial, or refer to the historical past. There are different kinds of *klama*, which vary in tune and rhythm, for different occasions. Usually it is performed in ritual or ceremonial situations, with the exception of funerals. *Klama* may only be played at funerals of priests because they have a special position among the ranks of the ancestors (Coplan 1972: 36). During *dipo* it is played as a background to ritual activities, at points of relaxation between ritual performances, and to celebrate the completion of ritual phases (ibid.1972: 27):

> *Klama* can thus be seen as not merely a musical type appropriate to specific events in the *dipo*, but an essential part of the very atmosphere of ancient tradition in which the *dipo* as a whole takes place. *Klama* helps to create this atmosphere in a psychological sense by its evocation of tradition in the minds of the Krobos; and in a literal sense by keeping the gods and ancestors informed of the proceedings with invocations and songs in their own language; and by providing a context in which the entire community of the divine, the dead, and the living can take part (Coplan 1972: 33).

A number of ritual rules and taboos adhere to most shrines and their veneration. Some only apply to the priests, others to the whole 'house' or the whole

---

[303] Chiefs are also installed with priestly symbols such as beads, white calico and a staff, which are designed to invest leaders with spiritual power (Quarcoopome 1993b: 125).

clan or society as a whole. For all Krobo it is a rule that men should be circumcised and women should have passed through *dipo* before their first pregnancy, thereby originally following the regulations of the Nadu and Kloweki deities (I will deal with male circumcision in the next chapter). Only then are they allowed to enter a shrine or the family houses. Other rules and regulations concern food taboos. Krobo people say that they, in contrast to the Asante, do not eat snails. They also do not eat pigs, in contrast to the neighbouring Ga people. Some food taboos only apply to, for example, twins, for whom the taboos can vary. Other rules only apply to a particular shrine. According to mythical history, the Volta river refused to give water to the Krobo when Kloweki and her 'children' crossed it. Therefore the head priests of Kloweki are not allowed to drink water from the Volta or eat food prepared with water from this river (cf. Coplan 1972: 3; Huber 1993: 246). This means that they are not allowed to eat fermented food or drink pipe-borne water (which comes from the Volta). This also applies to the *dipo* initiates during the main phase of the *dipo*. If these rules are neglected, special purification rites have to be performed (cf. Huber 1993: 245).

"If I don't serve her, she will kill me": the call of the gods

> "They consulted the oracles again and came back to tell that she [the Kloweki deity] had said: 'if I don't serve her, she will kill me'." (*'A kpale ba ya gba wo ke ke I ba somo we le o e ma gbem'*) (Interview with a Kloweki priestess, 10-9-1998)

Priests have a special social status and hence should be treated with respect. It is expressed, for example, in taking off one's shoes before entering a priest's house. However, I observed how many Christian Krobo often speak about the so-called 'fetish priests' in derogatory terms. They feel the priests are 'pagans' and perform 'primitive rites'. Many of them have not been to school before. Family members of priests often try to convince them to convert to Christianity, as their relatives are also held responsible for the 'paganism' of the priests. People often try to avoid being associated with 'pagan' practices, at least publicly. My Christian companion was reprimanded by her Presbyterian church elders for being seen with me in a deity's grove. Her cousin, who had American visitors, sent them to us to witness the *dipo* rites, as she as a stout Presbyterian refused to visit a 'fetish house'. If Christianity is so dominant today and if it has a greater status, who are the persons who become 'traditional' religious specialists and why do they accept this position? I will investigate these questions in this section. The stories of different priests I interviewed about their line of work not only reveal how 'traditional religion' is viewed nowadays, in a society largely dominated by Christianity, but also that the symbols and ideology of Christianity have become internalised as reference points for all Krobo, including non-Christians.

A priest or priestess is said to be called or chosen by a deity.[304] However, a deity often 'selects' someone from a particular family, which makes the priestly functions more or less hereditary. Most priests and priestesses only come from certain 'houses' where the particular god is worshipped. Many priests have other priests in their family or have taken over this function from one of their (grand)parents. Usually these are also the people who taught them their priestly tasks. The call of a god may manifest itself in the form of sickness or madness. If the chosen one refuses to respond to the call, this may result in permanent sickness or madness, the loss of a child or even one's own death.

Various priests told me that the signs of their call became apparent when they were children or even when they were born. One priestess named Ako said that she could not walk, was blind and had boils all over her body when she was a small child living in the village. When she was sent to hospital she became even more sick, and the moment she just about had to go to school her sickness came back again. She explained that "no matter where you are, when the gods need you, they just find you and possess you".[305] This was also the experience of other priests. One priestess told me the call came upon her while she was in Abidjan, Ivory Coast. Other priests also experienced a setback or strange opposition when they went to school or church, while they were not yet ordained as priests. One priestess narrated how she first went to register with the Sra Presbyterian church (in Yilo) after she had a dream about a chapel and a pastor. However, when she was about to be baptised, her baptismal card mysteriously went missing. This was interpreted as a sign from a certain deity, who wanted her to serve him.[306]

Another male priest in his forties told me that he was not willing to respond to the call of Nana Klowɛki, because he attended school and was a churchgoer.[307] But he also experienced a range of adversities. The call first manifested itself in the form of strange occurrences:

> Whenever I went to farm, I would hear people talking close by, but I never saw anybody. Sometimes, I went to collect foodstuff, I would hear people talking closely behind as though they were following; other times they push my load down destroying everything. When such things happened I couldn't do anything. (Original in Dangme)

---

[304] However, some priests, like the *Okumo* priest, are chosen. The latter, the head of the *djéméli*, has been elected from the Akwɛno division by a council at least since the 18th century (see chapter three).

[305] Interview with *woyo* Ako, January 24, 1999, Odumase. The force that called her was 'the stool' (*sɛ*), the symbol of the *kono*'s power and representing his ancestors' power. Her task was to sweep the shrine (the 'stool house') during the *ngma yemi* festival. She also decorated people with a particular type of white and black clay to prepare them for rituals.

[306] Interview with *woyo* Maku, November 21, 1998, Somanya.

[307] Interview April 24, 1999, Kodjonya.

I asked him how he knew it was a call from the gods. He told me that:

> As things continued this way I went to some 'spiritualists'. I first went to Kojo at the Asitey junction. He [..] told me: 'This is the work they want you to do. If you don't you'll die.' My mother-in-law is a diviner; she invited me and [also] told me that this is the work I was destined for and to reject the call will create problems. (ibid.)

Interestingly, this priest said he first went to 'Kojo at Asitey juntion'. This Kojo is a pastor of a 'spiritual' (African Independent) church. The priestess in the example above, Ako, also said that her relatives first took her to a pastor who told them that it was a call from the gods. Next, they went to traditional diviners who confirmed the call. Other priests showed a pragmatic attitude towards different religions as well, while at the same time they felt that the call of a deity is too strong to resist.

This male priest further told me how he experienced impotency, then sickness. Once he went for an interview for enrollment in a police school in Koforidua (the regional capital of the Eastern Region), however the documents he needed to bring along went missing in a mysterious way. He told me: "It was after I lost my child through my defiance that I finally gave in. The gods were set to kill me as well." After all, he said, who would bury him after his death if he would loose all his children? "I resolved to take up the position. I came home to tell my people here and they tied the *la* (priestly beads) for me." However, this was not an easy choice. He felt that he could have attained a higher position in society if he had stayed in school and that he had lost the respect of many people. He told me:

> Indeed *manyɛ* Dale, this is my sad story. Sometimes when I think back on the tragedy I feel like drinking my head off. Other times you'll see people younger than me speaking to me with impunity, as though I were a baby all because of these fetish jobs I do. (ibid.)

This priest had now been in function for about twenty years. Part of his work, he explained, was to perform rituals to purify, for example, a ritually polluted house. He also officiated the yearly *dipo* rites in his house. He described himself as symbolising Kloweki's wife or her soul (*klawa*). His little daughter had also been mysteriously ill and a diviner had revealed that her task was to cook in Kloweki's shrine (during the festivals and ceremonies). Many of the female priests have to perform domestic duties in the shrine. For example another priestess, the Kloweki regent's wife, told me that besides her tasks in performing *dipo*, she maintained the shrine: sweeping it, weeding, and filling the pots with water. She called herself 'the servant in Nana's house'.

Other priests narrated how they experienced problems in a similar way when they tried to ignore the 'call of the gods'. The old priestess Tɛko-*yumu*

170

described how she had already been marked as a priestess when she was a child, when she was still nursed by her mother.[308] She became ill, and the oracles had concluded that it was Klowɛki who caused the problems:

> My grandfather [Klowɛki's senior priest] who brought the deity from Krobo Mountain had a sister who was to occupy this position as priestess. That sister is dead and so the deity has picked me. As I was very young, my mother took it upon herself to observe all abstentions from food and other taboos until I was old enough for *dipo*. (Original in Dangme)

Her grandfather, the Klowɛki priest, provided her needs during the *dipo* rites, so that her future husband Akwɛɛtɛ was able to perform *dipo* for her:

> During my *dipo*, I requested that the then *dipo* priest provides everything for my *dipo*. That was my grandfather *Asikpe,* who accepted the request and provided everything for Akwɛɛtɛ to perform the *dipo* ceremony for me. After *dipo* I was given to him for marriage and had seven children by my husband. I declined serving as a priestess at the Klowɛki shrine and consequently lost five children. When the fifth death occured we consulted the oracles and the deity claimed she was responsible for the deaths. I was left with two children - a boy and a girl. I then agreed to become a priestess to save the lives of my two children. Indeed, I started to serve with a sorrowful feeling. (Ibid.)

Still she also tried to find a solution to her setbacks in church:

> I suddenly decided to be baptised into a Christian church to ward off the devil. I joined the Apostolic Church. When I joined the Church I became paralysed for four months and I couldn't walk. When I was served a moderate meal, I would reject it until they served the quantity I desired. In fact I became a glutton and I was even getting annoyed when they served food to people in the house. They consulted the oracles again and came back to tell that the Klowɛki deity had said that if I wouldn't serve her she would kill me. (Ibid.)

However, Tɛko was still worried. How would she provide for the upkeep of herself and her children if she became a full-time priestess?

> It was then when my daughter Fatuma stepped in to convince me that she was prepared to provide my needs while I serve. I agreed and we came to *Dom*. The day they sent me to the shrine for the cleansing rituals I started walking and returned home from the shrine unaided. I walked back to Akwɛɛtɛ's house. When we came home they cooked for me, but I could only eat a little to already feel satisfied. I then asked myself why I had eaten so much when I was still a Church member. They [the people from the shrine, MS] came back to tell me the deity claimed responsibility for my abnormal food consumption. She quickly dissolved all I ate, so that I would crave for

---

[308] Interview September 10, 1998, Kodjonya.

more food. Now that I've agreed to serve her, I'm going to change to be fine and indeed, this is what happened. I demanded that she gave me work, so that I could feed and clothe myself. I was a widow, poor and without any property. The deity said she had something for me. She gave me some plots of land acquired for her at Ahabaso, Otlokpe, after the descent from the mountain. These plots were given to me. I should engage people to work in them so I will use the proceeds to fend for myself. I agreed. (Ibid.)

According to her story, when she finally accepted the *la*, Tɛko became well again. She ascribed the death of her five children and her own sickness to her initial failure to take up her position as a priestess in Klowɛki's shrine. Her tasks in the shrine were sowing millets and preparing millet for meals and beer during the *dipo* rites and the 'millet-eating' (*nma-yemi*) ceremonies: "If I fail to do this, I may die early. As of now, I will never become a Christian again. I would also never go chasing after any other [traditional] deity [except Nana Klowɛki]. If I do that I would die. I will continue this way as a priestess, now I am only suffering from piles and waist pains." Tɛko-*yumu* also was an expert *klama* singer. She said she earned some money by performing some of the rites for the *dipo* candidates. For example, she always washed the heads of the *dipo* girls' on Monday during the closing celebrations of *dipo*. And when a Klowɛki priest died it was her task to wash the corpse. Finally, she also knew how to perform purifying rituals that are necessary in some traditional homes when a man wants to bring in an Akan woman through marriage: "My duties are heavy, and if I dare to untie this *la*, God knows what's going to happen to me. Let her [Marijke] know that if I die I will go with it", [with the *la*, i.e. as a priestess].

Another old *dipo* priestess told me that becoming a priestess: "was my 'parting word' or 'destiny' (*sɛsɛɛ*) from my birth. My 'destiny' was that I would not become a Christian."[309] She said she fell ill and the diviners declared that she wanted to succeed her grandmother who was a priestess as well. She also felt that: "At that time [in my youth] the [traditional] gods were very active and omnipresent. It is not like the present time, in which Christianity has taken total control of man's life." She meant to say that, in her opinion, Christian religion has gained prominence in public space over traditional religion in recent times. When I asked this particular priestess why she was not wearing her *la*, she said that she felt shy towards people who would then know right away that she was a priestess.

My friend Juliana told me that she and her sisters had often tried to persuade their mother, 'stool' and *dipo* priestess Lako Sakité, to be baptised. But for a long time to no avail. During a conversation I had with her mother in 1994 and between 1998 and 2000, maa Lako said she would never leave the job. She felt she was serving God 'in a good and peaceful way', as she used to say. If she

---

[309] Interview September 29, 1998, Atua; I will explain the word *sɛsɛɛ* further in the next chapter.

would go against 'the stool' (she is the priestess for the _kono_'s stool), and become a Christian, it would probably kill her, she said. She also explained that she had seen examples of what she called 'fake priests', who go for baptism and die. Juliana tried to prove to her that the time had come for these people to die as they were baptised on their deathbed, but her mother could not be convinced. From her point of view, the 'soul' of these persons did not want the baptism and therefore caused them to die.[310] Such non-Christian presuppositions that continue to underlie people's concept of a person were also evident in different examples given by the Basel missionaries. For example, Basel Mission catechist Quartey reported on the death of one Jakob Latei in 1904, right after his baptism. His relatives were said to believe that his soul did not want the baptism. Had he not become a Christian, he would not have died.[311]

Therefore, I was initially highly surprised to hear through a letter from Ghana in 2002 that 'maa' Lako had been baptised. At the same time different messages reached me that she had been frequently ill. During a short visit to Ghana in January 2003 I had the chance to briefly talk to her about these changes. Lako Sakité was then wearing a chain with a cross around her neck as a sign of her membership of the Roman Catholic Church. She told me that one day, when she had tried to reach some place in her little courtyard, she fell down and nobody was home to help her. She was lying on the floor for a long time, crying for help, but nobody came to her rescue, even though her neighbours (relatives) were only behind the shared compound wall. Many people, even her own relatives, especially some of the young women in the house, had been calling her a witch, so maa Lako felt they did not want to help her. She thought she might die soon. According to Juliana, she told another daughter she then had a vision of a pigeon. Later she told her daughters to call the pastor for her, as she wanted to be baptised. The Presbyterian Church representatives refused to come to this 'fetish woman'. Then the daughters went to the Roman Catholics in Agomanya, who came and took her to church. She was baptised and Catholic priests visited her in her house. According to her, these priests told her that they did not mind that she performed _dipo_ or other ceremonies, which did not harm anybody.

Some authors have suggested that a Christian burial, which is much more prestigious, is such a major concern for many Ghanaians, that it is one reason for conversion to Christianity (Gilbert 1988; Witte 2001: 139). Did maa Lako want to be guaranteed a 'decent' Christian funeral for her family's sake by converting? Or did she want to make sure that she would not end up in hell when she thought she was dying? 'Eleventh hour' baptisms on a person's deathbed have been quite common ever since the Basel missionaries came to the country. For-

---

[310] See the next chapter for an explication of non-Christian ideas of the 'soul'.
[311] BMA, D-1,80 Afrika 1904, Odumase 137, W. A. Quartey, 10.03.1905, Odumase, 'Jahresbericht'.

tunately maa Lako recovered and she is still alive. At present I do not quite know to what extent she is continuing her activities as a priestess.

As some of the examples above show, some priests rather reluctantly succumbed to the gods, while others seem to have less problems. Accepting the task of serving a deity has economic as well as social consequences. The called ones have to find a means of living. Often the gods prevent them from being educated and engage in certain (higher-earning) jobs. They often farm or get some income through performing certain ceremonies. At the same time they have to deal with public opinion, which is dominated by Christianity. Some priests use humour to cope with the situation. When I asked one *dipo* priestess what her name was, she jokingly said: "My name is Tɛko and my Christian name is *wawoyo*, 'the priestess'." Her colleague priestess laughed when I asked her whether she had been going to church before and said: "Yes, I go to church in my shrine."[312]

The actions of the priests and priestesses upon their calling exhibit a pragmatic attitude towards different values and institutions, indigenous religious practices and Christianity. Some first went to the church to search for answers, where sometimes even pastors sent them to diviners. As Lako Sakité's example also shows, people in practice do not think and worship in terms of religious orthodoxy. They may switch from one religion to another in order to advance their own interest.

However, nowadays priests are forced to defend their position vis-à-vis the growing influence and status of Christianity and particularly Pentecostalism. They are able to do so by stressing the power and unavoidability of the calling. A call by the gods comes from outside the self and is outside one's control, while the Christian concept of the person would emphasise the choice of the individual. Therefore the headline above the story in the Ghanaian weekly *The Mirror* in June 1993, about the young man who was to become the Okumo priest at the time but converted to Christianity, quotes the converted priest saying: 'I am now free'.[313] In general, non-Christian presuppositions of the person persist. The type of illnesses, for example, described by the called priests, such as mental illness, impotence, and blindness, are seen as spiritual illnesses and caused by the gods, as Senah (1997: 142) also observed for the Ga. Whether one is a Christian or not, if a person is called by the gods, he or she has to respond to the call, or else it is believed that it may have serious repercussions for one's health and well-being.

---

[312] Interview December 24, 1998, Agomanya.

[313] "'I am now free". Dipo priest converts', *The Mirror*, 19-06-1993. In an interview I had with this young man in 1994, it became clear that he was still in training for priesthood at the time, as he did not wear the priestly hat yet.

'May the year go and come again': Calendrical rituals

Oklibone. Kpanyamuo o. Jeha a ya nε ba na wo'. Oklibone. Kpanyamuo o
Annual greetings: 'May the year go and a new one come to meet us.'

Migrating ceremonies are a common feature of the West African landscape. Piot (1999: 136) argues that they add substance to the claim that the groups of this area are anything but neatly bounded. The *dipo* rites rotate as well. *Dipo* is celebrated in some form among other Dangme speaking groups, especially the Shai (or Sε) and the Osudoku. *Dipo* comes from the west each year, moving from community to community, starting from the Shai around the towns of Dodowa, Agomeda and Kordiabe in January,[314] before arriving in the communities of Yilo Krobo around Sra and Somanya, usually in March. The smaller Osudoku groups are said to celebrate *dipo* at the same time as the Krobo. After the Bonya division in Yilo Krobo starts the *dipo* performance in the following weeks, and then it moves through other divisions and clans to Manya Krobo, where it is carried further by the Susui division, who in turn send it to the Akwenor. The migrating ceremonies again show that religious ceremonies are mainly, though not exclusively, organised on a clan and divisional level rather than by the group as a whole. There is overlap in the different performances, as each priest will have two, three or even four successive groups. The Manya division of Manya Krobo under the Nause priests are the very last people who finish with *dipo*. When I was there in 2000, the very last *dipo* was performed in the last weekend of May. After that nobody was allowed anymore to perform *dipo* for the particular season.

All the principal communal celebrations and festivals of the various clan-sanctuaries are part of a ritual calendar, and are successively celebrated in a more or less regular cycle throughout the year. Although they have separate paramountcies and hence are politically divided, the Yilo and the Manya Krobo share the same ritual calendar. Table 1 roughly shows the celebrations in chronological order. The traditional ritual calendar is organised around the sowing, planting and harvesting of millet. The millet-planting and millet-eating ceremonies are introduced by Nana Klowεki and celebrated by most other indigenous Krobo deities. The yearly festivals for the war-gods are more distinctive for particular clans. The time of the festivals and ceremonies, at least those connected with agricultural rites, naturally coincides with the corresponding season (cf. Huber 1993: 244). The *dipo* rites are performed during the main planting season.[315]

---

[314] Ayi (1966: 64) states that among the Shai *dipo* starts in March among one of the sub-divisions of Krobo origin called Numerse. Their *dipo* is more similar to that of the Krobo.
[315] All agriculture ends in September, therefore the old calendar ended in October with the 'millet-eating' festival. If the farmland is situated in secondary forest or forest, the clearing of the land starts

Table 1 The principal communal celebrations and festivals of the various clan-sanctuaries in rough chronological order. (Based on Huber (1993: 244)).

Month	Weekday	Deity or Sanctuary	Festival/ Ceremony
January	Sunday	Nako	*Wǫnya-yami/ngma-yemi*: / 'millet-eating'
Jan.-Febr.	Sunday	Various *djemawǫi* of Yilǫ-Krobo	*Wǫnya-yami/ngma-yemi*: / 'millet-eating'
February	Sunday	Ayɛbida	*Wǫnya-yami/ngma-yemi*: / 'millet-eating'
March-April	Sunday	Various *djemawǫi* of Yilo-Krobo	*Dipo* rites
April-May	Sunday	Various *djemawǫi* of Manya-Krobo	*Dipo* rites
May	Sunday	Nause	*Wǫnya-yami*
May	Sunday	Kotoklo	*Wǫ-domi*: 'war-dances' for the war god Kotoklo
May-June	Sunday	Nadu	*Wǫ-domi*: 'war-dances' for the war god Nadu
June	Sunday	Mɛɛtɛ	*Wǫnya-yami*
June	Friday	Kofi-Dade	*Wǫnya yami/pa-yami*: /'going to the stream'
June-July	Sunday	Totrokú	*Wǫnya-yami*
June-July	Sunday	Various *djemawǫi*, esp. Nana Klowɛki	*Koda-kpami*: 'Hooting at evil-doing'
August	Sunday	Likpotsú	*Kwǫǫ-djǫ-fǫmi*: 'to bless and cleanse the throat'
Aug.-Sept.	Sunday	Nause	*Ngma-yemi-ngɛ-ngmǫ nǫ*
Aug.-Sept.	Friday	Aflam	*Wǫnya-yami/pa-yami*: / 'going to the stream'
October	Thursday	Klowɛki	*Ngma-yemi*: 'millet-eating'
October	Thursday	Okumó	*Ngma-yemi*: 'millet-eating'
October	Friday	Lɛɛte-Na	*Ngma-yemi*: 'millet-eating'
October	Friday	Adjimɛ	*Ngma-yemi*: 'millet-eating'
October	Sunday	Various *djemawǫi* of Manya-Krobo	*Ngma-yemi*: 'millet-eating'
October	Tuesday	Hiǫnǫ	*Ngma-yemi*: 'millet-eating'

Millet is the old staple food. The cultivation of maize, root crops, oil palms and plantains has become more important in the Krobo diet since at least the 18th century. Growing millet is said to be time-consuming and its yields are less than those of maize: "Although millet is superior, dietetically, to maize, it is a more uncertain crop for it is difficult to protect from birds and shows small returns in sheer bulk for greater labour" (Ayi 1966: 11). However, millet has kept its importance in rituals, and most of the high-ranking priests, those connected with the worship of Nana Klowɛki, are still bound to have their own millet farms especially for ritual use. During the *dipo* rites, for instance, the grind-

---

in January. This is the less busy time preceding the first rains. Maize can be planted from January and cassava in February. In March the first rains start. Until mid-May corn can be planted. From early June to the end of July people harvest corn. Then in July or August the lean season starts. The only thing that can be planted then are groundnuts or beans and also millet, as millet-planting rites (*kodá-kpami*) take place during this season. After this the land can be prepared again for planting.

176

ing of millet, the preparation and distribution of millet 'beer' (*ngmada*) form part of the ceremony, and the traditional millet porridge is presented to the girls as the ancient Krobo diet (cf. Huber 1993: 47). In the past, as described in chapter three, every *dipo* candidate's father would make a millet farm, the crops of which were used in preparing the *ngmada*. If a *dipo* initiate had been betrothed in infancy, her future husband had to clear the farm of his future father-in-law on which the millet was grown. Millet is regarded as a symbol of fertility and health. During the *dipo* rites and other ceremonies, millet is therefore smeared on the forehead, chest and waist of participants, accompanied by praying formulas such as: 'that your heart may be gentle'. A priest told me that if a person gets sick, one way of trying to cure him or her is tying a piece of white calico around the person's waist with some millet inside. This little ritual can be done by an elder in the 'house', or a medicine man (*tsupatsɛ*). It means that the gods are beseeched to give back the person's health.

The next section will show how the *dipo* rites are seen as an integral part of the Krobo ritual calendar and of the Klowɛki cult. Although Huber (1993) places *dipo* on the ritual calendar, he describes *dipo* only in the context of 'initiation and separation rites', while no other existing study has made the link with the ritual calendar. Following the chronology of the main ceremonies, I first give a description of how the priests determine the time for *dipo* and how the *dipo* season is started by 'putting the millet in water' and by 'blocking the road' (mainly based on my observations in 1999). After that, I will give an impression of the principal annual celebrations around the planting and harvesting of the millet that I witnessed.

Starting dipo with 'Dede'

The 'opening of the *dipo* season' (*dipo blimi*) was done by the Bonya division of Yilo Krobo. A messenger was sent to the market areas. This so-called 'gong (*gogon*) beater' announced *dipo* on the market in the following way:

> *Agoo* [usual greeting to announce one's arrival] to all you here, I bring you the day's greetings. The market chief has asked me to inform you that in four weeks from next Sunday, the *dipo* celebrations will start. I'm a messenger, I don't answer queries, don't go and misquote me.[316]

---

[316] '*Agoo ha nyɛ ha nyɛ tsuɒɔɛ, i ha nyɒ i haa nyɛ Jua matsɛ kɛ e ha nyɛ tsuɒɔɛ. Hogba nɛ ma nɛ o tsi eywiɛ a ngɛ dipo sisije nɛ a kɛ ma fiɛ ha nyɛ tsuɒɔɛ. Fiɖo gbo we wo nyɛ ko ba wo i kuɒsi bɛ.*'
This particular announcement was recorded on the Manya Krobo market of Agomanya, March 10, 1999.

177

However, the priests and elders had to perform some rites in advance to prepare everything. The people of the Bonya division in Yilo Krobo were responsible for first 'putting the millet in water' (*ngma-nyum-wom*), which always has to be done on a Thursday, the sacred day of Kloweki. They also have to come up with a 'Dede', a common name for a first born girl, to start the *dipo* period with. If there is no Dede in their 'houses', a Dede can be taken from a different family. For this Dede the *dipo* will be performed free of charge. However, nowadays people do not seem very willing to bring their daughter as the first one.[317]

I interviewed Dede Tɛko, a slim, friendly looking woman with long grey hair in her sixties, who was an elder from one of the responsible Kpemor Bonya 'houses' about this matter in her compound at Sawer.[318] She said that some people believe that a Dede will not have any offspring, but according to her: "It is not true. I was a 'Dede' [used for the opening of *dipo*], and I have many children and grandchildren." Furthermore, she told us that the matter was becoming urgent now (it was the third of March). If no Dede would be brought to them the next day, the matter would be taken to the *kono* of Yilo Krobo. He would then be urged by the priests to send drinks to his *Asafoatsɛ* of Bonya, to summon him to bring a girl from his house. Dede Tɛko told us that normally this coming Thursday the ceremony of 'placing the millet in the water' would have been performed, but now that would probably be postponed for one week. It was important to start in time, or else the rest of the events to follow would be messed up too. According to Dede Tɛko, people were also eager to start so that they could start making money through performing *dipo*.

In the second week of March 1999, the millet was 'placed in water', and *dipo* was indeed started with a 'Dede'. When I wanted to know how many groups a particular priest had, I asked how many times he went to the *tɛgbɛtɛ*, which is always on a Sunday. In the whole of Yilo there were four or five consecutive Sundays on which the girls went to the *tɛgbɛtɛ*. In mid-April the celebrations for the war god Kotoklo would start. Traditionally, the *dipo* had to be finished by then. The Yilo *kono* would also perform his stool cleansing rituals on April 22nd. For this performance too it is against custom to do it at the same time as *dipo*.

In brief, every year the *dipo* season has to start in Krobo with the Bonya people in Sawer. There has to be a first girl and that first girl has to be a first born. It seems that in the past it was custom that the first group of *dipo* candidates always consisted of first born girls. For the very first group at the Kloweki

---

[317] Traditionally, a first born daughter called Dede would be preferred not to marry and bear children for her father by lovers. This 'Dede' often became a ritual expert and keeper of the traditions of the house. It was said that '*Dede gba wo*', 'Dede weds the deity', and she often became a diviner and a priestess if there was a shrine in the house (cf. Huber 1993: 89, 98). Many of these women were famed *klama* soloists and respected 'old ladies' in the house (Coplan 1972: 77).

[318] Interview with Dede Tɛko, March 3, 1999, Kpemo Bonya.

shrine in Kodjonya this still was the case. It is said by some that the second group would consist of second born girls, and the third group would consist of the third born girls. However, all the groups I saw were mixed and girls were initiated together with their younger sisters and cousins.

'Putting the millet in the water' ceremony

By mid-March the preparations for *dipo* had started all over Yilo Krobo. Some families who lived in the cocoa farming areas all over (Southern) Ghana, had come with their daughters to their hometowns. Lako Sakité in Odumase had also already started to string beads and make the decorations the girls would wear. This is a typical task for the old ladies in a house.

Two weeks after the millet ceremony had been performed at Sawer in Yilo, I witnessed it at Plau, another part of Somanya town, on March 25, 1999. Two elder women sat opposite each other with two brand new, large clay pots in between them. They were elders from the family. The priest (Tetteh Gaga) told me that women who performed this ritual had to be women who were past their menopause. When I had asked them why they were the ones to perform this ritual, one of them simply answered that they were continuing the work of their forefathers. Each of them first poured a libation to invoke Nana Kloweki. The first woman said:

> Children of Nana Kloweki, when we give birth to children they grow up, it is to you Nana that we turn for consultation to determine what the children require (for the *dipo*). Here are children who have come of age and need to be (ritually) bathed. We've been invited to come, and the preliminary rituals of millet soaking we are doing, is to be followed by the actual *dipo*. We are here as children, you (Nana) have seen yourself the changes taking place in the world. We have come to join hands and together we have put the millet in water. We never know failure, so this millet that we've put in water, may it sprout well, so we can treat it for the ceremony. What we are doing now is just like what we used to do. We invite you to come and witness; we are (just like) children. We appeal to you to make the soaked millet sprout, so that all relatives come to assist, so that we may know success. (Original in Dangme)

The second woman replied:

> That's it, because we who are here performing these rituals, we were also made Krobo women. We know how satisfying it is when you go through *dipo*. When we are called we come to help to do it. Any time we do it, it turns out as a big success, as you Nana promised. This is our 'drink' that we present. We present it to you Nana Kloweki to solicit your help to make it successful, just as we have had it in the past, we are young and ignorant. (ibid.)

179

By stating 'we are young and ignorant', she apologised for any mistake she may have made. A third woman then poured a little schnapps on three sides around the pots as a libation. One pot contained millet. She took a small quantity out with a small calabash. When she threw it round against the roof at three places she said: '*Kloyo jimo*' (literally: 'You are a Krobo woman', i.e. referring to *dipo*). Then she threw millet grains round in the compound and on the veranda. After that, the millet was placed in the other pot and water from a stream was poured around the pot at three corners as a libation, as pipe-borne water cannot be used, because it is Volta water and therefore taboo for Nana Klowɛki, as I explained earlier. Then the brownish looking water was added to the millet. The first two women were stirring the content. An earthen dish (*ka*) was placed on top as a cover and it was left like that. One *dipo-yo*, fourteen-year old Abena, was already present, and danced around the pot together with the elder women. She had to lower her cloth so that her breasts would show. She was shy, but obeyed and pulled it back up again after she had finished the dancing. She and her mother and some siblings had travelled all the way from their farm in Sefwi in the Western Region (over 300 kilometres) to their hometown for *dipo*.

A few hours later around noon, the millet was taken out of the pot by the two women and spread out on a piece of cloth in one of the dark little rooms of the house. They covered the millet with leaves and another piece of cloth. They poured a small libation again, drank a little bit of the liquor and then placed the bottle of schnapps next to the millet. In three days, the next Sunday, they would come back to sort out the millet and perform the first rites for some *dipo* candidates.

The following Sunday the women happily showed me that the millet had germinated as expected. This meant that none of the *dipo* candidates was pregnant. If larva had entered the millet, it would have been taken as a bad omen. They sorted the millet, then dried in the sun and later ground it. After that, the women brewed the *ngma da*, the millet drink. Again, if the pot containing the *ngma da* would break during the brewing process, it would be taken as a sign that one of the *dipo* candidates was pregnant. The fertility of the girls and the fertility and blessing symbolised by the millet are therefore closely connected.

'Blocking the road': the dipo blo̱tsimi ceremony

The 'blocking' or 'closing of the road' ceremony (*blo̱ tsimi*) is performed by groups of priests and priestesses at three places along the main roads in Asitey, Atua and Nuaso, adjacent towns of Odumase, and the three 'gates' of Manya Krobo.[319] I attended this ritual first at Asitey and then Atua on the same Thurs-

---

[319] I was not aware of any such ceremony performed at Yilo Krobo before the *dipo* rites.

day morning, April 1, 1999. I was told this ceremony is performed to 'block the road' to the area of the *dipo* shrines, so that no evil spirits should come to disrupt the *dipo* ceremony.[320] The ceremony consists of purification and pacification rituals. Such types of rituals generally form an integral part of Krobo 'traditional' life. They can vary, but the common aim is to remove the 'pollution' or 'evil thing' ('*musu*', in case of a more general calamity called '*yaya*' or '*koohio yobu*'), which has brought a ritually dangerous and disastrous situation. This can manifest itself in sickness or death (cf. Huber 1958).

The particular place at Asitey was said to be chosen to mark the boundary between '*yono*', 'upcountry', and, '*dom*', 'in the valley', the place of the hometowns. As the head priests, dressed in their full priestly attire, joined in the common ceremony, it was meant to benefit the whole of Krobo. The priest Okumo was the head of the ceremony here. He did not allow Julie and me to greet him or take photographs. Other priests and priestesses with whom I was also familiar, however greeted me enthusiastically. After the ceremony (very similar to what I will describe below) was performed here, the group of priests split up to go to either Nuaso or Atua. A group with the priest Okumo as head went to Nuaso. The other group consisting of eight men and five women with the priest Ajase as leader went to Atua. Because Okumo would not allow me to film or take photos, I went along with the latter group. I was told that the place where the ritual was performed at Atua was supposed to indicate one of the places where the Krobo had settled after 1892, marking another boundary.

At Atua I was allowed to record everything. The ceremony at Atua went as follows. The priestesses sang some ancient *klama* songs in which they asked the god Nause to command rain to fall. A branch was cut off by the men and stuck in the ground with a piece of white calico bound around it on one side of the road. Some stones, which were first swayed over the performer's head to ward off evil, were buried with the pole. At Asitey this pole was said to be a branch of the *buna* tree, which is traditionally used to mark any boundary. Ajase then spread a square piece of calico in the middle of the road. He placed rocks at the edges so that the cloth would not be blown away. A group of priests, all barefooted, surrounded him. Two priestesses and Ajase's messenger (called a *labia*), stopped the cars that approached from Somanya side, therefore entering Manya Krobo. They asked the drivers for a small financial contribution to the offerings. Most complied, some refused. In the meantime, Ajase drew a line with white chalk from one side of the road to the other as a ritual barrier. Ajase then stood among the group of people again on the calico and poured a libation with water over the line in order to appease the spirits. The others hooted with their arms in the air. At Asitey they had also called out for water or actually rain

---

[320] According to Huber (1993: 273), this 'blocking of the road' only happens when a great disease or calamity is said to be threatening the towns.

(*'Nyu oo nyu!'*). He poured the second libation with his small priestly cup, the *likoko*, filled with schnapps. He spoke the following words:

> Today is the day we perform the ritual (*kusum*) of peace in peace. God, father and his mother earth, bless it all, today is *blotsimi*; so that evil (*yaya*) from over the seas and beyond the river banks coming with the intention of destroying the rituals and the custom of *dipo*, may be interceded by God, so that this ritual road block stops evil from coming here, so that God may lavish us with peace and security during this *dipo*, so that no evildoer dips his hand into it. (Original in Dangme)

Everybody hooted again in response. The evil or disaster mentioned above, *yaya*, refers to a general calamity threatening or worrying the whole town, which is thought to be carried from the sea by the wind (Huber 1958: 162).

Then Ajase slit the throat of the white fowl he held for cleansing.[321] He sprinkled some of the blood that flowed from its throat around the poles in the ground and along the 'barrier'. Then he walked back while he plucked the feathers of the cock and threw them over the 'barrier' until he had reached the other side of the road. He came back to stand on the calico and cut the fowl somewhere once more. This produced a strong reaction by the muscles of the already lifeless fowl and he had to hold it firmly. He plucked the rest of the feathers. Now the dead animal lay in front of him across the line drawn with the white chalk. The priests left the street. The fowl was taken along to be cooked. Some women were still stopping cars that passed by on this busy road.

On the other side of the road, the priests Ajase and Klemesi and three other men stuck a pole with a stripe of calico like a flag in the ground as a marker. The group of priests, men and women, went to stand in the middle of the road once more. Ajase poured another libation with schnapps, the appropriate 'white' drink for Kloweki to render her favourable:

> Yes ye God of Thursday, God, the father, mother earth. Nana Kloweki, come bless this prayer. We can't even tell the genuine side of a cloth from the woof. Long ago, at the time of the ancestors, you descended the Krobo Mountain, and what you have been doing is what we are doing as today's grandchildren in your place. We appeal to you every *dipo* season around Easter (*Ista*), we perform the *blotsim* ritual as a prelude to the *dipo* rites. So that the candidates, young girls who will undergo the *dipo* ritual, should have peace. That they may be fertile and give birth to many. We still appeal that our errors that stem from our ignorance may be overlooked; whatever mistakes we may commit in the course of this ritual, may you put it right. So that you turn misfortune (*yobu*) away and bring us fortune. Peace is what we request, peace, peace. It's me Ajase the priest. May our wishes be granted. (ibid.)

---

[321] The white fowl may have substituted the customary white sheep, maybe for economic reasons.

Fig. 5: The priest Ajase performing the 'blocking of the road' ceremony, April 1, 1999.

Here Ajase referred to Easter (*Ista*) to determine the time for the *dipo* rites. He asked for Nana Klowɛki's pardon for any mistake he may have made during the ceremonies. Again everybody hooted in response. Now Ajase grabbed a cutlass (*dadesɛ*), and moved from one pole to the other across the road, while making zigzag movements on the ground with the cutlass, apparently as I was told, to mark the border once again. The other priests sang *klama* songs. In the end Ajase struck the pole with the cutlass thrice, as every ritual movement is usually repeated three times. After this he stood on the calico a final time, with the others surrounding him, uttering a formula of prayer while holding the cutlass in the air. Three other men did the same thing, while the others hooted. They repeated this act thrice. Ajase then spoke the following words before pouring out a bucket full of water over the white line:

> Indeed this Thursday, we the commoners, behold our drink; we are the common folk. You Nana Klowɛki, you are the leader [elder] of all. So we implore you, what we're doing now, whether right or wrong, we don't know the head or tail of it. We the commoners, wherever we err, do put it right so that we will enjoy peace and tranquillity; may those who wish peace have it; may those who wish war have it; peace, peace may our wishes be fulfilled. (ibid.)

Now the way was free for the *dipo* performance in Manya Krobo, celebrated in April and May. These rites will be described in detail in chapter seven. After the different divisions in Yilo Krobo had already finished with their *dipo* rites in March and April, the annual celebrations for the main war god Kotoklo took place there in May, which I will not describe here. The celebrations for the Manya Krobo war god Nadu were supposed to take place a few weeks later, but because there was no main priest at the time, the celebrations were not as grand as normally.

'Hooting at evil-doing': The koda-kpami ceremony

The millet-planting rites took place in July. The acting Klowεki priest (*seyelọ*) at Kodjonya and the priest Okumo at Mampong were the main officiants. The 'hooting at evil-doing', the *koda-kpami*, took place at the main Klowεki shrine in Kodjonya on the first Sunday in July,[322] as a first ritual toward the celebration of the climax, the 'millet-eating' (*ngma-yemi*) festival. On the same Sunday, the Okumo priest celebrated the *koda-kpami* at his own shrine. The aim of this ritual is to dispel any evil and cleanse one's conscience before the gods can bless the growing of the new millet seeds. It reveals the traditional conviction that there is a causal relation between human guilt and the sterility of farms. In order to guarantee fertility, the priests, their assistants and elders publicly bear testimony that they have committed no evil. All guilt and innocence is placed under the deity's sanction through oaths. If any evil-minded person would take part in this public calling of the deity's sanction (described below), the god would cast the sanction, i.e. harm and death, upon that person. The public ritual is preceded by a secret ritual called *koda-yemi* (eating on the occasion of *koda*) that is performed in the 'bush' grove of Klowεki. Until at least somewhere in the 18th century, when millet was still the principal food grown by the Krobo, the *koda-kpami* rites and ritual sowing of the new millet on the priests' farms was a sign for all people to start sowing on their own farms and await the blessings of the gods (Huber 1993: 247, 253). In the next paragraphs I will describe the rites as I witnessed them.

At about six in the morning the priests started gathering in the Klowεki regent's house. I arrived with Julie, her sister Angmọkwọ and her cousin Lucy around 6.30 am. Julie and Lucy had not witnessed this ritual before, so they were curious to see it. We greeted the people around and were officially welcomed. Julie explained why we had come and asked if I could see everything. Permission was granted after paying 16,000 *cedis*. Customarily, it would have been proper to give a drink with which a libation would be poured. However, I

---

[322] I witnessed this ceremony in 1998.

noticed that different priests were often satisfied, and probably even preferred, cash. My 16,000 *cedis* represented a foreign, i.e. Dutch, schnapps at the time.[323] A libation was poured for us 'to pave the way'. I was allowed to take photos with my camera and observe the rites. However, first I had to change my clothes. I was wearing a blue skirt and a black shirt, which colours were not allowed in Klowɛki's sacred grove. I also had to remove my red earrings and my black watch. Wearing gold jewellery is also not allowed in Klowɛki's shrine. 'Red' metals (gold and copper) are considered destructive to spiritual power, and are rejected in general Dangme priestly ideology. Instead, silver is considered as mild or 'soft', and is preferred by the gods (cf. Quarcoopome 1991: 64). Like the other priestesses, I tied a white scarf around my head, and wore two blue and white coloured wrappers. We also removed our shoes before entering the sacred grove behind the Klowɛki priest's house.

The main priests Ajase and Klɛmesi sat in front of the entrance of the round hut, the sanctuary of Nana Klowɛki. The interior of the hut was hidden from view by a white curtain. Both priests wore the tall conically shaped straw hat (*komi pee*). Klɛmesi's hat was decorated with feathers. Apart from the priests Ajase and Klɛmesi, several minor male priests, about ten female priests and a number of elderly men and women had entered. An earthen black pot went round with an ablution of water and millet. Everybody sipped a bit from the drink, and then both men and women smeared some in their neck and on their chest for health and fertility. They sang the *klama* song that is typically sung at the end of the year during the *ngmayem* festival, welcoming the new year: '*Oklibone lee. Kpanya muo jeha ya nɛ e ba. Bone lee kpanya muo jeha ya nɛ e ba*': 'May the year go and come back again'. The women danced and sang and bottles of local gin went round, which increased the festive mood. The people wanted me to dance as well, but I felt shy. Julie danced in my place for now.

Then we went outside to do the ritual hooting, which we would repeat another two times. Men stood on the left and women on the right, both directed towards the sun, towards the Akuapem hills. They were hooting at evil by holding their left hand in front of their mouth, in this way making a sound like me and my friends used to make when we were children and played 'cowboys and Indians'. The priest Klɛmesi started by coming forward, uttering his grievances, while he pushed the stick he was holding into the ground.[324] Whoever wanted to harm him, he said, it should rather turn against the person. Should he himself

---

[323] See Akyeampong's interesting study of alcohol for the history behind the use of Dutch 'schnapps' in ritual in Ghana (Akyeampong 1996).

[324] The Klowɛki's main priest's position being vacant for many years now, the priest Klɛmesi came forward in his place.

have harmed anyone, the deity's sanction should fall upon him.[325] When he had finished, everybody started hooting again, and the women started digging in the earth and stamped their feet on the ground to bury evil and all evil thoughts. After Klɛmesi, Ajase came forward and later also other priests. In the next round individual worshippers came forward to utter their complaints about the wrongs that were done against them and ask the gods to grant their wishes. In the meantime, Ajase and Klemɛsi received people in front of the round hut inside the grove who had come to offer drinks. Following this, libations were poured for them. The women kept on singing and dancing and they also smeared some millet in my neck. In the third round it was the women's turn to challenge the deity's sanction. After that, we were served a meal of ground and cooked millet. When we left we were told to come back on Wednesday,[326] when another ritual was going to take place.

The following Wednesday morning the ritual sowing of the millet (*ngma dumi*) was performed in Kodjonya by the priest Ajase. Less people were present now. Two priestesses took along some calabashes with millet seed to the farm, which was not far from Klowɛki's grove. With his hoe Ajase started hacking the ground thrice, while the hooting went on around him. The assistants and priestesses then followed him. The men made little holes with hoes, the women filled them with seeds. In the end, Ajase made one large round heap of earth, in which many seeds were placed so that they could be replanted later, as I was told. To me it looked as if the heap took the shape of an altar. After we got back into the house, we were all given a little bit of millet to eat. The schnapps bottle went round, and some libations were poured. The priestesses sang *klama* about the millet, that 'if you sow, you will eat'. From this time until the celebration of a ceremony called the *kwoo-dzo-fomi* seven weeks later, no hooting or drumming was allowed at the places of worship.

Three weeks later, again early in the morning, Julie and I headed off for Kodjonya again, where the *ngma tlɛmi* was going to take place. According to Julie, this means 'weeding under and replanting'. When we arrived in Kodjonya, the Klowɛki regent was surprised to see us. He did not mind that I wanted to see what was going to happen again, but according to him it was nothing special. Apart from him, only seven priestesses were present. The Klowɛki regent worked with a pickaxe and women used cutlasses to weed the millet farm and replant some of it. They broke off the tops, so that the plants would grow better. After about ten minutes the Klowɛki regent said I could leave now, because this was all they were going to do. However, I stayed of course, and tried to help

---

[325] Huber thought that the swearing and solemn cursing on the part of the priestly officials and individual worshippers was disappearing, therefore he gave the full samples of the texts recorded when he witnessed the ceremony (Huber 1993: 249-252).

[326] At the *Okumo* priest's shrine the sowing of the millet would take place on Tuesday.

186

weeding with the cutlass. After an hour we were finished. There was an earthen open basin with water where Ajase had made the heap of earth the last time. Everybody washed their hands in it and sprinkled water on the little millet plants for them to grow as a nice little ritual.

The 'welcoming of food': the kw<u>oo</u>-dz<u>o</u>-f<u>o</u>mi ceremony

Less than four weeks later on a Sunday, in the seventh week after the *koda-kpami* celebration, (it was August 23), the *kw<u>oo</u>-dz<u>o</u>-f<u>o</u>mi*, meaning something like 'welcoming of food' ritual (literally: 'to bless and cleanse the throat'), was going to be performed at the shrine of the Likpotsu deity of Djebiam-Agbom sub-division. This is a ceremony of the first fruits, the yams, which are offered to the deity before the priests and people eat them. In the morning and afternoon the preliminary rites of patching and renovating the old sanctuary and preparing the *sibaa*, which is mashed yam mixed with boiled eggs and palm oil, had taken place. The latter is normally the characteristic dish for those gods who have been introduced from the neighbouring Akan, while the 'real' Krobo gods eat *busie* (millet or maize porridge with small portions of meat or fish) (Huber 1993: 261). Although *Likpotsu* is also considered a 'real' Krobo god, he is also offered yam as food, because he is said to have originally been introduced from the Ewe people.

In the evening time I was accompanied by Julie, a male cousin of hers, the priest Gaga and my colleague researcher Veit Arlt. There were many priestesses and priests present. The essential rituals for this ceremony only happen at this particular place. This time the priest Okumo and his spokesman Asa, who presided over the ceremony, were there. The priest for *Likpotsu* who was the officiant of the whole ceremony, together with his chief assistant, sat under the roof of the open sanctuary inside the grove, while Okumo, Asa, Adjime and other guest-priests, assistants and elders sat outside in a semi-circle. The female priests and worshippers sat opposite them. We were late, asked to pay some money, but the main rites had just been performed already. Still Okumo wanted more money, and was the only one who made objections to my filming in the shrine.

Before we came, the *Likpotsu* priest had performed some blessing and purification rites by invoking the gods and washing himself with a purifying ablution. Then the ritual offering of the new yam in the form of *sibaa* followed (Huber 1993: 262-263). After this, everybody moved to the open courtyard near the priest's house. The singing and dancing of *klama* outside the shrine went on beyond midnight, and we sat watching for some hours. The old blind priest Asa was given a privileged place. He sat next to a large, round drinking pot (*takpa*) containing palm wine that stood in the middle of the compound. The small drinking cup, only used by the priests (*lik<u>oko</u>*), went round for them to drink palm wine from. Everybody else also drank from the palm wine and *akpeteshie* and some people became quite drunk by the end of the night.

The *kwoo-dzo-fomi* rites are believed to bring blessings upon the farms, houses and animals and protect against illness when eating of the new crops. After this the seven-week ban on drumming and hooting at birds is lifted again (cf. Huber 1993: 265).

'Eating of the millet': the ngma-yemi rituals of the priests

During a meeting in mid September, all the important priests including Okumo, came together in the Klowɛki grove in Kodjonya to decide upon the date of the *ngma-yemi* celebrations. The date depends on the growth of the millet, but for each sanctuary the celebrations start on the week-day that is sacred to each particular deity, so for Klowɛki people on a Thursday. A group of female priests sat separate from the men. They did not take part in the discussion, and were chatting among themselves. The men decided that their *ngma-yemi* should be celebrated in about five weeks time.

On a Thursday in October, the *ngma-yemi* celebrations at the Klowɛki shrine in Kodjonya were going to take place, as usual. *'Ngma'* is the millet, and *'ye'* means eating. Different priests and priestesses from other clans were coming to these annual celebrations as guests. Outside the house, at the cooking place, the women were busy preparing *kungmi,* a festive food made of millet. When they saw me, they were joking that this time I would certainly dance. Apart from Veit Arlt and me, two other strangers were present. One of them was a Filipino, a Roman Catholic father, the other, a Togolese man, who was still a seminarian. Before they were allowed into the Klowɛki grove, they had to negotiate about the money that had to be paid for schnapps. As obvious Christians, they had to convince the priests that they did not have any bad intentions to enter the shrine. The Roman father told me that he was stationed in a village in Upper-Manya. The Togolese man named Pierre was studying in Tamale, in the Northern Region of Ghana. They were accompanied by a Krobo teacher. The friendly Filipino Roman father explained to me that because he lived and worked in this area he felt that he had to learn about 'the culture of the people' (in chapter eight I will go into the 'inculturation' view of the RC Church).

While we were already inside the grove, Okumo, a person representing the old Asa (he was not able to come due to health problems) and the priest Gaga came back from a sacrifice they made at the hidden shrine in the bush.[327] Before they entered, Okumo objected to the bucket that was used in pouring a libation of water at the entrance, apparently for cleansing. He thought that a tra-

---

[327] See Huber (1993: 255) for a description of this ceremony.

ditional earthen pot should have been used. This time he also had become even more defensive in his reactions to us, the strangers. He and his assistant covered their face and refused to have any pictures taken of them. He reprimanded Gaga and Julie for speaking *blɛfogbi*, a foreign language, i.e. English, because only *Klogbi* (Dangme) should be spoken inside the shrine.

Inside the grove, many libations were poured by the spokespersons of the different priests, amongst others: Asa, Okumo, Klowɛki *seyelo̱*, Nause and Likpotsu. They asked for blessings and peace, and thanked the gods for the food. There was singing of *klama*. Klɛmesi and Ajase offered the first fruits in the form of millet porridge to the gods and ancestors on behalf of the people. After this, they sat at the entrance of the round hut again, ready to receive individual people who brought offerings of schnapps and money, and poured libations for them.[328] Julie expressed her surprise to see some people she recognized from the surrounding area. The school where she teaches was not far away from this place. She did not expect them to be worshippers of the shrine. Nowadays many people try to keep up Christian appearances and avoid open affiliations with the shrines.

We were given a mixture of millet and water to drink and had to smear it in our neck and on our chest for blessings. Later we were also given the *kungmi*, with a sauce that includes okra, fish and palm-oil. Not much happened after this. Julie and I returned in the evening for more celebrations. In Klowɛki *seyelo̱*'s house electricity had been cut off, so that we sat in the light of a few lanterns and oil lamps. A handful of people were present, most of them half asleep. It took another hour, until about ten p.m. before the action started. After a long libation outside the house by Klowɛki *seyelo̱*, one priest started singing *klama*, followed by some of the women. In the meantime, people kept arriving until there were about forty people present. Still hardly anybody stood up to dance, despite encouragement from different sides. According to Julie, the priestesses were reluctant to dance because they might get possessed by the gods. Then suddenly Klowɛki *seyelo̱*'s wife, a priestess, stood up and started running up and down, and dancing at the same time. She was said to be possessed. Even when the music stopped, she kept on dancing. When the singing stopped, she started singing herself. Some people encouraged the drummers to continue, to play for her. After about twenty minutes, her husband told the other women to leave her alone and let her go to sleep. Not long after that, we also went home.

These *ngma-yemi* celebrations were essentially priestly ceremonies. Nevertheless, the activities of the priests were considered to be important for the well-being of the whole community, and the latter were also represented by a number of important elders and individual worshippers. They asked for blessings for all. Parallel to the priestly *ngma-yemi*, the preparations for the public

---

[328] See Huber (1993: 256) for some examples of what was asked and thanked for in the libations.

Ngmayem festival that is celebrated in Manya Krobo at the end of October, were taking place,[329] in which the priests were also going to play their part, sprinkling food and millet for the ancestors. As I mentioned in chapter two, the Yilo Krobo had their annual festival, the *Kloyo-sikplemi*, a few weeks earlier.

The dynamics of Krobo religion

African religion is often regarded as not having any historical development. Critics of African religion therefore have considered it to be a brake on progress, while for the very same reason admirers have praised its contributions to solidarity, stability and community (Ranger 1988: 106). As an analytical category 'African traditional religion' has been very largely the product of Religious Studies, as it developed in African universities during the nationalist periods (Peel 1994; Shaw 1990), and of the "paradigmatic status accorded in religious studies to the Judeo-Christian tradition and of the associated view of 'religion as text'" (Shaw 1990: 339). Peel points out that traditional religion: "as such is the purified version of the missionary category of 'heathenism', constructed as a system of religious alterity to Christianity, a category for which those whose beliefs and rituals comprised it would originally have had no use whatsoever" (1994: 151).[330]

The term 'African traditional religion' remains problematic, even though the advocates of the acceptance of 'African traditional religion' as a mature religion (e.g. Idowu 1973; Mbiti 1969; Olupona 1991b; Parrinder 1976) made a major step forwards in comparison to the (missionary) designations 'primitive religion' or 'paganism'.[331] First of all, the heterogeneity of the African situation implies that the term 'plural religions' should be used instead of one 'African traditional religion'. Secondly, the word 'traditional' suggests a static and unchanging situation and connotes that which is ancient and pure (Ranger 1988; Shaw 1990: 341). The lack of historical data has contributed to this idea. However, African religions have been in constant change, interaction and adaptation, long before the coming of the colonizers. Therefore, as Blakely, Beek and Thompson suggest, 'continuous transformation' may be the best definition of 'tradition' in Africa (1994: 17).

The idea of an 'authentic situation' in pre-colonial times has also enforced the compartmentalised study of 'traditional religion' and African Christianity, in

---

[329] Huber wrote in 1963 that this public *ngmayem* festival had recently been introduced then (Huber 1993: 260), and therefore he does not describe it any further.

[330] Peel specifically studied 'Yoruba traditional religion' as an example of 'African traditional religion'.

[331] Parrinder's study, for example, was first published in 1954, in the era of independence for most African nations when there was a sharp increase in studies giving a positive image to African religions (see Mudimbe 1988). However, his study left little room for differences among African religions and contributed to the view of 'African traditional religion' as homogenous.

which they appear as two distinctive fields (cf. Meyer 1999: xviii). Different studies have shown the danger of a dichotomy of 'traditional religion' versus Christianity, as: "When used in too bipolar a fashion, the categories of traditional and world religion are simplistic and reinforce certain prejudices of the putative rationality of the modern world and the irrational traditionalism of the premodern" (Hefner 1993: 4). This compartmentalisation has rather been a result of the influence of Christianity, and the dualism introduced by the Basel missionaries has endured in the perceptions of religion in Krobo. As we have seen in previous chapters, it were the missionaries of the Basel Mission who defined which practices of the 'pagan' Krobo constituted their 'religion' (cf. Peel 1978: 443). This dualism has continued in everyday discourse and experience, in which Christianity is dominant, especially in the public domain. Nowadays there is a growing consciousness of non-Christians that they have to defend heir position vis-à-vis Christianity. This explains some of the priest Okumo's actions. In his minority position he insists on linguistic purity and the use of 'indigenous' items in ritual. He objects to intruding foreigners in order to retain his identity.

However, the emphasis of many priests on the unavoidability of the call of the gods to defend their position makes clear that pre-Christian presuppositions continue to underlie their concepts of the 'self' and the world, and not only theirs. The dominance of Christianity does not mean that ideas about religion in Krobo society or other African societies are coherent and static, or that they can be classified according to 'Christian' and 'traditional', or 'Western' and 'non-Western'. Christians, who do not all share the same ideas, participate, even if secretly, in rituals such as *dipo* and the communal millet rites, while non-Christians refer to Easter (*Ista*) to determine the time for the rites, or consult pastors when they are experiencing setbacks. As became clear from the description of the realm of the priests, and some of the practices around the annual ritual cycle, Krobo religion shows variability and flexibility, which accounts for its easy integration of foreign influences and elements and room for pluralism, as in the past. On the one hand, the worship of the old *djemawoi* integrates people on various levels, from a local to state level. Even though 'traditional' places of worship and practices have moved to a more hidden sphere, this is partly a continued situation in which secrecy also equates power and priests maintain their position as ritual specialists. On the other hand, individuals are free to consult any deity they deem capable of helping them achieve their ends.

This chapter was mainly about ceremonies that are performed as *kusumi* by ritual specialists for the well-being and benefit of the whole community, in which only a small number of the common people take an active part. However, as priests, family elders or otherwise, these people represent and act on behalf of a larger community. In the next chapter I will turn to life cycle rituals which show that *kusumi* is important in the lives of common people as well. Non-Christian presuppositions that continue to underlie ideas regarding the 'self' and the (unseen) world of individual Krobo, who mostly call themselves Christians (cf. Peel 1994: 162), become prominent during life cycle rituals, such as naming a child, the *dipo* rites and in rituals surrounding death, in which many people take an active part. These rituals are performed to constitute relations that define a person's social identity.

6

"First the custom, then baptise":
Life cycle rituals, Christianity and personhood

In the previous chapter it became clear that *dipo* is part of the ritual calendar, and as such is part of *kusumi* and occupies an important place within 'traditional religion'. Based on observations and estimations, it can also be assumed that a large majority of Krobo people have their daughters pass through the *dipo* rites. Whereas the previous chapter dealt with ritual specialists, this chapter focuses on 'common' people who mostly have Christian affiliations. How is it possible that despite the continued prohibition of *dipo* by the Presbyterian Church and other churches for their members, and despite the complete rejection of 'tradition' and hence of *dipo* by Pentecostals, most people still have *dipo* performed for their daughters? It seemed impossible and inconsequent to the Basel missionaries to be both a Christian and perform 'traditional' ('heathen') rites. A perception of Christians who (secretly) participate in non-Christian rituals as indecisive, insincere or inconsequent is rooted in Western assumptions about the person as a unique, autonomous unit, a separate individual with an inner conscience or 'self' who makes his/her own choices and is responsible for them. These Western cultural notions of the individual are rooted in Christianity (Dumont 1986; Murray 1993). In Christian teaching a person is held responsible for his or her moral actions that are of his or her own making. The Christian self is structured around the central identity of the soul, unique and eternal (Murray 1993: 19).[332]

The aim of this chapter is to grasp Krobo notions of personhood by investigating life cycle rituals. I propose that life cycle rituals constitute and gender a person, and the *dipo* rites partly have to be understood within this context. By taking a closer look at the complexity of Krobo personhood and (female) life cycle rituals, presuppositions about the (invisible) world, notions regarding a person and the importance of belonging become apparent. In this chapter I will deal with the following questions: What comprises the Krobo category of the person? What are the differences between Christian and Krobo conceptualisations of the person? How is a (female) person constituted and gendered during life cycle rituals? How do people deal with the, at times, competing Christian

---

[332] Murray (1993: 19) remarks that the Christian notion of selfhood is however complicated by the concept of conversion, in which understanding the self can be remade, or reborn.

and traditional demands? Do Krobo people themselves experience a situation of conflict? At the end of this chapter, I will examine my findings in the light of current anthropological debates on the self and the person.

Ideas about the self, the person and the (invisible) world

As in other African societies, the self in Krobo society is viewed as being diffusely spread into the non-human world of spirits and ancestors (cf. Piot 1999: 19). There is a general belief that before a person is born in this world, s/he has some kind of spiritual existence in another world. That world is called *huanim*. People do not seem to have a clear idea of what it is, or where it is. 'Stool' and *dipo* priestess Lako Sakite told me that 'everybody comes from somewhere', and that '*Mawu*' (God) has something to do with it. People think that when leaving *huanim*, each individual reveals the destination of his life on earth in his or her 'parting word' (*sɛsɛɛ*) (cf. Huber 1993: 137). Hence *sɛsɛɛ* can be seen as one's destiny. Maa Lako explained to me that my *susuma* (often translated as 'soul', see below) could have come from here, from *Klo*, before it decided to be born in *ablotsi* ('abroad', 'white man's land'). Laughing, but also serious, she hit her legs to illustrate what she was going to say:

> Tell her she [Marijke] should observe her legs. The legs are carved in a way the others [other whites] do not have. (...) We observed her critically before installing her [as a *manyɛ*, see introduction, MS]. Look at her calves. Tomorrow if she does not wear a gown, look at her calves. It's just like someone who has been wearing beads below the knee.[333] (Original in Dangme)

During divination rituals that were part of the preparation for *dipo*, I also encountered the idea that people's souls can come from different places (and decide to be born in a specific place) (for a description, see next chapter). At the same time maa Lako seemed to refer to ideas about reincarnation, by suggesting that I could have been a Krobo in a former life and reincarnated as a white woman.

Traditionally it is believed that each person born in this world has left a spouse in *huanim*, who is accordingly called *ohuanim-yo* (your *huanim* wife), or *ohuanim-huno* (your *huanim* husband), and who is wont to trouble her or his partner in this world (cf. Huber 1993: 137). So the spirits in *huanim* live in female-male-pairs. Another term used for the 'spiritual-spouse' is *gbetsi*.[334] The

---

[333] There is the general belief that beads shape parts of the body. Therefore little girls are given beads to wear below the knee that will give the calves the desired shape. For Krobo a person's calves are a central focus of personal physical beauty.

[334] The term *gbetsi* is most probably derived from the similar Ewe term. In Ewe, however, the meaning is slightly different and is used to designate the 'parting word' or 'destiny', similar to what Krobo call

gbetsi has to be asked for permission to leave the spiritual world. If this does not happen or one's spiritual spouse is neglected in this world, he or she (your *gbetsi*) can harm you or persecute you here. If this is the case, a diviner can advise you to have a special shrine, consisting of a pot with some cowry shells and white clay, dedicated to your *gbetsi*. Huber (1993: 139) insisted that not everybody possesses such a shrine. The only people I knew who had one were priests and traditional healers. Lako Sakite told me she keeps hers in a corner of her bedroom. People behaved rather secretive about it, as they often did about non-Christian 'fetish' objects. Nobody let me see it. *Dipo* priestess Tɛko-*yumu* told me that every Tuesday before the annual *ngma-yemi* festival of her deity Klowɛki, she celebrates her *gbetsi*'s anniversary by slaughtering a fowl. She uses the fowl to prepare soup for her *gbetsi* and prepares millet into a traditional (Ewe) dish called *akple*, and she gives it to people around her to eat.[335]

Where the *gbetsi* is believed to be an outside agent and the one that may cause bad luck, another spiritual entity, that of the *kla* (also *klawa*), is believed to be intimately connected with one's self, and at the same time is seen as one's protector. However, the significance of the *kla* is somewhat obscure.[336] The *kla* bears one's birthday name and, unlike the *gbetsi*, is regarded more often as having the same sex as the person to whom it is attached. Tɛko-*yumu* talked about her *kla* as 'the *kla* I came with [the day I was born]'. It is said that everybody born on the same day, has the same *kla*. Next to a shrine for her *gbetsi*, Tɛko-*yumu* also has one for her *kla*, and every Thursday after her *gbetsi*'s anniversary, she honours it the same way as the *gbetsi*. The *kla* shrine (*kla tsimi*) consists of a small bowl-shaped calabash. While Huber thinks not everybody possesses such a shrine (based upon his research in the 1950s), Field claimed (in the 1940s), writing about the Dangme people in general, that every adult had one, which was stored in the rafters of the house, so that it could not be harmed (Field n.d.: 20). Apparently the *kla* can also make demands. When I asked Tɛko-*yumu* why her *la* consisted of two blue beads (*koli*) around her wrist instead of one, she explained to me that her *kla* demanded her to wear a second one next to the one she wore for Klowɛki. The *kla* said that if she was serving somebody, she also

---

sɛsɛɛ (Huber 1993: 137). Meyer (1999: 63) also describes *gbetsi* as someone's fate or destiny, but at the same time as the personification of it; the *gbetsi* could be sent after somebody to bring him or her back to the 'land of spirits'. Abedi-Boafo translates *gbetsi* as 'ill-fate, misfortune'(1978: 48).

[335] Nana Klowɛki is sometimes said to originate from Ewe land. Huber (1993: 139) says that the Ewe in various ways "must be regarded as the teachers of many ritual observances of the various Adangme groups", and that among them "very similar beliefs are found".

[336] The word *kla* probably is derived from the Akan word *k'ra*, but like the Ewe *gbetsi* the Akan term semantically comes close to the Krobo word *sɛsɛɛ* ('parting word' or 'destiny') (Huber 1993: 138). In Ga the *kla* is likewise said to correspond to a person's destiny and originate from creation (Senah 1997: 131). However, as in Krobo, the *kla* in Ewe was also believed to determine a person's character. It was introduced on a person's birthday and saw to his or her well-being (Meyer 1999: 64).

had to serve her. Both the *gbetsi* and the *kla* shrine are broken on one's grave at death (Huber 1993: 139).[337]

To Huber the *kla* was defined as 'the soul you come with on the day you are born', whereby he translated the word 'soul' from the vernacular *susuma*.[338] Tɛko-*yumu* also talked about her *kla* in a manner suggesting that she was born with it, but she did not use the word *susuma*. There is no adequate English translation for the word *kla* itself (cf. Meyer 1999: 64), and I doubt whether *susuma* can be properly translated as 'soul' in Judeao-Christian terms. *Susuma* is a crucial factor in one's personal identity. The word *susuma* was often used in relation with the divination during *dipo*. Like the *kla*, it is connected with one's self, and even more with one's personality. During the divination for *dipo* girls, the *susuma* makes demands similar to those of the *gbetsi* or the *kla*, as I will describe in the next chapter. According to Field, the Ga and Dangme believed that the *kla* was that part of the human makeup which departs at death and becomes a ghost. The *susuma*, however, could leave the body without causing death (Field n.d.: 20). It is believed that it can leave persons and wander about when they are asleep, and at death it leaves them for good (cf. Huber 1993: 138). It is not clear where the *susuma* goes to. However, part of the human personality is believed to survive after death. What is thought to persist is commonly called *kpade*, which means a ghost or 'dead spirit'. The dead spirits are said to live in the world of death (*gbeje*) (so not in *huanim*). This world is thought to consist of ancestral communities, similar to earthly kinship groups, and their occupations and social status are said to be the same as they held in this world (Huber 1993: 220). Hence *gbeje* in many ways is a mirror image of the known world. Some believe that the world of the ancestors can be found in the eastern direction of Sameh, the (mythical) place where the first Dangme once migrated from, and therefore a Krobo person's coffin is buried facing in the direction of the east. Others maintain that it must be somewhere on or beyond the ocean (Huber 1993: 221).

For other Dangme groups Field described that a man's *kla*-doll was set up beside his body as he lied in state before burial. After death the *kla* departed from the doll and the doll became an ordinary doll (Field n.d.). One time I noticed a wooden doll at a sub-chief's (*asafoatsɛ*) funeral in Odumase, but this doll rather resembled the dead man himself and not his spiritual wife. My compan-

---

[337] Field clarified the concept of *kla* by stating that incubating eggs were thought of as possessing *kla*. Also, witches could destroy a person's health and finally take his or her life by eating away the person's *kla*: "In this connection the *kla* is thought of as an invisible double with limbs, for if the *kla*'s arm or leg is attacked or eaten, the corresponding bodily limb of the patient becomes diseased or paralysed. Sometimes a witch will achieve longevity by reinforcing her own *kla* with a stolen *kla* of a victim who dies prematurely" (Field n.d.: 20).

[338] The word *susuma* is often translated as 'soul', and could also be referred to as 'personality'. It seems etymologically connected with the Akan word *sunsum* (spirit) (but does not mean the same thing). Senah (1997: 131) refers to it (in Ga language) as a spiritual element on which a person's individuality depends.

ion, however, explained to me that it represented the man's *kla* as he was a chief. This seems to be an Akan influence and particular for chieftaincy rituals. Nowadays the term *kla* is also used for the boy that represents the *kono*'s *kla*. During the annual *Ngmayem* festival he sits in front of the *kono* when they are carried together in the latter's palanquin. To be the *kono*'s *kla* is an honorary and hereditary function. The boy in question has to be ritually clean, and therefore preferably a virgin.[339]

Nowadays rituals are still observed to assure a peaceful transition of the dead person's soul to the other world. When one elderly woman I knew had died, I was told something strange had happened to the body. As soon as the body had come out of the morgue, it started to decompose. The dead woman's relatives came to maa Lako to ask her for advice. She told them that they should reassure the body (i.e. the 'soul'), and tell her that they would wash and dress her well. It turned out that the young man whose assignment it was to cut the dead woman's nails and hair (the dead person's hairs and nails are kept in her family house) had a grudge against her, which was seen as the cause for the decomposing. So the *kla* had to be reassured before it could leave peacefully.

In sum, the different terms such as *sɛsɛ*, *susuma*, *gbetsi*, and *kla* are partly exchangeable, are difficult to translate and have different origins. As I already established in the previous chapter, this should not be taken as a sign of inconsistency, but rather shows the hybrid and dynamic character of Krobo 'religious beliefs', which are the product of both local and trans-local forces. The conceptualisations are different parts of a person's self and personality in this and the other world. Especially the concepts of *sɛsɛ* and *susuma* can be regarded as that part of each person that is a unique and exclusive element of his or her personality. There is no fixed system of representations and practices to be shared by everyone. Different ideas and terminology mostly point to the dynamic, changing and flexible character of Krobo ideas about the self and relations with 'the unseen world'. Nowadays, mostly ritual specialists still look after their soul's or spiritual husband's or wife's shrine on a daily or very regular basis. For ordinary people beliefs about the invisible world emerge in particular during crises and life cycle rituals, as in rituals surrounding death, but also during *dipo* as will become clear.

Christian notions of the person

As I mentioned in the introduction of this chapter, a Western perception of the person as a unique, autonomous unit, a separate individual with an inner con-

---

[339] At the time of my research the boy was Kofi Adjoka, who took over this function from his grandfather. In 2002 his little brother Kweku took over. I happened to live in the same house with them in Odumase during my fieldwork. 'My' family is closely related to the 'royal family' in Odumase.

science or 'self' who makes his/her own choices and is responsible for them, is structured in Christian teaching around the central identity of the soul, which is unique and eternal. In this way Christianity makes a distinction between the body and the soul, whereby the soul has everlasting life.

Presbyterian Christianity believes that God communicates directly with the individual person, who may in turn communicate directly with God. So God is the sole force to know the inner thoughts and wishes of the individual and may reciprocate in ways known only to him or her. According to the church, a person is responsible for his or her own moral actions, and therefore for his or her own worldly success "provided that [s/]he can keep a proper relationship with God and not allow it to be destroyed by actions that lead to sin or moral separation" (Middleton 1983: 11). The Basel missionaries stressed that it was a person's own choice whether to end up in heaven or hell after death. So there was no predetermined character defining a person's course of life in the Christian concept of the individual person as in the Krobo notion of the sɛsɛɛ. One effect of the missionaries' teachings has been that the religious importance of the local group was reduced in favour of that of the individual, as Middleton (ibid.) argues in the case of Akuropon town. Furthermore, the focus of Presbyterian Christianity is on the nuclear family and individualisation, while traditionally the primary unit of social organisation and identity in Krobo society is the patrilineal extended family.

Besides a similar focus on the nuclear family, Pentecostal Christianity even propagates a total severance from blood links (Meyer 1999: 208). While, ideally speaking, a Christian in Presbyterian Christianity is a self-conscious individual who devotes her- or himself to God, in Pentecostalism it is possible to experience being possessed by evil forces and at the same time being delivered from them through the Holy Spirit. So interestingly a person can be, as is possible in traditional conceptualisation, conceptualised as being overwhelmed by an external force, and as being open and susceptible to forces from outside. Taking this as a point of departure, Meyer argues that: "Pentecostalism, often suspected of promoting Westernisation, does not however promote a Western concept which teaches people to understand spirits as aspects of themselves. Pentecostals regard not only evil spirits, but also the divine, as the presence of an Other" (Meyer 1999: 211). This point is important in understanding why Pentecostalism is so attractive to many people in Ghana, and, as I will discuss later on in this chapter, to understand how it is possible that, despite the complete rejection of *dipo* by Pentecostal Christians, most of them still have the rites performed for their daughters.

Introduction and incorporation into the physical world

Outdooring the child (bi-kpo-jemi)

Until the eighth day after its birth, a newborn baby is regarded as a stranger, not a human being, on this earth. If it dies before that no funeral rites will be performed.[340] The baby first has to be ritually introduced to the physical world. As one man put it: "We make it known to the child that he has come to live among human beings." It will simultaneously be incorporated into its paternal kin group and also be socially accepted by its maternal relatives. Throughout (Southern) Ghana, the ritual through which a new-born child enters society and becomes a person among persons, is called 'outdooring' in English. But the content of the ceremony differs. The subsequent namegiving and the tying of the *la* string by the Krobo is often done on the same day, but is sometimes performed at a later date, usually a Sunday, when more relatives, at least the baby's father or grandfather, are able to be present, and offer the mother gifts. The following description is based on a total of six outdooring/naming ceremonies I witnessed. The exact order of the rituals may differ at different places, but they basically follow a similar pattern.

As I already mentioned, the outdooring is performed on the eighth day after the birth of a child in its family house, the house of its patrilineage. Not many people need to be present. At dawn, around 4.30 am, preferably the (grand)father of the baby, throws water on the roof from a calabash. An old lady holds the baby under the drops that fall off the roof. I was told that this is to tell the baby that once you have come to this world, you will experience rain. Huber thought that this ritual was only still performed occasionally at the time of his research in the 1950s (Huber 1993: 146), but to my knowledge it is still common. Then the same old lady of the house, or preferably a 'Dede', a first-born girl, who often is a ritual expert, carries the child on her back to the road or path outside the compound and crosses the road thrice with it (*blọmi pomi*). Maa Lako softly spoke the following words when I watched her doing this for a baby girl from her house in October 1998:

> A new-born person will certainly walk and so we take you across the road, so that when you go out to farm you come, when you go out to hunt you return, when you go out in peace you should return in peace. When they ask about you, the people should be told you are alive. When you walk, your posterior should be protected [i.e. so that

---

[340] Death in pregnancy or childbirth is believed to be abominable. In such a case a priest who specialises in cleansing rites like the priest Asa, must be called to perform the necessary burial and purification ceremonies. The corpse is not laid in state and used to be buried 'in the bush'. The death is thought to have been caused by an evil spirit or force. The ghost of the deceased may not be able to join the ancestors and roam about as a bad spirit, because the person has been prevented from living a full life and therefore becomes dangerous (Huber 1993: 220).

you can't be attacked from behind, you should be safeguarded, MS]. Grow up to fetch water, to go for firewood, to learn to sweep, to cook, you should grow and go to the market and come to cook so that we eat. When a person is born these are the things (s)he does. We beg that your posterior be entirely sealed (so that you can't be attacked). (Original in Dangme)

People explained that 'this is custom' [kusumi], and that a person can only become a human being and a family member after outdooring. You are shown that as a human you will walk.

After the rituals the old lady bathed the naked little baby girl. While she gently splashed water on her, she talked to her to inform and advise her by saying:

> What we have done/performed [is to show you this:], if you go to the farm; return. If you go out hunting; return. May your posterior be sealed, your way forward be opened wide. You say 'father' before you call 'mother'. You call your mother Maayo, you may call her 'maa'. 'Father', 'mother', 'father', 'mother' that is what we say. Grow up to come and fetch water. Women bathe (regularly). You should bathe and apply (traditional) cosmetics (mɛnɛ). [She repeated 3x:] Your eyes be clear (to discern the genuine from the spurious). Born in the Nam clan you can't be silly or stupid. Nam people are never foolish. If they tell you something that you consider foolish, speak wisdom to them. If a person doesn't tell you anything, don't tell him/her anything (only speak when it becomes necessary). (Ibid.)

With these and other words, maa Lako showed the baby what people do in this world and who she is. She told her that she has a father and a mother and how to address them. By telling that you say 'father' before you say 'mother', she referred to the social importance of the father for his children and of the patrilineal family. She also informed her that she is part of her patriclan, the (Djebiam-)Nam clan. She told the baby that as a woman she should fetch water, and take care of her body. There seems to be no special preference for a male or a female child. One special name that can be given to a girl even means: 'a woman is never surplus' (Yo-trowe) (Huber 1993: 150). For this particular baby the namegiving was done at a later date.

Namegiving

At the namegiving ceremony not only the baby, but also the baby's mother is the centre of attention. She is dressed in white and blue to match the white beads she wears for everyone to know that she has just given birth. This is common for nursing mothers all over Southern Ghana. The white colour symbolises victory in childbirth, success and happiness (Kumekpor, Bredwa-Mensah, & Van Landewijk 1995: 20). The namegiving usually takes place after the outdooring that was performed earlier in the morning. It is often held on a Sunday morning, usually between six and nine a.m., so before church time, in order to give all relatives, friends and neighbours the opportunity to attend. In particular the father of the child, that is to say, if he has performed the marriage rites for the mother, has to be there. If not, and the baby is a *yo-bi*, the baby's maternal grandfather has to be present. The ceremony starts with a libation, but very often also a Christian prayer. Some people claim they only do it in 'the Christian way', so without any libations, but usually it is a combination of both. At the namegiving of one baby boy, I recorded the following prayer. It shows an interesting incorporation of 'traditional' elements into Christian prayer when it is said that God received His name on the eighth day:

> Heavenly father (*Mawu*), we thank you for the care throughout the weeks, and for assembling us here this morning. We give you our heart-felt thanks. Amen.
> We are here this morning by Your grace; you said we should go to the four corners of the world and reproduce and be plenty like the sand on the beach. It is because of this saying we are here. Amen.
> By Your grace, you have given us a son through our brother Tɛɛ and the wife, and on this day, as you, Christ, were given a name on the eighth day, we are also here to name the baby in Your name. We are here to ask Your blessing for the boy. Father we again say thank you. Amen.
> We commit today's celebrating into Your hands, being the head of the seat and also the chairman. You have knowledge and wisdom. Everything we do here must resemble You Christ and be blessings to us. Amen.
> We know you are keeping everything in control and Satan (*abosiam*) has no way here. Let the naming ceremony be peaceful. The boy should grow and become somebody. Be among us from the beginning to the end. Amen. (Original in Dangme).
> [English:] Praise God. Hallelujah.

After this prayer by a pastor, the father of the baby presented its mother with some money, wax print cloth, baby clothes, a bottle of schnapps and the *la* beads. If the father of the baby is absent, the baby's (paternal) grandfather or his representative will be the one who presents this type of gifts. If the baby belongs to his or her mother's patrilineage, its maternal grandfather will be the one to present gifts. The name of the baby was announced. Usually a family name is given, in this case Ossom-*tsɛ* Narh (after its paternal grandmother's grandfather (Ossom),[341] and the fourth boy (Narh)), and a Christian name, in this case the biblical name Seth. The basic rule for namegiving is that the name is determined by the order of birth for both males and females. This indicates that a classification of seniority among siblings according to order of birth is important. An older brother has authority over younger siblings etc. As there will be many people with the same name, sometimes a qualifying adjective is added to distinguish an individual person, for instance Dede-*wayo* (small Dede), Tɛko-*tsu*

---

[341] This is possible in case the father of the baby was a *yo bi*, therefore belonging to his mother's patrilineage because his (grand)mother was not (fully) married.

(reddish Tɛko) or Tetteh-*yumu* (dark Tetteh). The practice of naming babies according to the particular day of the week on which they are born is common among the Krobo, and both a week-day and an order-of-birth name may be given. However, the practice appears to be of Akan origin, as the same names are used as the Akan terms for weekdays, while the Dangme have their own designations for weekdays.[342]

After the presentation of the gifts the baby's uncle poured a libation, which in its turn resembled elements of the Christian prayer:

> Holy Sunday, day of our grandfathers. Lord (*Mawu*) we ask your blessing. We ask you to listen to us. You gave the command that we should go into the world and multiply. Today, my brother Tɛɛ has added another soul to us. He brought him here and all the family members came and named the child Seth Narh. We ask your blessings upon the name and the child. Let him grow and come to attend school and be somebody in future. The ways of the devil (*abosiam*) (should) be sealed and thrown away. (Original in Dangme)

Both prayers asked for protection against the devil who is called *abosiam* in Christian teachings.[343] This particular baby was actually believed to be a 'replacement' for the son who drowned in a well a few years earlier at the age of two, or even the returned son himself. Different people kept on emphasising how much the baby resembled his dead brother. So the parents were particularly happy.

If a baby dies soon after its birth, there has to be a mystical cause, which can be revealed by a diviner (*gbalɔ*). The child's *sɛsɛɛ* may have decreed that he be born into this world and leave it again soon afterwards in order perhaps to be reborn (cf. Huber 1993: 164). Usually if a mother has lost two or more babies before, it is believed that it concerns a child who 'does not want to stay in this world' and therefore it should be prevented from returning to where it came from. This can be done by giving it an 'ugly name', for instance *Odɔkɔ* (slave), or by disfiguring the child's face by cutting three marks on each side of its mouth. I met several adult people with these marks. The aim is to dissuade the child's family in the other world from calling him or her back.

After the prayers and presentation of the gifts by the father, the *la* string and the *kɔli* bead are tied around the baby's right wrist by an elderly woman,[344]

---

[342] There are other specific names that, for instance, mark a special event on the day of the child's birth. For twins the rules are special. All the sub-groups (*wɛtso*) and clans (*kasi*) also have their own peculiar names for their first-born sons and daughters. See Huber (1993: 148-151) for more details about the general rules for naming a child in Krobo society.

[343] The Krobo concept of *abosiam* or *abonsam* is a corrupted derivative of a borrowing from the Akan language. According to Meyer (1994), the concept *abonsam* in traditional Akan discourse either refers to a witch or wizard, the bush-monster (*sasabonsam*) or the deities (*abosom*). The concept has been incorporated into Christian terminology, where it is used in reference to the devil or demon.

[344] A baby girl will have the *la* tied to her left wrist.

preferably a first-born-woman of the house, on behalf of the baby's father, its grandfather and grandmother. The *la* consists of a raffia fibre with the white *nyoli* and the black *tovi* bead. In addition, the blue coloured *ko̱li* glass bead is fixed to the child's wrist. These beads, the priestly beads, are seen as a symbol of ancient cultural and ritual tradition, as I described in the previous chapter, and are always worn by traditional priests and priestesses. Some say the black *tovi* bead represents one's *kla*, and the white *nyoli* bead one's *gbetsi* (Huber 1993: 148). This tying of the *la* is therefore considered to be 'fetish' by some Christians. It is accompanied by words such as:

> Your father's beads is what is being tied for you.
> Today we shall give you a name.
> When a person is given birth to, (s)he has to be named.
> Your name is (name)
> If somebody calls you, say *'agoo'*.
> Go with victory and come with victory.
> Your heart should be strong.
> If they ask you of your whereabouts, they should say you are there.
> You must respect.
> If you go and you get something without a problem, then bring it.
> (Original in Dangme)

After this, the baby is ritually 'shown water and drink' by first putting a few drops of water and then some schnapps on its lips and in its mouth. Hence the infant is introduced to the two most powerful fluids in the life of a Krobo: water (a 'cool' drink), indispensable for life here on earth, and liquor (a 'hot' drink), necessary for communion with the ancestors (cf. Akyeampong 1996: 33).[345] Now the baby is regarded as a member of the 'house', its lineage, with its own personality and social status. After this ceremony more relatives present gifts of money 'to stamp the name', usually ranging from 1,000 to 4,000 cedis (between less than fifty cents and two USD at the time). Each name and amount is read aloud. Often the ceremony is ended with the singing of some *klama* songs, to which the mother dances and thereupon receives more gifts. In the meantime drinks will be served to the guests, either minerals or beer, whilst the *akpeteshi* (local gin) bottle may also go round. I did not witness any special thanksgiving ceremony a number of weeks after birth which, according to Huber, took place 'in most houses'. At one namegiving ceremony the patrilineal family of the baby was invited for drinks after church by the baby's father's family (who had not (yet) performed the rites for the child's mother) on the same day.

---

[345] The use of water and alcohol in the namegiving ceremony came to be adopted among the Akan and the non-Akan groups of (Southern) Ghana, probably after the 1930s (Akyeampong 1996: 32).

Male circumcision

Little girls are immediately distinguished from little boys after birth. They are given waist beads to wear, and have their ears pierced. For little boys it is very important that they get circumcised. In a myth of origin of *dipo*, which was also told to the Basel missionaries in the 19th century (see chapter three) an analogy is made between male circumcision and *dipo*. Usually the story goes that a man had two wives, of whom one only had sons and the other only had daughters. The one with the daughters was jealous of the gifts the other's sons received after their circumcision. In order to compensate her, the *dipo* custom was instituted as a celebration for her daughters. The mother of girls wanted her children to be treated equally as boys. By introducing *dipo* it is assumed that girls are compensated.

All male Krobo are to be circumcised, usually eight days after birth. According to Odonkor (1971: 54), this used to be the case only for children in the priestly families. For those children of other families it could be done from the second to the sixth year. Circumcision is an old institution that distinguished Dangme people from the Akan-speaking peoples, perceived as distinguishing the ritually 'clean' from the 'unclean'. In Krobo, uncircumcised men are not allowed to enter the sacred grounds of the native Krobo gods, especially the war gods *Nadu* and *Kotoklo* and the principal deity *Nana Klowɛki*. In the past Krobo families would not give their daughter to marry an uncircumcised (i.e. Akan) man. Only banned girls who had become pregnant before *dipo* would marry into Akan families, such as the neighbouring Akuapem. According to Huber: "It is this rule of circumcision that, apart from the difference in language, most distinguishes the various Adangme groups from the neighbouring Akan, and which, in ancient times, was imposed upon any group of people that wanted to join the Krobo on the Mountain" (Huber 1993: 154). As Akan people were considered to be unclean people, some Krobo told me that in the past when for example an Akwamu person came to their store to buy something, they would have to put salt in their mouth for cleansing before they could talk to such an unclean person. Nowadays most Akan people, except for the chiefs and the king (*Asantehene*), are circumcised: "[…] until recently (and to this day in principle) it [circumcision] was considered a deformity which disqualified a man from traditional offices" (Sarpong 1977: 12). Sarpong claims circumcision among the Asante was passed on from the Muslims (ibid.). When I discussed the topic of circumcision both men and women in Ghana in general reacted quite amazed when I told them most Dutch men are not circumcised. Circumcision has become the norm. Men said that they were teased in boarding school for not being circumcised, or they were the ones to tease others. Men and women believe that 'sex is sweeter' when a man is circumcised, and they asked me jokingly which one I thought 'tastes better'.

Despite the great importance attributed to a boy's circumcision, there are no rituals involved. Moreover, it does not need to be done by a Krobo.[346] Seth Narh's father declared that he preferred to have it done in hospital, which he considered to be more hygienic. For my landlord's grandson Kofi it was done in the house. The mother of the baby assured me that the circumciser (*wansam*), in this case a 'Northener' and Muslim named Mohammed, would do a better job than the staff in hospital. In addition, she said that it was much cheaper, with a difference of about 5,000 *cedis* at the time. I felt sorry for the little boy though, who had to endure the circumcision without anaesthetics and was crying for a long time while his great-grandmother tried to soothe him.

Even though the circumcision is accompanied with very little ceremony, and in this respect the distinction with the Akan has almost disappeared, people still realise the importance of circumcision. Without being circumcised, a Krobo boy is not considered a full Krobo, and above all, is ritually unclean. For girls ritual cleanliness is achieved through *dipo*, which will be discussed in the next chapter.

Becoming a woman

Signs of womanhood

In former times, an uninitiated girl could be distinguished from an initiated woman by the way she was dressed. One characteristic element was that she wore her wrapper below her naked breasts, as described by the Basel missionaries. The elder women in the house could tell by watching the development of a girl's breasts that she was coming of age. This would mark her readiness for the initiation rites into womanhood. Elder women whom I spoke specify their age by referring to their breasts, they may say for instance: "I was a little grown, my breasts were just bulging out (when such and so happened)." There are different names for different types of breasts. For instance, small and pointed breasts are called *nyo-tso* ('stick- like breast'), and breasts that are round and big 'like calabashes' are called *kpaku-nyo*. When I asked older women at what age *dipo* was performed for them, they proudly said that they had breasts when it was done for them. Janet Otuwa Opata, my landlord's mother who was over eighty years old,

---

[346] In the past there would be feasting and merry making after the circumcision, staged at the *Nadu* shrine for the Manya Krobo, and the *Kotoklo* shrine for the Yilo Krobo. This would mark the initiation of the circumcised boy into manhood and his capability to go to war in future (cf. Ashie n.d.: 47-48; Teyegaga 1985: 22-23). I have not been able to witness it and I doubt whether this was a general practice. However, apparently the dedication of little boys to the war gods still takes place on a limited scale during their annual ceremonies. One priest from Yilo told me that: "If you belong to a pagan home, you will present your child to Kotoklo. If you don't do this, it will affect you."

told me that at the time of her *dipo* performance, around the mid 1930s, you should be in your teens before *bobum*, the dressing-up, was performed for you, having big breasts. She said that it should not be the "shooting ones", but the breasts should have come out clearly for everyone to see that "these are breasts".

In the past, massaging breasts to delay the onset of puberty was a common practice, which is called *nyo-kpami*. It is not directly related to *dipo* as such, but different people with whom I spoke made this connection, as it was seen as a step on the road to maturity. It was an act that a mother would perform for her daughter, when she thought that the girl was becoming sexually mature too early. Therefore she would massage the breasts of the girl with a stone early in the morning. According to Lako Sakite, 'the lump' could be massaged away in this way. Her daughter Juliana told me that the aunt she grew up with had done it for her "when I was in [elementary school] class 6". It seems this was a kind of an indigenous form of controlling sexuality. Maa Lako explained:

> This happens when the parents want their daughter to grow up before *dipo*: they massage the breast. Those days when they may perform the massage three times before you undergo *dipo*, the initiate becomes pregnant and gives birth soon after *dipo*. She has matured. Today, they don't massage the breasts. Girls are still young and they go through *dipo*. Not long after, they will give birth. One after the other girl gives birth. Then a young woman becomes a grandmother and considers herself grown up. [No], you're young! Girl's breasts begin to develop and we think she's matured. She may be in school, around primary class three, and then she gives birth [disapproving tone of voice]. (...) When the lump has developed in the breast before you massage, it won't break [therefore it should be done in time]. (Original in Dangme)[347]

So the purpose of the *nyo kpami* was to delay the onset of puberty. One informant thought it would also delay the start of the menstrual cycle. Ashie's writings (n.d.: 43-44) confirm that the massaging would be done three times, with an interval of a few years. During this period a girl would be called a *smuggle*, he wrote, probably pidgin English for 'small girl'. When finally the breasts started growing, the girl was considered to have become old enough for *dipo*.

The *dipo* rites do not coincide with the first menstruation, but the menstruation is monitored, as its absence may be an important sign of a pregnancy. A pregnancy was and still is only legitimised when the *dipo* rites have been performed. A few menstrual taboos are still observed in some houses. For instance, my friend Juliana would not eat in her family house for about three days during her period. Menstruating women also should not cook. When a new chief or queen is confined as part of his or her installation, only men or young girls are allowed to cook for them, out of fear for possible contamination with menstrual blood.

---

[347] Interview April 22, 1999.

Until the early twentieth century, uninitiated girls could also be recognised by their hairstyle. The hairstyle of girls in an old Basel Mission photograph was recognised by my informants as *smuggle*, for 'small girls'. The hair would be divided in little buns. They said that after *dipo* was performed a girl would not have this hairstyle again.[348] Another characteristic feature of dress that used to be a sign of maidenhood, and now visibly worn by *dipo* girls as a symbol of femininity and womanhood, is the long, red cotton loincloth (*subue*). After *dipo* and after giving birth, according to Bell (1893: 10), the *subue* would be supplemented by a 'baby-pad' in the past, which is a kind of cushion the women carried around the waist to carry their babies. During *dipo*, the *subue* is worn with the ends hanging down to the floor at the back and front. It is a marker of *dipo* girls. The *subue* is also a standard wedding gift. I was told that in the past all women would use it as underwear. Older women said that it was a pity that many young women do not use it anymore as such. Still women of different ages with whom I discussed the topic told me that they preferred it over modern underwear. They felt that the *subue* is more hygienic and preferable to panties for erotic reasons. One woman called Naki told me for example: "If a man comes in right now, he would love it! That is why men love the Krobo women. If you wear *subue* your private part becomes warm, so that if a man takes you, your vagina titillates. If you don't wear *subue*, your vagina is moist and watery." The *subue* is said to have a ritual cleansing effect as well as a protective effect. People told me that a *subue* can cure the convulsions of babies and ward off evil powers, and that it therefore is often kept with infants, as they are vulnerable to witch attacks. One woman told me: "Whenever a child gets a convulsion, remove the one [*subue*] you are wearing and use it to wipe the child's face, then tie it around its head, and (s)he'll be free of the convulsions immediately." I once witnessed how a woman used her knickers to get her baby's convulsion under control, since she was not wearing the *subue*. This shows it apparently is not so much the *subue* itself, but the contact with female genitals or its secretion that gives it its power.[349]

The *subue* can only be worn together with waist beads to which it is attached. In normal daily life women wear one to three strings of the so-called waist beads under their clothes around their waist, whether they wear a *subue* or not. When I once asked Lako Sakite why women wear waist beads, she exclaimed: "A woman must always put on beads!" What she meant was that a woman without beads is not a real woman. It is an expression of femininity. Therefore beads play a special role during *dipo*. During the outdooring stage they not only express wealth, they also exaggerate the girl's femininity by em-

---

[348] BMA D-30.06.053, 'Mädchenanstalt Odumase'.

[349] The Dangme speaking Prampram priestesses wear the *subue* around the chest and the abdomen as part of their religious dress (Quarcoopome 1991: 64), which also shows it can have mystical power.

phasising her hips. The beads make the girls move in a very graceful and feminine way.

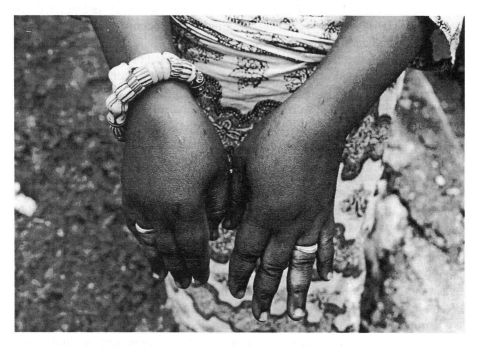

Fig. 6: Awoyaa showing the marks of *dipo* on her hands, Odumase, July 2000.

Until recently, young women would have cicatrisation designs incised after *dipo* to prepare their bodies for adult sexuality and to mark them as Krobo women. Huber wrote that: "There is the conviction, dating from ancient times, that no Krobo girl can ever become a mature Krobo woman and a wife worthy of a Krobo man, unless she can show on her body and on her hand the visible marks of her initiation" (Huber 1993: 165). Today the 'sweeping marks' on the hands (*bɛɛmbo*) as a proof of passing the 'sweeping test' are still given to some girls. With a razor blade small cuts are incised, after which irritants are rubbed inside the wounds to encourage the build-up of scar tissue. Most adult Krobo women can still be recognised by these marks. When I asked different priestesses when they would give the marks to the girls, they, however, indicated that many girls said they would not be able to stand it. It would be too painful for them, and they did not insist on it. Nowadays, the photos made after *dipo* are regarded as sufficient 'proof' and the marks are often considered to be 'primitive' and non-Christian by the girls and their families. Some of the earlier educated and Christian girls already did not receive any cicatrisations in the past. A

208

seventy-two year old woman told me: "They didn't give me the *bɛɛn'bo* at the time I was a schoolgirl [around 1940]. None of the schoolgirls did this." She also said that her *dipo* was done 'secretly'. Most school girls in those days were Presbyterians. And to hide that they had been initiated, they did not receive these marks. I met other old women whose marks had become invisible, because the skin of their hands had become wrinkly.

Apart from the marks on their hands, women used to receive scars around the waist (*aplamdɛ*), and on the belly (*yisi wombo*).[350] According to Tettey (1977: 6), *aplamdɛ* means 'marriage taboo marks', indicating that no man but the husband would be allowed to touch his wife's waist. Ashie (n.d.: 11) calls these marks *adjedu*, and wrote that the belly marks went along with the blessing to 'be fruitful and multiply'. Elderly women I met who were over seventy years old still had these marks, but also a befriended market woman who was in her forties showed the marks on her belly to me. The women, often chuckling, said that only their own husband was allowed to touch them there, so apparently they had an erotic significance. Lako Sakite said it showed a woman's capability of giving birth, another way of linking it with sexuality. Another old woman said that with these marks you can be recognised as a (ritually) cleansed person.

We can learn more about these cicatrisation designs in the past from a number of Basel missionary reports about the confirmation of some early female converts. By coincidence, it was discovered in 1904 that the confirmed girls had their belly and back cicatrised, similar to what used to be done to girls who passed through *dipo*. The missionary Wilhelm Erhardt called it 'an invitation to immorality',[351] as he apparently was aware of the Krobo meaning that they were erotic signs of female sexuality. As they were applied after *dipo*, they proved the readiness of girls for sexual relationships. Cicatrising was immediately forbidden after this discovery. To mission worker W. A. Quartey they were:

> Signs of concubinage, having some obscure songs in connection; and are generally cut on the chest, belly and back of the waist. To be able to show them as often as possible, a girl must abruptly uncover herself now and then with a queer presumption of preparing her clothes, and that in the street, in the house, everywhere.[352]

According to Quartey, with the scars a girl showed her willingness to marry and that she could do 'anything she liked'. He continued: "What the motive is by which our Christian girls are so willing to have these incisions cut on their bodies is a puzzling question." Indeed it is a very intriguing question why the Chris-

---

[350] Elsewhere the marks on the belly are called *fomi bo* (Schroeder & Danquah 2000: 5).
[351] BMA D-1.83 Goldküste Ga 1905, Odumase 124, W. Erhardt, Odumase, 22.01.1905, 'Jahresbericht'.
[352] BMA D-1.83 Goldküste Ga 1905, Odumase 126, W.A. Quartey, Odumase, 27.02.1906, 'Jahresbericht'.

tian girls had their bodies cicatrised. Did these confirmed girls and their families try to integrate some elements of *dipo* into the Christian confirmation, or does it rather prove that *dipo* was performed for them before they went through the confirmation? I think the fact that it was mentioned that this cicatrisation was done by 'pagan women' indicates the latter. In addition, performing *dipo* before Christian rituals has become the norm, as will become clear later on in this chapter.

Ages of dipo girls

One of the most common complaints about *dipo* these days is that people say that girls are initiated too young, which is supposed to have undesired consequences. They are said to enter into sexual relationships at an early age, as this is allowed after *dipo*. It is also felt that this deviates from 'the original practice', and that it was different in former times. However, I found that a majority of the girls passing through the rites was around fourteen years old, which may not be so different from the past. It seems that most girls will have their first period around this age. Only 27 out of 110 girls (24,5%) I interviewed at the time of their initiation in 1999, was below eight years, while 60 out of these 110 girls (55%) were twelve years and older.[353] Of those young candidates below the age of eight, the most extreme case I encountered involved two initiands whose mother said they were one year and four months old. They were a pair of twins, a boy and a girl. Only one girl said that she was seven years old, which was an exception, because it is a socially desirable answer to state that you are eight years or older, as I will explain.

Different people told me that they considered an age of eight years and older an acceptable age for initiation, and pleaded for an age limit of eight years old and higher.[354] It seems that from eight years onwards girls are considered to mature: they may start to menstruate and become sexually active, and comprehend what is happening. At the same time they therefore also enter 'the danger zone'. Hence Huber's explanation that girls were initiated below the age of eight because their parents were afraid of a pregnancy before the rites, (and the consequent punishment of expulsion) seems plausible (Huber 1993: 166). The parents want to be on the safe side. However, Huber does not clarify why there would

---

[353] I asked the age of 110 *dipo* candidates at the houses of seven different *dipo* priests. This age may not always be correct. In some cases it can be assumed that the girls did not know their exact age, as many people in Ghana do not know the precise date of birth. The largest number of girls (15) was found in the category of fourteen years old, eleven girls were fifteen and twelve girls said to be sixteen.

[354] In a public speech, the new *konọ* of Manya Krobo, however, called for a restriction of the ages of girls going through *dipo* to fifteen years and higher (Doku 2000; GNA 2000).

be a greater fear for a possible pregnancy at the time of his research than before. Paramount queen mother of Yilo Krobo, *manyε* Nana Korlekwor Adjado III, was one of those people who pleaded for girls to be initiated at the age of eight and higher. In an interview I had with her in July 2000, she explained that she had investigated the *dipo* rites in 1999. She established that there was dissatisfaction among her people about the young ages of many *dipo* initiates. She then proposed to the Traditional Council and later in a meeting with traditional priestesses to set an age limit for *dipo* with a minimum age of eight. In another interview I had with the old *wonọ* Asa in July 1994, he suggested the same. However, the supposed change in age for *dipo* initiands is not a recent change. Remarkably, the same minimum age was even mentioned already about 125 years ago, when missionary Weiss noticed in 1877 that not only mature girls went on Krobo Mountain, "but also girls of six or seven years old".[355] This mainly seems to have been a result of the increasing impact of missionary and colonial influence (see chapter three and four). Interestingly, Huber (1993: 166), based on his research in the 1950s, considers the same age of 'seven or even less' to be deviating from 'the original practice'.

The fact that the ages of initiands are felt to be younger now than used to be the case is a matter of perception. A girl of fourteen may have appeared to be more mature in the past than today. In the past girls hardly attended school. As I explained earlier, when a girl's breasts began to grow she was considered to be maturing. After *dipo*, which was (and is) the main precondition for socially accepted pregnancy, girls were encouraged to have children early and even outside of legal marriage. At the same time, girls probably used to marry at a young age. The ideal was to marry right after *dipo*. Janet Opata, for example, remembered one woman who had passed through *dipo* together with her (back in the 1930s). She was very lucky, she said, because she married immediately after the rites. She was "still in her (*dipo*) beads", when her future husband came "to perform the (wedding) rites". However, now that more girls attend school, the time gap between the onset of puberty and marriage has widened, as Oppong (1974: 4) already pointed out in 1974, while girls still often conceive early. 'Teenage pregnancy' is experienced as a dilemma now, partly in relation to the high number of female school dropouts, as pregnant girls are not allowed to attend school, partly because the hegemonic Christian morale places sexuality within marriage.

The reasons why girls pass through the rites at a younger age than deemed desirable, are mostly of an economic nature and have to do with convenience. When investigating these 110 initiands, only one girl of four years old was said to have come to *dọm* without any older siblings or relatives to participate in *dipo*. I found that all other very young candidates had come along with one of

---

[355] BMA D-1.29, Weiss, 18.2.1878, Odumase, 'Jahresbericht der Mädchenanstalt pro 1877 (als Beibericht zum Jahresbericht der Station Odumase)'.

their older sisters or cousins because it was time for the latter to be initiated. The younger ones had been added out of convenience. It is relatively cheaper to initiate young girls and to initiate different girls together in one group (see next chapter).

Another important reason for parents to have their daughters initiated at a young age is the influence of Christianity. Huber does not say much about this subject. He only adds in a footnote that, apart from his already mentioned anxiety over a possible pregnancy before the rites, another reason for the young age of some *dipo* girls is that churches forbid *dipo* for their baptised members. Therefore parents let their daughters pass through *dipo* before baptism (Huber 1993: 166), as I will discuss in the next section. This reason especially applies to the members of former mission churches and in particular to the Presbyterian church, as it inherited this cultural policy from the Basel missionaries. Paradoxically, the same Christians who often complain about the young ages of the girls going through *dipo*, and regard it as proof that it is an 'outmoded custom', because they do not think that they learn much from it at such a young age, are therefore the ones who let their daughters be initiated at a young age.

One may indeed wonder why it remains important that girls are initiated, even at the age of two, although many people think that the rites 'loose their function' in this way or have no purpose, while they should mark the transition to womanhood. As the previous chapter already showed, the reason is that *dipo* has a wider meaning. This will become clearer in the next chapter where I will discuss the rituals in detail.

Apart from influencing the ages of *dipo* girls, it may be partly due to Christianity that a number of rituals referring overtly to sexuality have disappeared from the ceremony. I was told that a ritual called *yo-sami* is sometimes still performed during the time of confinement. I have not witnessed it, but some people with whom I discussed this thought that the function of *yo-sami* was to teach girls about sex (also see chapter four). One male priest also told me it was a 'women's affair', so he did not really have a clue about what went on. Huber described this ritual as follows:

> While the girls lie in the *dipo*-room, a young man of their kin group is, like the candidates, anointed and dressed in a white loin-cloth, beads and a hair-dress of silk. Like them he has to stand on the antelope skin, while the women sing and dance around him. They mark him with white clay and place a little piece of wood into his mouth which should remind him to perform the ceremony with dignity and in strict silence. With a long walking staff in his hand and accompanied by the women, he solemnly and slowly marches over the place towards the room of the initiates. (...) One of the principal old ladies leads him into the room. In some places it is customary that a libation is poured first and the gods invoked to bless the girls with fertility. Without being seen by them, the young man is then three times seated upon each girl's buttocks, where he remains for some moments. The old lady, simultaneously with this performance, may repeat the following words: *Munɛ no wa ngɛ mo nyumu se blo hãhe-oo, nɛ*

otso bimɛ fuu! (from today the way to men is free to you. May you bear many children!). The whole ceremony is discretely performed and has nothing to do with deflowering. It signifies that through their initiation the girls have become mature and that henceforth, i.e. after the closing rites, they may begin sexual relationships with a man, and that consequently they may have conceptions without incurring ritual contamination (1993: 181-182).

Lako Sakite described the rite in a similar way to me. She stressed that the boy would be dressed gorgeously and only old ladies would be present to perform the rite. She called it (freely translated) a 'mock sexual act', which was both a playful way of teaching and a source for entertainment. During the rite one of the *klama* songs, which is usually also sang after the final rites, could be sung. The lyrics of one of the songs was: 'My father nursed and guarded me to this matured age and so I look plump and attractive' (*Tsɛ pua mi tsotso, tsɛ wo he nu*). She said the boy would be called 'husband of *dipo*yi' (*dipoyi a huno*). Maa Lako said that the reason it is not performed everywhere these days is that it is very hard to find "somebody's child" to perform a non-Christian ritual. Where girls are not confined, this rite will always be omitted.

Competing demands: Christian ceremonies

After her initiation, a girl may go through some Christian ceremonies. These may not be considered as life cycle rituals as such. But as many people aspire to be baptised, and this will usually be done *after* the *dipo* ceremony, I need to go into the practice. Moreover, the Basel missionaries have tried to substitute *dipo* by the Christian confirmation from the very beginning, while the Pentecostals claim that (adult) baptism is the only ritual that is necessary. The descriptions shed further light on how people deal with apparently competing demands.

Christian churches do not acknowledge that traditional rituals make a Krobo child into a person. They consider them to be pagan or even of the devil. The Presbyterian Church sees the rites of baptism and confirmation as the proper substitutes for outdooring a child and for *dipo* rites. The late Presbyterian reverend Teyegaga stated that the social aspects of *dipo* have been replaced by Christian schools, and that the moral and religious aspects have been "enshrined in baptism and confirmation of Christian symbolism" (Teyegaga 1985: 65). In practice, however, most people have been 'outdoored' as well as baptised, and most women have passed through *dipo* and also have been baptised or confirmed in church.

Nowadays, there are only a few Christians who fully reject *dipo*. A small number of descendents of the first Basel Mission converts, who have their family house in what was once part of Salem or *Lebo* in Odumase, (a Christian quarter set up by the Basel Mission as a safe haven for Christian converts who were rejected by their families), still do not perform *dipo* in these family houses.

These few families are usually still active and proud members of what is now the Presbyterian Church. They are part of the old local elite. As described in chapter three, girls who became pregnant before *dipo* and were therefore banned from their old family house and became social outcasts, often settled or married into Christian families in these Salems at the time of the Basel Mission. At present, it is still a solution for a girl who becomes pregnant before *dipo* to become a Christian.[356] *Wono* Tetteh Gaga told me that: "People have been announcing in churches that banished girls can come to their churches, they can stay in town, but not in the family house." Traditionally such a girl would be punished and ritually expelled. I have not heard of any recent ritual expulsions. Huber described that he witnessed such a case once in 1956 (Huber 1958: 168).

I will take a closer look at the example of a descendent of an early convert, a woman named Lily Janet Ayerkwor Odzawo, a retired primary school teacher, who was born in Odumase in 1935.[357] Lily Odzawo's family house in *Lebo* was built by her maternal grandmother's father, her great-grandfather named Daniel Batsa Nyako, who had fled from a village near Somanya to *Lebo* in Odumase after converting to Christianity, probably in the 1870s. At that time it was not uncommon for Christian converts to even be declared dead by their 'pagan' family members (see chapter three). He and his Christian wife had six children, of whom only one was a girl, Lily Odzawo's grandmother. Her grandmother's children from a relationship with a non-Christian were *yo bi* ('woman's child', see chapter two), and her mother's children, including herself, are *yo bi* as well, hence all belong to the great-grandfather's house. This is due to the fact that *dipo* was not performed for the women, and the families of the children's fathers did not allow them to become part of their lineages. Lily said: "Because my mother did not perform *dipo*, our father's side [of the family] neglects us. (...) We go there, but we do not do anything together with them (...), things such as funerals and marriages." As Lily Odzawo's father was not able to build his own house and never fully performed the marriage customs, his children remained part of his wife's old family house (of the great-grandfather) in Salem. Lily herself married a Christian Krobo man, a devout Presbyterian, Paul Odzawo, who was able to build his own house in Odumase, meaningfully called 'the House of Joy'. Her sisters however, had children, but they never married and stay at the old family house. Lily has one daughter who was not initiated either, and she married a man from Akropong. Three of her four sons have married, but none with a Krobo. Her in-laws influence her to tell her last unmarried son to marry a Krobo woman. According to Lily, she has never regretted not going

---

[356] According to Ayi, writing in the 1960s: 'This [the settling in the Christian community] is very much so in Krobo but in Shai [Dangme-speaking neighbours] she may leave the town completely and settle somewhere else"(Ayi 1966: 49).

[357] Interview with Lily Odzawo, June 20, 2000, Odumase; Interview of Veit Arlt with Paul Odzawo, November 23, 1998 and of MS with Paul Odzawo, March 3, 1999, Odumase; all in English.

through *dipo*, even though people in town do not regard her and her sisters and daughter as 'pure Krobo'. They see this as the reason why her sisters did not marry and her own children have married 'strangers', i.e. non-Krobo. Her husband made a similar remark and added that sometimes people rebuke them for looking down upon their own customs. However, both say they do not mind this. Lily feels she is 'better off', because all her children have been educated and one of her sons even is a reverend minister. However, rumours in Odumase say that some of her unmarried sisters have secretly had *dipo* performed for their daughters.

The example shows that refraining from *dipo* mainly has consequences for relations with the (extended) family. Descendents from early converts either marry other such descendents, non-Krobo persons or not at all, as they can only stay in the original Christian family houses, or, if they would have money, in a house of their own without other relatives from the extended family. Sometimes uninitiated women have relationships with Krobo men (outside *Lebo*), but hardly ever full marriages (I will return to marriages later in this chapter), which means that their offspring belongs to *their* family house, usually founded by the first male convert. Ironically, this is often the cause of several generations of *yo bi*, (while having children outside of marriage is not condoned by the Presbyterian Church).

Baptism

The majority of people let their daughters pass through the *dipo* rites, but they also want their children to be baptised. They have developed a strategy to 'combine the two', even though churches do not allow *dipo* for their members. People feel that the 'traditional' rites of outdooring a baby and of *dipo* can only be done *before* Christian baptism. I asked the same 110 *dipo* initiands who were mentioned earlier whether they were Christians. Many said they belonged to some church, but those had not been baptised yet. In an interview (in English) with Gilbert Nartey,[358] a 59-year old representative of the Anglican Church, he admitted that the practice for Krobo Christians is to have *dipo* performed before baptism:

> Marijke: "You were talking about the conflicts between the Christian Church and traditionalists. What does your own church think of it?"
> Nartey: "Well as far as our church is concerned over here, we don't take sides. We feel if a child is in school and at least about six years old, the child must be baptised. When the child is baptised, it immediately severs connections with the old tradition and is ushered into Christian tradition, according to Christian principles."

---

[358] Interview July 22, 1994, Odumase.

Marijke: "She severed..., you mean she breaks with the old custom?"

Nartey: "Yes, she breaks with the old custom. Our emphasis is that we've seen the light [of Christianity], therefore if you are ushered into the light there is no need trying to come back to the old system of tradition, so what I mean is there are many innovations in the old traditions."

Marijke: "So, what do you mean, once a child is baptised you don't want her to go through *dipo* anymore?"

Nartey: "That is what is argued a lot over here. That as soon as the child is baptised prior to the *dipo* custom, there is no need to send the child back for this *dipo* custom, because it means from then on the child becomes a new person all together. It does not belong to the old society [anymore], so everything it gains in the new society [of the church] is what the child has to follow. That is the main argument."

Nartey's view is the view of the former mission churches. As Nartey explained, as soon as a child has been baptised, she is seen as 'a new person altogether', so from that time on she should not 'go back' or 'backslide' as the (Basel) missionaries used to call it. This point of view has been repeated in several discussions I have had with Christian representatives of (former mission) churches. It is in line with the strong boundary the missionaries felt should be drawn between 'paganism' as belonging to 'the past', and Christianity as 'the modern'. Once the line has been crossed, one should not 'slide back'. Still the formal point of view of the Presbyterian Church is that people should desist from *dipo* altogether. The Roman Catholic Church, with its headquarters in Agomanya, propagates a more liberal view. People repeatedly told me that Roman Catholics not only condone the performance of *dipo* before baptism, but even encourage it.

In an article in *The Watchman* (1998), the author named Kumah considered the problem of *dipo* and Christianity as an explicit struggle between family obligations and individual choices. According to him, parents of young Krobo girls sometimes make their daughters pass through the *dipo* rites at a young age to make it impossible for them to avoid it. The parents are said to be afraid that the girls might become members of any of the so-called 'young' or charismatic churches and subsequently would make an 'individual choice' and not participate in the rites. I encountered women who conveniently used this viewpoint as an argument to defend their situation. They said that they felt that *dipo* is unchristian and that they did not like it that they had to pass through the rites, but it was not their fault, because the parents had performed it for them when they were very young. Such a woman was Emilia, a presbyter in the Presbyterian Church in Odumase, who said she was five years old at the time of her initiation and could hardly remember any of it. Other women also claimed they could not even recall the event. A Shai woman, when interviewed about *dipo* in the weekly *Mirror*, had the following to say about her age:

I was initiated through the Dipo rites when I was a child, so I did not exactly remember the various processes I went through. Now that I am of age I have read the Bible extensively and realised that my parents were not fair to me. What I see today and the things I hear people say about Dipo increases my fear, and I even regret now that I went through the Dipo rites. Since I realised the practice was heathen, I have been praying to God to forgive me and those who supervised and made me go through the rites (Felicia Maku Tetteh, Trader).[359]

So by blaming the performance of *dipo* on the parents or those who supervised her, this woman was able to pass the responsibility onto someone else, but she still had complied with traditional demands and Christianity at the same time. At a young age she was initiated and became a member of her family, at an older age she chose to become a Christian. Claiming that they do not even remember their *dipo* and that somebody else was responsible allows Christian women to dissociate themselves from *dipo*. However, their own daughters will usually be initiated as well, either by them or by a relative such as an aunt. Paul Odzawo recalled how at one time *dipo* was nearly performed for his only daughter: "One time one of my aunts asked to spend the holidays with my daughter during Easter in April. At first I didn't realize the danger. Normally I never allowed the children to stay with anybody." He accidentally heard that the aunt wanted to perform *dipo* for his daughter: "But I managed to snatch her away. Otherwise she would have undergone the ceremony." His story, however, shows how *dipo* can easily be performed for children of unwilling parents, as they often do not only stay with their parents, and other relatives can take responsibility.

Initiation, often 'secretly', performed before baptism may go back to a tradition started with some of *konọ* Sakite's daughters in the 1880s. The Basel missionaries were hoping that the education of daughters of chiefs would be the right strategy to influence and convert the rest of the population. However, *konọ* Sakite's father, Odonkor Azu, had refused to give out any daughters to the missionaries for education, whereas *konọ* Sakite 'gave' several of his daughters to the mission in the 1880s. One daughter of Sakite was baptised in 1884, but she had already passed through *dipo*. In the following year, another two daughters of Sakite (of different mothers), Makutu, born in 1873, and the younger Maku, were about to be baptised before they had passed through the *dipo* rites. But their mothers protested. The missionary couple Weiss reported that the mother of Maku took her to Krobo Mountain under the pretext that she might be pregnant and had to be tested. The Weisses stated that Maku returned to them "on Sunday afternoon, in sweat and in tears", insinuating that she had refused to pass through the rites. But we are not told how long she had been on the mountain. It is possible and even likely she had passed through *dipo*, maybe in an abridged form. After threatening Sakite with a report to the Governor because of his lingering, the missionaries baptised Maku anyway with the name Eleonora on January 17, 1886. It is not clear whether Makutu was also involved. However,

---

[359] In: 'Forum. Panelists from Dodowa talk on: The Relevance of *Dipo* Today', *The Mirror*, 22.08.1998.

after this she was referred to by the name Juliana, a Christian name, which indicates she was baptised, and the missionaries reported that these two girls were the first of Sakite's daughters who "declared to have forsaken *dipo*" with their baptism.[360] Nonetheless, it is very unlikely that they had 'forsaken *dipo*' or that these girls could decide on their own to 'forsake *dipo*'. First of all, Makutu was only twelve or thirteen years old, and Maku was even younger. It would have been almost impossible for them to disrespect their elders by making their own choices. Secondly, Juliana Makutu would later become the first Krobo (paramount) queen mother in history (probably in the 1930s. She died in 1944). Even though queen motherhood can be called an invented tradition in Krobo, Krobo people assured me during my fieldwork that only a 'real Krobo woman', i.e. an initiated woman from the right descent, can become a queen mother.

The members of the currently popular Pentecostal and/or Charismatic churches are also known as 'born-again' people. Baptism is their most important ritual and they do not know a ceremony such as the confirmation or communion (see next section). This baptism can be performed from about the age of fifteen. It often involves a total immersion in a river or a basin of water, after which the person comes out as a 'new person', as if she or he were 'born again'. It symbolises a 'complete break with the past', which usually includes a severance from the relations with the family. Contact with the ancestors, which in the former mission churches is usually regarded as harmless, is seen as a possible cause of trouble. Ancestors are seen as analogous to the devil. Therefore people need to be delivered from all previous ties with spiritual entities they have come in touch with, for instance during the *dipo* rites. After deliverance from such evil spirits a person can become conscious of her/himself as an individual. The following quote from a 35-year-old representative of the Pentecost Church may provide a typical view of Pentecostal baptism in which the Holy Ghost could descend upon a person after the actual baptism:

> The spirit of God enters the person after baptism. The Holy Spirit will make you a matured Christian. We have something called the Holy Ghost Baptism. (...) Some people get it just after baptism. When they are raised from the water, you see them speaking in tongues. Somebody may speak English who has not been to school. Or somebody may say some certain words, which he himself doesn't understand. (...) Now it is the satanic spirit that is ruling human being. So only if that evil spirit disappears, and the true spirit, that is the Holy Spirit, comes into you, then you can call yourself a Christian or a child of God.[361]

---

[360] BMA D-1, 42 Afrika 1885, Odumase 120, Weiss und Weiss, Februar 1886, Odumase, 'Jahresbericht der Mädchenanstalt'.
[361] Interview in English with Peter Muala, June 30, 1994, Odumase.

In the above-mentioned quote the view is expressed that one can be possessed by an evil spirit, which represents the old customary ways, and then experience deliverance from it through the Holy Spirit. As is the case with evil spirits, the divine is also experienced as the presence of an Other.

Considering the age at which people are being baptised in Pentecostal churches, performing *dipo* at an earlier stage would seem to go together easily with a later baptism. However, these churches reject anything they consider 'traditional', and therefore 'fetish' and 'satanic'. Their formal point of view is that *dipo* should be abolished. Dissociating themselves from anything 'traditional' is an important part of the Christian identity of their members. Hence they will consider *dipo* as part of the baggage of 'the evil spirit', which has to be rejected before one can become a 'true Christian', possessed by the Holy Spirit. In practice, however, this allows them to deal with the spirits 'of the past' from which they are not yet able to detach themselves.

One reason people mention why they do not make a clear choice as a Christian individual, is the fact that they are poor and depend on their relatives in many ways. They need them to help them in performing ceremonies such as funerals and marriages. They claim to have little choice but to abide by the rules of the old (ancestral) family house where they live and therefore cannot withdraw themselves from participating in non-Christian ceremonies. Most people cannot afford to build their own (family) house, where they, ideally speaking, would be free to stick to their own (Christian) rules. (However, their obligations towards the old family house would not automatically disappear). In most family houses the traditional rules that no uninitiated Krobo girl is allowed to sleep, eat and drink in the house, are valid due to fears of pollution, while the extended family usually plays a decisive role in matters such as marriage.

Confirmation

The Basel missionaries have always tried to replace the *dipo* ceremony by the Christian confirmation, in which a convert makes a confession of faith to become a practising member of the church.[362] But they never succeeded. In discussions I had with their successors, the Presbyterians, an analogy was made. People said that, as is the case with *dipo*, girls should only start having children after their confirmation. Representatives of the church felt that the confirmation should replace *dipo*. Others felt that it does not mean the same thing and does not have the same impact, because the confirmation is something which is only celebrated within the church.

---

[362] The Roman Catholic and the Anglican Church do not celebrate a confirmation ceremony with this meaning.

At the end of the 19th century, converted Christian girls of whom the Basel missionaries thought they had forsaken the *dipo* rites appropriated the confirmation in their own way, despite missionary protests. Already before the official abolishment of *dipo* in 1892, Christian girls started to include aspects of *dipo* rites in their confirmation celebrations. It was reported in 1891 that after their confirmation, six girls involved "seemed to think", according to Basel missionary Josenhans, "that dressing up and wearing gold jewellery was part of the whole thing",[363] similar to what was customarily done during the outdooring rites of *dipo*. They also seemed to "imitate the heathen girls", feeling that after their confirmation they were grown ups and free to engage into sexual relationships to which their parents did not object, according to the missionaries.[364]

The Basel missionaries tried to minimize rituals and outward appearances in their ceremonies. They disapproved of excessive jewellery and dressing up during the confirmation, although at the same time they felt that the fact that their Krobo converts seemed to regard confirmation as an equivalent to *dipo* was a good sign and proof of their influence.[365] Even though they wanted *dipo* to be replaced by the confirmation, it was absolutely unthinkable for them that the two would be combined, as was happening now. To the missionaries this was a sign of syncretism. However, some missionary reports show that ten years later, when *dipo* had officially been abolished, confirmation rites had become even more elaborate and more similar to *dipo* rites, or what was called *bobum* at the time. A pastoral epistle from the missionaries dictated that during confirmation it was not allowed to wear 'unworthy' jewellery, which shows that this was still practised. In the same year it was reported that a white sheep was demanded for the confirmation of Christian girls. Friends and family would come and eat for days on end. Other parallels with *dipo* and *bobum* were that the girls would not work for a week and let their mother take care of them. Furthermore, their parents would buy jewellery and clothing for them. The fact that many girls became pregnant one or two years after the confirmation, even if they were not married and therefore subsequently excluded, again shows the similarity to *dipo*.[366] In reality, the confirmed girls usually had *dipo* already secretly performed for them. Only a rather limited number of Christian families living in the Christian quarters of the town, or certain people who were part of the Djebiam-Nam clan from which the Christian paramount chief is chosen since 1892, were known to favour the elaborate confirmation ceremony.

---

[363] BMA D-1.54 Goldküste 1891 Ga, Odumase 169, G. Josenhans, Odumase, 11.03.1892, 'Jahresbericht der Mädchenanstalt'.

[364] BMA D-1.64 Goldküste 1896 Ga, Odumase 162, W.A. Quartey, Odumase, 1896, 'Halbjahresbericht'.

[365] BMA D-1.64 Goldküste 1896 Ga, Odumase 168, M. Brugger, Odumase, 22.01.1897, 'Jahresbericht der Mädchenanstalt'.

[366] BMA D-1.102 Goldküste Berichte 1914, Odumase 10, W. Erhardt, Odumase, 10.02.1915, 'Jahresbericht'.

Members of this 'royal' family, with its strong links with the Basel Mission Church, continued to withhold themselves from the *dipo* practice. According to Obeng-Asamoa (1998: 172), Azzu Mate Kole's household even included a large number of social outcasts, among whom were girls who "did not pass the virginity test of the *dipo* rites". However, other people say that the children of the *konọ*s passed through the rites secretly. The *konọ*'s stool priestess Lako Sakite told me about a secret ritual that was performed for members of the royal family and other Presbyterian families. She implied she had also been involved in performing it, so that may have been since the late 1950s.[367] According to one informant, this secret ceremony was only performed in Odumase because of Odumase people's allegiance with the Presbyterian Church. Juliana called it a ceremony for "those who said they are baptised and they won't like their children to go naked".

Lako Sakite described it the following way. She said that after completing school, the girls concerned would be ready for their confirmation in the Presbyterian Church. Then before the confirmation was to take place, a secret ceremony was performed on the preceding Saturday. Deep in the night, the girls were made to stand on the antelope skin also used in *dipo*,[368] a libation was poured, a goat was slaughtered and the blood made to flow on their feet to purify them. She also claimed that there was a piece of stone from the *tɛgbɛtɛ* brought to the 'stoolroom' in the *konọ* 's palace, which was used in these girls' initiation, as normally 'climbing' the *tɛgbɛtɛ* is regarded as an essential part of *dipo*. The goat meat was cooked and eaten. Then the next day, on Sunday, the parents of the girls invited their relatives. They then presented a white sheep as a symbol of the girl's confirmation and the completion of school, and also to let people know their daughter was ready for marriage now, as in the *bobum* ceremony. They feasted with *kpokpoi* (a festive meal with yam), rice and *fufui*, and invited the whole neighbourhood to come and eat, as also described by the Basel missionaries. The girl was now considered an adult, but the Saturday night ceremony was not made known to anybody. Therefore the Odumase variant of the ceremony caused problems sometimes. In some cases, Odumase girls did not marry Krobo men because they supposedly were not initiated. In other cases, some men divorced their wife because their problems were blamed on the wife not undergoing the proper rites.

---

[367] Although the signs of 'the stool' calling her to take up the role of its priestess had been there since her birth, she only accepted this role after she gave birth to her daughter Juliana in about 1958. She had lived with the father of Juliana in Kumasi. Then she also started to perform the *dipo* rites like her grandmother had done before.

[368] The Roan antelope skin is associated with Nana Klowɛki and held sacred. *Dipo* girls are warned that they will turn crazy when they step on it whilst trying to conceal a possible pregnancy. So it is a kind of test of the girls' integrity.

While the Basel missionaries always complained about girls leaving school after *dipo*, somewhere along the line the trend was reversed. Girls would pass through *dipo* before they were baptised (like Sakite's daughters Makutu and Maku), and also before they went to school. The sisters Sophia Lakwor Akwetey and Lydia Koryo Akwetey, about eighty and sixty years old at the time of the interview I had with them,[369] remembered how *dipo* was performed for them when they were young, maybe seven or eight years old. It was done 'quickly', i.e. in an abridged form, as they were Christians, and immediately afterwards they were sent to school. Sophia's *dipo* must have been at the end of the 1920s, as she was confirmed in the Presbyterian Church in 1937 at a marriageable age. What the old ladies remembered most about their confirmation was that they wore shoes or sandals for the occasion, where they normally would go barefoot.

What is left of the old confirmation ceremony today is that people just buy a container of rice and a tin can of corned beef or tuna to prepare a stew in order to celebrate the event. The young new practising member of the church will take this food to school to hand it out. Perhaps it is partly due to economic reasons that people do not seem to buy a sheep anymore.

Marriage

Dipo is seen as a precondition for sexual relationships and for a successful marriage. *Woyo* Maku told me: "If you go to marry a woman for whom *dipo* is not performed, there will be disorders in your family. You will never prosper and nothing will go well for you." People told me again and again that without *dipo*, a marriage would never be successful. One woman named Comfort explained: 'Then by and by if something happens in the home your husband will say: 'Because my wife didn't perform *dipo* custom, that's why we don't get money, that's why we are having many troubles in our marriage'." One Krobo woman living in Accra said that *dipo* was not performed in her Christian family. During marriage negotiations they would tell the other family about this so that "they should not come back later and complain". When I narrated this to my friend in Odumase to see her reaction, she said: "Complain about what? They know that by all means it will have an effect. Some trouble will come and the marriage will break." I was often told that even non-Krobo men, for instance Ewe men, would find it important that *dipo* was performed for their Krobo wife, because, as *wono* Tetteh Gaga explained to me: "They care because misfortune can easily follow them." So non-Krobo also take the mystical implications of *dipo* seriously.

---

[369] Interview June 20, 2000, Odumase.

Family marriage (wɛku-gba)

In former times, parents would usually choose the particular marriage partner for their children, although this choice was never obligatory. Girls often were betrothed by their father in their youth. The father of the boy approached the parents of a particular girl by bringing her a *subue* "to tie the loin-string for the infant", and a quantity of cowry shells "to buy the waist beads which hold fast the loin string". Such infant engagement had the value of a promise and was by no means regarded as a legal marriage (Huber 1993: 99). Different people told me that 'the Krobo like family marriage', marriage between members of the same 'house', but normally not including first cousins. However, a person is allowed or even sometimes encouraged to marry his or her cross-cousin or even parallel cousin (cf. Huber 1993: 89). In the past, a family marriage had particular advantages with regard to economic life. As Margaret Field wrote in 1941:

> [T]he custom of 'wekugbla' or 'family marriage', strongly developed among the Krobo, is, according to their own assertions, encouraged mainly from prudential motives. By this custom, the marriage of parallel cousins (regarded as incest by most Gold Coast people) is condoned. By such a marriage not only does a man pay less for his wife than if he procured her from strangers, but his obligations to his father-in-law, in the matter of farm labour, are not additional to those due to his father's brothers, and in general the money and effort he expends on his in-laws turn directly to his own advantage (Field 1941a: 15).

Such a family marriage was not only advantageous for the men as Field claimed, but for the women as well. For example, one old woman who had a family marriage and probably married in the 1940s, told me that she liked it, because after the death of her husband nobody could send her away from his house, as it was *her* (grand)father's house too. Apparently women sometimes fear that they will no more be tolerated in the house by their husband's family after their husband's death. Although theoretically there should always be a place for her in her own family house, her return is not always welcomed or may even cause tensions. Both the farmland of this woman's husband and her own farmland at the village were close together, and her children were in the same house with her. Family marriages are also reported for the Dangme neighbours the Shai (Ayi 1966: 32). Therefore, in contrast with many societies with unilineal descent, in Krobo, marriage within the lineage (*wɛku*) is allowed and is, or at least was, even preferred.

Thereby a marriage between two different 'houses' could involve an 'exchange of women', often resulting in a cross-cousin marriage. But when one of the partners is a *yo bi*, a marriage between cross-cousins can mean, like a marriage between parallel-cousins, a marriage within the 'house'.[370] For example, Tetteh Gaga told me his sister was married to his father's sister's son. So they are cross-cousins. But his father's sister was not married, so her son belonged to the same 'house' as Gaga's sister. Their children are again part of the same 'house'. "So", he said, speaking as the head of the 'house', "I cannot send her children out [of the family house, MS]." People often share the same family house through family marriages, as we also saw in the example of the old woman. Family marriages are still frequent, although many young people now prefer to choose their own partner. However, if the family does not approve, they have a problem.

If a Krobo woman marries into her husband's family outside her own 'house', she always remains an integral member of her own 'house'. After she has died, she will be buried by her own patrikin after the funeral has been performed in her own family house, and if she divorces or becomes a widow there is, ideally speaking, always a place for her in her own family house. Therefore, as Senah (1997: 78) also observed for the neighbouring and related Ga people, even in marriage, a person's allegiance to kinship bonds is greater than to conjugal bonds. At the same time, marriage is largely conceived as a family affair or a bond between two kinship groups, rather than between two individual people.

According to Field, whose writings date from the 1930s and early 1940s, almost every 'popular custom' in Krobo was subservient to the passion for farming and land expansion. She wrote that Krobo who had their farms in Akwamu, Kwahu and Akyem Kotoku would still never associate themselves with the people of the places they colonized. They would still eat their own food, speak their own language, bury their dead in the hometowns, return home for all major special occasions, and "a Krobo who marries an Akan becomes an outcast, but this rarely happens" (Field 1941a: 19).[371] Field described a kind of trial marriage as an example of a 'popular custom' that was related to farming. Hereby a man and a woman would live together on his farm for a year or so before they decided to commit themselves to marriage. He would "test her abilities as a hard worker, a thrifty manager and a successful market saleswoman". She was "equally determined not to marry the man if she finds him a bad or lazy farmer" (Field 1941a: 14). She also found a, what she called, *kplangbi*, the child of an unmarried mother (*yo bi*) in almost every household she examined (ibid.).

---

[370] In strictly unilineal societies, a marriage between cross-cousins would mean a marriage between members of different lineages. As your parallel-cousins, your mother's sister's children and your father's brother's children belong to your group, while your cross-cousins, your father's sister's children and your mother's brother's children, belong to different lineages.

[371] In such a case, special purification rites would have to be performed, which nowadays only happen if a Krobo man comes from a 'traditional' house and wants to marry and bring an Akan woman into his family house (also see previous chapter).

Today, there are probably more interethnic marriages than in the past, but still it is the exception rather than the rule. I would say that intermarriage between Krobo and other Dangme and Ga speaking groups, and also Ewe-speaking people, occurs more frequently than between Krobo- and Akan-speaking peoples. Sporadically, Krobo women marry a 'notherner', a Muslim. One such woman who I knew well, had become a Muslim after marriage, but her husband had also performed all the necessary Krobo rituals for her, as they lived in Krobo area. They had performed *dipo* for their daughter, so that she would have no problems to stay in her mother's family house. Women who are married to non-Krobo men who are from homes where initiation rites are not performed, still have the *dipo* rites performed for their daughters. One woman who has children with a Ga man told me that the Ga variant, the *otufo* rites, were performed for her daughters, which are seen as equivalent to the *dipo* rites, and because the children belong to her husband's house, as necessary for them.

In the next section I will first describe the customary marriage ceremonies, then briefly discuss the 'church wedding'. The customary ceremonies are described in much greater detail, because the rituals are more elaborate and a marriage is only considered authorized when these rituals are performed. The description shows how relations between families are established through marriage.

Customary marriage

I attended nine marriage ceremonies between June 1998 and June 1999, both customary and Christian marriages or a combination. In 2000 I also witnessed an Islamic wedding in the *zongo* (Muslim area) of Somanya.[372] Although every ceremony I attended was different, with few alterations in the order and routine of the rites, the general form was much like the description below. Customary marriages do not necessarily take place in hometowns, but usually they do, as the main family house is there. According to Huber's descriptions, the different stages of these marriage rites used to take place on different days (Huber 1993: 99-110). This is no more the case, unless we talk about the initial rites in which the husband introduces himself to his wife's family (see below). Most of the time the main stages are celebrated in the weekend, either on a Saturday or a Sunday. Sometimes the customary marriage ceremony takes place on a Saturday, and the Christian ceremony on the (following) Sunday. Sometimes both take place on the same day, sometimes they are separated in time, and sometimes only the customary marriage ceremony is performed.

---

[372] I will not describe Islamic weddings, here it is sufficient to note that a small part of the population celebrates this type of marriage ceremonies.

The customary marriage ceremony has to be held before the Christian wedding, and consists of several stages. Sometimes when I asked people whether they were married, they would answer: "It is left with some stages", or: "Only the initial rites were performed". They meant that only the 'knocking the door' ritual (*agbosim*) had been performed, and the man had officially introduced himself to the woman's parents in this way by offering them a drink. He therefore expresses his wish to marry their daughter. Usually the drink is accepted and often the woman is either already staying with the man (but now it is made official) or will live together with him from now on. For many people only this first stage has been performed. Ideally, a man has performed the full marriage rites for the mother of his children. That way the children out of the marriage become part of his patrilineage, and are his responsibility, so that he contributes at least financially. However, due to economic circumstances, many people are not completely married, as a full marriage ceremony is expensive, and therefore often postponed until a later date. Families may spend (an equivalent of) a few hundred USD. Many women I met are not (fully) married. They often have children from several different partners. I know a woman who has five children from five different men. Another has children from three men. Others have children from one man only. Many men have different children with different women, but only relatively wealthy men can afford a polygynous household, which is now much less common than in the past.[373] It depends on his personality, status and personal financial circumstances whether a man will contribute sufficiently to the upbringing of his children or not.

A marriage ceremony takes place in the bride's family house. When the groom's people are entering the compound/homestead of the bride, they are welcomed with some *klama* songs. The singing continues until the visitors have been given seats and they get set. The bridegroom's family carries the wedding gifts to the bride's house. It is often an impressive sight to see women in a long line carrying things on their head. After all the groom's family has arrived in the bride's house, they formally greet the bride's family by going round from right to left and shake hands with the seated bride's family. When the groom's family is seated facing the bride's family, the latter get up and come to greet them the same way. The spokesman for the man's family first introduces the groom, his parents, and the other people he came with. The groom is usually dressed in wax print cloth or *kente* cloth, and wears expensive, light coloured glass beads around the neck and wrists. Many of the guests are also dressed in wax print cloth. The ceremony usually starts with a libation by the head of the house (*we ku matsε*) to inform the ancestors, as a rule including the deceased former head

---

[373] With regard to the 1950s Huber (1993: 117) estimated that "somewhat less than 50 % of the married men have made full marriage payments for more than one woman while their first wife is neither divorced nor dead". To have several wives added to a man's prestige, and in case he owned several farms and farm houses, it also facilitated the management of his property (see chapter three).

of the house, that their (grand)daughter is going to marry, and ask for their bless-ings so that she should be fertile. Often the libation is followed by a Christian prayer. The bride will still be inside a room, surrounded by female relatives and friends. They may sing: 'From today onwards, you'll be called a married woman' (*Kε je muε nε kε yaa, a ma tsε mo kε yo hunotsε*). The women are fan-ning her and are loud and boisterous. Some will shout repeatedly for the fun of it: *'So la ti!'*, and then others answer: *'donnooo!'* The bride may smile a bit, but she has to compose herself and remain silent. A schnapps will be presented by the man's family as a 'greeting drink'. A *klama* song that may be sung in the meantime to console a bride whose mother or parents died before her wedding goes as follows:

Kọkọ nọko be nε e be nọko
Kọkọ, there's nobody who doesn't have someone to call his/her relative.[374]

Then the gifts of the man to his wife are presented (*yo-sibim'*, meaning 'asking for the hand of the woman').[375] The man's gifts consist of money repre-senting drinks and a suitcase or trunk that contains other presents, like a head kerchief (*duku*), *subue*, waist beads, jewellery, clothes and wax print cloth.[376] He gives gifts to the woman's parents to show his appreciation that their daughter was nursed and raised by them. The father of the bride customarily receives items such as native sandals (*ablade*) and an umbrella. The mother of the bride is given an amount of money to 'cleanse her back'. As Julie explained to me: 'she needs to be compensated because when the daughter was a baby she uri-nated on her back'. Before the gifts are accepted, a large delegation of the family of the bride goes to consult the proverbial 'old lady'. Some *klama* songs may be sung in the meantime. The first song quoted here is a reminder to the audience to be aware that the waiting moment is a time of anxiety and silent prayer to the gods to blind the bride's family in consultation so that they return with a favour-able verdict. The other two songs are meant to reduce the anxiety of the bride and her family about the outcome of the consult:

---

[374] Paddi Odonkor explained the song to me as follows: This song is sang to console and assure a girl during her wedding or *dipo* ceremony. It is purposely sang for a girl whose mother or both parents died before her wedding or *dipo* ceremony.

[375] Before the *yo sibim'* is performed, a first drink would customarily be sent to the bride's parents the night before 'to bid them a good night's rest' (*sih womi*), and a second one early in the morning 'to awake them' (*sitremi womi*), and a third one 'to wash their face' (*nyami womi*) (cf. Huber 1993: 102).

[376] Many of the wax print cloths have names and meanings. At one marriage ceremony that I attended, a wax print cloth was given to the bride with the name (in Twi) '*abua bi bẹ kawua nẹ efiri wu ntama*'. I was told that this meant: 'if anything bad will happen to you, it will come from your own family'. It meant that there had been a difficulty within the family, and the groom's family's gift was a warning that problems would not necessarily come from them.

1. *A ho a jla ya nɛ wa li he nɛ wa ngɛ lolo.*
The family of the bride have gone to confer and consult. We are not sure about the fate of our mission yet

2. *Ko̱yo ko ye gbeye, no̱nɛ o klo̱ he sui Mau pe mi*
Koryo don't be afraid, those things that keep us anxious are taken care of by God

3. *Ko̱yo ko ye gbeye wa ngɛ o se*
Koryo don't be afraid we'll stand by you[377]

It is customary to additionally request one, two, or even three bottles of 'Holland schnapps', as people call it, when the man's family come back from 'the old lady', under the usually joking pretext of some offence by the groom. One time, for example, I heard that the groom was accused of having kissed the bride before the wedding. However, the outcome is not determined in advance, and sometimes more money is demanded for some serious offence. This is also the time when the whole family is involved, and not just the parents of the bride and groom. Another time I witnessed how the bride's brother claimed very seriously that he was not informed in time about the wedding, and that a certain incident showed that his sister's future husband did not respect him as representing his deceased father. Therefore he wanted a foreign schnapps to be pacified. After serious consultations he was given an amount of money representing the schnapps. When the bride also presented him a gift in return, both were obviously emotional. It seemed to remind them of the absence of their deceased father.

The bride comes out of the room in her first dress to greet the man's family, then she will go back in and change again. First her friends and female relatives may have fun by coming out with a different woman hidden under a piece of cloth pretending it is the bride, or they may claim that the bride is not around. When the bride comes out a second time in another dress, she is seated with her family opposite the man's family. Sometimes she changes a third time. At one place I witnessed how the bride was decorated with *mɛmɛ*, traditional cosmetics.

---

[377] The songs were explained to me by Paddi Odonkor as follows:

Ad 1). During the first stage (*yo-bami*) stage in the marriage ceremony the family of the bride usually goes out to take a final decision on whether to consent to the marriage or not. This can also be done at the pre-*fiaa* ceremony stage. If someone in the course of investigations into the groom's background discovers some social enigma, it could be dealt with or reported here. Then the issue can be discussed and a decision can be made, before the final consent of the family is announced. It is the last review of the credentials of the man. For instance, it could be that the man's relative (brother or uncle) has had an 'affair' with the bride's sister or relative, which may not permit this marriage to hold.

Ad 2). Song to diffuse the anxiety in the bride, the groom and her relatives who fear that the in-laws may come from the consultations with a shocking revelation that may block the marriage.

Ad 3). Song to encourage and assure the bride that even if people should return with an unfavourable tiding 'we are there to plead on your behalf to turn the wheel around'. Sometimes they return to demand rather huge sums of money for minor offences.

Circles were drawn with it on her arms, chest and back. Her backside was made to look big by tying several cloths around her waist. After this, it is the turn of other relatives on the man's side to present gifts, usually donations of money. After that the woman's own family present her with gifts. Gifts to the woman can be a sewing machine, a bible, drinking pots, earthenware dishes, cutlasses and consumables such as shallots. The mother of the bride at the very least presents her with a cooking pot, a dish used to grind pepper in and a ladle. The father of the bride presents her with new clothes or money. Finally, anybody else can come forward and donate an amount. All names with the donated money are written on a paper and read aloud. Every time people call out: 'Mo ni ba ooo!' Literally meaning that more should come, but used as a special word of thanks to show appreciation of a gift. It is important to know, as with any ceremony in Ghana, how much was given by whom, in order to be able to reciprocate at a later time. The whole ceremony of money donations can last about an hour. Sometimes the reading of names can be interrupted by donators giving small speeches peppered with jokes, for example to give the groom advice about women. In between and afterwards the dancing and singing continues. There usually is a lot of *klama* singing, however in Christian, often Pentecostal, homes people also sing Christian songs.

The fiaa ceremony

Of principal importance, at least in Manya Krobo (in Yilo it is not done in all houses (Huber 1993: 103)), is the *fiaa*. This is a ritual in which the bride and groom are not present. It is performed by both families. One woman representing the woman's family, sits inside on a stool on the doorstep of the room. I was told that she should be married as well, as that would invoke blessings. She places her left foot on the doorstep, a first-born woman representing the man's family sits outside facing her, and places her right foot on top of the other woman's foot. They introduce themselves and report the reason for the ceremony.[378]

---

[378] Words like the following will be exchanged by the two women: W(oman's representative): Say it loud: To where (will you take her)? (*Nyɛ de nɛ e he e wa: Kɛ ya jie?*). M(an's side): To (name) (*Kɛ ya* ...). W: But now that you're going (with my daughter) if I call in times of troubles, would you come? (*Nɛ nɛ o kɛ ya no nɛ pu no nɛ i tsɛ mo o ma a ba lo?*). M: Yes. I will. *Ee-e ma ba*. W: Even if in danger/fire will you come? *Ke lam hu o ma ba lo?*. M: Yes I will come. Even if you request for a vehicle/car I shall buy for you. *Ee-e, ma ba. Ke o kɛ wa he lole ha mo wa ma he ha mo*. W: If I call you in the rains would you dare and come? *Ke hio m ngɛ nɛɛ nyɛ ma nyɛ no lo?* M: Yes we shall oblige. (*Ee-e wa ba o*). W: What is your name? (*Kɛ a tsɛ mo kɛɛ*). M: My name is (name) (*A tsɛn ...*). W: What about the man? (*Nyumu o nɛ?*). M: (Name). W: Which of my daughters do you want? (*Bi o te nɛ o ngɛ hlae o nɛ?*). M: The first daughter of (name) (*bi Dede o*).

Both women drink from a red coloured alcoholic drink (for example something called 'mandingo bitters') three times in turn. Then they do the same thing with a little glass of schnapps. Both sides pour libations with the drinks. Then they both pass one arm under the knee and both hold an end of a straw and pull it, so it breaks (*yi ba pomi*). They exchange the straw parts, while the representative of the bride says: '*I ha mo*' ('I give unto you'). The other woman representing the groom's family says: '*I hee*' ('I accept it'). As usual they repeat the rite thrice. This ritual is a symbolic expression of the 'giving away' of the bride, and of the partial rupture with her kin (Huber 1993: 104). The tradition of *yi ba pomi* bears resemblance to the practice of land transaction that was in use at least until the end of the 19th century (Azzu Mate Kole 1955). This traditional system was known as *sugbayie ba pomi*. It involved the breaking of a leaf or vine by the buyer and the vendor of the plot of land. The ends were kept as proof of the transaction. In addition, a sheep was slaughtered to pacify and inform the ancestors of the transfer of ownership (Obeng-Assamoa 1998: 132). To the Krobo this was a deal that implied the transfer of sovereignty.[379]

In some places this ritual is omitted. Instead the female representatives exchange money by swapping it over to each other underneath their knees. The amount may vary. At one place for example, I saw how the 'Dede's' exchanged two coins of 200 cedis, at another place they exchanged two notes of 2,000 cedis. Then the women rub their hands together while some more schnapps is poured over their hands by somebody, while saying '*fiaa fiaa fiaa!*' After this, everybody around drinks from the schnapps, and the wedding is sealed. The words *fiaa* and *hiao* have about the same meaning. They are often connected with blessing formulae and "express the confirmation or ratification of the blessing" (Huber 1993: 104). A libation often ends with the words: '[*fiaa, fiaa*], *manye ba!*' ('May blessing truly come!'). Then people around respond by saying: '*hiao!*' Therefore the whole *fiaa* ceremony can be understood as invoking a blessing. The *fiaa* means that the family of the husband has promised to take care of the new wife. The exact order of the *fiaa* rituals varies. Every time I witnessed it (about four times), there was a lot of discussion or even confusion by people around about what exactly needed to be done. Nevertheless, this ceremony is considered of principal importance by the Manya Krobo. Without this ceremony a wedding would not be recognised by the mutual families.

After the *fiaa* ceremony, people celebrate with *klama* singing and dancing. The women dance in the particular way they learned during *dipo*. Here are some extracts from popular songs:

---

[379] According to the Krobo, this custom was similar to the Akyem *guaha*. However, the Krobo believed that the transaction implied the transfer of sovereignty, while for the Akyem this was not the case, which caused misunderstandings in land transactions between the two (Obeng-Assamoa 1998: 132).

Otumo ba mo, mo ha lɛa ba nɛa ba
If Otumo demands (something) from you, give him,
(because give and take is part of normal life)
[Meaning that no one is self-sufficient]

l kpe yotsu ngɛ Adase we,
I've wedded a red woman from Adase's house,
l kpe yotsu nonoono
I've wedded a very reddish woman
[A 'red', light-skinned, woman is considered more beautiful than any other woman]

Fia fia amanye he, amanye se wa ye o
Blessed, blessed, success, success/victory is ours
[see the explanation of *fiaa* above]

Some people sing Christian songs. Everything is concluded with a libation and often a prayer. At this point the exchange of rings and vows is sometimes part of the whole ceremony as well. If this is the case, pastors, priests or their representatives of the couple's church(es) are present to witness the whole ceremony and officiate this part. They give a speech and pray and take the vows of the couple. Sometimes the bible is then given as a gift and the couple is advised to rely on the bible in times of sorrow and times of joy. After everything is finished, people are given a meal like, for instance, rice with stew or 'Fanti kenkey' (a coastal variety of the fermented maize) to eat. People also drink quite a lot of liquor, although families that are members of Pentecostal churches sometimes refrain from this. They will only serve minerals.

Christian wedding

There is a tendency these days in Christian circles to call the customary marriage ceremony 'the engagement' (in English). Christian people want to show that the ceremony comes before the church wedding, which is more important in their view. I will briefly describe this below.

People usually make special printed invitations for the Christian wedding. For example, an invitation may include the text 'Solemnisation of Holy Matrimony'. The texts include an appropriate verse from the bible. I received printed invitations that stated the names of the 'officiating priests' (for Roman Catholics) or 'ministers' (Protestant). It seemed like a matter of prestige to have as many priests, reverends and/or pastors present as the lists contained the names of six or more. Furthermore, the invitation stated the programme for the 'order of service', a long list for the 'order of photograph' (for example 'couple and priests', 'couple and groom's parents', etc.), and finally the 'reception' ceremony, which may include the 'cutting of cake'. One invitation simply stated: 'The (name) and (name) families respectfully request the pleasure of the company of (name) to witness the wedding ceremony between their son (name) and their daughter (name)'. In the programme no reference is made to any of the traditional rites.

The people who are normally invited are the family members and friends of both sides of the family, but the church is also quite full with church members. The bride and groom dress in Western clothes for the wedding blessings in the church. A groom will wear a suit. Brides wear 'Western' wedding dresses, usually with 'lace' in soft colours such as pink or white, and a veil, and carry (artificial) flowers. Sometimes the church in question hires these dresses to the bride. During the church services the church musicians or choir play a lot of music and the whole congregation sings and dances. A pastor, reverend or priest will pray and preach to advise the couple to be faithful to each other, and ask for God's blessings. He performs the wedding ceremony in which the couple says 'I will' to one another and exchange rings and finally a kiss, under loud cheering and clapping of the audience. Somebody may be present from the local council to legalise the marriage for the (national) law. It is not very common to marry before the local council in a separate ceremony, although this is possible. Afterwards, the guests are served with food, usually at the bride's house. Appropriate food may be fancy food such as fried rice, or rice with stew, and snacks such as kebab, cookies and minerals. A disc-jockey plays loud music, often high life, to which people dance for some time in the afternoon.

The full status of womanhood is only attained after a woman has given birth, ideally within marriage. Where the status of a man is largely derived from having a house(hold) of his own, the status of an adult woman is mainly derived from her children. A woman without children is pitied and often not much respected. Sometimes a particular girlfriend would point out a woman to me and say with a low voice: "She has no child". She knew what that felt like, because she herself only had her first and only child at the age of 38, after trying in vain for a long time. However, both men and women generally regard children as very important. Ideally, children will take care of a you in old age and help with organising your funeral when you die.

Death and funeral rites

After starting this chapter with some of the non-Christian beliefs concerning the self, the person and life and death, I moved on to those life cycle rituals that constitute and gender a (female) person. Personhood is finally validated at the death of the individual. Traditionally, a diviner will be consulted to determine the cause of death in order to make sure that the death was not a 'bad death. A 'good death', that is to say, a death not caused by an evil spirit through an accident, death in childbirth or through suicide, is a death obtained from the ancestors. Then deceased persons can become ancestors, but only if they have chil-

232

dren. The completed person is therefore the product of a whole life (cf. La Fontaine 1986: 132). Therefore the main purpose of the rituals performed during the burial and funeral is to make sure that the soul of the deceased person is able to join the ancestors in *gbeje* and become an ancestor, rather than remaining in the world as an evil spirit to trouble the living.

It goes without saying that a dead person's sex and social status influence the particular burial and funeral performances, but I will not describe or discuss funeral rites elaborately here, as this would require another chapter or book. The death and funeral rites of the Krobo have been described in detail by Hugo Huber (1993: 192-225). Now, forty years after he first published his findings, many of the practices he described are still valid, although many others have disappeared and new ones have sprung up. Usually a wake-keeping takes place in the night between Friday and Saturday, although wake-keepings have been contested in recent years and often skipped from the official programme (see chapter two), to be followed by a burial for a Christian, which is also called a 'thanksgiving' service, in church and the actual burial on Saturday. Some funeral celebrations close with a church memorial service on Sunday. The funeral celebrations are frequently postponed for weeks after the death occurred for financial reasons and matters of convenience. The introduction of mortuaries, however, where a body can be preserved even for months, has now made the postponing of the burial itself possible, which adds to the prestige of the funeral. It is important to note that Huber did not mention any Christian ceremonies and memorial services, which form an intricate part of most funerals today, varying from simply including the singing of Christian hymns and praying to a full Christian burial at a Christian cemetery.

Funeral celebrations take a very central place in social and cultural life of (Southern) Ghanaians (see e.g. De Witte 2001). People spend a lot of money on them and they are regarded as very important to attend. A main feature of a funeral is that it is an occasion where relationships are highlighted. As Huber already observed for the Krobo in the 1950s, there is no other occasion, except perhaps during the *dipo* rites, on which "the responsibilities of consanguinity and affinity relationship are equally felt and expressed" (1993: 208). Both maternal and paternal relatives and friends are present in mourning attire, and contribute in the form of money donations. The greater the number of sympathizers, and the more spectacular the funeral-play and show, in the form of music and dance, food and drinks, the style of the coffin and the decorated corpse, the more fame and esteem is reflected upon the deceased and his or her 'house'.

The head of the house (*wɛ nokotoma*) has to 'bury' any dead member of his 'house', including daughters who are married to outsiders. This actually means that he has to pour libations before and after the burial as well as during the closing of the funeral in the name of the group, and preside over the meeting where the elders of the lineage decide on the dead person's properties (Huber 1993: 31). It used to be common to bring all dead bodies to the hometowns for burial, but these days, partly due to the costs of transport, they are also buried in the village. Still, if somebody's corpse cannot be brought to his or her hometown, some hairs and finger- and toenails that are always cut right after death will be brought to the hometown to be kept by the head of the 'house'. The main funeral rites will still take place in the 'family house', and relatives and friends will come to _dom_ for it. So funeral rites are part of the 'homecoming' rituals.

Here a non-initiated woman is left out and cannot become a completed person in the traditional sense, as she is no longer a member of the 'house'. Practices such as keeping wake, placing items in a coffin or using alcohol to communicate with the ancestors, which are deemed necessary within Krobo conceptions of personhood to safeguard the arrival and good position in _gbeje_ of the deceased, all emphasize that the deceased is part of a community that entails both the earthly and the spirit world. However, as De Witte (2001: 157) points out for the Asante in Ghana, such practices have no cosmological meaning for Christian churches. They are categorised as 'traditional' and rejected as 'pagan', or partly accepted as 'African culture'. Funeral performances evoke a constant dialogue between Christian churches and doctrine, and local cultural practices. For a Christian person the main concern is to receive a Christian funeral and be buried at a Christian cemetery. In the Christian notion of the self, a person's choice regarding heaven or hell entirely depends on his or her own deeds, decisions and moral life. The type of funeral performed cannot change the destiny of the spirit of the deceased. However, many 'traditional' practices are still performed for Christians, while Christians also think it is important how the funeral was performed, for example whether their body was laid in state in the church, and whether they are buried at a Christian cemetery or not, in order to receive a 'ticket to heaven'.

Personhood in a complex world

The focus in this chapter has been on the performance and attendance of life cycle rituals that constitute and gender a person and are either mediated by Christianity or traditional religion. For many people 'Christianity' and 'paganism' are important categories. However, people in Odumase, like the (Presbyterian) people in the town of Akuropon as studied by Middleton (1983) and Gilbert (1988; 1993; 1995),[380] perform or attend different types of rites that "remind them of their existence and fortify the faith held in their powers" (Middleton 1983: 12). As has become clear in this and the previous chapter, they may take part in rites dealing with their ancestors or ritual practices involving deities, and at the same

---

[380] The town of Akuropon is known in Ghana as the seat of the main educational facilities of the Presbyterian Church since the arrival of the BM on what was the then Gold Coast in 1828.

time attend a church service on Sunday in one of the various churches. In the event of sickness, they may consult a pastor, but also a diviner. They may have their children baptised in church, but also by all means have *dipo* performed for their daughters. Performing and attending rites of different religions, which are in many ways opposed to one another, may seem contradictory to an outsider. African intellectuals and theologians (e.g. Baëta 1968; Fasholé-Luke, Gray, Hastings, & Tasie 1978) have seen members of former mission churches who (secretly) participate nowadays in non-Christian rituals as 'victims of the missionaries' who are bereft of their African identity (Meyer 1999: 134-135). From this perspective people are indecisive, insincere, inconsequent, and have a 'split consciousness'.

Do people really experience a split consciousness or 'inner self', when they observe Christian and non-Christian rites, as argued by the Basel missionaries? This question is the consequence of a Christian viewpoint that starts from the notion of the moral individual being responsible for his/her own actions, which seems to clash with the non-Christian notion of the self. What does the complexity of Krobo personhood as constituted by life cycle rituals tell us about presuppositions about the (invisible) world and notions regarding the self and the person? And how do Krobo people attempt to reconcile themselves to the sometimes competing demands? In order to deal with this issue adequately, we first have to delve into some of the anthropological literature on the self and the person.

Marcel Mauss argued that the idea of the individual is unique to Western thought, and that this idea is rooted in Western philosophy and in Christianity (1986 [1938]). He introduced a distinction between the 'self' (*moi*) and the 'person' (*personne*) (the public role one learns to play).[381] The Western concept of the 'self', often equated with the Western person as an individual, has been widely described as individuated, detached, separate and self-sufficient, and as involving a dualistic metaphysic (Morris 1994: 16). In non-Western societies a person was hardly thought to have an inner conscience or a self-awareness of a unique human being, because s/he derived identity from the clan, the kinship group or tribe. Although in anthropological writing the latter point of view has been dismissed as a product of the Western construction of Primitivism (e.g. Cohen 1994; Lienhardt 1985),[382] and the Western concept of the self as essentialist, autonomous, bounded, egocentric and individualist has been shown to

---

[381] Mauss' argument is far more complex. However, his essay has had little impact until recently (see e.g. Carrithers, Collins, & Lukes 1986). Until the late 1970s concern with the self has been limited to the (American) sub-field of psychological anthropology (Cohen 1994: 2).

[382] In Africanist writing (by non Africans), the idea that African individuals would have their own consciousness, their own inner life, only appeared from the 1950s with the works of (female) anthropologists such as Bohannan (Bowen 1964 [1954]) and Smith (1981 [1955]), and later Shostak (1983 [1980]). See Riesman's overview (1986: 103).

represent merely one (relatively recent) theory among many (philosophical, theological, and literary) traditions (Morris 1994: 16-17; Murray 1993), the tendency to distinguish between a Western sense of uniqueness of the (person as an) individual and a non-Western idea of the person as defined by relationships, still dominates many ethnographies and anthropological essays (e.g. Marsella, DeVos, & Hsu 1985; Shweder & LeVine 1984).[383]

Much has been written about the lack of 'individuality' among African peoples in particular, suggesting that a person is 'absorbed' into the social group (Morris 1994: 118). In Africanist writings on 'the person', the 'relational self' is usually emphasised (Riesman 1986). It is a person that cannot be considered apart from his or her ontologically prior social context, from the community of relationships into which a person is born and within which he or she lives. As Piot argues in his study of the Kabre society in North-Togo:

> To abstract out the individual, and his or her 'interests' and property, would seem, then, to be an inappropriate starting (or ending) point for theoretical analysis. Further, the divide between individual and society [in Euro-American theories, MS] is not part of the construction of sociality in many African societies (Piot 1999: 17).

Every person is always related to other human beings and each person is defined through relations. However, Piot argues (1999: 18) that persons do not 'have' relations in many African societies, they 'are' relations. A person should be seen as composed of, or constituted by, relationships, rather than as situated in them.

The sociocentric and egocentric view of the person should be regarded as different *ideologies* of personhood in Western and non-Western societies that may tend to highlight aspects of individual or social identity and mask other aspects (Borsboom 2002). Although Western as well as non-Western notions regarding the person show part of both aspects in everyday practice (Jackson & Karp 1990; Lienhardt 1985; Morris 1994), and highlighting either the 'sociocentric view' or 'egocentric view' regarding 'the person' can be called an artefact of context (Jacobson-Widding 1990; La Fontaine 1986: 124), these different ideologies may clash, as the case of the Basel Mission showed. Their Western notion of the individual person, the Christian teaching of a direct communication between God and the individual and of the individual as someone responsible for his or her own destiny, was in contrast with 'traditional' Krobo notions of the person, where decisions and choices that people make can also be determined by non-persons such as gods and spirits, and rituals constitute and gender a person.

---

[383] Murray (1993)] argues that even those academics who propose a 'pluralist', 'fragmented', 'relational' 'inconsistent' notion of self for *all* human beings, also contrast their own conceptions to a presumed hegemonic Western construction (e.g. Ewing 1990), which he reveals as an 'invention of a Western tradition'.

Morris (1994: 11) states that a person is often clearly expressed in a ritual context and rituals often have an ideological function in a conception of 'the person' as a cultural category, which is a conception articulated specifically in the cultural representations of a specific community. The ritual context defines and shapes various identities, and the importance of life cycle rituals in Krobo society must be seen in this perspective. The integration into the social world and gendering of the self to become a person starts from birth, and is mediated by life cycle rituals. The ritual recognition of the accumulation of roles and statuses marks the progress of Krobo men and women towards full personhood, hence the *dipo* rites are part of a cumulative social (female) identity. The *dipo* rites create potential mothers and wives (cf. Grimes 2000: 109), while marriage and especially the birth of children are essential prerequisites to obtain full personhood. From this perspective, *dipo* is only one, but crucial, part of the female life cycle rituals.

In these life cycle rituals the ideal of the socio-centric person is the focal point. During the rites, which are all family occasions, the ancestors of the family, or in case of marriage, the ancestors of the families of the groom and bride, are called up to be present and bless the ceremony. In this way continuing relationships with the ancestors are established. In the case of *dipo*, as described in the previous chapter, a relationship with the deity Nana Klowɛki is also established. The socio-centric ideal is confirmed in the way people talk about *dipo*. As people *are* relations, no woman will say 'I did *dipo* (personally)'. When asked whether she passed through *dipo*, she will rather answer in a passive and plural form: '*A sɛ mi dipo*,' meaning that: '*Dipo* was performed for me'. The proper question to ask in Krobo is: '*A sɛ mo dipo lo?*', literally: 'They performed you *dipo*?', ('Was *dipo* performed for you?') Or: *Nyɛ sɛ dipo lo?*' 'Have you people performed *dipo*?' (i.e. 'Have you been initiated?').

Hence the rituals mark group membership and are designed to ensure fertility and prosperity and ward off misfortune. As Middleton argues: "By observance of rites people mark their adherence not only to a superior or constraining power, but to a way of seeing their society and their experience of the world" (1983: 12). Rather than indicating indecision or insincerity, Krobo people's behaviour reflects a need for ritual protection and ritual purification in a world of moral and cosmological complexity, rather than in a world of contrasts. As in the Akuropon case, a need for ritual protection, and I would like to add, ritual purification, is central to Krobo thought:

Throughout life it is essential to have supernatural protectors against dangers that beset people, jut as in all highly stratified societies it is necessary to have political and familial protectors and patrons. In both spheres it is advisable not to limit oneself to a single source of protection but if necessary to change protectors from one situation to another (Middleton 1983: 12).

In practice most people do not experience problems in incorporating Christian elements into many non-Christian life cycle rituals. Conflicts between Christians and non-Christians and among different Christians regarding the outdooring and naming ceremonies and marriage rites usually concern aspects of rituals that some deem 'pagan', such as the pouring of libation or the tying of priestly beads, while others accept them as 'African culture'. Even though most people call themselves Christians, non-Christian presuppositions continue to underlie notions about the person and as such the life cycle rituals are regarded as important. Krobo notions of personhood definitely contain ideas concerning individualism, although this individuality is sanctioned through spiritual conceptions. Krobo notions of 'the person' are an interplay between being the locus of a social network, of kinship ties and of a sense of individual identity in the form of a person's *susuma* ('soul') and especially *sesɛɛ* ('parting word'). It should be kept in mind that Krobo conceptions of the person are complex and do not deny the agency and autonomy of the self. They involve biological (material), spiritual, social and individual dimensions. They also do not express a radical dualism between the spiritual and the material, or between individual autonomy and the social context (cf. Morris 1994: 20-21).

Although no Christian elements have been incorporated into the *dipo* performance, and the performance as a whole is deemed 'pagan' and is therefore rejected by Christian churches, some of the *dipo* rituals that refer to sexuality have changed as a result of Christian influences. People also rather refer to Easter, the Christian calendar, than to the traditional ritual calendar to indicate the time of the celebrations. While some practices simply have disappeared, people have also developed strategies 'to combine the two', that is to say, the performance of *dipo* and attending church service. Involvement in traditional practices is normally seen as 'backsliding', which a Christian should avoid. The Basel missionaries introduced the expression 'back-sliding into heathendom' to emphasise the spatial and temporal difference constructed to distinguish Christianity and 'heathendom' (see chapter three). They thought that *dipo*, like a number of other 'heathen' practices, would become obsolete in time, as it was regarded a matter of 'the past'. However, Krobo people were not willing to give up on *dipo*. Nevertheless, they took the boundary between 'paganism' and Christianity very literally and accepted its existence. Going through Christian ceremonies after *dipo* has become the norm among members of the former mission churches. This shows that it is considered to be important to first become a member of Krobo society, a 'real' or 'pure' Krobo, so as to emphasise the 'relational self' and become a clean and acceptable person according to traditional standards, before one can make more 'individual' choices in order to become a full church member. However, this is an individuality of sorts, as a person establishes new relations that can help create a Christian identity. After her initiation, a girl may be baptised and, in the former mission churches, be confirmed or have her first communion. This norm, which is the result of the continued strong

238

rejection of *dipo* by most churches, is paradoxically another reason of the younger ages of initiands, and hence of teenage pregnancies, which Christians always complain about. The Presbyterian Church has never succeeded in replacing *dipo* by the confirmation ceremony. The confirmation lacks the ability to ritually cleanse a girl to protect her from evil, and does not gender a person. I will discuss the 'inculturation' or 'Africanisation' debate in chapter eight.

The separation from 'the past', that is, from family and ancestral relations, propagated by the Pentecostal churches in order to become an individual 'born-again' person, is an ideal that has not been achieved yet. Although Pentecostals, in the name of Christianity, challenge the notion of traditional life cycle rituals as constituting a person, they cannot fully detach themselves from these notions. However, the Pentecostal category of the person can go easily together with traditional notions. A person is conceptualised as open and susceptible to forces from outside. As Meyer (1999: 171-172) argues: "during [Pentecostal] deliverance sessions, people (re-)enact their possession by non Christian powers, thereby integrating these entities into Christian worship, albeit in a subordinate sense." Hence, by taking ancestral and non-Christian spirits very seriously, the Pentecostals give believers the opportunity to be a Christian without giving up the concerns of traditional religion, although they are asked to distance themselves from traditional religion. Pentecostal churches mediate between traditional religion and mission-church Christianity:

> On the one hand, they profess individualisation and separation in the same way as the mission church. On the other, by providing believers with an explicit and elaborate ritual praxis, they make up for the shortcomings of the mission church, which have existed even since the introduction of Christianity to the Ewe [and the Krobo, MS] (Meyer 1999: 173).

From a Pentecostal perspective, conversion is conceptualised in circular terms, which allows believers to move back and forth through the sequence of possession by evil spirits, exorcism and possession by the Holy Spirit: "Pentecostalism provides a bridge between individualistic and family-centred concerns and allows people to express and reflect upon the tensions between both" (Meyer 1999: 212).

By regarding *dipo* priests as agents of the devil and all non-Christian ceremonies as his realm, Pentecostalism therefore gives its believers room to manoeuvre. This explains part of the attraction of Pentecostalism. Adult baptism allows people to have *dipo* performed for them. After their baptism they can be delivered from the 'evil spirits' they encountered and start anew. Despite the complete rejection of *dipo* by Pentecostals as 'tradition' and 'of the devil', most of them still have the rites performed for their daughters, although often in secret.

The *dipo* rites are part of the life cycle rituals that constitute and gender a Krobo woman as a person, for whom belonging to her family, kinship group and society as a whole is of crucial importance in life. However, some of the changes in *dipo* suggest that the importance of *dipo* as a life cycle ritual has decreased, while other aspects have remained significant or even have become more distinct, as will become clearer in the next two chapters. In the previous chapter it was stated that *dipo* is not just a life cycle ritual, but is also part of the ritual calendar. In the next chapter, in which the *dipo* rites will be described in detail, the importance of belonging to one's family, kinship group and society as a whole, as expressed in the rites, and hence the importance for the whole group, will become more explicit.

7

" A pure Krobo": Performing dipo

"A pure Krobo means that the custom has been performed for you. (…) You have to be pure, clean and pure." (*Wono* Tetteh Gaga, March 25, 1999, Plau, Somanya)

"*Dipo* is like washing the dirt from your dress, because you can't send your dirty dress to a gathering. *Dipo* is like washing your dress to look clean. Anybody who doesn't want it misses a great thing." (*woyo* Maku, November 21, 1998)

"*Dipo* will continue, because it is cleansing. It is in every woman's mind that she wants to be clean to be able to go anywhere." ('maa' Adjoka, July 3, 2000, Odumase)

The Ghanaian movie 'the Taboo' (1993), which was largely shot in Kodjonya, one of the Manya Krobo hometowns in *dom*, depicts the story of the girl Kosi who violates the *dipo* taboo: she becomes pregnant before passing through the rites.[384] Even though her pregnancy was the result of her teacher raping her, Kosi is eventually sent away from her home and is told she is not part anymore of her family and should never come back to her town. Misfortune started to befall her family as a result of the initial silence over her illegitimate pregnancy. Even though she is driven from her home, pollution and ritual danger have not gone with her. Therefore her family house has to be ritually purified by a priest to prevent further supernatural sanctions. *Wono* Asa is the ritual specialist in charge of all such cleansing ceremonies among the Krobo (cf. Huber 1958: 168). Ritual cleanliness is an important concept in Krobo society, an important tool to draw boundaries and one of the main aims of the *dipo* rites. Like circumcision cleanses a Krobo boy and distinguishes him from the uncircumcised (see previous chapter), *dipo* is regarded as cleansing and purifying a Krobo girl. In this chapter, I will focus on the performance of the *dipo* rites, the multi-faceted meaning of its rituals, and on the ways in which its continued, although changing, practice by women (and some men) contributes to the reproduction of a Krobo identity.

Most studies dealing with initiation rituals take Van Gennep's model of *rites de passage* (Van Gennep 1960), which was further developed by Victor Turner (1979; 1991), as a starting point. The *rites de passage* ('rites of passage')

---

[384] Part two of 'the Taboo' appeared a few years later. Another popular Ghanaian film about *dipo*, probably shot in the Shai area, is called 'Dede' (Ghana film Industry Corporation, 1985).

consist of rituals and symbols that accompany the transition from one life stage to another, marking a change in status, and usually take a threefold structure: the separation, the liminal and the incorporation stage. In order to study the basic structure of the ritual and to get more acquainted with the people involved, this chapter concentrates on a description of one *dipo* performance, which took place in Odumase in April 1999.[385] I chose this specific event, because I was very familiar with the priestess, Lako Sakite and her family, and consequently with some of the children passing through the rites. Therefore the description of the *dipo* performance that will follow here is mainly based on the week that I followed *dipo* in Lako Sakite's compound most extensively. I was allowed to film the rites with my video camera and take photographs, except at the sacred site of the *dipo* stone (*tɛgbɛtɛ*). Although every *dipo* performance was slightly different, with few alterations in the order and routine of the rituals, the general appearance was much like the one described below. However, for the analysis I will not only make use of the knowledge I gained from this particular rite, but also at other places and from other people.

Preparations: divination and cleansing

Introducing Doe, Ata and Lawɛ

The first time I met Doe was in Lako Sakite's compound in 1998, when she was ten years old. She was a cute looking little girl, who usually had a broad smile on her face. The name 'Doe' indicates that she followed a twin. Her mother Ako had a daughter and a pair of twins, Ahulu (a boy) and Ahubia (a girl), before her. *Dipo* had already been performed for them. By coincidence, Doe was also followed by another pair of twins, Ata (a girl) and Lawɛ (a boy. Ako, a woman in her early forties, also has a twin sister herself, called Akweley. Therefore twins in this family is not exceptional. According to Krobo tradition, having twins is a sign of blessing.[386] Not all of Ako's children have the same father, and

---

[385] See Bloch (1986), who uses a similar approach to analyse a circumcision ritual in Madagascar.

[386] As in other Ghanaian societies, twins (*hawi*) have a special position in Krobo society. While in Ga society there is even a special twin ceremony during the annual festival (*homowo*), in Akan-speaking Fanti society, for example, twins used to be killed at birth because they were seen as an anomaly. In Krobo society the birth of twins is a joyful occasion, but twins are also feared and regarded as troublesome, because they have special needs and are always jealous of each other. Some say twins originate from baboons, others believe that twins, like other mysterious beings, originate from the sea (Azu 1929: 36; Huber 1993: 156, 158). This belief is recorded elsewhere in Africa. Van Santen (1993), for example, describes that twins in Mafa society in Cameroon are thought to have a close relation with water spirits. After birth, Krobo twins have to be convinced to stay in this world. Twins have special names. If both are boys, they are named Akwete and Akwetɛ, Atɛ and Lawɛ, or Kani and Kponkpo. Twin girls can, for example, be named Ata, Ahubia, Ako and Akwele, and Akoko. The child born

242

as she is not married, she mainly has to cater for them. As this is practically impossible especially due to financial constraints, several of her children are actually being raised by different relatives. This practice of fostering is common in Krobo and in many African societies. Often the foster parents either are more affluent than the real parents, or they do not have children themselves.[387] Doe was staying with maa Lako in 1998, who shares a complicated kinship relation with her, at least so it seemed to me. Doe's grandmother was the second wife of maa Lako's first husband. That marriage was a family marriage: maa Lako's first husband was her cousin. Therefore his children with the second wife also are her relatives, as they all originate from the same 'house'. Julie, maa Lako's daughter from a different man, calls Doe's mother Ako, maa Lako's husband's daughter from the second wife, her 'cousin'. Because Ako's children are *yo bi* (mother's children), she and her family were responsible for their *dipo*.

Ako had already told me in August 1998 that she would let Doe pass the *dipo* rites the following year in Lako Sakite's house, and that she would allow me to film everything. I was excited and always kept her promise in mind. So about eight months later, when the time for *dipo* was approaching, I asked her whether she still planned on having *dipo* performed for Doe and her twin sister and brother, Ata and Lawɛ.[388] Ako explained that she could not afford it, she would have to postpone *dipo* until one year later. She had spent all her money on the death of a cousin in 'the village'. I then proposed to pay for all expenses and told her again that I would like to be part of the whole process. Ako immediately agreed and started making plans. She said she would instantly see maa Lako to ask whether we should start the coming weekend, or rather one week later. Then we would have to go to the market soon to start buying the necessary items.

Divination

Before maa Lako started to perform the initial *dipo* rites for the whole first group, all girls had to prepare themselves individually with their relatives. This

---

after twins will also receive a name that indicates its place in the order of birth. A boy born after twins can be called Tɛwia, a girl Doe. In case a woman gives birth to three sets of twins, she is specially honoured (cf. Huber 1993: 160).

[387] See Notermans (2003) about practices of fosterage in Cameroon.

[388] Because it is believed that "the lives of twins are intimately linked together by a kind of mystical bond" (Huber 1993: 159), they should be given the same kind of food and dress. If one child is given a piece of land to farm on, the other child should get the same area of land. For the same reason they have to go through *dipo* together and perform certain rites at each other's wedding. If one of them dies, a wooden doll representing the dead twin is carved and taken care of, in order to prevent the deceased from returning to his living twin brother or sister and taking him or her to the other world. Twins are also believed to have a peculiar connection with the *abodoi*, a kind of fairies or dwarfs, which are seen as children or messengers of the gods.

meant that the girls would go to a diviner (*gbalo*), ask the *susuma* of the girls for permission to perform the rites and ask them what they needed for a successful *dipo* performance. *Woyo* Dede Gbao explained to me:

> If someone [a *dipo* candidate] detests something you don't force it on her. This is one of our rituals and if you don't go through it you lose your identity. Sometimes the candidate's *susuma* [translated to me as 'soul', see previous chapter, MS] taboos something [i.e. detests something, MS], in that case, you need to coax the *susuma* to say what token or fee it would require for reconciliation, so that the *dipo* ritual is performed. (Original in Dangme)

I asked her what would happen if a candidate's *susuma* says she does not like to have *dipo* performed for her. The *woyo* answered:

> Some say they do not like it at all. Then we go ahead to explain that *dipo* is a precondition to become acceptable in this society as a Krobo woman. We keep coaxing until the spirit agrees. It may say: 'I am Hausa and so I require some cultural artefact of the Hausa on me.' Another may require the Ewe fashion and so demands a *dipo* in Ewe outfit. You may need to see a Hausa to tell you about their symbols which you use. (Original in Dangme)

It is very interesting that, as *woyo* Dede clearly states, a person needs to have *dipo* performed in order to become accepted as a Krobo woman in Krobo society. One is not born a Krobo, one's soul or spirit needs to be ritually incorporated into Krobo society. That the origin of one's *susuma* can be, for example, Ewe or even Hausa, also points at the past, when strangers from different places sought refuge on Krobo Mountain and became part of one Krobo society. At the same time, the divination acknowledges each individual's needs and concerns.

Some of the parents went to a *gbalo* of their choice by themselves. Others did not want to be seen in the house of a 'pagan', and therefore sent a relative in their place. Maa Lako used to take her *dipo-yi* to a *gbalo* named 'papa' Tetteh, a relative of hers. However, these days he came to her house for the soothsaying, because she was not able to walk herself. Maa Lako said she liked it. It was not good to use somebody's shrine, she said. In this way she could keep an eye on what happened and help bargaining to reduce the amount of requested items. Maa Lako and papa Tetteh had a close relationship anyway. He would come to help her with the *dipo* performance every year, and I had seen him in her house before, throwing cowries on the floor when maa Lako wanted to know whether she would ever recover from her hip injury and walk again.

Papa Tetteh was going to use the same method of divination with cowries to find out about the *susuma* of the sisters Doe and Ata and also Ata's twin brother Lawɛ.[389] The girls did not need to be present themselves. It was an afternoon, because, papa Tetteh said, by that time the souls would be playing. In the morning they would be sleepy and more difficult to call. Me, Julie, maa Lako, the mother Ako and papa Tetteh were sitting in one of the small rooms of the house with pink walls, which they called 'the hall'. The idea was to be more or less out of sight and have more peace and quiet. However, the noise by the children and other people in the compound still penetrated the room. Nobody seemed to care, and they just continued. One of Julie's sisters walked in and out, and at one time even interrupted the session to ask me whether I wanted to buy some food items from the seller who was passing by. This little incident indicates that, although the divination is taken very seriously, it is not done very solemnly. Similarly, I also often saw maa Lako pouring the necessary libations before proceeding with a certain rite, while hardly anybody listened or kept quiet. It seemed to be a routine matter. At the same time I could not have attended the divination so easily at other places or even at the same place with different children, if I had been a stranger to them. People did not do this in the open.

Since I was paying for their *dipo*, and in this sense the 'mother' of the children, I was asked to pay an amount to papa Tetteh for his services. He demanded 3,000 *cedis*. He started to throw the cowries on the floor and looked up: "What are the children's names?" Ako answered: "Ata and Lawɛ, and sister Doe." Papa Tetteh again threw the handful of cowries on the floor a few times and studied them each time they fell on the floor in a particular pattern. He then asked: "Who is doing it for them?" This time it was Julie who readily answered: "It is '*manyɛ*' (referring to me) who performs it." Papa Tetteh then said: "Tell her they [the souls] are thanking her." Everybody in the room consequently thanked me. Papa Tetteh threw the cowries on the floor again: "Tell her…" (*De le kɛ…*). Julie translated: "Your children said they are from Krobo Mountain." She laughed in a content way and said: "They are big people, not small children. You see them as small children, but they are old, they are older children!" Apparently, it was understood that these children were reincarnations or old spirits of Krobo who had lived on Krobo Mountain, the old ritual home. Papa Tetteh threw the cowries on the floor again: "Tell her…" Julie translated: "You being the mother, you have to perform the rite; they will dance." Papa Tetteh threw the cowries again several times on the floor, and each time he mentioned the items the souls were demanding. Julie assured me that "everything will come down", and she mentioned the items to me: one gallon of palm wine, one gallon of *akpeteshie*, two bottles of schnapps. After this, a full bowl of water yam, plantain and a special kind of meat of the *afugbɛ*, which according to Julie was antelope

---

[389] The cowri shells used for the divination are deemed as pagan by Christians. Although the cowri shells were the currency in the past, nowadays they are especially associated with the so-called 'fetish priests'. In other parts of Ghana, some priests wear them in their hair. On the Krobo markets, female priests sell the shells and other comparable items used in performing rituals.

meat to be used for a dish called *wuwi*, was needed.[390] Furthermore two fowl, a cock and a hen, an empty snail shell, seven cowries and seven pesewas were demanded (the number seven is imbued with mystical power). I asked what the empty snail shell would be used for. "They will use it" was all Julie said, "My mother has some". Papa Tetteh threw the cowries again. Julie told me: "After all this you will go to Agomanya (market) and dance with them. When you see the people go 'boom boom boom boom boom', you will go round the whole market." (They laughed because of the sound she made to imitate the music). The souls further demanded old beads and old *kente* cloth, "because they are old", Julie smiled. They also demanded an 'old lady' to dress them. The last items that were needed were some hairs from the fur of an animal called '*dongobwomi*', and three two-yard pieces of white calico (*klala*).

The whole session lasted for about half an hour. Maa Lako then asked papa Tetteh that if they would perform all this for the children, would they become free and good people? He confirmed this. Julie translated with a smile: "Doe said that she is happy for what you are coming to do for her." (Papa Tetteh threw the cowries once more). "Ah!", Julie exclaimed before translating his words, "It is Doe who is thanking you, but as for Ata, she is the one saying [demanding] all these things!" She looked disturbed. Papa Tetteh threw the cowries on the floor again and stated in Krobo that Ata was a bad girl. I heard people make these kinds of comments about twins more often. Twins are considered to be troublesome. Maa Lako discussed something with papa Tetteh. Julie told me she said that they should be very lenient with me: "Because supposing it is their father who is here coming to do these things, then, she will back them to collect all these things they are asking from him. But because somebody else is willing to pay the rites for his children, they should reduce the costs." In the end, after some bargaining, the *akpeteshie* and palm wine had been reduced to one bottle instead of two. The money to be paid to papa Tetteh for today's services had been reduced to 2,000 *cedis* after more pleas from Julie and her mother.

Maa Lako wanted to know whether I was satisfied. I said it was fine. But maa Lako herself was not happy about 'going round the market'. Julie translated: "My mother said that their sisters and cousins had told they are all Christians [and hence unwilling to perform certain rites], so there is nobody to send them to the market and go and beg for those things, so they should see to it and also talk about that." "On the market they have to beg for money?" I asked. "*Ee*", Julie said confirming, "Beg for food and money. They will carry a calabash and you will go round. That is not good". As if to stress it, she had a disapproving look on her face. Papa Tetteh then made sure that this demand was substituted by 'one gin' and 'something he would bring from the market'. We had

---

[390] According to Huber, the *afugbɛ* is the Krobo word for Maxwell's Brown Duiker (Huber 1993: 257).

finished the session now. Besides all requested items, we had to buy some more foodstuffs to feed the prescribed food to the children. Ako said she could arrange for palm nuts and oil. In addition, we had to buy corn and dried fish. Maa Lako also had some large calabashes we would need as well for the ritual bath. Again, it was said we needed big ones, since the children's souls had informed us that they were from the old mountain home.

After we had finished, four women with five children came to also have their divination. They had come all the way from their farms in Assin-Fosso in the Central Region, about 160 kilometres in a straight line from Odumase, but a much longer way to travel. They were relatives of each other. Odumase was their hometown, however, and that was why they came to do *dipo* here. They were staying with some relatives in their family house opposite the palace. The mother of the eighteen- and sixteen-year-old girls Mamle and Maku was a tiny figure, who did not have any teeth left in her mouth. It made her look much older than she probably was. She had brought her mother-in-law along. The names Mamle and Maku indicate that they were the third and fourth daughters of their mother. The other mother among them was a beautiful younger woman, who was the first mother's cousin. Her name was Comfort Koko. She carried a two-year-old named Mamle on her back and had another daughter Koko ('second-born') with her, who was six years of age. They were both going to be initiated. Another child named Domɛyo was about three years old and was Comfort Koko's sister's child, who could not be present herself, because she was sick. The fourth woman among them named 'Baby', was the one who had announced their coming to maa Lako the evening before. She was the mother-in-law's niece (the woman's husband's brother's daughter), so she came from the same 'house'. She had been asked to pay 25,000 *cedis* for the *dipo* performance of all the children, which was said to be mainly for Mamle and Maku. The small children were added in order to reduce the total costs, as the relatives would share and small children were cheaper.

Besides all the requested items, Ako and I bought food stuffs such as palm oil, dried fish and yams on the Saturday market that same day, so that we could feed the prescribed food to the children during the rites. We also bought red cotton to make the *subue*, the loincloths that the *dipo* girls wear, and a few yards of white calico. Ako said we also needed rope for threading beads, raffia, new towels to use after bathing, powder, new sandals and wax print cloth to use for the 'outdooring'. We bought everything and were therefore well prepared for the rites.

Cleansing

On the same day, it was Saturday late afternoon, the *dipo* candidates who had come from Assin-Foso were cleansed in maa Lako's little compound. They had brought a red and a white fowl, like we did, two tablets of white clay (*nguo*), small calabashes, a little black earthen pot, one yam that was to be cooked, one egg and a blue '*koli*' bead. One of the calabashes contained money, coins of 200 *cedis* each, and two kinds of (medicinal) leaves. All these items had been requested by the children's 'souls' (*susuma*), although papa Tetteh had to make inquiries to remind him for whom each particular thing was meant.

Whereas 'my' children's souls claimed they were from Krobo Mountain, the souls of some of these girls had claimed they were from elsewhere. Accordingly, different rituals had to be performed. The big girl Mamle's soul, for example, said she was from Ho in the Volta Region. "She is from the river", Julie translated papa Tetteh's words. "She deceived the husband [apparently meaning: her *gbetsi* or *kla*, i.e. her 'spiritual spouse'] before coming. Before she will allow the mother to perform the rite for her, the mother should compensate the husband." Little Domɛyo's soul was also from the mountain home, as papa Tetteh found out. "Look at her face", Julie said, "She is an old person". Indeed, little Domeryo's face had a sorrowful and serious expression and looked as if she could be the reincarnation of an old lady. "She is from the mountain. She is one of the old, old ladies. Because of that, she is always falling sick. She needs cleansing." The fowl had been bought for her cleansing.

Papa Tetteh filled a big calabash with water and medicinal leaves or herbs and added millet. He swayed a smoking torch, made of the fried flower of a palm tree (*tsitsii*), thrice around the children, who stood next to each other.[391] He repeated this act with the calabash and the other items. Then he threw the '*tsitsii*' in front of the house at the doorstep. The '*tsitsii*' had cleansed the children and the items, and would keep any bad spirit away. In the meantime maa Lako poured a libation invoking the ancestors in order to ask for their consent and blessings and apologise for any mistake she might make in performing the rites:

> Stool priest Opata, his son Tɛtɛbio, he brought his daughters for a ritual bath, we went to consult the diviner to know their descendants, so we can perform the ritual accordingly. They showed us and all the things are ready for the rites; you the owner of this house, behold your drink so that you ensure a peaceful (*dipo*) ceremony. May they come in thousands, may they arrive in millions to request that I and I alone should perform *dipo* for them. We appeal to you, we're young and, as we begin [the rites] tomorrow, those omissions through our ignorance, right them all. Those we don't know let them appear in our dreams so that we see and do the right (thing) for peace to prevail; we appear for your blessings. I am performing the rites in your name. It isn't by my own initiative; this is the drink that I present to seek your consent. May they go hunting and return safe, if they go treasure hunting may they return with bags full. Give me strength, we appeal that our endeavours and enterprises succeed so that we could be counted among the successful ones. (Original in Dangme)

---

[391] A *tsitsii* is the dried flower of a palm tree. It is the customary torch for ceremonial cleansing of a house or a place of worship or for personal purifications.

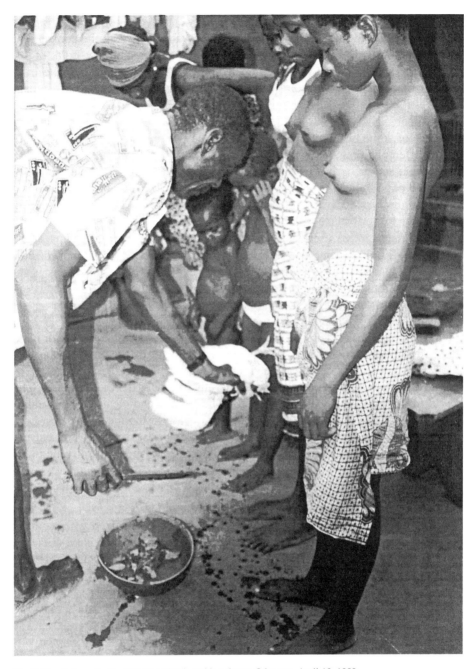

Fig. 7: The diviner ritually cleansing Mamle and her sisters, Odumase, April 10, 1999

The children were made to stand in a line. The diviner, papa Tetteh, also poured a libation, stressing the purpose of the rites:

> Yes today, on this Saturday, you born on Saturday, God bless it. Invite all (spirits of the land) from the Volta River (*Jo̲tso*) to the boundary at Ako̲le,[392] Dome̲yolu̲o̲ son of Dome̲yo, it's true what the old lady has said, the year has come; he who comes from *Kloyom* [Krobo Mountain], Yagaga [another nearby hill], from stone hills, from the rainbow; this (rite) is known only among the Krobo. We mark them with your symbol so that they may tread on safe paths. It's the norm that I, the accomplished, should perform the ritual bath [the purification] for them so that they may go and come in peace. Peace be to peace lovers, war to war mongers. If on their arrival they had no fortune may they meet fortune on their return. May they be fertile and produce so they can name children after their fathers and mothers. Whoever follows the elephant never knows a wet foot. It's our appeal that after the *dipo* they get men to marry them so that we enjoy the peace. (Original in Dangme)

Next, he thrice swayed the red fowl around the heads of the children, then cut its throat in one single move with a knife, and sprinkled the blood on the children's feet. He did the same with the white fowl. The girls were threatened that they would have to pay for two bottles of schnapps if they cried. Julie explained to me that they should not cry "because it is something holy". In the meantime rather the grandmother of the girls was crying, because she was moved by the fact that three of the girls were orphans, and their parents were therefore not there to witness their initiation.

After this, papa Tetteh took the calabash with the water, the clay and the millet, and also swayed it around the children's heads. Then he washed their heads and feet with the cleansing water. After that, he stood behind the children and threw the content of the calabash with the leaves and coins over their heads. He took some of the millet and sprinkled some of it on the children's heads and threw some in front of them. This was the end of the ceremony. The two oldest girls Mamle and Maku immediately started plucking the dead fowl. The floor was scrubbed with a broom and water to wash the blood of the fowl away. Maa Lako prepared the yam by cutting it in little pieces that she mixed with palm oil and the boiled egg, in this way making a dish called *sibaa*. One bowl (*ka*) was put down with plain white yam, another one with the (red) mixture. This was how the souls had requested it. The girls ate of the food.

Then Ako arrived with Doe and Ata after six, when darkness had fallen already. I was a bit annoyed that she was late, because by now it was almost too dark for me to film as I had intended to do. The cleansing for 'my' children was going to be similar to the one of the other children. The major difference was

---

[392] *Jo̲tso* means the banks of the Volta River at Kpong. It stands here for the northern boundary. The village Ako̲le on the Accra road forms the southern boundary of Krobo territory. Therefore when these boundaries are called, it refers to: "in the whole Krobo land" (Huber 1993: 263).

that some special actions had to be taken because Ata was a twin. The leaves that were used to bathe the children were of a special kind for twins, called *nyanyla*. These are 'twin leaves', because they grow in pairs. Papa Tetteh started to wash the children with these leaves. He swayed the calabash containing the water and the leaves over their heads. Ako was blowing a horn (*'e ngɛ koli ngmlaa'*) in the meantime, and the women were singing songs especially for twins. Another woman was rasping a horn in a rhythmic way, while singing. These horns are antelope horns, and they are also used to celebrate the birth of twins and their turning six months old. The pair of horns, like the leaves, symbolises twins.

When papa Tetteh had killed another red and white fowl, he not only sprinkled the blood on the children's feet, but also dipped his finger in the blood flowing from the fowl's throat, and touched the girls' forehead and temple with it. After the red fowl was used first, one of the women stroke the bodies of the girls, who still stood next to each other with the horns. She repeated this thrice. After each time she hit the ground with the horns. Then papa Tetteh finished with the white fowl. In the end, he grabbed one hand of each child with his own hands, let go, crossed his arms, grabbed their hands again, let go once more, and finally pulled the girls behind him.

After everything was finished, maa Lako told the girls, while soup of the slaughtered fowl was being prepared, that they were going to learn how to wash and cook. She also asked them whether they had had their period before. She called Mamle, the eighteen-year-old girl, to come to talk seriously to her. She wanted to know if the girl was seeing a boyfriend, but the girl said no. Then she went on to investigate about her menstrual cycle and asked her when she had her last menstruation. Mamle said she was in the fourth week since the last time. Maa Lako then said: "If it is the truth that you're speaking, we expect that we will see your menses by Sunday. If it is not seen between now and Sunday you might have to visit Atua before you are allowed to go to the *tɛgbetɛ*. You don't count the days. You are just here and it comes, isn't it? We are never challenged; you claim to have no boyfriend and we live to see the truth." There is a government hospital in Atua. Julie told me before that her mother sometimes sends some of her *dipo-yi* there when she has a suspicion that they might be pregnant. In order to exclude any risk, she lets them have a pregnancy test before proceeding with the rites. As mentioned before, there is no direct link between *dipo* and the first menstruation. However, when a girl menstruates during *dipo*, it is seen as a blessing. She is smeared with white clay (*nguo*) as I witnessed myself. The women then sing in honour of her.

The cleansing rituals above show characteristic elements of Krobo purification and pacification rites that are such an intrinsic part of most of their 'traditional' ritual ceremonies. For instance, bringing a living animal in contact with a person and letting the blood flow over the person's feet and touching the feet with it are characteristic details of purification rituals (Huber 1958). According to the explanations of Julie and maa Lako, the red chicken used in the cleansing, represents 'dirt'. With the subsequent white chicken this ritual pollution is taken away. The white fowl is seen as a sign of blessing, i.e. it pacifies. Maa Lako explained: "If a red fowl is used to remove the problem on you, the white fowl is used as a sign of victory. It is also to prevent disaster following you back to the ceremonial grounds." The purification of a person through the use of a red and white fowl can also be done in other instances, if necessary. For example, I once witnessed it when it was done for a man who had been involved in a motor accident. And I have also seen it performed during the installation ceremony of a chief. Similarly, the colours red and white were used in designating ritual food, as described above.[393]

The aspect of going to the diviner is not mentioned in published descriptions of *dipo*. Huber (1993), for example, does not mention it at all. Some people claim that traditional priests have added these rituals to the whole ceremony in order to make it 'more fetish'. This particular aspect of *dipo* is regarded as specifically appalling and extremely pagan by most churchgoing Krobo. For instance, Alfred Ablaidu Ambassaky, a former headmaster of the Presbyterian Primary school in Kodjonya told me: "There are some aspects [of *dipo*], which go against Christianity. (…) Sometimes you see some oracles being consulted during the process of the ceremony. (…) That's why they have a conflict with Christianity. According to the Bible we should not consult oracles."[394] However, these rites are important to include in the description of the *dipo* ceremony. Most parents have them performed for their children They show the importance of ritual cleanliness and that Krobo ideas about what constitutes a person (the way the body, soul and spirit are related) are very much alive, and therefore contribute to our understanding of why rites are considered to be important.

Separation

Sunday: tying of the soni

Lako Sakite received her first full batch of *dipo* girls (*dipo-yi*) of that season in her house on Sunday morning April 11th, 1999. This first day this first group in April only consisted of nine girls. Three of them were siblings as I described above: eleven-year-old Doe and her nine-year-old sister and brother Ata and Lawɛ. Because their mother Ako was a relative of maa Lako, she agreed upon

---

[393] The use of the colours red, white and black, in particular in ceremonies and initiation rites, has been noted elsewhere in Africa. See e.g. Turner (1967: 60-74) and Richards (1956: 59) about colour symbolism among respectively the Ndembu and the Bemba in Zambia.
[394] Interview June 22, 1994, Kodjonya.

an amount of only 20,000 (twenty-thousand) *cedis* for the performance of the three of them, instead of 15,000 *cedis* (around five USD at the time), which people claimed was the usual sum for one child. The other five girls from the same family were the ones that had been cleansed together with Doe, Ata and Lawε: the two sisters, Mamle and Maku of eighteen and sixteen years old, and their mother's cousin's daughters, Koko and Mamle of six and two years old and another niece of three years old named Domεyo. Finally, there was twelve-year-old Maku, daughter of Awoyaa from Agomanya, again a relative of maa Lako. A Sunday is the usual day to start with marking the *dipo* candidates as *dipo-yi*. In the past it would either be a Sunday or a Thursday, the holy day of Nana Klowεki, according to Huber (1993: 166, 169). Younger girls are often added to the group on the following Friday. For those candidates the whole ceremony can be finished in one weekend.

As usual at the beginning of a ceremony, maa Lako started with a libation. Her female assistant, an old woman named Mawo, cleansed the girls with a '*tsit-sii*'. The girls removed their wax print wrappers now. They also had to remove their underwear. Especially the older girls felt reluctant to undress, although there were only women around. At another place I observed how an older girl felt so shy that she was allowed to undress inside the room. The elder women had grumbled about it. They always assured me that the naked breasts are necessary. In this way, they can tell whether the girls are pregnant or not by looking at their breasts and stomach.

Maa Lako and her assistant shaved part of the hair of the girls with a razor blade (*yi-si-pomi*) to create the characteristic Krobo style of the past called *klohuε*. The girls were lined up to wait for their turn. After that, the *soni*, a particular palm fibre (see chapter five), was put around the neck of each girl, one after the other. This ritual was called *soni muomi*. Lawε was made to sit next to Ata for it. Maa Lako thrice put the *soni* around the neck of Ata and fixed it the third time with a knot. She gave her a second one for Lawε. Then she cut the ends and held them in her right hand and touched Ata's forehead and her chest with them, while using the following prayer formula:

> May you be bold, may you be fair and firm, may your heart be strong, may you work and prosper. Go in peace and return the same, if they inquire about you they should be told, you're healthy. May you be fertile and produce. When you are born and you grow up you are made a Krobo woman. Lawε is your twin brother. All that must be done for Lawε will be added to yours. (Original in Dangme)

To Lawε maa Lako said:

> Lawε, as a man behold your *soni,* we add it to Ata's. All that needs to be done for you Ata takes up, but at the outdooring stage you will be dressed up like Ata. And so Lawε, give them your blessing. If you go hunting, come back with game. If you go

treasure hunting come with success. Lawɛ your part is added to Ata's. (Original in Dangme)

In order to be certain that everything was understood she asked: Are you satisfied? (*Tse o bua jɔ?*). Lawɛ was urged to respond and answered: "*Ee*" (Yes). Maa Lako then ended by saying: "*Dipo* taboos/detests any illness" (*A sɛ we nɔ dipo nɛ e dɔ la*). She asked Lawɛ one last question: "Do you understand?" (*O nu?*). Lawɛ answered: "*Yoo*", he did.

The girls were all given a new string of waist beads. After this, a simple white string made from pineapple leaves (*glo*) was put around the waist. The women were cutting a shining red fabric, with either black or white patterns, to turn it into long stripes of loincloth. They subsequently pulled such a *subue* between the legs of a girl, both ends being held by one woman. Then they tugged it under the string of waist beads and the *glo* to let the *subue* almost reach the ground both at the back and in front. A wax print wrapper was then tied around the waist on top of the *subue*. In the meantime, some of the women were singing many *ha*, a type of *klama*, songs. Most girls had quite short hair already, so nothing else was done to it. Only Maku, Awoyaa's daughter, had longer hair. Koryo, a 'sister' of Julie who also lived in the house with maa Lako, dressed her hair for her in another traditional style called *yi-hɔɔm*. This style has a religious connation and can be seen in old photographs from the Basel Missionary.[395] The hair is divided into five buns arranged in a circle, with one in the centre.

Now the girls were called one by one to the grinding stone by maa Lako's assistant Mawo. It was a large, flat stone that stood on the cement floor on the veranda. Mawo charged 200 *cedis* per child. She put some millet on the stone and grabbed a girl's hands and put them thrice on top of the grinding smaller stone. Then the girl in question started to grind. In the background the women were singing *ha* songs: 'Come closer to the grinding stone, so that we may grind the millet' (*Hɛ mo su wɛ he ne wa gblɛ ngma*). Mawo helped, and in some cases she showed how it should be done. The ground millet was put in the girl's calabash and she made room for the next candidate. After Doe had finished her turn, she picked up her calabash and took it to maa Lako who sat at the other end of the open compound. Maa Lako mixed the millet with some water and made Doe drink some, but only after the third offer. Then she had to chew some, but only swallowed it the third time. Doe's face betrayed the tastelessness of the substance. Maa Lako smeared the rest of the mixture on Doe's chest and made her turn around and lower her cloth a bit. She also smeared the substance on her waist while murmuring: "Go and return with peace. You shouldn't be frightened

---

[395] BMA D-30.08.044, 'Ein Otufo Mädchen'; BMA D-30.08.045, 'Otufo Mädchen'; According to Quarcoopome (1991: 62), this hair style called *akuku*, *akoko* or *akukuli* is common among both the Dangme and the Ga, and at Prampram and old Ningo towns is a privilege only accorded priestesses of indigenous deities. Maku actually is a priestess, just like her mother, for the clan deity Mɛtɛ.

Fig. 8: Grinding millet the traditional way, Somanya, March 1999.

255

by these rituals, never. Be bold" (*Ke o ya tsl<u>oo</u>. A pee we n<u>o</u> ha n<u>o</u> nɛ e tsui po k<u>o</u>k<u>oo</u>k<u>o</u>. O tsui ko po*). Finally, some millet was smeared on her knees and feet.

Around nine o'clock in the morning everything was finished. However, the dancing continued. Ata and Lawɛ danced as a pair and all the women were cheering them. Even maa Lako danced while she was seated on her stool, by swaying her upper body and arms. I could see she was in her element. As she often said, she simply loved the *dipo* performance, and nothing would ever stop her from doing it. Awoyaa, Maku's mother, made another attempt to let the two 'big girls' dance by demonstrating to them how to dance. The evening before the girls were encouraged to practice the dancing, but they had felt shy, and because they did not live in the Krobo area, the dancing seemed quite new to them. The group of curious children that gathered in the compound teased them by singing: 'If you don't know how to dance, you'll only get chicken feet to eat!' But for the time being these two girls still refused to dance, despite warnings from Ako that they'd better practice in time. She said they would have to dance later on, whether they liked it or not, as every Krobo woman is supposed to know how to dance. The dance consists of very graceful hand movements. The rest of the body is held rather tight. Ata and Lawɛ shuffled forwards and backwards by just moving their toes, swaying their head elegantly to the rhythm of the music. Some women were singing, accompanied by the beating on a gourd. This is a female instrument, consisting of a calabash harnessed with beads, coins or shells.

This time of the day on Sunday morning was also the time for many people in Odumase to get ready to go to church. Bold and wild Awoyaa started to sing mocking songs. I understood she sang about the pastor, and how he would see buttocks and that we were ready for him. And why, she sang, does the pastor always come and watch when the *dipo-yi* go for their bath? Everybody laughed. I also recorded a song with the following lines: 'Reverend minister/pastor, your daughter was among those candidates we tied the *s<u>o</u>ni* for' (*Papa Os<u>o</u>fo o bi <u>o</u> ngɛ mi nɛ a mu<u>o</u> s<u>o</u>ni*).

After this, the *dipo-yi* went to fetch water, to fill the big barrels in the compound. They would carry out chores like this the rest of the week. There was water for bathing, washing, and drinking. For the period of their initiation the girls were not allowed to drink tap water, because it comes from the Volta river (see chapter five). The girls were also not allowed to eat any corn 'which has been put in water'. This means no *kenkey* (Krobo: *otim*) or *banku*, as these meals are prepared from fermented corn. I was told that it is 'foreign food', food that is not regarded as indigenous Krobo, but as of Akan origin. Therefore corn and also cassava are not allowed during *dipo*. Leftover food, in particular soup, according to Julie, is also forbidden, apparently because of the fear that anybody could tamper with it during an unguarded moment. Everything has to remain pure and clean. During the rest of the week most girls slept in their own family houses. Only her close relatives Doe and Awoyaa's daughter Maku stayed with maa Lako. Although Maku was relatively young, she looked quite grown, and her mother Awoyaa wanted to do everything 'the proper way' for her. She preferred her to stay with maa Lako for a longer time than the rest, especially since Maku was already a priestess (*woyo*), like herself. Only two weeks later she would add her younger daughter Lajɛ, who was eleven years old, and her granddaughter Afi Dede, who was six years old, to the group, in order to do the final outdooring together with Maku. The other girls visited maa Lako's house every day. They fetched water, cooked and swept the compound. Every evening they practised their dancing skills. They were recognisable to anyone as a *dipo-yo* for the whole period. They only wore the *subue* and a wax print wrapper on top, leaving the chest bare, plus the *soni* around their neck. They did not wear any sandals or shoes.

Friday: Preparing the millet drink

The preparing of the millet beer (*ngma da*) took place on the following Friday, April 16th. Maa Lako's assistant Mawo swayed the *tsitsii* around the heads of the people present in maa Lako's compound that afternoon, and then laid it at the doorstep where it remained smoking. That day, the millet, mixed with some maize, was put on the fire to prepare the *ngma da*, literally the millet drink, which was going to be drank over the weekend during the main rituals. Maa Lako poured a libation before she started. She and Mawo already let the millet ferment. Then they mixed it with water and used two pots for the *ngma da*, a huge one and a smaller one. They put the small pot on the earthen fireplace that was lit with firewood first. They did it very carefully, because it was common knowledge that if one of the pots would break during the process, it would indicate that one of the girls was pregnant. Mawo scooped the foam off the boiling liquid inside the small pot. Some coins were placed next to the fire. Maa Lako explained to me that they gave money and poured libations in front of the cooking pot for the spirit of the hearth, so that "any evil spirit hovering around to spoil the drink can't do this" (*Noko yaya nɛ ngɛ bee nɛ ma ba puɛ da a e be nyɛ*). Another *tsitsii* laid smoking on the other fire for the same purpose (to chase away evil spirits). Later on the large pot was put on that fire. Maa Lako poured another libation in front of the fire. After the cooking, Mawo put both pots inside a small storeroom. She placed three old cutlasses straight up against the big pot. She covered the pots with a calabash and made black scratches on the back with a crayon, probably a piece of charcoal. She repeated this with the small pot. She finally stroke each pot with one of the old cutlasses. She murmured something that I could not understand. When I asked what she was doing exactly, I was told that it was for protection and anyone who saw the pot would know that it had to be left alone. The two old women were involved with the work the whole day, although maa Lako still prepared her tobacco to sell it in between the preparation phases of the *ngma da*. She, Ako and other women were also busy threading beads all day. Old ladies like maa Lako are usually experts in naming and validating beads.[396]

In the morning, a mother brought her daughter to be added to the group. Naki was a pretty girl of five years old and she lived in the house just opposite maa Lako's house. The *soni* was tied for her alone and she was made to grind the millet. Papa Tetteh came later to carry out the divination for her. Now maa Lako's first small group numbered ten girls. The second and third group would be bigger. In 1994 I observed a first group that consisted of only nine girls. Then the two oldest girls had also been 'big girls' aged nineteen and seventeen, who had started on a Sunday. The rest of the younger girls had been added to them on the Friday before the weekend of the 'grand finale'. The second and the third group of *dipo* candidates is the largest for most priests.

Ritual cleansing

Saturday morning: the ritual bath

Many small rituals are used to symbolically cleanse the girls, the main ones are the ritual bath and the sprinkling with goat blood performed on Saturday. I paid Mawo 5,000 *cedis* as a fee for accompanying us to the ritual bathing on Saturday morning, April 17th. Maa Lako herself could not go, because it involved walking. She poured a libation before we went. Then, around seven in the morning the girls were all lined up, with the tallest girls in front. Comfort-Koko, one of the women from Assin-Foso, closed the procession carrying her two-year-old on her back. Only Maku, Awoyaa's daughter stayed behind with an annoyed face. She wanted to come along, but had to wait for another week before it was her turn. All girls, even the youngest on her mother's back, had white walking sticks in their right hand and carried a calabash on their head.[397] The calabash was filled with a towel, locally made soap, a traditional fibre sponge, a string of waist beads and a new piece of *subue* and cloth. Accompanied by their female relatives who were beating the gourds and singing, they walked about 500 metres to a nearby stream.

---

[396] Many of the old ladies have their own treasure-chest with old beads at home. They consider them as part of their legacy. Maa Lako also has a large box full of precious beads. Many people come to borrow beads from her for a special occasion, sometimes against a small fee.

[397] This type of stick is also used by the priests and the installation of chiefs. Quarcoopome calls it a 'mystical stick', which is made out of the wood of a tree called *okoli-awotso* (*Ochna membranacia*) that has religious significance (Quarcoopome 1993: 147, 150).

Fig. 9: Dipo girls going to the stream for their ritual bath, Somanya, April 3, 1999

When we reached the stream, the girls were given instructions where to stand and what to do. We were at a secluded place surrounded by palm trees and green bushes. The road was near, but passers-by could not see us. Only some curious children from a neighbouring house stood by and watched. However, it looked as if they were more curious about me, a *blɛfono* (white woman), than about the *dipo-yi*. Still anybody who passed by could know something was happening here, because the women were not exactly quiet. They hardly tried to keep their voices down. Ako and Awoyaa repeatedly sang with loud voices. Ako obviously had already drunk a bit too much of the schnapps. She sang excitedly: 'My daughter Dede, are you among [the *dipo* candidates]?' (*Ye bi Dede lee o ngɛ mi lo?*).

I was surprised that there appeared to be no water around. I asked Julie if there really was a stream. "It's just here. There is the stream line", she answered. My eyes followed the direction in which her finger was pointing, but I did not see anything. "But there is no water?" I asked. "Right now there is no water", Julie said, with no further explanation. I contemplated for a moment. "So what water do they use then", I asked in confusion. "Oh, they are going to bring the well water here", she said, as if that was very obvious. Then she added with a serious tone in her voice: "You see, they are not allowed to use any other water, except from the stream or well." Some women actually soon came back with a few buckets of water from the well. One of them was scolded by Mawo for not taking off her shoes when she approached the girls. She walked back to remove her slippers. I asked Julie whether I should take off my shoes as well, but she said that "only those who are performing the rites" had to remove them. Here I obviously was the outsider, the researcher and filmer, despite my help with Ako's children's *dipo*. Ako helped Doe and Ata to wash and bathe. Men were not allowed here, so Lawɛ was not part of the bathing ritual, but as usual Ata did everything double for him. Each girl received some water in her calabash and had to take off her *subue* and waist beads. Then they proceeded to wash their *subue* with water and soap. After that, they washed their whole body with a sponge and a lot of local foaming soap. The sponges made out of the fibres of a plant are no longer commonly used these days. Most people bathe with 'sponges' that are actually strips of fishnets in different bright colours. However, old ladies like maa Lako always preferred the indigenous sponge. "How can I bathe with something people use to catch fish?" she said. She felt that the indigenous sponge fulfilled its purpose, cleaning, much better than the 'fishnet'. During the *dipo* period, it was considered to be necessary that participants used the 'original' and 'indigenous Krobo' items as much as possible.

After the bathing the girls were smeared with 'traditional powder', which looked like sawdust, in their armpits, neck and chest. After this, the women helped them to fix the new *subue* to a new string of waist beads. On top of that they wrapped a fresh wax print wrapper around the waist. Ata wore two cloths, one for her and one for her twin brother. The girls took off their *soni*. When they had finished all this, the girls were lined up again with calabashes on their head and white walking sticks in their hands. They were told not to talk on their way back. Julie said that from this time on they had to be serious. The girls were admonished that if anybody would try to make them laugh on the way they should compose themselves. It was remarkable to see how the faces of the children were in general calm, almost apathetic. One could interpret this as the dislike of the children to pass through *dipo*, but I believe this is generally not the case. I also observed a similar posture during different happy ceremonies such as weddings. The persons who are the centre of the rites are supposed to compose themselves and act worthy and dignified. They should not show their emotions. The people around them, however, were laughing and singing and dancing. They were obviously enjoying themselves.

On the way home the women beat the gourds and started singing again. After we returned to maa Lako's house the girls were dancing to *ha* songs. Mawo and maa Lako prepared a red kind of dye (*boa*) out of some leaves and white clay, which was mashed together. They sprinkled the girls with it. Julie explained that it is "just for decoration". In the meantime, we, the adults, drank palm wine and were fed with water yam and stew, prepared with palm oil, a dish called *wuwi*. The *ngma da* was on the fire again. A woman came by and spoke softly to Julie, after which Julie delivered the message to her mother. There were more whispers. Julie later told me that the woman was a member of the Pentecost Church, but that she wanted to enlist five children, who she was representing, for *dipo*. Because of her church she had to do everything 'in secret'.

Maa Lako called the girls who were present one by one again. She thrice put some roasted corn on each girl's lips and made them eat after the third time. She repeated the same with pieces of sugarcane and groundnuts. Then she threw hands full of each into the girl's *subue*, which she held in front of her like a knapsack. The explanation was that after this the girls were not allowed anymore to eat these 'forbidden foods' until after the final rites on Monday. According to Julie, this was also to remind them of the old days, when people would carry this type of food with them on long journeys. In the afternoon 'Saturday's *fufui*' (*Ho fufui*) was served. A special aspect of this *fufui* was that only plantain was used for its preparation. Normally people would use cassava, but from now on it was considered as non-indigenous, like corn and other foodstuffs, and therefore it was forbidden food. Mawo, maa Lako's assistant, simply told me "It is *kusumi*" and could not offer any other explanation. Again maa Lako first introduced the food in a ritual way to the girls by letting them spit it out thrice and then eat it. This was to teach them how to eat, she merely explained. She also said that it was to teach the girls that they should not eat in a house that is not 'clean', maybe because the *dipo* is not performed there. In that case they should not swallow the food. The girls were served with a nourishing palm nut soup to accompany the *fufui*.

After eating, the girls practised dancing again. The women were having fun, especially Awoyaa and Ako were joking a lot, as usual. Ako pulled one of her breasts out of her yellow dress, which caused hilarity, and held the breast in front of her daughters as if she wanted to say proudly: 'Look I'm your mother who nursed you and who helped you to reach this stage'. They sang a few special songs for twins. For example, they sang the following song, which tells us that ceremonies for twins and their support are expensive:

That bitter fish of the sea, it has touched my lips (*Wo lo dodomi wolo ba sa i nya he*)

And a favourite song in which the mother of twins is teased and insulted, goes as follows:

Dale [name of the mother] you are strong headed, your face is like something partly eaten by sheep (*Dale le o gbe o he nya, o hɛ mi yaya kaa nonɛ to ye*)

Awoyaa was making growling sounds when she ate, and also came to 'steal' food out of my bowl. Maa Lako asked her amusedly if she was out of her mind. Everybody was laughing about Awoyaa's funny behaviour. She told me I would have to do the same thing when it was her children's turn.

Late in the afternoon some distant family members passed by to greet maa Lako as they happened to be in the neighbourhood for a funeral. It was busy in the little compound all the time. The women continued to thread beads. Others were singing and were accompanied by the gourds. Some of the following *klama* songs were sung:

(Soloist): Today for this performance, the people come from *manyɛ* Lako's house and the occasion is *dipo*. We've assembled because of our yearly customary rite. (*Mwɛno wa ngɛ fiɛe, nɛ wa je manyɛ Lako we o nɛ wa ngɛ dipo pee. Wa kpe ngɛ wa jeha kusimi o he*)

The Chorus responded with a song that means to say that a woman looking for a husband must ensure the man is the industrious type, or somebody she can build on. Or it could also be explained as 'Major enterprises must be entrusted to the care of very competent people', referring to the *dipo* girl who traditionally would be married soon after *dipo*:

(Chorus): It's to a strong tree that we tether the cow. (Exclamation), a beautiful one, behold, is coming. (*Tso o nɛ e he wa a ngo na a mwo he. Ja lellee yo nɛ hi ma*)

Awoyaa really seemed to be into the songs that mock pastors. She sang another one:

Pastor stop looking at me, the *dipo* we are performing you are also doing it (for your daughter). (*Osofo lee joo mi wotsi mi nio nɛ wa wo o mohu o ngɛ mi nɛ wa wo*)

262

Papa Tetteh, the diviner, arrived after four p.m. that afternoon to finish with his job. He was going to fix certain items that were requested by the girls' *susuma* on a string around the girls' neck. Their *susuma* had told him they wanted to wear these things during *dipo*. He was late, because he had done the same job first at another place, the Klowɛki shrine in Kodjonya. He called the girls one by one. They sat on a stool in front of him. He then put the string around the neck that hung on their back right down to their waist. He tied the necessary items to this end. For example, for sixteen-year-old Maku he used the ancestral bright blue *k̰oli* bead and some white hairs. For Ata he used three cowries and four other shells. She had a double thread, one representing her twin brother. Papa Tetteh used four cowries for Doe, all as instructed during the divination the week before. Naki who had just joined the group, was last in turn.

Around eight o'clock in the evening, all girls assembled in maa Lako's little courtyard. Maa Lako gave all girls some millet to eat. Then she thrice wrapped a piece of white calico around all the girls' chests in a ceremonious manner, while they were standing on the Roan antelope (*b̰o*) skin that was spread on the ground. The Roan antelope skin is held sacred and *dipo* girls are warned that they will turn crazy when they step on it while trying to conceal a possible pregnancy. So it is a kind of test of the integrity of the girls. The food was "because of the custom", maa Lako said, "That is what they ate in the olden days". She gave it to the children very inconspicuously out of a tin can instead of using a special bowl. That is, she explained, because these days the young men are wicked, and they might use '*juju*' (sorcery) to affect the children, so they might put something in the bowl if they see it. While she was wrapping the calico around the girls, maa Lako spoke out words like the following:

> This is cloth with which your father makes you a Krobo woman. May you go in peace and return in peace. May you be courageous and prosper. If you are called may you respond to your name. This cloth is a symbol of your *dipo* rites, go in peace and return in peace.

As ideally it is the father who is responsible for his daughter's *dipo*, it is said that the father provides the cloth. Then papa Tetteh was holding a black goat by its legs and maa Lako was sitting by his side. The girls were lined up in front of her. Papa Tetteh swayed the goat towards a girl's forehead and she thrice pushed the goat back with both hands. Maa Lako then touched the goat's forehead with both palms of her hands, then took her hands off and touched the girl's forehead and chest. She repeated this act thrice. She explained to me later that it is supposed to remove all sins from the girls. I also asked her why it was papa Tetteh who helped her with the rites. Maa Lako explained that not only did she need a man to hold the goat for her because it was heavy, but papa Tetteh also was 'a child of Klowɛki'. The goat cried out of fear and rolled its eyes. Some girls looked afraid, but were still laughing. The goat swaying in general caused great merriment, but the youngest girl was scared and cried, and her mother had to hold her. Papa Tetteh spoke the following words while performing the rite for Doe:

> Doe your father Tɛwia presents you with a sheep with which he is making a Krobo woman of you. May you go in peace, and return in peace. May you go to prosper and return with prosperity.

Her 'father Tɛwia' was Doe's mother's brother, who acted on behalf of the dead grandfather as head of the household. In the past every father would provide a goat for each of his daughters, but nowadays people cannot afford it. Therefore the priestess buys one goat that is used for the whole group. Lawɛ was also among the initiands, but was referred to in a slightly different way. Papa Tetteh wished many children in future for Lawɛ. And he said *dipo* should help him to find a wife. After the first children, the ceremony became like a routine for all the girls that followed. Papa Tetteh repeated the same words (with different names) for all the different girls. When he had finished, maa Lako poured a libation to the ancestors. Now papa Tetteh called out loud the small donations that were given to the *dipo-yi* by their relatives: "Doe, your mother gives 150 *cedis* as a token of your *dipo* victory. Your father Tɛwia presents you with 200 *cedis* as a token of your *dipo* victory" (etcetera). Afterwards there was more singing and dancing again. One *klama* song recommended the 'good things' in maa Lako's house, with which the *dipo* itself could be meant. Or it might mean that one only meets beautiful *dipo* candidates at maa Lako's house. In other words it meant: 'The best is found at maa Lako's house' (*maa Lako we nonɛ hi ngɛ*). This was a popular song I heard in other houses, only then it referred to the particular priest residing there.

Sunday morning: killing the goat

Around four a.m. the next morning, I woke up Julie to accompany me to watch the 'killing of the goat' (*to-gbemi*) ritual. Castrated goats are the usual sacrifice used for the goddess Klowɛki, and the blood is meant to cleanse the initiates.[398] Maa Lako said she wanted to do it early in the morning because she was afraid of the sanitary health inspectors. I think she also was afraid to do this thing openly, because we were close to the so-called Christian quarters (*lebo*) of town.

---

[398] In the neighbouring (but Akan) area of Akuapem a castrated ram is likewise considered to be symbolically clean and peaceful (Gilbert 1989: 67).

264

It also meant that she was not going to use the goat's fat and intestines to decorate the girls when they would go to the *tɛgbɛtɛ* later on, which used to be a custom in the past. She would use white calico instead.[399]

This ritual slaughtering did not take much time. The girls were standing in a wide circle in the courtyard. Only the light of a single bulb lit the place and I did not have enough light to film. Papa Tetteh simply slit the throat of the goat unceremoniously and then sprayed the blood that gushed out of the goat's neck over the feet of the girls. He did this by swaying the goat round. When I asked maa Lako later why he did this, she simply said that "this is custom and as usual, we don't explain all of it". However, she also added that it is one of the very necessary rites of *dipo*. She explained that the spilling of the blood of the goat is among the very essential parts of *dipo*. In case anyone would challenge one's passing through *dipo*, she said, one could refer to this rite as a defence and call in the *dipo* priestess as witness. Huber (1993: 173) wrote that: "The blood is thought to wash away anything in the adolescent girl which could be harmful for her healthy development towards mature womanhood and motherhood; in other words, everything which could endanger her future conceptions and parturitions."

Maa Lako poured a libation in which she informed the ancestors about the stage reached in the *dipo* and asked for their help. When papa Tetteh had finished, the girls went to wash the blood of their feet and papa Tetteh started to cut the goat into pieces that were going to be distributed to different members of maa Lako's family.

The Climax

Sunday morning: going to the old lady's house

On Sunday early morning around 6.30 a.m., April 18th, after I had taken a little nap in Angmokwo's (Julie's sister) bed, the girls were lined up again in a row, from tall girls to short girls. This morning we were 'going to the old lady's house' (*a ya yomo o wɛ*). Lawɛ also went along. The initiands were all holding a walking stick in their hands. Maa Lako had put the white calico around their waist three times again. Mawo prepared a small black pot containing millet beer that had to be taken to Kodjonya to see 'the old lady', referring to Nana Klowɛki. I was waiting for Julie who had gone home earlier and promised to bring me a

---

[399] A few priests may still use the goat fat instead of white calico. At the Okumo priest's place in Mampong, in 1994, I saw the goat being slaughtered immediately after the 'touching-of-the-goat-ritual' in the evening. He did use the goat's fat that was dried over night to use it as a veil to decorate the girls' heads the next day. In the past, the more intestines were used to decorate a girl, the greater the wealth of the father's family (see chapter three).

cloth that I could wear inside the shrine to which we were going, but we had to leave without her.

On the way it was clear the girls were tired after the short night they had. Little Domɛyo's cloth kept on coming down, and little Naki cried and said she was feeling hungry. When we reached Kodjonya, we saw that many other groups also had arrived. The house and courtyard of Klowɛki were crowded with people. I was worried, because Julie still had not shown up and I realised I could not go into the shrine without a cloth. And even though I had been at this place before and the priests knew me, without Julie as my companion my position was much less secure in this large crowd of strangers who were all looking at me. Some people were just curious about me, the white woman. Others made a less hospitable impression and warned me that I could not go inside the shrine. I decided to take control. I did not want to miss this ritual that I had not witnessed before. After all, perhaps Julie would not come at all.

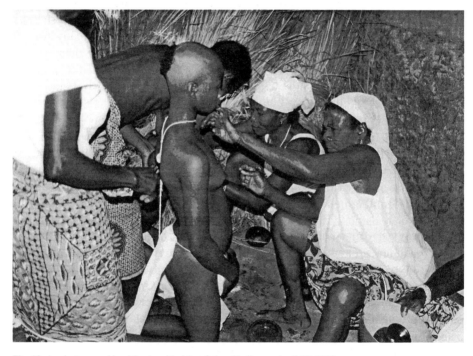

Fig. 10: A priestess marking Mamle with dabs of clay, Kodjonya, April 18, 1999

I went to greet the Klowɛki priest's regent (*seyelo*), and asked a cloth from his wife, 'auntie' Mamle, another *dipo* priestess. She gave me one. I undressed in her room and wrapped the cloth around like a dress. I went outside the house and crossed the courtyard to enter the grove where the Klowɛki shrine

266

was. One priestess wanted to stop me, but I told her I wanted to accompany 'my' children, Doe, Ata and Lawɛ. Mawo then led me to the place inside the grove where four elderly women were seated next to each other in an open mud hut. Two of them were the twins Ako and Akweley, the Klowɛki *seyelọ's* sisters, who I had met before. The other two were priestesses who knew me as well. I was allowed to film, but I was asked to give the priestesses some money as they were 'hungry'. Then suddenly Julie had arrived after all, accompanied by two white American girls who had also come to witness *dipo*.[400] Without Julie they would not have been allowed inside and I felt slightly irritated that they kept 'my' research assistant away from me and had obviously followed in my tracks.

It was quite crowded inside the grove. The *dipo* girls from groups of different 'houses' were standing in lines in front of the four women. There were also several other twins (boys accompanying their twin sisters). The women marked each girl with dots of clay on their temples, breasts, lower back, back of their knees and her feet (*bua siami*). The accompanying women in the room were singing. The marks were 'for blessing'. These marks indicate the stage in which the girls were at that moment. They show that they were ready for the climax (*tɛgbɛtɛ yami*). I was told that different shrines have their own type of marks, so that people can see where they are from. It is also believed that the old ladies are able to make out any possible pregnant girl during this ceremony by studying the girls' bodies.

According to Lako Sakite, she offered food to the ancestors at this stage, but I had not observed it. However, three weeks later on a Sunday, I observed how, after the marking, food was presented to the ancestors by the priestesses in Asitey, a nearby town, during a *dipo* performance. The diviner (*gbalo*) and a priestess first poured a libation of palm wine and schnapps to invoke the ancestors and inform them about the food. The priestesses cooked leaves of the *lẹno* tree and filled bamboo sticks with water, palm wine and schnapps. They prepared a mixture of cooked millet with palm oil and dried fish. This was placed on fragments of broken clay plates. The diviner threw the leaves and pieces of white calico in front of the house where he had already laid down pieces of meat. The flies feasted on it. The man said that if the ancestors would not be fed, they would come and do bad things. Finally, the rest of the food and drink was put down outside the house under a big tree in 'the bush' for the ancestors to come and eat.

---

[400] I had met these two girls for the first time a week or so earlier in Odumase. They were exchange students who studied for one semester at the African Studies Department of the University of Ghana in Legon. They would stay in Krobo for a few weeks to study the *dipo* rites. After that they were going to write a long essay on these rites.

In the afternoon, back in maa Lako's house, the standard party meal for 'traditional' Krobo festivities, *kungmi*, was prepared (see chapter five). Mawo had filled a large calabash with white clay, leaves and water. After eating, all the girls had to come and cleanse themselves with it. The older ones were having fun and splashed the cooling water on their almost naked bodies. Two-year-old Mamle cried and had to be held by her mother. Julie said the 'bathing' means that they were getting cleansed and ready to go to the *tɛgbɛtɛ*. On the way to the *tɛgbɛtɛ* an elder walking in front of them would also sprinkle this type of water from a calabash over the girls. Now the women were preparing the raffia string that was tied to the upper arm of each girl together with some black seeds (*kutukpa*). An elder female relative was busy mashing lemon with a particular root (*kpanyatsrɛ*) to obtain a colouring. It is used to colour the *kutukpa*, which according to the people around "just serves decorative purpose". However, the raffia fibre also has a mystical meaning because of its ancestral associations, as mentioned in a previous chapter. Again Ata received two strings, one for her and one for her twin brother. In the meantime Maa Lako was roasting the goat meat. The goat had still been jumping around a day earlier, now his head was lying next to the cooking pot. Koryo and Angmokwo, Julie's sisters, declared that they would not eat the meat, because they were Christians.

We left the house around three in the afternoon. This time when we reached Kodjonya, it was even busier than in the morning. Now outside, around the house, there were women and girls selling foodstuffs and sweets, wax print cloths, shoes and *akpeteshie*. In the 'kitchen' (a shelter of wooden poles thatched with a roof of foliage), other women, some of them priestesses, were stirring their ladles inside huge cooking pots on the fire. They were also preparing the *kungmi*. Inside the house, at the courtyard, I saw that a large number of *dipo-yi* had gathered. I counted at least thirty, and their number was still growing. There was an impressive crowd of male and especially female relatives. The excited buzzing of their voices filled the air. Some young women were beating their gourds vehemently, at the same time jumping and singing at the top of their voice. I joined them for a few minutes, much to the amusement of the bystanders. By this time I had already changed my clothes, because I knew that the women who wanted to accompany the children later on should not wear a top and no jewellery, even though nobody would be allowed inside the shrine itself.

The priestesses thrice pulled each girl to stand on an antelope skin. The mothers and other female relatives decorated the girls with many beads around their upper arms, knees, neck and in particular their waists. The mothers also placed strings of white calico and raffia around their shoulders and put a piece of calico on their head in order to provide them with spiritual protection. A priestess sprinkled white clay on the faces and chest of the candidates for decoration, but mainly to portray purity. Late in the afternoon the girls, accompanied by

Fig. 11: Lawɛ, Ata and Doe, ready to go to the tɛgbɛtɛ, (as a boy, Lawɛ will not go all the way), whilst their older brother and an auntie are looking on, Kodjonya, April 18, 1999

their (mainly) female relatives, took off for their journey of some 500 metres to the sacred grove where the *tɛgbɛtɛ* was. Some women held a white cross, the symbol of Klowɛki, behind the girls' heads, others beat the gourds and sang. Dozens of girls and a large crowd walked the small path through the bush, further and further away from town. The girls held a leaf between their lips, which prevented them from making any noise. Some of the smallest children who were carried on the back of their mothers had been given cola mixed with *akpeteshie*. It made them feel sleepy and prevented them from crying. The crowd that accompanied the girls, however, was highly excited and very boisterous. The climax was near. This would be the moment of truth. If any of the girls would fail the test on the *tɛgbɛtɛ*, disaster would definitely follow. The girl in question would have to be banished from her family house. The responsible family would have to pay for the purification of the *tɛgbɛtɛ* and their house with an amount of money, seven sheep, seven bottles of schnapps and seven pieces of white calico. No need to say that this would ruin them.[401]

So there was a tangible tension in the air. I was excited too. I had been planning towards this ritual that I was eager to see with my own eyes. Normally only the female priests have the privilege to enter the grove with the *tɛgbɛtɛ* during the *dipo* rites. The minimum requirement is that you have to be an initiated woman yourself. And even the priestesses had "to keep themselves holy" as Julie expressed it, during the *dipo* celebrations. This meant that they stuck to the same food taboos as the *dipo-yi*, and refrained from sexual intercourse. Many people on the way seemed to be worried that I might enter the grove. They made comments about this, some quite hostile. I had experienced this before at a shrine in Somanya (at *Tɛɛ Dugbᴏnya*) where women had sung: 'It [*dipo*] has not been performed for you, so you cannot go with me' (*A pee we ha mo (3x), o bi nyɛɛ ma ya*). It seemed that they did not like to have strangers around here. Earlier I had set my hopes on my familiarity with the people around the Klowɛki priest, and the fact that 'my' children were among the *dipo-yi*. However, I knew that my chances were ruined as soon as the two American students had arrived on the scene. With 'so many' white people around I would not have any chance. I was more or less placed in the same category as 'my sisters', the other *blɛfono*, with whom the people were not familiar.[402]

---

[401] As I mentioned in the introduction of this chapter, the ritual expulsion is the task of the priest *Asa*. I have not witnessed such an expulsion. Huber mentions he witnessed one in 1956 (1958: 168). Tettey mentions an expulsion in Madam (one of Odumase's suburbs) in 1975. The girl in question was taken in by a Christian family (Tettey 1977: 22).

[402] Huber, although a man, writes that he was permitted once to watch the climbing of the *dipo* stone, of which a photo in his book is testimony. Even though Beckwith and Fisher (1999) state that one recent photograph in their book shows the sitting on the *tɛgbɛtɛ*, this may have been staged: the priestess performing the rite is wearing gold jewellery, which is strictly forbidden around the Klowɛki and other indigenous shrines.

Therefore, I devised an alternative plan. Was it not possible for Julie to try to enter the grove with my video camera? As she was also 'a child of Klowɛki' and maa Lako's daughter, she might not have too many problems to enter. Klowɛki *seyelo̲* had agreed, but as he was staying behind in the house, he would not be able to exercise any authority at the grove where only women were allowed. When we arrived at the junction with the big mango tree, beyond which the crowd was not allowed to go, I handed over my video camera to Julie. The two American girls also gave her their photo cameras, so she was quite packed. We waited among the other people who stayed behind. After a while, some ten minutes, the first *dipo-yi* came back from the *tɛgbɛtɛ* under loud cheers of relatives and others. They were carried on the back of their mother or another female relative. A few weeks before in Somanya I had also had the honour to carry a *dipo* girl from the *tɛgbɛtɛ*. The proud grandmother shared this story with many people. Here some of the girls, especially the older ones, were handed over to the young men who were waiting for them. Despite the very heavy weights of the girls caused by the many kilos of glass beads around their waists, most of the carriers tried to run back to the house of Klowɛki as fast as possible, like winners with their trophy. In the past they would truly be the future husbands of the girls. In order to rush them more, people were saying 'the Ashanti were coming', in this way reminding them of the olden days when there was a danger of raiding Akan tribes during wartimes, who sometimes captured Krobo women. Men with old-fashioned rifles were shooting in the air, some deliberately shooting off branches from the trees around. The atmosphere was wild and excited.

It took a long time before Julie finally came back from the *tɛgbɛtɛ*. The last *dipo-yi* had already passed by. I saw her talking to some of the priestesses who were also returning. I was disappointed when she said she had not been allowed to enter the grove. However, her story was nevertheless interesting. Later she narrated to me what had happened at the grove and why the whole procedure had taken so long. Julie told me that the *tɛgbɛtɛ* consisted of a large flat stone with some smaller rocks under it. It was enclosed by palm branches woven into a fence. There were about eight priestesses. She had bowed to them. The moment she entered, one of them started shouting: 'Somebody has entered! Somebody has entered!' Julie said that the priestess was possessed and would not calm down until she had stepped back. However, Julie was sure the priestess had not seen her, but I was not convinced of this when I heard which priestess she was talking about. This same woman had also not been willing to receive me during *dipo* in Somanya. Julie continued to narrate that the priest Klemesi (a male Klowɛki priest) who was just outside, had also noticed her and told her that she could come inside, but not with 'the things' she was carrying. He meant the video and photo cameras. If she would take a picture she would turn blind, they warned her.

Julie described how the girls had entered on their own in small groups. All accompanying women were waiting outside, very anxious. They had also wanted to come inside, but the priests outside had even used canes to keep them at a distance. I asked Julie what they did with the small girls who were tied to their mother's backs. She said that those were handed over to the priestesses, who were the only ones inside. They stood around the *tɛgbɛtɛ*. I knew from other accounts that the rite is quite simple. They will seat each girl on the stone three times. According to Julie there was no talking inside: "The place is very silent!" According to Huber (1993: 178), the priestesses simply say: 'Sit down! Stand up! We are making you a Krobo woman' *(Hisi!-tesi!-wa ngɛ mo Klo-yo peehe-oo!)*. They repeat these words thrice, simultaneously with the action. The rite does not take long, just a few minutes for each girl. Yet, as Bowie (2000: 153) points out for initiation rites in general, the invocation of fear is a powerful way of inscribing meanings on the body and mind of initiands at its most receptive and vulnerable. This fear is also invoked in the girls' mothers. Julie depicted how they were at the left end with four or five girls: "Then a message came out that something was wrong. So all parents should be very careful. If it is your child, you should get prepared to pay. There, a parent started urinating out of fear. Her heart! If it is your child, seven goats, seven schnapps, money!" "Did they think that one of the girls might be pregnant?", I wanted to know. Julie confirmed this and recounted how the priestesses had to perform a special rite to make the girls get up from the stone, as it seemed that the stone somehow did not want to let the girls go:

> They left the girls on the stone and they turned towards the eastern side of the fence. They started singing and clapping, singing and clapping. All the mothers also prayed! The whole family was there. You see, they were five in number, but they were from one family. They started singing a song and the song literally means: 'We are at a place where we don't know whether we will come back or stay.' So these people started singing outside, a priestess was also singing inside, but the voice was not coming out. They were performing the rite. You see that there was a gap, when everybody left and these people were still there.

According to Julie, the priestesses were able to lift the girls up from the stone after about fifteen minutes, and after trying a few times. They were all relieved. According to the priestess Julie had talked to, incidents like these often happened when grown-up girls were involved and people were suspicious about their conduct.

After the girls of maa Lako's group had safely returned to the house, they were seated next to each other on the antelope skins, which were spread out in the courtyard. All their hair was shaved off by some of the elders of their family. Naki's mother, however, had paid 1,000 *cedis* to save her daughter's hair. She explained that she did not like the hair to be shaved, "because the girl goes to school". After the shaving, maa Lako thrice put a conically shaped straw hat on the heads of the girls. It was amusing to see how difficult it was to find a fitting hat for little Domɛyo. The first ones maa Lako tried, covered her eyes. A strip of calico was then tied around the smallest hat, so that it would not come down. After that, Mawo grabbed the hands of each girl and placed them thrice in and out of the black earthen bowl, which was filled with the goat meat in front of them. This was the special bowl maa Lako had not wanted to take out the day before. Then they were given some of the meat to chew. The women around were having fun and laughing. One woman tried to 'steal' the meat from one of the bowls. Afterwards the girls, heavy with beads, were thrice lifted off the skin, one by one. Mawo and another woman performed this job. When they reached the 'big girl' Mamle, the other woman stopped. She made unmistakable sounds while she shook her pelvis forwards, much to the hilarity of the spectators. While dusk was falling, all the girls danced, including the girls from Assin-Fosso who had felt shy during the first days. All relatives around were very de-lighted about the happy ending of the final rites and praised the girls for their dancing skills. They sang *ha* songs like the following one, in which a *dipo* girl is compared to a ripened fruit:

> The fruit is ripe. Fellow friends come and we do the harvesting.
> *Adamo, e fo ngɛ bo he. La lo bi nyɛ ba o o.*

Some old ladies I interviewed reminisced about the time they had passed through these rituals (in the 1930s-1940s). After the Sunday's rites of going to the *tɛgbɛtɛ*, they would stay in confinement for one week before the Monday's closing rituals were performed for them. In this week they were taught more songs and they killed the time with storytelling. As I described in chapter three the period of confinement was much longer on Krobo Mountain, where *dipo* had been performed until the end of the nineteenth century. After coming from the *tɛgbɛtɛ*, the hair of girls was shaved in the same way as today, and the girls wore a priestly hat. While they wore the hat, they were well-fed. The longer the fam-ily could afford their upkeep on the mountain, the more beautiful the girls would finally come out. Until the day the parents wanted to finish their stay, the hair was not cut or even washed anymore. So the final 'washing of the head' ritual signified the end. According to Huber (1993: 182-183), when the hair had grown back after about three months, the girl would be allowed to work again. If the parents could afford it, the girl would still remain on the Mountain for some time. In an informal way she would be taught crafts such as basket weaving or pottery making. Nowadays the confinement lasts just one night, and *dipo* is largely concluded with the 'washing of the head' the following day.

Bold and Beautiful: the final rites

Monday: washing the head

Early in the morning on Monday April 19th, the 'proof pictures' were made of the *dipo-yi* while they were still dressed in the white calico, with the beads and in particular the hat. With this picture they would be able to prove to everyone that they had undergone the *dipo* rites. Usually a number of professional photographers hang around the *dipo* scene, because most people do not have their own cameras. However, I made the pictures of Doe, Ata, and Lawɛ. I had to make one of each of them separately, then one with the three of them, one with their mother Ako and uncle Tɛwia, and then Julie took me with the children as well.

Now a 'cousin', an elderly woman named Dede who did this work every year, was grinding a red colouring with water on a grinding stone. Two normal buckets of water stood beside her, one with soapy water, one with plain water and a towel. One by one the girls came to sit on the small stool in front of her. Dede cut the yellow raffia string unceremoniously from the girl's upper arm. It left a mark, because it was very tight. She also took off the *nyakpa*, the 'necklace' with shells they were given the other day by papa Tetteh for their *susuma*. After lifting the hat thrice, she subsequently took it off the third time. Then she touched the bold head of each girl thrice with the red colouring, which looked like blood. After that, she washed the head with the soapy water and then rinsed it by wringing out the towel over her head. I paid Dede a fee of 2,200 *cedis* for Doe and Ata: 1,000 each for this 'washing of the head' ritual *(yi-fọmi)*, and 100 each for cutting the string.

In the meantime, maa Lako had been seated on a stool in the middle of the courtyard. Mawo assisted her. All the girls and Lawɛ came to her after their head had been washed. Each girl was given a broom and had to sweep for a few seconds. Then she had to grind an imaginary pepper in a grinding bowl, put it in a pot and stir the imaginary soup with a spoon. Ako got overexcited when it was her children's turn and she imitated their actions and made additional sounds. The others around were shaking their heads about this silly woman. In the end, Mawo simulated making the small cuts *(bɛɛm'bọ)*, twelve in number, on the back of the girl's hands with a razor blade.[403] She spoke the following words to accompany the symbolic actions the girls had to perform:

> You'll wake up and sweep, after sweeping, you fetch water. 'What will we eat?' They instruct you to prepare food of the dough or some other food. You prepare the stew, get the dough food ready, you prepare soup and we eat. Should somebody challenge your *dipo*? You tell the person it was done, and show him the marks at the back of

---

[403] In the past a piece of bamboo or a sharp shell was used.

your hand or you name witnesses to come and testify that you were made a Krobo woman. (Original in Dangme)

Although I have still seen real cicatrisations with a majority of adult Krobo women, it seems that it is not done often these days, as mentioned in the previous chapter. I never saw it actually performed and it does not seem to be a must these days. One woman told me that if you have them, "people will know that you are an illiterate".[404] In the past these cuts formed proof that *dipo* had been performed. Literally they meant that a girl had gone through 'the sweeping test'. In addition cuts were made on her back and waist (see previous chapter). The photos that are taken now serve as proof. A photo is also easier to hide than the visible marks, as most church-going people will not want others to know that *dipo* was performed for their daughter.

Another final ritual followed after everybody had finished outside. We moved to 'the hall'. Maa Lako swayed the head of the girl sitting in front of her, while she held a plume of elephant hair (*gani*), on top of her head. This plume was said to represent fertility. She and Mawo, Ako, Julie and the women of the other family sang *klama* songs. Then each girl was given mashed plantain with palm oil, which she spit out thrice before eating. Now the ban on forbidden food was lifted. I had to pay 1,000 *cedis* for each *gani* for 'my' three children, but maa Lako and Mawo were satisfied with a total of 2,000 cedis.

After all had finished, I accompanied Ako with her initiated children and the girl Naki and her mother to visit some relatives. The children danced in each house and they were given small donations. Ako and I were congratulated. We ended at papa Tetteh's house, where his sister prepared a special decoration out of white rope and two or three black beads. She made a kind of bracelet with a plume. It was not clear to me if this was just for adornment or if it had a mystical meaning. At least it was regarded as a unique ornament for *dipo*. Each initiand wore one on the left upper arm. The dressing would be completed the same afternoon.

'Beautifully adorned girl!' [405]: *The outdooring*

It is Monday, April 26, 1999. My colleague Veit Arlt and I are in a compound house in Agomanya. My friend Awoyaa, a woman of 54 years old, is overexcited with joy.

---

[404] I also read and heard that some people think that the razor blade is used for cutting several girls and therefore might be a factor in the spread of AIDS in the district. However, I have not seen the cuts being made on the spot. I learnt that if the cuts are actually made, it is preferred to do it after the rites for individual girls. A new blade is usually used for each girl when her head is shaved. It is therefore unlikely that razor blades constitute a high risk for HIV infection in this way.

[405] Many of the favourite *ha-ye* (a type of *klama*) songs sung during *dipo* finish with the words *Ajawale saa yo*, 'beautifully adorned girl' or 'maiden', also translated to me as '*dipo* befits a woman'.

275

There they are, sitting like queens on their throne in the middle of her courtyard: her fourth daughter, twelve-year-old Maku, her fifth eleven-year-old daughter Laje and a six-year-old granddaughter named Afi Dede. The gifts they received have been put in a basket that stands in front of them. They are beautifully adorned with precious, yellow and reddish glass beads around the waist, neck, arms, wrists and legs. They wear wigs decorated with beads and many yards of expensive wax print cloths. This afternoon their female relatives and friends have spent hours to dress them. Now people around form a square with a dancing ground in the middle. The initiated girls are sitting on a couch that has been placed outside at a central place. To their right some five young women are beating the gourds. To the left and opposite, visitors, house members, friends and relatives sit and watch. More women stand around. The girls in their final, so-called outdooring stage of their *dipo* rites, sit stiff and still. They look serious and composed, until they are called one by one to show their now perfect dancing skills. Afi Dede starts, followed by Laje. Awoyaa bursts out with joy and pride. She dances wildly around her gracefully moving daughter, spraying her with perfume, swaying her wrapper in front of her feet and embracing her. She just does not know what to do out of happiness. She pulls out one of her breasts, holding it in front of her daughter and then turns towards my video camera to show it to me. She makes me laugh. When it is Maku's turn to dance, Awoyaa crawls on her hands and feet and it looks as if she is going to be possessed. Some of the other women around lift her up again and put her on a chair to calm her down. However, they also sing, dance and enjoy. Many pictures are made of the girls for future remembrance and to show their *dipo* performance to people who had not been able to witness these events.

The last stage of *dipo* called 'dressing up' (*bobum*, also see chapter three and four), was the coming-out of the fully-fledged Krobo girls on Monday afternoon and the following days, as described above in Awoyaa's house. For the group in maa Lako's house this all happened a week earlier, except for Awoyaa's daughter Maku. The older girls in maa Lako's first batch then departed with their younger siblings to their own family house. For the *dipo-yi* this stage means they are dressed up and have to show their dancing skills. The women, Naki's mother, Ako, Mawo and other female relatives, devoted the whole afternoon to the dressing of their children. They seemed to enjoy it a lot and I was amazed again about the patience of the children, who hardly uttered a complaint. In particular the tying of the many beads to the right size took many hours. Ako and her friend were folding the long, new pieces of wax print cloth and attached them to the waist beads. Long ends hung at the front and back. They used yellow or reddish beads and other jewellery was added, such as gold earrings. Yellow and red beads are thought to signify maturity (Kumekpor, Bredwa-Mensah, & Van Landewijk 1995: 20).

When the women finally were satisfied with the results of their efforts, it was time to take more pictures. Divine, one of the photographers, had already passed by another time to find out whether he could earn some money here. None of the girls, except for Naki, wore any headgear. Because her hair was not shaved, Naki had to cover it with a headgear (*duku*). The girls now showed their dancing skills, and an increasing number of curious people filled the little courtyard. The *dipo-yi* moved even more gracefully and serenely than ever, now that they were beautifully dressed with cloth and precious beads. The women sprayed them with perfumes. They even spread the wrapper they were wearing on the floor for them and danced excitedly around them. When it was not their turn to dance the girls sat on the armchairs that were put outside for them. They were like queens on their throne and gave the impression that they felt like this. Their hips were made bigger with beads and headgear, so even the smallest girls looked like little women now.

Fig. 12: Ata and Lawɛ dancing during their outdooring, Odumase, April 20, 1999

The dressing up was repeated the next day. This time the *dipo-yi* wore different wax print wrappers and beads, and they all wore either a *duku* or a black wig. They danced in the houses of different relatives and received gifts, often in the form of money. Some of the girls were 'decorated' with an item hanging around their neck, which expressed the profession of the parent or the responsible relative. For example, one girl whose mother was an *otim* (fermented corn dough) seller wore a chain of maize, with a small portion of *otim* wrapped in maize leaves attached to this chain. Lako Sakite's *dipo* girls, as part of the 'royal family', always danced at the *kono*'s courtyard in front of the palace on Tuesday afternoon. Now she was represented there by her assistant Mawo, who encouraged the girls to dance. People donated small amounts of money and sprayed the girls with perfume (*laventa*). In his study of Krobo *klama* music, Coplan beautifully describes the dancing of *dipo* girls during their outdooring, and the way it enhances the Krobo notion of femininity:

> The entire impression is of a slightly bent and swaying torso with gently bouncing arms and folding fingers, floating across or around the floor in feet and legs that barely appear to move. 'Hangme' is a very constrained, feminine style of dance, and it is strangely identified with *dipo*, where it is marvellously calculated to show off feminine charms in a demure fashion. 'Hangme' at *dipo* also demonstrates how costumes may be conceived as a means of extending or enhancing the movement complex. The yards and yards of thick, luxurious cloth gathered round the girls for their *klama* display gives them a doll-like, almost conical shape, the cloth billowing out around the hips and falling straight to the ankles. The 'mincing' movement of the feet is therefore barely visible, and the dancers truly seem to float across the floor almost as if they were suspended just off the ground, while their arms and torsos gently move and sway in cross rhythm three against four. (...) Through its identification with *dipo* 'hangme' is a symbol of Krobo womanhood and an artistic expression of their concept of true femininity (Coplan 1972: 128-130).

After the dancing at the courtyard, the girls entered Lako's house and danced there, until all *dipo* girls returned to their respective homes in the neighbourhood, where they also danced until evening time. People who wanted to also went to the Wednesday market in Agomanya with their *dipo-yi*. Doe, Ata and Lawε did not go, but I observed other girls on the market. They had to pay a fee to the market collectors at the entrance of the market, and then went round to display themselves. Anyone there could request a *dipo-yo* to dance, and give her a gift, either money or goods such as tomatoes or cassava, to show their appreciation.

Between April and early June there were still small groups of *dipoyi* everywhere in town, usually accompanied by their mother and/or some other female relatives. They went round to the houses of relatives to dance and receive some donations, and at the same time thank them for their support. After a few days they would stop dressing up, and return to their home in the village or elsewhere. However, they continued to wear their arm decorations, beads around the wrists and knees and necklaces for some weeks, while it also took some time before their hair had grown back.

'A pure Krobo': ritual and belonging

Rituals are multi-faceted and have many functions, both on the level of the individual and for groups or societies (Bowie 2000: 151-152). For individual girls going through these rituals, the *dipo* ceremony is a rite of passage that signifies a transition in life, a change in status and identity. As *dipo* as such is a precondition for motherhood and marriage, one of the main themes of *dipo* is fertility, which was expressed in several of the discussed rituals and symbols.

The three stages that mark the change in status of an individual girl can easily be discerned in *dipo*. Although the period of seclusion, which could be defined as the *liminal* period, has practically disappeared from the *dipo* performance, we can still see certain so-called 'thresholds' (*limen*) in *dipo* in other ways, which mediate between one physical space and another and between one social state and another (Van Gennep 1960). The whole period between marking or separating the girls as *dipo-yi* on Sunday, and re-incorporating them by dressing them usually a week later on Monday, may be regarded as a main *liminal* phase. In this phase the girls are 'betwixt-and-between', using Turner's words (1979) to designate the state in which the girls are dressed alike, have to remain silent and adopt a servile posture, representing submission "to an authority that is nothing less than that of the total community". The community in turn "is the repository of the whole gamut of the culture's values, norms, attitudes, sentiments, and relationships" (Turner 1991: 103). Nudity is a feature of this stage, as a levelling and humbling is necessary before a new status can be achieved. The use of red and white colours in this context symbolises the dangers inherent in liminality that is commonly associated with most rites of passage (Quarcoopome 1991: 61; Turner 1979). The red and white colour, for example, of the dye and clay that is used to sprinkle the *dipo* girls' bodies, of the fowl killed to purify them and of the food given to them, embody both misfortune and good fortune, danger and purity. It is also possible to focus on the boundaries between stages and see the threefold pattern repeated at every stage of the initiation, as Bowie points out (2000: 163). For example, the sitting on the *tɛgbɛtɛ* first involves the preparation of the girls by sprinkling them with white clay and putting a leaf in their mouth to prevent them from speaking, then involves the key crossing of a threshold, entering the sacred grove with the priestesses, after which the girls are triumphantly carried back from the 'bush' to the compound as future brides by their (potential) fiancés.

The *dipo* rituals are effective, as they depend on inherited value-laden images that are driven, by repeated practice and performance, 'deeply into the bone' (Grimes 2000). People take great care to perform the rites correctly. Many of the rituals involved in the *dipo* performance are experienced as very efficacious, as really 'working'. Failure, for example, to pass the pregnancy test on the *tɛgbɛtɛ*, the sacred rock, can have disastrous consequences. In such cases the rituals have the ability to effect transformations. At the same time, the participants in the rites act very casually and these rites are performed in a relaxed atmosphere. The *dipo* performance also has the purpose to entertain through dancing and singing. There is a lot of merriment and feasting during the rites. Simultaneously these actions evoke feelings and emotions related to deeper meanings.

Even more important than the theme of fertility is the focus on ritual cleanliness and belonging, as I will discuss next.

Although some other Ga-Dangme speaking peoples perform similar rites, especially the much smaller groups of the Shai and the Osudoku, the *dipo* rites are associated with 'Krobo-ness'. Even though non-Krobo and also Krobo people might at times criticize the performance of *dipo*, associating it with paganism and backward traditions, the insistence of Krobo people on its continued performance conveys a sense of ethnic pride. Women enjoy participating in the rites and parents feel very proud of their daughters when they have passed through. *Dipo* distinguishes them from outsiders and they feel that *dipo* makes real Krobo women of the girls, while Krobo families generally insist on partners who have passed through the rites for their men.

A number of aspects of *dipo* convey a relationship between *dipo* and an essential Krobo-ness. First of all, *dipo* is a homecoming ritual. In the past, before 1892, every Krobo who wanted to perform *dipo* for his or her daughter, had to return from the farmlands to the hometowns on Krobo Mountain. Nowadays, *dipo* can only be performed in the hometowns in the plains (*dom*), and Krobo families return from all over the country and beyond between March and May for this event, in this way renewing family ties and observing their 'custom'.

Secondly, it is believed that *dipo* makes one 'a real Krobo', that is to say, a 'clean' person according to Krobo concepts. The *dipo* rites make the distinction between the ritually clean and the unclean, the initiated and the uninitiated. Through *dipo* a girl becomes pure and 'clean', like a boy becomes clean through circumcision. If a girl is found to be pregnant before she has passed through the rites, she is considered to be defiled, and extensive purification and pacification rites have to be performed to get rid of her pollution and dangers following her. Such a girl may harm the well-being of others, so she becomes an outcast in society. The strong taboo on a pregnancy before the rites shows the fear of rejection by the family in particular and Krobo society in general. The importance of belonging to your house and Krobo home through *dipo*, and therefore the importance of *dipo* for Krobo identity, is expressed in *klama* songs such as the following:

> My daughter if it is not done for you, you can't eat in many homes
> But as for me, I will eat from East to West.
> If it is not done for you, you can't eat in many homes.
> *I bi a ke a yi no nge nio me a we ke a pee we ha mo o*
> *Se i mi lee, ke je la ga ke ya pue nako tse me a we ma ye.*
> *Ke a pee we ha mo o e yi ni nge nio me a we.*
> I want to tell you something.
> Be patient and you will see and hear.
> Do not rush my daughter. If it is not done for you,
> you can't mingle with people and you can't eat in their homes.
> *I nge nye dee ke nye gbu gblasi.*

A girl who has not passed through *dipo* literally cannot eat in her family house, which also means she is not really part of the family. At the same time she is advised not to eat in 'unclean' houses during *dipo*, that is to say, houses where *dipo* is not performed. Through the food taboos during *dipo* a girl is taught to be careful about where and what she eats. It is also implicitly implied here that a Krobo woman who has not passed through *dipo*, would not make a proper wife for a Krobo man, as being an unclean person she could not cook for him.

The cleansing rituals performed for a 'defiled' girl and the ones performed during *dipo* show characteristic elements of Krobo purification rites that are such an intrinsic part of most of their ritual ceremonies. Libations, ritual ablutions (leaves and white clay), ritual smoking, sacrifices of animals and cleansing through blood, ritual shaving, tying a girl with strings and ritually cutting the latter, ritually blocking the road and hooting and trampling down ill-luck and disease, are some of the basic rituals that can usually be found (Huber 1958). The bathing on Saturday can be added as a special cleansing ritual during the *dipo* ceremony.

As we saw, the women who have to handle the girls, the priestesses, were also supposed to stay ritually clean during *dipo*, like the girls themselves, especially when they go to the *tegbete*. They have to stick to the food taboos and abstain from sexual contacts. The *dipo* priestesses also do not bathe any corpses and do not attend funerals during *dipo* time. I was also told once during the *dipo* celebration of 'my' children that I could not attend the funeral of an old queen mother who had died, because I would become 'dirty'. The woman named 'Baby', who had brought the five children from Assin-Foso, did not come to the *dipo* site anymore later on, because somebody in her house had died.

Only ritually clean people can wear the conically shaped hat (*komi pee*). Besides *dipo-yi*, only senior male priests are allowed to wear these hats that are imbued with immense religious significance (cf. Quarcoopome 1991: 63). This is because the palm fibre has ancestral associations (see chapter five). The same fibre (either *soni* or *komi*) is used at other moments during *dipo*. That only ritually clean people are allowed to wear the hat explains why the hats are worn after the *tegbete*, when the girls have undergone the ultimate test and have come out as 'pure' Krobo women. Giving the hat to the *dipo* girls also symbolises the girls' engagement with Kloweki in the manner of newly initiated priests (Coplan 1972: 28).[406] Furthermore, the fact that the rites are performed as part of the

---

[406] The investiture with white calico, the killing of a black goat and the cleansing with its blood, the confinement with specific food prohibitions and the dressing up with beads, are also all features that the *dipo* ceremony has in common with the installation ceremony for a priest (Huber 1993: 189).

veneration of one of the indigenous and most senior deities, Nana Kloweki, distinguishes Krobo *dipo* rites from initiation rites performed elsewhere among Dangme or other neighbouring people. It is believed that the girls, dedicated to Kloweki, become clean and pure like the goddess herself. The role of millet during the rites is typical in the veneration of Kloweki, and the *dipo* initiation has many other features in common with peculiar elements of her cult, such as the use of white calico, the sacrifice of a black goat, the usual sacrifice for Kloweki, and the cleansing with its blood and the use of the Roan antelope skin.

A third aspect that stresses the importance of *dipo* for Krobo identity during the performance of the *dipo* rites is the use of old, inalienable things and traditions that are regarded as authentically Krobo. For example, there is the emphasis on 'indigenous Krobo food' and well-water during the critical days of the rites. The use of 'indigenous' items such as natural sponges, clay pots, traditional grinding stones and traditional cosmetics is stressed. Glass beads and other typical decorations too are perceived as Krobo items. Whereas gold is of the greatest importance to the Asante, beads represent wealth in Krobo. Furthermore, the hair of the girls is shaved or groomed in an old, traditional Krobo style. Another element that used to identify a Krobo woman according to her ethnic origin were the scars that would remain a visible result of the twelve small cuts given on her hand as proof of her *dipo*, and therefore of being a Krobo woman. The use of the Krobo language is emphasized and foreign languages are forbidden during *dipo*, and in particular in the shrine. The singing of *klama*, its specific lyrics and the typical dancing learned by the *dipo* girls also constitute an essential part of an atmosphere of 'ancient tradition'.

Interestingly, while the use of 'traditional items' is promoted during *dipo*, it does not seem to be a problem to use 'foreign items' such as razor blades, plastic bags, photographs and even modern pregnancy tests. Apparently, the emphasis on certain items does not mean that 'modern' items are excluded, but it is rather an emphasis on 'typically Krobo' items than on 'old' items. And what is regarded as 'traditional' may easily change. For example, the red loincloth (*subue*), which is worn nowadays, is an imported cotton cloth (Quarcoopome 1991: 64). On old Basel missionary photos, most of which were taken between 1896 and 1917, it can be seen that *dipo* girls used to wear a strip of old *kente* cloth called *titriku*.[407] This is Ewe *kente*, probably woven by Ewe weavers living in Krobo. When I showed these old photos to different old Krobo women and

---

Huber (1958: 168) states that: "Both before and during their puberty rites the girls are to a certain extent regarded as 'spouses' or 'wives' of the gods, i.e., of the gods' guardians, the priests".

[407] Malika Kraamer, working on a forthcoming PhD thesis (SOAS) on *kente* weaving in the Volta Region, told me that this type of *kente* originates from Agotime in the Volta Region. With this type of *kente* the warp is not visible. Only the weft of the cloth can be seen. The Agotime people are considered to be Dangme people, 'left behind' during the migration from the East, but they no longer perform *dipo*, it only survived in the form of folklore.

priestesses, they thought that the girls in the pictures were not Krobo as indicated by the captions, but rather from the neighbouring Shai or Osudoku. This may be possible. According to Ayi, Shai *dipo* girls still used to wear the *titriku* at least until the 1960s (Ayi 1966: 44).[408] It is also possible that they forgot that fashion may have changed. The fact that changes are possible shows the extent to which these rituals can be adapted to modern demands. Some aspects, such as the goat fat being worn as a veil and the cicatrisation, are regarded nowadays as being out of date. The Basel missionaries introduced photography, and hence photos have also already testified to the performance of *dipo* since two generations. (Nevertheless, the use of video or photo cameras inside the sacred grove was strictly forbidden). School girls who are either Christians or want to avoid being ridiculed (or both) can 'buy' their hair. The *klama* songs that are seen as part of ancient tradition can also be renewed. Sometimes existing songs are adapted to local circumstances, while new lyrics are also composed, which occasionally mock those Christians who claim they do not perform *dipo*.

All these ancestral items and aspects represent a sense of continuity and group unity in a material and cultural sense, despite the fact that certain features of *dipo* are changing and various intra-Krobo disputes, for example concerning chieftaincy affairs, the politics between Yilo and Manya Krobo districts and Christian points of view, persist. The use of old or 'real Krobo' features such as *klama* songs and beads and the strong relationship with the mythical figure of Kloweki convey a 'given-ness' to *dipo*, which in turn contributes to a seemingly 'primordial' perception of Krobo ethnic identity. It is felt as something which is unchanged and authentic (cf. Renne 1995: 134). This feeling was, for example, expressed by a woman who said: "They cannot abolish *dipo* at this time, because the great-grandfathers and great-grandmothers have been performing it." Many people stress that dipo is part of their 'custom' (*kusumi*).

However, at the same time that Krobo men and women emphasize that *dipo* is a 'custom' and cannot be stopped, people acknowledge that (unwanted) changes are occurring in the performance of *dipo* and/or they associate the rites with paganism and backward traditions. One supposed change that people often complain about are the age of the girls going through the rites, as I explained in the previous chapter. Old women stress they had to spend at least one week 'in seclusion' in their time, and people are aware of the fact that the rites ranged from three months to more than a year on Krobo Mountain before 1892. Ayi (1966) and Coplan (1972), describing the *dipo* rites in 1966 and 1972 respectively (but heavily relying on Hugo Huber's descriptions of the 1950s), claimed that the Krobo *dipo* rites they studied lasted between 10 and 20 days (Ayi) or three weeks (Coplan). Nowadays the confinement lasts just one night and the

---

[408] However, on contemporary photographs they also wear the red cotton loincloth (see e.g. the photographs in Beckwith & Fisher 1999).

whole *dipo* period may be as brief as four days, however for the majority it lasts about ten days in total. In the first place this change is due to various socio-economic reasons. Most parents cannot afford to provide for the needs of their daughters for a much longer period. At the same time their different responsibilities often do not allow them to spend more time in their hometown. Some parents do not want their children to miss out on school. *Dipo* partly coincides with the Easter holidays, however, and many parents take the opportunity to have the *dipo* rites performed during that period. Some people wish to limit their participation in the non-Christian rituals of *dipo* to the minimum or try to hide this from their church as much as possible. For example, five-year-old Naki's *dipo* was reduced by a week compared to the one of Doe and the others, and her hair was not shaved. She just went through the essential rites from Friday to Monday. Another woman I knew even let her granddaughter skip most of the 'outdooring'. She had to go through *dipo* in Somanya instead of ManyaK-pongunor in Manya Krobo in order to limit the chance of being observed. This happens more often, however this occasional 'hiding' mainly applies to those who live in the hometowns. The great majority of the Krobo who come from rural areas usually spend at least a whole week in their hometown.

In short, the *dipo* rites with all the ancestral connotations and associations with the hometown and used indigenous items, which relate to the cult of Nana Kloweki and the annual ritual calendar and are part of the life cycle rituals that constitute a Krobo person, belong to the dynamic realm of *kusumi*. Ethnic pride, purity and fertility, which are symbolised in the rites, prove to be crucial elements in the resilience of the rites. As part of *kusumi* the dipo rites are part of the main rituals whereby a Krobo consciousness and identity is continually constructed and reproduced. Being regarded as 'a real Krobo' implies a willing acceptance of this *kusumi*. The *dipo* rites are therefore effective means of defining individual and group identity, which means belonging to the family, the hometown and society as a whole.

However, the question of young ages and changes in the duration of the rites is debated. At the same time, *dipo* is criticised for its assumed pagan and backward aspects of the rites. Most changes are experienced in the context of Christianisation. Christianity has made *dipo* subject to dispute since the Basel missionaries arrived. At the same time it provides another circle of identification, as already demonstrated in the previous chapter. I will return to the Christian discourse in the next chapter, in which I will specifically examine debates about culture that are related to Christianity and state policy.

8

Debating dipo:
Discourses of culture in Ghana

[C]are must be taken that Christian doctrines are not sacrificed on the altar of traditional religion which often comes by the name 'culture'. Some half-hearted biblically
ignorant Christians fall into that trap, but they are warned of their accountability in life
after death! So, Christians must beware of the religious trappings of our traditions
(Ahinful 1999).

Current Ghanaian Christian perspectives on culture and tradition often echo the
point of view of the 19th-century Western (Protestant) missionaries. They
equate 'culture' with 'tradition' and often associate both with 'traditional religion'. In the eyes of European missionaries, conversion to Christianity in Africa
meant the advancement of European 'civilisation' and 'enlightenment'. They
successfully created a dichotomy between traditional religion, perceived as a
matter of 'the past', and Christianity, associated with 'modernity', which has
been very influential in Ghana. In chapter three I have discussed how the Basel
missionaries strove after converting the Krobo to Christianity, and how they regarded this as a transition from one state of affairs to another, from 'paganism'
to Christianity. As they perceived *dipo* as part of what they called 'heathendom'
or, later, 'traditional religion', conversion therefore implied a complete rejection
of *dipo*. The British colonial administration reasoned along similar lines, but
emphasised the 'uncivilised' character of *dipo* versus the 'civilisation' of the
nation state. The British even 'criminalised' *dipo* by placing it under the banned
'customs' mentioned in the Native Customs Ordinance. Ever since, the colonial
and missionary cultural policy has led to continuous debate and ambiguity on
the part of the local population.[409] Most Krobo Christians did not reject 'traditional religion' as they were required to, especially because they were not willing to give up *dipo*. Conversely, Presbyterian and other churches still do not allow participation in *dipo* and have been unsuccessful in attempting to institu-
tionalise elements of *dipo* into Christian ceremonies such as the confirmation.
The Presbyterian Church has therefore left the '*dipo* problem' completely unre-

---

[409] For similar debates among the Guan/Akan people in the neighbouring Akuapem traditional state,
see Gilbert (1995).

solved, while the opposition to *dipo* received a new incentive with the rise of the Pentecostals in Ghana.

Today, almost on a daily basis, local Ghanaian newspapers and journals disseminate perspectives on how modern (Christian) Ghanaians should relate to 'culture', and sometimes to *dipo* in particular. They reflect debates that Krobo people and Ghanaians in general regularly take part in, either in the home or in public arenas. The Manya Krobo District Assembly for instance, occasionally organises discussions on *dipo* aimed at bringing 'traditionalists', church leaders and government representatives together to resolve conflicting ideas. On May 28, 1998, for example, a symposium on *dipo* took place at Krobo-Odumase. Local politicians and chiefs and queen mothers also address problems relating to traditional practices (perceived as 'culture') at public gatherings. The state-owned newspapers *Daily Graphic* and *Ghanaian Times* are daily read by many people, while different other weekly or daily newspapers and magazines are widespread and their publications often discussed. The Christian magazine *The Watchman* of May 1998, for example, carried an article by its editor Divine Kumah, entitled 'Our girls on the Internet: why are we feigning surprise?' (Divine 1998)'. It expresses concern about 'Internet pornography', relating to photographs of bare-breasted *dipo* girls on certain web pages advertising 'Ghanaian culture'. Kumah further comments on what he saw after passing through Odumase on a trip he made:

> I was plain shocked to see a long queue of half naked girls in a *dipo* procession. (…) I was even more amazed to find out that the procession included an unusually large number of little girls, some even carried on their mother's backs. (…) What is all this mess about in the name of culture - but a licence to indulge in premature sexual activities?

Such backward rites should be stopped, he feels, because: "of what benefit are the so-called puberty rites any longer in a civilised world like ours?" The author expresses the popular Christian view in Ghana that these rites are 'immoral', because the girls are 'half naked'; that the rites are supposed to be 'puberty rites' and therefore should not be performed for little girls; that 'culture' should be regarded as 'performing traditional practices'; and that the rites, due to the young ages of the participants, lead to premature sexual activities, as having passed the rites legitimates sexual relationships.

Cultural practices in Ghana, such as (girls') initiation rites, the *trokosi* practice,[410] female circumcision,[411] the Gambaga witches' village,[412] chieftaincy

---

[410] *Trokosi*: a practice in Southeast Ghana (particularly the Volta Region) under which young girls are pledged into servitude in a shrine to atone for the misdeeds of their parents or families (see ch. 8 in Akyeampong 2001; Ameh 1998; Kofi 1998).

[411] Female circumcision, although forbidden by national law, is practiced in some areas in the North of Ghana.

and the 'ban on drumming',[413] are regularly discussed in the media and among the partakers.[414] Articles addressing these and other practices with headings such as: 'Modify Cultural Practices', 'Abolish Outmoded Customs', but also: 'Let's strengthen cultural values', 'We must redeem our cultural values' and 'Preserving the *dipo* Culture', can be frequently read in Ghanaian newspapers and other media.[415] These discussions show that 'culture' is part of a local Ghanaian discourse (cf. Coe 2000). However, as the headings show, there are different interpretations of what culture means and different values attached to culture. Whereas some people advocate the protection of and respect for 'culture', others condemn cultural practices as being 'immoral', 'backward' and 'uncivilised'. These practices are blamed for blocking development in a world where Christianity is linked with 'enlightenment' and 'modernity'.

This chapter details the various discourses of culture in contemporary Ghana in order to understand how people talk about and interpret the *dipo* rites, and to what extent their interpretations reflect the old missionary perspectives. Drawing from the discussions people had with me about *dipo* in conversations and interviews, and from statements about *dipo* in newspapers and other media, I will investigate how people strategically make use of different concepts of culture in order to either reconcile their Christian identity with participating in *dipo* or occasionally distancing themselves from *dipo*. Different institutions promote the discourses: evangelical churches, government ministries, the Institute of African Studies and 'traditionalists', and they form a repertoire available to many Ghanaians. However, the discourses reason within a limited discursive space on 'culture' as 'tradition', which the missionaries and the colonial administration successfully laid out. The different interpretations of culture indicate the continuous struggle of Krobo people to negotiate between the government policy, which views culture as relevant to the nation and to its development, the demands of the family and their ancestral traditions and the Christian views of the churches of which they are members, in which culture is identified with the realm of the devil. The different discourses are occasionally combined. Sometimes people seek to achieve a synthesis between different opposing ideas. There is a continuing discussion to try and bridge the dichotomies they perceive as

---

[412] The Gambaga witches' village in the North-East of Ghana is a special quarter of Gambaga town where (old) women, often widows, are expelled to after being accused of witchcraft in the Mamprusi kingdom (see Drucker-Brown 1993).

[413] The 'ban on drumming' concerns a monthly ban on drumming and noisemaking in the 'Ga traditional area' to prepare for the annual Ga *Homowo* festival that commemorates (driving away) hunger (see e.g. Van Dijk 2001).

[414] See e.g. (Addy 1998; "Editorial: Freeing the Trokosi girls" 1998; "Editorial: The Gambaga outcasts" 1998; Sawyer 1999), to name just a few recent articles from newspapers addressing these particular practices.

[415] See different headings in the *Ghanaian Times* and the *Daily Graphic* (1998; Asiedu 1999; Dei 1999; Okyere & Ampratwum-Mensah 1998; Oppong Kyekyeku 1998).

real, between tradition and Christianity, culture and progress (cf. Coe 2000). Yet, although the discourses have a strong orientating function, they are not neatly separated in daily life.

As Baumann (1996: 9, 14) remarks, the word 'culture' need not mean the same in political rhetoric or in the usage of informants as in anthropological analysis. The concept of culture has been much debated in cultural and social anthropology. There is an overall consensus nowadays that culture is not a real phenomenon, but an abstract and purely analytical notion. It is not bounded or homogeneous, but encompasses the whole of the practices of everyday life, 'what people do' (also see chapter one). Nevertheless, outside anthropology the word was borrowed and assigned a new, and far more concrete, meaning. The reification of culture does not make sense for analytical purposes. However, in a discourse of contestation, reification may be desirable, and even seem necessary, to effect mobilization, and therefore important to study as such.

'Dipo is pagan': Christian discourses

A Christian dipo?: The 'Africanisation' debate

In some Christian circles, especially among Roman-Catholics, there is a heightened Christian self-understanding of the necessity of adapting the Christian message to its cultural environment, referred to as 'inculturation' (cf. Bowie 1999 67).[416] This is called 'Africanisation' within an African context, which means: the development of a supposedly 'authentic' African variant of Christianity. Already at least since the 1950s, the former European-oriented mission churches in Ghana started to loose members to African Independent churches that were closer to 'traditional African' (religious) practices. Hence the mission churches also started to 'Africanise' their services, for example, by allowing drumming and dancing in church. In theological circles it has been recognised that the implementation of European values in Africa is not necessarily desirous or successful as a mission strategy (Bowie 1999: 67). African critics of Western hegemony have, for example, argued that Jesus Christ can be perceived as an 'ancestor' and 'priestly mediator', in this way placing Christ in an African context (e.g. Bediako 1990). Christianity has failed to take root, after over 150 years of evangelisation, if one is to judge from phenomena such as the rejection of monogamy by many Africans (Bowie 1999: 67), and the performance of rituals

---

[416] The term 'inculturation' usually preserves a specifically theological agenda, while the term 'acculturation' is more commonly used by anthropologists to refer to culture contact (Bowie 1999: 70). Recently the term 'dialogue' has also been used within Roman Catholic circles (see Notermans 2002).

such as *dipo* among the Krobo. Therefore Christian theology is still seeking for new solutions.

The rhetoric of 'Africanisation' implies a dichotomy between 'authentic tradition' and 'true Christianity', from which, according to critical (African) theologians, a synthesis should be created, assuming that something can be recognised and defined as 'authentic tradition' or 'true Christianity'. As Bowie observes (ibid.: 68), the models underlying these assumptions tend to be static and in practice can be seen as an attempt by the mainstream church authorities to maintain definitional control over the faith of the former mission churches. Who is to decide who is a Christian and who is not? And how to define what constitutes African culture? While I do not want to further explore the inculturation debate here, it is important to examine how the Africanisation debate took shape in relation to *dipo*.

The term inculturation is usually defined in opposition to syncretism. Inculturation is regarded as the legitimate adoption of selected aspects of idealised features of indigenous culture into Christian practice (ibid.: 69). Within the Basel Mission discourse on African Christianity, the term 'syncretism' has been negatively reserved for a perceived distortion of Christian essence. African Independent churches and non-Western practices performed by Christians have therefore often been dismissed as 'syncretism'. As the pastor of an evangelical church explained, any Christian taking part in *dipo* is considered to be practising syncretism: "[A]nd not pure Christianity. They mix Christianity with idol worshipping." The same is stated for the Independent or 'Spiritual' churches, as (some of) the pastors are polygynous and they make use of items such as incense and candles. In the view of the former Basel Mission Church, now Presbyterian Church, in Odumase, there is only a thin line between inculturation and syncretism. It still typically regards perceived characteristics of Krobo family life, which includes pre-marital intercourse as legitimised by the *dipo* practice, as a stumbling block to church growth. The reverend minister Odjidja, for example, a Krobo and Basel Mission trained scholar, recognised that the advent of new Christian churches since the early 20th century has complicated 'the battle against *dipo*', as some of these churches, including the Roman Catholic Church, were more lenient towards 'African culture' (1977: viii). Teyegaga, a reverend minister who as a Krobo was trained by the Basel Mission (see chapter five), specifically addressed the issue of how to relate to *dipo* as a Christian. He warned against Africanisation, which in his view could easily turn into syncretism, or what he calls 'paganising Christianity':

> The desire to Africanise Christianity must not mean paganising Christianity. The Church would be able to help the youth and the new convert better if the Church itself knew the meaning and significance of the old African tradition and customs. Salvation cannot be found in any other name than in Jesus Christ, who is the Way, the Truth and the Life (Teyegaga 1985: 10).

According to Teyegaga, this meant that *dipo* does not belong in the Christian church, and a synthesis is not possible:

> *Dipo* is an ancient traditional institution for puberty rite and training for marriage. It belongs to the traditional community. It does not belong to the Christian Community. Christianity has rites for Baptism, confirmation and Lord Supper for the believers. This is what Christians in Krobo, Shai and Osudoku *must know and therefore shun away from the dipo* custom (Teyegaga 1985: 49) (italics by the author)

The loss of members of the Presbyterian Church to the new African Independent Churches in the 1950s forced the Presbyterian Church to 'Africanise' its services to some extent. Despite the sustained prohibition of *dipo* by church authorities, members of the church continue with it 'in secret', which usually simply means, out of sight. It is a public secret that most church members have had *dipo* performed for their daughters. Benjamin Tetteh-Ofoe, a Krobo and a student in Religious Studies at the University of Ghana, wrote about *dipo* in Yilo-Krobo in 1979 that:

> The effect of the performance of this customary rite on Christianity seems to be gaining upper hand. Because according to recent information I had, even some clergymen gave out their daughters to some relatives to have the custom performed for them secretly (Ofoe 1979: 34).

The type of rumours Ofoe referred to are still common today. Ofoe showed a great concern that the performance of *dipo* "has now grown worse" and restated "the *dipo* custom as it is performed now, should not be done by any Christian. This is so because it is entirely idolatry and a Christian should in any case not worship any other gods apart from the Almighty God" (Ofoe 1979: 39). Like Teyegaga, he tried to show that confirmation should have the same value for Christian girls as *dipo* has for 'pagan' girls. The Basel missionaries had already tried to substitute *dipo* by the confirmation ceremony in the 19th century, but without much success (see chapter six). Formally the Presbyterian Church is still an advocate of this idea, hence continually drawing a strict boundary between 'heathendom' and 'Christianity', between 'culture' as equal to 'tradition', and 'modernity'.

Others try to find solutions in 'christianising' *dipo*, in a way taking the 'inculturation' process the other way around. For example, under the heading 'Preserving the *dipo* Culture', a certain author named Kofi Dei published a series of two articles about the *dipo* rites in the *Ghanaian Times* (Dei 1999). He argued that *dipo* could become a Christian institution protecting the virginity of Christian girls. This would mean that *dipo* could be preserved, but only if it was 'modified'. From his writings it becomes clear that, in line with the tradition of the 19th century Basel missionaries, the writer regards Christianity as the next stage after the 'elements-based religious rites', as he calls them, in the evolution of mankind. In this line of thought the invocation of 'elemental spirits', for example, should be substituted by the invocation of God, Christ and the Holy Spirit. The writer further proposes that with certain changes *dipo* and *bragoro* (Akan puberty rites) could be more powerful social and cultural institutions. Some of the changes he suggests include the awarding of certificates to *dipo* graduates, signed by a traditional authority and a medical doctor that would declare them certified virgins and the sponsoring of girls, for example, by NGO's to allow them entrance into vocational schools. He feels that in this manner women would be empowered with "virtues of hard work, personal hygiene, self-respect, selflessness, love and a sense of dignity, and confidence". He then writes within the Christian idiom, but with a sense of the value of 'traditional culture': "A loss of self identity and self-esteem leads to confusion, an inordinate drive for self interest leading to the mass production of Delilahs and Jezebels, at best, instead of the Sarahs, Esthers, Marys, Naomis, Deborahs etc." Even one of the charismatic pastors in Odumase, Immanuel Dadebo of the 'Deeper Life Bible Church', told me that according to him the *dipo* rites could be modified in such a way that Christians could participate. He said that he specifically had a problem with traditional priests performing the rites, otherwise it could be performed as far as he was concerned.

Typically, the Roman Catholic Church, however, is mostly involved in the 'inculturation' debate. Anthropologist and Catholic Archbishop of Kumasi Peter Kwasi Sarpong is the most well-known protagonist of the inculturation debate in Ghana (Sarpong 2002). His booklet on the 'traditional' practice of the pouring of libation to the deities and/or ancestors, which he sees as compatible with Christianity, has been widely debated in Ghana (Sarpong 1996). Another author even wrote a study particularly about 'Asante Catholicism' (Obeng 1996). Most of the Catholic clergy working in Ghana are advocates of inculturation. I once met a Filipino Roman Catholic priest working in the Krobo area at a traditional priest's grove during the celebration of the annual 'millet-eating' rituals (see chapter five). No Presbyterian or Pentecostal reverend or pastor would have shown himself there. However, the Catholic priest explained to me that he felt that because he lived and worked in this area, it was necessary for him to learn about "the psychology and the sociology of the people", as he expressed it.

Another Roman Catholic missionary I met was stationed in Asesewa, a large market village in Upper Manya. He was an Indonesian priest from Flores. In a lengthy conversation about *dipo*, he also argued that *dipo* should be transformed into a Christian ritual. He talked about inculturation and that this was a matter of a change in mentality and, according to him, would therefore take about two generations before the change would be accomplished. Besides that, he felt that people had greater problems than *dipo* and more serious things to worry about, which also was the reason that it would take a long time before changes would be introduced. It is another public secret among the Krobo that the R.C. Church (as well as the small congregation of the Anglican Church) has been condoning the performance of *dipo* in the meantime,, as long as it takes place before baptism (as I described in detail in chapter six). Although many Catholic church members share the view that *dipo* could be turned into a Christian ritual, whereby the elder women in the church could for instance be trained in such a way that they would be able to instruct the girls, in practice most of them have been following this tacit rule of 'first the custom, then baptise'.

Pentecostalism and the dissociation from culture

> Today, although the majority of Krobos claim to be Christians, there are some die-hard exponents of tradition who seek, in the name of preserving cultural heritage, to force everyone to submit to the ideals of the dipo rites, several aspects of which, Christians contend are purely idolatrous (Mbinglo 2002: 110).

As I described in greater detail in chapter two, the Pentecostal churches have proliferated in Ghana in particular since the 1980s. Whereas Roman-Catholic, and some Protestant, theologians advocate 'inculturation' and the 'Africanisation' of Christianity, the present-day influential leaders of the charismatic Pentecostal churches preach a rigid dissociation from 'African culture' and local traditions. The notion of a rupture, to 'make a complete break from the past', forms a key in the understanding of current Ghanaian Pentecostalism (Meyer 1998). As Meyer (ibid.: 183) argues:

> The appeal to 'time' as an epistemological category enables Pentecostals to draw a rift between 'us' and 'them', 'now' and 'then, 'modern' and 'traditional' and of course, 'God' and 'Devil'. In this way Pentecostal discourse takes up the language of modernity as it has spoken to Africans through colonisation, missionisation and, after Independence, modernisation theory. Indeed, a clear analogy exists between the Pentecostal - and, for that matter, the Protestant in general – conceptualisation of conversion in terms of a rupture with the past and modernity's self-definition in terms of progress and continuous renewal.

The increasing popularity of general Pentecostalism therefore stems from the fact that it ties into historically generated, local understandings of Christianity in Ghana. The language of Protestantism and that of modernity shows an analogy. The constant rejection of 'tradition' and spirits has been vital to a Christian identity in Protestant Basel missionary times, and still is today. Conversion to Protestantism meant to become modern in social, economic and political respects (Meyer 1992b; 1999). Hence Christianity has been localised in Ghana, but in ways that heighten the dichotomy between 'tradition' and 'Christianity'. The paradox is that through its rejection, 'traditional religion' is actually taken very seriously and not simply discarded as a kind of 'superstition' or a matter of 'the past'. African Christians continued to believe in the power of 'traditional' gods and spirits, but demonise them as only causing evil in the world. Pentecostal

Christianity classifies ancestral spirits, witches and ritual practices related to veneration and protection as demonic and diabolises them. It objectifies 'tradition' as a past wrapped up in ancestral and devil worship, which continues to influence present-day events. The Pentecostal churches believe that every Christian has a past that affects his or her present condition, such as past sins and ancestral cultural practices, which exposed that person to demonic influence (Meyer 1999) (also see chapter six).

Although believers were either not willing or not able to fully break away from what the churches conceptualise as 'the past', as I have described in previous chapters, Pentecostalism allows them to address their ambivalent stance towards modernity (cf. Meyer 1998: 184). The Pentecostals clearly see the *dipo* rites, which emphasise the connection to the family and the deity Nana Klowεki, as an important practice among the Krobo that can keep a person trapped within the realm of an ancestral curse from which she needs deliverance. As already emphasised in chapter six, where I discussed life cycle rituals and the tensions with Christianity, the aim of deliverance sessions is to turn people into individuals who are independent of and unaffected by family relations. Members of charismatic churches are asked to separate themselves from rituals such as *dipo* that have traditionally served as occasions for those living elsewhere to come home and reaffirm ties to their families and hometowns. Pastor Frederic Opata of the Christian Outreach Mission, who was 43 years old at the time of the interview, explains:

> They believe *dipo* initiates you into the Krobo society, but that is a false belief, because we are created by God, we are all God's people, we are not created by the Krobo. So we must give all honour and ascribe everything to God alone, not to any other shrine. But that is how the Devil is working to shape the people's mind away from God.[417]

The pastor claims here that the wider identification with being a Christian is more important to him than to identify with Krobo society. He also considers the Christian God to be higher than any of the local gods. He feels that the Devil is behind *dipo* and that the local shrines try to 'keep people away from the Christian God'. The pastor also told me that he has had women come to his church to be delivered from evil powers caused by *dipo*:

> We have found that many people come into contact with witchcraft through dipo and it is giving problems, because in due course we have to pray for some people to deliver them from these powers (...). We realise that the spirit says that he came out of *dipo* into the person (...). So dipo is purely paganism.

---

[417] Interview with Frederic Opata, August 3, 1994, Odumase.

The same concerns are expressed among other, smaller Dangme-speaking groups where *dipo* is performed, particularly among the neighbouring Shai. On a similar note a Shai 'businesswoman' called Theresa was quoted in an interview about the *dipo* topic for the weekly newspaper *The Mirror* as follows:

> When the *dipo* girls are made to go about almost naked there is the possibility of these spirits (operating in darkness) getting attracted to the girls and spiritual marriage is contracted. (...) Our women give birth to bastards and a lot of Dangme women dominate prostitution. All these are due to the evil spirits behind dipo.[418]

Interestingly, this woman also makes the popular connection between 'paganism' and immorality that the Basel missionaries used to make.

Julie gave me another example of an occasion where the *dipo* rites were addressed as belonging to the realm of the ancestors or the devil from which deliverance is necessary. She told me about a healing session that she attended recently in the Presbyterian Church in Odumase. All the women who had passed the *dipo* rites in the past were asked to raise their hands and come forward. The majority complied. The pastor, who had been invited from Accra and had 'spiritual gifts' granted him by the Holy Spirit, 'delivered' them from the god they had been dedicated to during *dipo*. Apparently some of the women had screamed, others fell on the floor. The battle between God and Satan is enacted on the bodies of believers during such deliverance services. This battle is also visualised through other popular means, such as films, stickers and calendars (see also Meyer 1992a). For example, a popular calendar from Lagos, Nigeria, entitled 'the Downfall of Satan' depicts Jesus (a white man) and Satan (a black man with horns and a tail) in a comic strip as boxers in a boxing match. Jesus is declared winner of the match after a heavy fight in the box ring.

Particular aspects of *dipo* are regarded as specifically appalling by Christians. The pouring of libations, divination practices, the sacrificing of animals and pouring of their blood and the going to the *tɛgbɛtɛ* are regarded as 'pagan' practices. This was, for example, expressed by Irene, daughter of a Presbyterian presbyter (her mother), and at the time of our talk married to a pastor from the 'Assemblies of God' church. She told me that, although *dipo* was performed for her when she was four years old, she would not have her daughter go through, because: "They perform rituals that go against Christianity." When I asked her which rituals she meant, she answered: "Rituals such as the pouring of libation, slaughtering a goat and pouring the blood on the feet." Another aspect many Christians object to is the fact that local priests supervise the rituals being performed, as was mentioned before. The Pentecostal pastors even call these 'fetish' priests 'worshippers of the devil'.

---

[418] *The Mirror* (1998).

In other conversations many of the same aspects were mentioned time and time again. For instance, I once had an exchange with three middle-aged members of the Women's Fellowship of the Presbyterian Church in Odumase about *dipo*, among whom was Lily Odzawo (see chapter six). They said they rejected the '*juju*' and 'fetish' aspects of *dipo*.[419] I asked what those '*juju*' or 'fetish' aspects were. Lily Odzawo commented:

> If Christian priests perform it, there is nothing wrong about it. But a fetish priest, performing the custom for a Christian, is very bad. Because they will take you to the bush and you have to sit on a certain stone. There are certain things under it, nobody knows.

With 'the things under it', Lily referred to the common knowledge that many, sometimes very unobtrusive, shrines derive their power from the 'things' that are buried under it (see chapter five). Here the 'certain stone' is the *tɛgbɛtɛ*. She continued: "And secondly, before you go to that stone, a goat will be slaughtered and its blood put on your feet. And the goat they will knock against your head three times." I asked her what was 'fetish' about the goat. Lily Odzawo answered: "The blood, because Jesus Christ has shed his blood once for us all. So we don't need any blood to purify ourselves again." Here one of the other women, Juliana Mamle Tetteh, came in:

> And then, we Christians, know that there are some kinds of spirits behind what they are doing. It isn't just the mere goat that they slaughtered or the mere stone that they put you on. But there is a bad spirit in it, behind everything that they do and because of that bad spirit it is why we, Christians, are advised not to go in for that custom.

The women also mentioned the consulting of oracles, the pouring of libation, and the high costs involved in *dipo* as 'bad aspects'. Juliana Tetteh added: "Because of this *dipo* they fail to send the children to school, saying they have no money, but when it comes to that custom, they go and borrow money and perform it."

The purification with blood by sacrificing a goat is explained by Christians as being redundant, because Jesus Christ sacrificed himself and gave his blood "once and for all (...), which has secured an eternal redemption for all who cease from their own works of purification and instead trust in him" (Bediako 1990: 45). Several people I talked to not only objected to the goat because of the blood involved, but also claimed that it led to immoral behaviour. For example, pastor Samako, the founder of a local charismatic church, said:

> "They are provoking the image of that goat into the woman's spirit. The goat is a prostitute beast. Then it enters into you. The bible says that men should not take blood."

---

[419] With the term *juju* people refer to negative spiritual and magical powers.

I asked him: "What do you mean with saying it is a prostitute animal? Do you mean that that behaviour will come to the girls too?"

Pastor Samako: "Yes, if you take the blood. The bible says every blood, there is a life in the blood. And if I have a life in my blood and I give it to a human being, the human being will have that life. The human being will behave as the goat."

Marijke: "So to you there is a relation between *dipo* and prostitution?"

Samako: "Yes, *dipo* brings prostitution in Krobo land."[420]

Samuel Teye, an Apostolic pastor and also a Krobo man, explained that performing *dipo* was wrong by referring to an often-cited bible story of Moses and his people at the Mount Sinai, when Moses climbed the mountain leaving his people behind. When he was gone they made an image of a calf out of gold and worshipped it as an idol. Teye explained: "It is not the way of God to worship an idol. If you believe in God you should take your distance." In his view performing *dipo* and therefore serving the traditional gods was similar to worshipping an idol. He also referred to the story of king Nebuchadnezzar to explain that those who worship idols – including those who perform *dipo* - will be punished, and those who do not will be rewarded:

> These three children were not worshipping and they were thrown into the fire. That is where the Lord showed that He is God and took them from the fire. So at present people worship Satan. Churchgoers fear that if you do not make the *dipo* custom they will be sacked from the house. But we believe that those who really believe, if you sack them from the house, God will prepare a fine place for them. And really He has been doing that. Those who have been driven away by their parents, God gave them better places.[421]

Like pastor Teye, who said that 'God gave these girls better places', several Krobo told me that Krobo girls who had been banned from their family houses, because they had become pregnant before passing through *dipo*, had later become wealthy in life. For some girls this may have been true. One reason may be that these girls, as a result of their forced severance from their family ties, actually managed to achieve individual riches in times of greater economic opportunities at the end of the 19th and the first decades of the 20th century. Another reason is that, as I described in chapter three and four, conversion to Christianity has become a way out for these girls ever since the Basel missionaries came. Some of these girls became educated, married Christians, and in this manner became part of the educated elite. Others who were banned, ended up in, for example, the neighbouring Akan states, such as Akuapem, married there and were said to be blessed with large families. The popular Christian explanation

---

[420] Interview with Samako, founder of the 'Christ City Church', October 7,1998, Odumase. Samako was baptised in the Anglican Church, he changed to a Pentecost Church in 1988 and was then baptised again. In 1990 he was 'called' to start his own church.

[421] Interview with pastor Samuel Kweku Teye, Apostolic Church of Ghana, August 7,1994, Odumase.

obviously was that God rather had blessed these girls as they were saved from paganism. Another likely option open to this kind of girls to earn a living was prostitution. As explained in previous chapters, Christian female converts had a dubious reputation.

In short, the general Pentecostal point of view and many successors of the Basel Mission with regard to 'culture', and *dipo* in particular, can be summarised as follows: *dipo* means the worshipping of 'idols' and the devil. The 'fetish priests' use their witchcraft (*juju*) to perform the *dipo* rites. These rites are seen as the catalyst of teenage pregnancies, prostitution and subsequent immoral behaviour. As they represent 'paganism', Christian leaders do not allow their followers to participate in the rites. The Christians who do participate are called 'backsliders' (people who 'slide back' into 'heathendom'). The Presbyterian Church members often just pay lip service to their church's official standpoint, as they continue to perform *dipo* secretly. The Pentecostal churches offer their adherents a way out: people can be delivered from 'the past', which ties them to family relations. However, with their increasing influence, the rhetoric of a strong dissociation from *dipo* and other 'traditional' ceremonies has received a renewed incentive.

'Dipo is kusumi': Culture as custom

Whereas in the Christian discourse 'culture' is seen as the realm of the devil, culture is positively regarded as tradition or 'custom' in another discourse, which comprises the important realm of chieftaincy and the ancestors, including ritual practices and ceremonies, 'drumming and dancing' and festivals. From this perspective culture is partly something distant or abstract and a selection of the totality of everyday and ritual practices. It refers to specific activities or practices, something in which priests, elders and chiefs take part. Partly it is secret knowledge, only known to those who should know (see also chapter five). When asked about it, many Krobo people assert that *dipo* cannot be abolished, because it is custom (*kusumi*) (see previous chapters). With regard to the Asante initiation rites for girls Sarpong (1977: 12) observed that: "If an Ashanti were asked why girls' nubility rites [*bragoro*] are performed, he would almost instinctively reply that they were instituted by the ancestors and failure to comply with their injunctions would infuriate them." By saying likewise that *dipo* is an ancient custom, which was started by the forefathers, people not only express the viewpoint that *dipo* is part of a cultural heritage that should be handed down to future generations and that one should be proud of, but also that 'custom' is something you cannot withdraw yourself from. 'Custom' binds a person to his or her hometown and makes him or her a person, as became clear in the previous chapters. One queen mother from the Susui division, for example, told me the story of her brother who, even though his family opposed, married a woman who was a

Jehova Witness and therefore had not passed through the *dipo* rites. Worms appeared in the drinking pots of the brother's household. This was believed to be a bad omen, caused by his wife's uncleanliness, and later on he divorced her. Stories such as these, in which the importance of *dipo* for a successful marriage is stressed, abound in Krobo.

However, those who have interests in this realm, have to reason within the discursive space the Christians have successfully laid out, and therefore try to argue that culture is 'not just pagan'. Newspaper articles in the *Ghanaian Times*, the *Daily Graphic* and *The Mirror* carry headings such as: 'Customary practices aren't demon-inspired – Nii Tetteh' (Noonoo 1998). One *asafoatsɛ* (sub-chief), for example, told me: "Why do they say *dipo* is fetish? We inherited it from our forefathers, it is part of our culture." In the same way traditional priests who supervise *dipo* emphasised to me that '*dipo* is not pagan', but *kusumi*. Christianity and *dipo* therefore should go side by side. *Wonọ* Asa, for instance, emphasised that *Klowɛki* is not pagan. He called *dipo* a 'living custom' and said that it is 'purely custom', through which someone becomes 'a Krobo woman' and a 'whole Krobo'.

At the same time, 'custom' is placed in the past, in agreement with Christian rhetoric. When referring to culture as a custom or tradition, people often refer to the past, even though with nostalgia. They were told that when *dipo* was performed on Krobo Mountain, girls were taught the domestic duties of a wife and mother. They would be mature before entering into marriage. One old man in Odumase, for instance, told me that his house was a Presbyterian house in *lebọ*, and that *dipo* was not performed there (however, his daughter told me that *dipo* was performed for her at her mother's house). According to him "they use *juju* ways" and that is why *dipo* is not good. In the olden days, however, when *dipo* was still performed on Krobo Mountain, it was "a good thing". Then the girls "were preserved until a certain age" and would marry straight away after *dipo*. Now, according to the old man, prostitution has become rampant due to the young ages of *dipo* girls. Likewise, Presbyterian reverend Eric Aminarh said:

> When you see what they are doing now it doesn't reflect the aim they first had, because now children of even five, four, three, two years old pass through this custom. It is very, very bad. When a young girl knows this thing has been performed for her, it gives her license to start flirting with men. Because she feels she has matured. That is the cause of teenage pregnancies these days here.[422]

According to divisional chief (*Wɛtso Mantsɛ*) Angmortey Zogri, *dipo* used to be different:

---

[422] Interview June 6, 1994, Odumase.

Dipo has commercialised. It used to be domestic science. The confinement would be for one year. It was a vocational institution. They learnt how to make pots and mats from raffia leaves. Before you would marry, you would be at least 20 years old. That was the purpose of *dipo*, but they adulterated it. Children who are nursed on the back, now undergo the *dipo* performance. They don't know anything. It has become something like a fashion when even infants are going through. In the olden days there were no teenage pregnancies. In the olden days you'd be brought up in moral discipline, now it is a fashion as the girls are so young. (...) If we go back to the old system, it will help us to come down on teenage pregnancy.[423]

Complaints such as the above can be heard frequently. It is said that 'in the olden days' girls were well matured before passing through *dipo*. Paradoxically, both Christians and non-Christians ascribe the perceived decline of morality to the decline of the rites, whereas in the past the missionaries and their converts ascribed what they perceived as immorality to the very performance of the rites. In the ideal *dipo* of the past, girls always married as soon as they had passed through the rites, as the sexual freedom for Krobo girls and women after *dipo* does not match current dominant Christian gender norms.

People also claim that *dipo* has become 'more fetish' than it was in the past. Just as the idea that *dipo* used to be a kind of training, or a school, this line of thought follows the Basel missionaries. As outlined in detail in chapter three, the Basel missionaries considered *dipo* as part of Heathendom, which had to be conquered by Christianity. In line with the myth of the construction of the tower of Babel, the missionaries thought that the Krobo had originally believed in one high God and had degenerated into 'tribes' with 'dialects' and 'local gods' in the course of time. Separated from the God they had originally worshipped, they were serving the devil in the meantime. Their religious ideas and practices of the time therefore were represented as typical examples of 'Heathendom', but it was thought that originally *dipo* had not been 'fetish' and was a kind of native school. Paul Odzawo, a strict Presbyterian, whose wife and daughter did not perform *dipo* (see chapter six), said:

I did not like the idea [of *dipo* for my daughter] because of the processes through which the girls pass. (...) I like the original idea of training children, the girls, to be good wives. But then this thing was attached to fetishes and priests, so it became commercialised and the original idea was spoilt. It has changed into money.

Pastor Samuel Teye of the Apostolic Church of Ghana told me in a similar vein:

When civilisation came, some of the leaders [of the Krobo] began to explore some dirty custom. (...) they had turned it into a fetish custom, whereby they will kill some goat. They take the intestines and make the child wear it around the neck. It has a dirty

---

[423] Interview with *Wɛtso Mantsɛ* for Piengua division, Angmortey Zogri, March 11, 1999, Agomanya.

scent. They will take the head of the goat and use it to hit the head of the child three times. (...) We got to know that that custom was different from what our forefathers were doing. What they did was to educate the children to know how to sweep and other things. But now the *dipo* custom has turned into the worshipping of idols. The fetish priests with their *juju*, they perform the rites. We the Christians say that that is consciously teaching of their religion. (...) So we as Christians we do not allow our members to do that *dipo* custom. But when a child is one week old, you can bring the child to the chapel for a minister to dedicate the child to the almighty God. And when it grows up, at the age of about fourteen, fifteen years, we baptise the child into the Christian religion.[424]

The idea that the traditional priests have pulled the rites towards them is understandable in the light of the events around 1892. In 1892, as described in detail in chapter four, the old women performing the *dipo* rites and the traditional priests were driven off Krobo Mountain. The priests lost a great deal of power and sought ways to re-establish some of their authority by continuing to perform the rites at their hidden shrines in the outskirts of the town. At the same time, of course, the idea that *dipo* is fetish and the rejection of 'traditional religion' has been the flip side of converting to Protestantism from the onset of Christianisation.

'You give to Caesar what is for Caesar'

On the one hand, the tradition-modernity dichotomy is part of people's lived experience. One expression different people used in conversations with me was: 'You cannot serve two masters at the same time', meaning that they felt they had to make a choice between traditional demands and those of Christianity. Tetteh Gaga told me how he, as the oldest son of his father who was a traditional priest, was destined to become a farmer. He was nevertheless eager to be baptised and receive an education, which his father allowed in the end. And much later in his life, after his father had died, he was pointed out as the successor of his father. In his view it meant that now he had 'to combine the two', as he put it, because he was both educated and a priest.

Hence, on the other hand, experience shows time and again that in practice 'tradition' and 'modernity' - as far as one can distinguish them from each other - are not opposites, but exist side by side, and do not exclude each other. The Krobo chiefs especially, who are usually regarded as 'custodians of culture', embody both 'custom' and 'Christianity'. As I explained in chapter three and four in particular, the history of the paramount chieftaincy and Basel Mission Christianity cannot be separated in (Manya) Krobo. Krobo historians are

---

[424] Interview August 7, 1994, Odumase.

300

usually proud to point out that Odonkor Azu was one of the first people to embrace Christianity, even though he never converted (e.g. Odjidja 1973). He was the one who allowed the Basel missionaries to settle in Odumase. Since the installation of Emmanuel Mate Kole in 1892, the paramount chiefs have been Christians, but they are also involved in many customary practices. The Manya Krobo paramount chief who is ruling at present, *konọ* Sakite II, is aware of the delicate position he holds as a (Presbyterian) Church member and a traditional leader. He told me he is trying to understand, not to condemn traditional practices. However, as a Christian he disapproves of sacrificing a goat, displaying naked breasts and the young age of *dipo* girls during the *dipo* performance. He feels that *dipo* should be modified, so that it ultimately can become a Christianised custom. *Konọ*'s father was a presbyter, and he claims that his three sisters never went through *dipo*.

The juggling with different views on culture is, for example, shown in the interview I had with the Presbyterian reverend at the time, named Nakotey, in Odumase, who is a Krobo from Somanya.[425] I asked what, according to him, is the significance of *dipo*. He answered:

> The *dipo* custom trains young girls for future marital life. So, the importance is that, after they have gone through the *dipo* custom they are fully prepared for marriage. And when they enter into marriage they'll be in a position to play the marital role very, very well. They will be taught how to stay with their husbands, peacefully, they will be taught how to manage the home affairs effectively, they will be taught how to care for the children in future. They prepare them for all this. They will also be taught the culture, I mean the total civilisation, the people, and it is the culture that identifies us as a people. They will be taught the culture of the people. How to put on cloth properly, how to dance, as they are doing right now.

While we were talking inside the house, we could see and hear *dipo* girls who were being 'outdoored', as it was the month of May, passing by in the street. They were accompanied by their singing female relatives. He continued:

> Even [they are taught] how to eat and cook food. And then they are also taught financial management, financial control. When your husband gives you money, you learn how to manage it. And all these things bring about peace in the home. So that you see is the importance of the *dipo* custom. It is this that identifies us as a people, so it is very important to us.

Here the reverend formulated the idea of culture as a way of life of a people, which is important for its identity. Like others he presents the ideal image of the *dipo* performance as a training. However, when I asked whether he had performed *dipo* for his daughters, he answered: "Because of my Christian belief, I

---

[425] Interview with reverend Nakotey, May 19, 1999, Odumase.

don't perform it." The reverend said that he feels that aspects such as killing a goat are very pagan and should be revised, and that:

> Because of Christ and because he has died for us, our sins are forgiven because of this. He sacrificed himself for us once and for all. So I don't see any reason why I should go and perform any other custom to make my children perhaps clean or so. So I told her [my wife] and thank God she understood me. She agreed.

As a devout Christian, the positive view of culture in terms of useful and 'heritage' did not correspond with his view of *dipo* as a 'pagan custom'. However, he showed that he was familiar with both views and did not start off by condemning *dipo*.

Another example of the struggle with the perceived dichotomy between 'tradition' and 'modernity' comes from a woman named Dedo from Odumase, a 54-year old principal of a primary school in Accra, who told me that when she was a child, a diviner had told her family that she was destined to become a priestess and it would therefore be 'useless' to send her to school. Nevertheless, she was sent to school and training college. Ever since, however, she had been "troubled by the [paramount] stool".[426] Especially during festivals, or rituals and ceremonies concerning the chiefs, she experienced becoming possessed. For thirty years she had been trying to resist the call of 'the stool'. However, in the year 1998, just before the annual *Ngmayem* festival, she decided to give in. The day after the interview I observed how she underwent a purification ceremony, after which the *la* was tied for her. This meant that she accepted to serve 'the stool'. When I asked her how she dealt with it, being a Christian, she defended herself by saying:

> Well, well, you know this is custom. Custom and Christianity, they are two different ways, two different things. We are only making a mistake by saying... we are confusing ourselves by saying 'if you perform custom, it means you are going against Christianity'. But when you have been to that house [her family house = the 'royal' family house], did you see any idol? Did you see any idol? I'm asking you a question [expecting an answer from me]. (...) You know the church [people] they are confusing, mixing two things. But the bible says, 'Give that which is for God to God, and that of Caesar should be given to Caesar'. It is a parable. Because in the bible, [it was written about customs of the time:] circumcision, it was a custom, yes, and the festival, they had festivals, which they celebrated.[427]

Dedo meant to say here that custom is 'not just pagan' and the opposite of Christianity. Custom meant ancient traditions, as also celebrated by people

---

[426] A particular stool can symbolise a traditional leader's power and be used as a medium for the veneration of the ancestors.
[427] Interview October 26, 1998, Odumase.

talked about in the bible. Paganism in her view means the worshipping of idols. Therefore she wanted to emphasise that there is not necessarily an 'idol' at the houses where custom is performed.

During the interview Dedo went on to explain things from a slightly different perspective, vindicating that the local gods and their priests had rules and laws 'just like us Christians', and that she admires the local priests for their righteousness. With a sudden intensity, she added:

> But they [the local priests] adhere to their rules! However, ministers, even when married, chase women; [Julie, who accompanied me, laughed cynically as if to confirm this]. They go after people's wives.
> Julie: Impregnating your children.
> Dedo: Yes! These Christians, they go in for abortion and so on and so forth. But that Tigare priest [a priest for a rather widely known (anti-witchcraft) deity that originates from the north, given as an example here] knows, if he does it, he will die! So who is faithful?

As I heard other people do when defending 'traditional religion', the woman pointed out the bad behaviour of some of the Christian pastors in contrast with the supposed righteousness of traditional priests. Such people complain that immorality has increased with Christianity. This is often explained by saying that in traditional religion one is punished immediately after doing something wrong ('the priest will die'), however in Christianity one can pray for forgiveness and will not be judged until Judgement Day. At the same time, Dedo wanted to demonstrate the relativist viewpoint that the indigenous gods and their adherents are part of a religion, just as Christianity is one of the existing religions. This idea is also taught in the government school textbooks for cultural studies, in which the 'Christian, Islamic and Traditional' religions are treated as analogous and referred to as 'the three main religions in Ghana'.[428] Even though people acknowledge that Ghana has three religions, many people in practice take Christianity as the point of departure and regard it as a superior religion, and 'Traditional Religion' in particular as inferior to Christianity.

In short, Christian discourses about culture have influenced much of the debate about cultural traditions in Ghana. So far, I have discussed discourses in which culture is either regarded negatively as the realm of the devil, or positively as the realm of custom. In the latter case, people have to reason within the discursive space as laid out successfully by Christians, and therefore try to argue that culture is 'not just pagan', but also place this ideal culture in the past. They struggle with the perceived dichotomy between tradition and modernity, and the meaning of culture that is highlighted often depends on the context in which people find themselves. In the next section we will look at a different idea of

---

[428] For example, see *Cultural Studies for Junior Secondary Schools, pupil's book 2*, Ministry of Education and Culture, 1988.

culture as expressed by the government and part of the academic elite (particularly the Institute of African Studies), who attempt to emphasise the positive aspects of culture by treating culture as functional and part of the Ghanaian national identity.

'Culture for development': dipo and the state

'Unity in diversity': national culture

> If any country wants to project itself in this modern world of globalization, that country must first project its culture. (...) Culture and traditions are the only means [through which] we can differ from the rest of the world (Oppong Kyekyeku 1998).

> In the face of the threat of foreign culture invading our very psyche, it is important that we try to maintain our identity through our music, food, dressing and social interactions (Abdulai 1999).

State-owned newspapers *Ghanaian Times* and the *Daily Graphic* articles, as quoted above, often write about the need to protect Ghanaian culture in the face of the threat of modernity and foreign cultural influences that might sweep it away. At the same time there is a growing awareness, stimulated by international organisations such as the UNESCO that want to safeguard 'traditional culture' and folklore, that Ghanaian's cultural heritage can be used to promote national development, in particular with regard to tourism.[429]

The Ghanaian state has developed initiatives for the enunciation of a national cultural policy, and therefore a national identity, that partly coincides with the quest of some of the mainline Christian churches for Africanisation.[430] It seeks to overcome the legacy of colonialism and missionisation, and the perceived threat of modern globalisation. *The Cultural Policy of Ghana* (n.d., but probably re-written in 1999), which the NDC (National Democratic Congress, see chapter two) government has designed based on the 1992 Constitution, declares, on the government's behalf, that:

> In our encounter with alien cultures and colonialism, strenuous and unrelenting attempts were made by extraneous forces to denigrate our culture and deny it of any value. Attempts were also made to supplant our traditions, ideas and ideals in order to ensure the imposition of extraneous ones aimed at keeping us forever in subjugation (*The Cultural Policy of Ghana* n.d.: 2).

---

[429] UNESCO stands for: 'United Nations Educational, Scientific and Cultural Organization'.

[430] At the time of my research between 1998-2000, the National Democratic Congress (NDC) was in power, with J.J. Rawlings as the president of Ghana. The New Patriotic Party (NPP) won the national elections in 2000 and formed the government from 2001 until the present day (also see chapter two).

304

The state's policy wants to use the past as a rich source for societal renewal, for achieving progress and development in a 'Ghanaian' way, and to augment the general public's awareness of their cultural heritage, aiming at fostering national cohesion. In contrast to the Pentecostal view, the past is not perceived as a curse, but as a source of cherished cultural identity (Van Dijk 2001: 46).

These ideas are part of the postcolonial debate, with the creation of a national identity as a major theme. Former presidents Nkrumah and Busia started to introduce forms of ideological education as mechanisms for effecting nationalism (Agyeman 1988). Many of the ideas have been a response to the idea of white supremacy instituted by the colonisers. To this very day Ghanaians are still extremely conscious of being regarded as 'backward' in the international arena. Writing about the cultural policy of Ghana's first president Kwame Nkrumah, George Hagan, professor at the Institute of African studies (University of Ghana) noted that:

> One abiding effect of the leadership of Nkrumah is that the peoples of Africa now have a consciousness of their cultural identity and possess a definite pride of culture. Africans are also aware of the need, in fact of the necessity, to discover their cultural heritage and develop it (1993: 3).

Some of Nkrumah's ideas have been the guiding principles of Ghana's cultural policy from the time of Independence to the present. A central thought was the concept of *African Personality*. This concept represented an attempt to seek the permanent and universal in the changing patterns of African culture and nurture the consciousness of African identity, while acknowledging Africa's cultural heterogeneity. It served to provide some principles for the quest and preservation of the African heritage and stressed that the African is part of world culture (Hagan 1993). Under Nkrumah some cultural institutions such as the Ghana Museum, the Arts Council of Ghana and the Research Library on African Affairs were started. He inaugurated the Institute of African Studies and charged it "with the burden of leading the effort to uncover Africa's heritage and make the African aware of his rich heritage" (Hagan 1993: 21). Cultural practices were also revived. After all, Ghanaians were to see their culture as a composite culture of diverse ethnic cultures. Within Ghana the concept of 'unity in diversity' formed the bridge between local and national identity (cf. Schramm 2000: 23-25). According to some of my informants, *dipo* was celebrated with more vigour again after Independence through the influence of Nkrumah's politics. Ayi also observes in his African Studies thesis that there was a general tendency towards a return to *dipo* in the 1960s. But he does not make a link with politics, instead he points to the church authorities that "are no more as severe as in the past" (Ayi 1966: 37).

The NDC government created a National Commission on Culture, which operates through a number of 'pro-cultural institutions and agencies' to implement the Cultural Policy. The Commission tries to preserve, develop and promote culture by, amongst others, paying tribute to the Regional and National Houses of Chiefs, and organising festivals. The national festivals have themes such as 'the preservation of cultural heritage'.[431] The state policy does not propagate the continuation of 'traditional customs' for the sake of tradition, but argues that the development of a people and its culture are an important condition for development in any other area.[432] The key symbol for the promotion of national culture is the concept of *sankofa*. The *sankofa* bird turns its head and looks back in the direction of its origin. The meaning was explained to me as 'go back to the roots', or also 'go back and take it'. The Cultural Policy states that the concept does not:

> imply a blind return to customs and traditions of the past. It affirms the co-existence of the past and the future in the present and embodies, therefore, the attitude of our people to the interaction between traditional values and the demands of modern technology and the existence of international cultural milieu (*The Cultural Policy of Ghana* n.d.: 3) (emphasis in text).

The Cultural Policy further declares that the government wants to enhance the national cohesion and national development through the teaching of culture in schools, the promotion of Ghanaian languages, the presentation of Ghanaian culture in the media and art forms and the protection of the Ghanaian identity and cultural heritage.

The idea that there is a distinct Ghanaian culture leads people to criticise aspects of culture that are supposedly foreign. One Shai chief quoted in *The Mirror* in a discussion article about *dipo* (see also above) said about this:

> [O]ur own people think the white man's culture is superior to ours. As a result of this misconception we are getting lost as a people, drifting away from our rich culture and identity and rather copying the white man's culture, which is not suitable for us (Azu 1998).

In this line of reasoning, for example, the naked breasts of *dipo* girls are seen as an authentic expression of indigenous culture that needs to be protected against the influence of decadent Western culture, whereas in the Christian discourse this nakedness is condemned as being backward and primitive. The same chief mentioned above was quoted in the same interview saying:

---

[431] The National Festival of Arts and Culture (NAFAC) of 1998, for example, had as its theme: 'The challenges of cultural preservation. The strengthening of our national identity in the next millennium'.

[432] This view is in line with Nkrumah's thoughts: "Within a society poising itself from the leap from pre-industrial retardation to modern development, there are traditional forces that can impede progress. Some of these must be firmly cut at their roots, others can be retained and adapted to the changing need" (Nkrumah 1963: 83).

306

> Those condemning *dipo* should stop. (...) They should rather campaign against the various beauty contests where women are made to parade the stage almost naked in swim suits and check the numerous alien culture on our television screens which the innocent teenage children are copying.

In an editorial of the weekly newspaper *People & Places*, the modern dressing of some Ghanaian women was characterised as going against Ghanaian tradition as 'no serious man would take such a woman for a wife':

> It's amazing and embarrassing when you consider what has become of Ghanaian womanhood. It is a shame to see our women, semi-naked in their dressing. (...) Some of the women dress showing part of their breasts; the whole of their abdomen; some with only blouses which look like undies, awaiting to be topped by the real garments, hanging tops they call them. They go with tight lycra leggings, which expose all the contours of their feminine figure. (...) No serious man would take a woman for a wife after she had exposed herself to the whole world. (...) The electronic media should also be selective in the sort of materials they broadcast, since it is one of the channels through which our ladies miscopy the Europeans ("P&P Comment: Let's save Ghanaian womanhood" 1998).

It is telling that women are criticised for copying Western dress where women are seen as custodians and the portrayers of culture:

> In the face of the serious invasion by alien values, systems, and vogues, Ghanaian women have become the frontlines in the country's struggle for cultural preservation and development, especially in the aspect of stamping the nobility of Ghana's traditional modes of dressing ("Women take the front" 1998).

In this manner, in all the quotations above, concern is expressed about the image of Ghanaian culture that is portrayed to the outside world. People worry about the impact of Westernisation on 'authentic' Ghanaian culture.

In the definition of culture as formulated in the Cultural Policy, culture is mainly seen as a means for distinction from other peoples and cultures and therefore as something people can identify with. In government discourse culture means *Ghanaian* culture, promoting a national identity. So those who criticise their culture are accused of denying their identity as Ghanaians. In a reaction to an Internet discussion on the 'Ghana Homepage' about the desirability of photos of 'naked' *dipo* girls on the Internet,[433] one writer calling himself Papa Kwame defended *dipo* in this manner. He argued that the girls only appear barebreasted in public on the first day of the ceremony in order to show and prove

---

[433] The initial letter that started off the discussion was entitled 'The Naked Truth of a Ghanaian Cultural Pride', and was posted by Bright Boateng in December 2000 on 'Say it Loud', which is a virtual discussion forum on the 'Ghana Homepage': http://www.ghanaweb.com/GhanaHomePage/say.

their chastity.[434] Papa Kwame therefore rebuked other participants in the discussion for not taking pride in Ghanaian culture: "It is customs such as these that keep Ghana alive for future generations." A female writer taking part in the same discussion also wondered why Ghanaians felt ashamed about their culture towards Westerners, instead of being proud of it. She used the similar argument of cultural practices of a people as their communal identity, differentiating them from other nationalities, by comparing Ghanaians to the Scottish men who: "(…) wear their kilts with pride, in spite of being ridiculed by men and women around the world. This is a part of their culture they are just not willing to compromise."

Coe (2000) argues in her study of regional and national school cultural competitions, that these competitions promote a regional and ethnic perspective on culture: "it is much more about learning about the practices of other groups to promote ethnic tolerance than about presenting a common national culture." I do not think that celebrating ethnic differences contrasts with constructing a national identity. Education of this kind is rather in line with Nkrumahs' 'unity in diversity' concept (see above). Many Krobo use the government rhetoric as a defence of the culture of *dipo* when they say: 'Just as other tribes have their customs, we also have our *dipo* custom'. *Dipo* has become the figurehead of 'Krobo culture'. The advertisements in newspapers for the annual Manya Krobo *Ngmayem* Festival and the Yilo Krobo *Kloyo sikplemi* festival, for example, always portray a *dipo* girl in her finery.

Although the government is trying to bring the message across that culture is 'not pagan' and 'not just drumming and dancing', but a 'way of life', it is nevertheless mainly understood in those terms. It does not refer to 'what we do' in general, but is perceived as something one can choose to participate in or not. For instance, culture often refers to the more material aspects of culture such as dressing and bodily decorations. A well-known traditional bead maker in Odumase told me in this respect that he 'loves African culture'. As Coe shows in her study, the teaching of culture in schools is mostly limited to the cultural competitions with poetry recitals, drumming, dance and drama competitions. My friend Julie's school, for example, has a cultural troupe that at times performs at public gatherings. At such occasions they perform with drumming and dancing, portraying 'Krobo culture' such as the *dipo* dances. Groups such as these perform at festivals, for tourists or at (local) political gatherings. This particular group, for instance, performed within the scope of a three-day seminar that took place in January 1999 at the University of Ghana under the auspices of the International Centre for African Music and the UNESCO. The seminar was based on the UNESCO's recommendation of the safeguarding of traditional culture and folk-

---

[434] As was explained to me during my fieldwork, the priestesses and elderly women leading the ceremony are able to tell from a girl's breast and stomach whether she has been pregnant before or is pregnant at that very moment. A pregnancy before *dipo* is a big taboo (see chapter six and seven).

lore. However, a few pupils from Julie's class (class 6, the eldest children) refused to take part in it, because they felt it was unchristian.

'Modify cultural practices'[435]

When culture is regarded as static and 'traditional', as something of the past, it is often regarded as 'backward' and a hindrance to progress. Bright Boateng expressed this clearly when he writes on the Internet in reference to *dipo*: "I do respect our culture, but I believe we have to be proactive in innovating our cultural beliefs and practices and to create new social models that will not continue to hinder our progress."[436] Here he refers to the idea that culture is valuable, but needs to be revised, or 'polished', as it popularly stated in Ghana. This view is often expressed in the state-owned newspapers, not only because they report far more on comments made by government officials at public events than on everyday happenings (Hasty 2000), but also because the columnists and editorials disseminate this ideology. For instance, in the *Daily Graphic* it was written that: "We are at the crossroad and must therefore make an informed decision as to which way to turn – whether to follow tradition to the letter at the expense of technological development, or to dance to the tune of globalisation to the detriment of our cultural practices" (Dery 1999).

Chiefs and queen mothers in particular, themselves often seen as 'custodians of culture', are regularly urged by government officials to modify or eliminate cultural practices "that are socially harmful and conflict with provisions of the constitution". Chiefs and queen mothers from different regions of Ghana at times even attend workshops to identify 'outmoded customs and cultural practices' and make recommendations for their review or removal (see e.g. Pratt 1998). Which practices should be identified as 'outmoded' or 'harmful' and which not, is the difficulty. The government often focuses on practices that (in their view) abuse human, in particular female, rights, such as female circumcision or *trokosi* (in which women serving in traditional priests' shrines are perceived as slaves, see also introduction of this chapter). Therefore queen mothers in particular, representing the women in their respective areas, are called upon from time to time by politicians, to play a leading role in educating people to "abolish outmoded, cultural and traditional practices with negative impact on women which retard their development" (Ankuma 1998).

---

[435] This title was derived from a newspaper article by William Asiedu: 'Modify Cultural Practices' (1999).
[436] 'The Naked Truth of a Ghanaian Cultural Pride', by Bright Boateng, (www.ghanaweb.com/GhanaHomePage/say), December 2000. The name 'Boateng' seems to be an Akan name, but it is not clear where the writer hails from.

Christians in particular also focus on 'pagan' practices they regard as 'harmful' or 'outmoded', and therefore subject to 'polishing' or rather abolishment, such as 'the ban on drumming', the pouring of libation and also the *dipo* rites. Speeches made by reverends, priests and pastors at public gatherings regarding these issues are regularly reported in newspapers, as well as those of government and local politicians. If *dipo* used to be about home management and the protection of the virginity of girls, these people wonder, why do girls have to go through at such young ages these days? Another criticised subject is the girls' dressing during the rites. People argue that the attire of the girls that is 'close to nudity' will present a negative, primitive image of Ghanaians to tourists, and may lead to rape and 'immoral behaviour'. A Pentecostal pastor told me: "It attracts men. If they expose the women, lust will enter the men and then they follow them. The bible says women should dress modestly".

At the same time, this functional view of *dipo* as able to enhance morality also leaves room for the argument that if it was modified, it could prevent teenage pregnancies and AIDS.[437] Frequently, the *dipo* rites are also mentioned as an example of a practice, which should be modified in order to promote good morality among female youths. As I mentioned in chapter six, both in interviews with me and in public, the Yilo Krobo paramount queen mother and the Manya Krobo paramount chief have therefore proclaimed before that *dipo* should not be performed under a set age (eight years and fifteen years respectively) (see also Doku 2000). At a symposium on *dipo* at Odumase, District Chief Executive at the time, Henry Hammond, in his role of local politician addressed his audience as follows, after having summed up the positive aspects of *dipo*:

> In spite of these achievements however, I regret to say that our cherished culture is being adulterated. This is because now children of one month are made to undergo *dipo* rites. In addition, most of the traditional shrines have been turned into "goldmines" thus, the real impact of *dipo* found in the relevance of the *tɛgbɛtɛ* in the detection of early sex before the rite is now almost deceptive. I therefore wish to emphasise that there is a need to review these negative attitudes so that we can save our children from teenage pregnancy and the disgracing inference to Krobos as "Prostitutes".[438]

Without offering a solution, he then called upon "Christians, Moslems and traditionalists alike" to come with ideas to modernise the rites, so that the negative effects would vanish, teenage pregnancies would be curtailed, and morality and tourism promoted.

Hence people say that if *dipo* would be 'refined' and 'polished', there would be no problem. The 'fetish' elements should be removed, naked breasts

---

[437] See e.g. Schroeder and Danquah (2000).

[438] Address by the District Chief Executive Captain Henry Hammond at symposium on *dipo* at Odumase-Krobo on May 28, 1998.

covered and 'innocent' aspects such as the decoration with beads, the dancing and the passing on of traditions should be preserved. To preserve some aspects and reject others is one way of uniting the Christian discourse that emphasises the negative aspects of culture with the discourse that regards culture as a 'living custom' or part of the cultural heritage that needs to be preserved. One male teacher, for example, said : "You see the question is, *dipo* is not a bad institution, but there are some aspects which go against Christianity, and if those aspects could be taken away then I think it is a very good custom." Likewise, a man in his forties, a nephew of one of the old *dipo* priestesses told me:

> *Dipo* is a custom and as a custom we have to maintain it. The problem with it is that of modernisation. The nudity, the dressing, we have to modify it. But to say that we should eradicate or stop it, me I will never do that.[439]

Apparently he wanted to express his view that in the context of the 'modern' world *dipo* has some 'backward' aspects that should be modified. Otherwise it is a 'custom' that needs to be maintained. Even traditional priest Tetteh Gaga said about *dipo* that "People have made it tóó fetish". Gaga claimed that: "We are redefining it, we are changing things so that everybody can appreciate it", and even the children of pastors could come and do it. He asserted that he had taken out 'fetish things'. The soothsaying was something he did not find necessary. Under his supervision the children also did not have to touch the goat's head, they wore white calico instead of the goat's fat and intestines on Sunday. And the hair of girls, if they were school children, did not need to be shaved. The latter two aspects are almost generally observed these days.

The taking of a picture as proof of the accomplished initiation has come to replace the 'primitive' scarification on the hands, waist and back, and is also being generally accepted, as we have seen in the previous chapters. However, the uncovered breasts remain a hot issue. Where the breasts are sometimes covered in cultural performances outside of the context of initiation, the dressing of *dipo* girls otherwise continues to be unchanged. Interestingly, many aspects of *dipo* that are mentioned in the examples as 'fetish' and 'obsolete', refer to supposedly 'backward' and 'primitive' aspects rather than to particular 'religious' aspects, which, however, points to the fact that people reason within the Christian idiom that regards 'traditional religion' as backward and primitive.

Where culture is regarded as part of Ghana's cultural heritage that should be handed down from generation to generation, the government discourse of culture partly coincides with the mainline Christian churches quest for Africanisation, and partly with the view of culture as custom. However, the state's approach of culture means an objectification of culture. The 'culturalisation', to

---

[439] Interview with 'lawyer' Akwete, September 10, 1998, Kodjonya.

speak with Peel, of religious culture such as *dipo*, transforms culture in that narrower sense in which it is the concern of Ministries of Culture and Arts Councils. It is an attempt to secularise traditional rituals, "to turn them into harmless culture" (Peel 1994: 162-163). 'Harmless culture' or folklore is especially highlighted in the promotion of tourism.

Performing culture: tourism

Dipo girls in their finery are a favourite subject of photographs that have to promote tourism. The first time I learnt about a people named Krobo was in the early 1990s when I noticed a photo of *dipo* girls in a little travel guide on Ghana issued by the Ghana Tourist Board (1991). The picture shows three girls with an intricate hairdo, numerous strings of beads around the neck, arms and knees. Long stripes of colourful wax print cloth are tugged in with the heavy waist beads, leaving the upper body naked. Under the heading 'Festivals and Culture', *dipo* is also one of the listed events on the Internet site of the Ghana Tourist Board. The caption with the photo of two dancing *dipo* girls that illustrates the advertisement for this 'recommended festival' says:

> *Dipo*: A Puberty Festival by the Krobos (of Somanya, Odumase) when girls at an adolescent age are initiated into womanhood with a parade. The attire of the girls is close to nudity (Ghana Tourist Board).[440]

The caption seems to intentionally focus on the attire of the girls that is 'close to nudity'. A Ghanaian named Bright Boateng (whom I referred to above) writes how he was browsing the website of the Ghana Tourist Board and encountered the photograph of these 'half naked and bare breasted' *dipo* girls. He comments:

> When I was growing up in Ghana, bare-breasted young women in customary situations were of no curiosity. Today, the picture is different, and it 'is worth a thousand words'. While the peoples and communities involved in this cultural pride may understand its significance, many others (foreigners included) who view this site and picture may not understand its significance and may interpret it to mean different things in their own perverted ways. (...) Yes, they see worse of some of our women abroad, but let us try to control what is within our control. A people's culture is not necessarily virile in its staticity, but rather in its dynamism. All I am saying is cover them up a little, please.[441]

---

[440] http://www.africaonline.com.gh/Tourism/ghana.html
[441] http://www.ghanaweb.com/GhanaHomePage/say, December 2000.

312

Boateng is worried about the image of Ghana the picture portrays to outsiders. In the contemporary world the meaning of naked breasts has changed he thinks, and he wants 'culture' to be revised.

In an interview with *The Standard*, a Ghanaian newspaper, Nketia, director of the School of Performing Arts (University of Ghana), clarifies what could be done in the way of cultural reform ("The Standard" 1998).[442] As the editor of the Ghanaian Times commented: "The thrust of his views is to the effect that traditional practices may be reformed without abolishing them" ("Editorial: 'Toward cultural death (3)'" 1998). Professor Nketia mentions the *dipo* rites as an example where some aspects could be modified. At the same time he feels that displaying half-naked girls on festive occasions in the name of *dipo* would amount to taking 'puberty rites' out of context and stripping the girls of their dignity. He is of the opinion that rites such as *dipo* should not be 'commodified'. According to Nketia, this means that *dipo* should not be pandered to the taste of foreigners and tourists by displaying virtually nude girls during festivals, as that would deviate from 'the original purpose'. To say that '*dipo* has been commercialised' or 'commodified' is a popular phrase in Krobo. This is usually not said in the context of tourism, but to emphasise that *dipo* is a costive undertaking and that people, especially the 'fetish' priests, make money out of performing *dipo*. This is often 'proved' by pointing out the growing number of *dipo* shrines. One of the divisional chiefs told me that: "Formerly there was only one [*dipo* shrine] in Klowεki area (Kodjonya), but now everybody has one, because of love for money, they have commercialised the whole thing."

Despite the criticism on tourism from persons such as professor Nketia, tourism is another area where the aims of preservation of 'culture' and at the same time development and progress come together. In this context culture loses its religious meaning and is made into 'innocent culture'. A process of 'culturalisation' is taking place (Peel 1994), as I mentioned above. Culture then becomes a product or is 'commodified', according to Nketia. The National Commission on Culture and the Ghana Tourism Board both feel that the promotion of culture for tourist purposes is one of the best ways to 'develop' the country. One of the methods they use to promote culture is through the support of festivals, because "Festivals play a vital role in a country's tourism development, especially in highlighting its artistic and indigenous technology for marketing and also in unifying the diverse cultures of the people", as a journalist of the *Ghanaian Times* wrote (Opoku-Acheampong 1998).

Most of these festivals are organised annually to celebrate, for example, the new yam harvest, and they are meant to portray people's 'ancient traditions and customs'. The festivals form occasions for chiefs and queen mothers to

---

[442] Professor J.H. Kwabena Nketia has been called Africa's leading musicologist, and is the writer of numerous books and articles on especially musicology (e.g. Nketia 1955; Nketia 1986).

show themselves at their best with a lot of pomp and pageantry at the so-called durbars where they sit in state.[443] Chiefs and invited guests, mostly government officials, take the opportunity to address the audience about development issues. Festivals in various areas in Ghana are being revived or invented for the purposes of tourism and the increased status of the given town (Clarke-Ekong 1995). One example of such a more recently invented festival is the *Kloyosikplemi* festival of the Yilo Krobo, which commemorates the descent of the Krobo from Krobo Mountain in 1892 and was first celebrated in 1992 (see chapter two). The theme of the 1995 festival, for example, was: 'Mobilisation of resources for effective development of Yilo Krobo communities'. The *kono* of Yilo Krobo, Nene Kpetekple Narh Dawutey Ologo VI, wrote in his 'goodwill message' in the festival brochure:

> I wish to assure you that my Divisional Chiefs and the political and administrative head of this District would work in tandem and in harmony to create an enabling environment for all citizens to realize their full potentials. I am extending a hand of welcome to wealthy citizens, both Ghanaian and foreign investors to exploit the vast economic, tourist and agricultural potentials of the Yilo State on very generous terms from the leadership.

The *kono* in this way used the festival as a forum to express his interest in attracting wealthy Ghanaians and foreigners for investments in Yilo Krobo area.

I observed how cultural troupes in Krobo performed *dipo* dancing at both the Manya and Yilo Krobo festival durbars to entertain the audience and display 'Krobo culture'. The minister of Tourism at the time, Mike Gizo, expressed his concern about the 'near-nudity' aspect of *dipo* in a speech given at such a durbar in another Dangme-speaking area (Hudson 1998).[444] A columnist of the *Daily Graphic* reacted and shared the minister's opinion by writing that: "With Ghana fast becoming a big tourist destination in Africa, we have to do away with practices that can earn us scorn rather than respect and admiration in the eyes of the international community" (Darko 1998). However, the 'problem' of nudity began to be resolved at the *Ngmayem* festival of October 1998. Here the girls who were dressed as *dipo-yi* and danced *dipo* dances wore a brown coloured top to hide their breasts. The question is whether the concern about naked breasts is really that of foreigners, or is guided by Christian norms in Ghana. Very few foreigners are present at local cultural festivals, as tourism is still relatively low scale in Ghana compared to typical tourist destinations in the world. During local festivals a *dipo* dance performance obviously is seen as belonging to the

---

[443] A 'durbar' is an occasion where traditional rulers and people gather, which has its origins in British colonial India (also see chapter two).

[444] The particular durbar was held to mark the *Asafotufiami* festival of the Ada Traditional Area at Big-Ada.

314

'cultural tradition' of the Krobo and therefore articulates a cultural or ethnic identity.

Vis-à-vis foreign tourists the *dipo* dance performance does not so much create a specific ethnic identity, but it has the effect of creating a difference between 'the Westerner' and 'the African'. It acquires meaning as representing the 'authentic' African Other. In this way the performers try to gain access to the resources of the global tourist industry. Here the *dipo* performance becomes something which represents 'typically Ghanaian' or even 'African' culture, as the story of the 'Afrikan Jewels' in the following indicates.

'Passage to Africa'

The 'traditional' aspects of the *dipo* rites enjoy an increasing interest from the outside world in the form of tourists and other visitors who search for 'authentic culture'. A series of articles in an online newspaper under the heading 'Passage to Africa',[445] narrates the story of a group of five thirteen to sixteen-year-old African-American teenage girls, who travelled to Ghana "to find keys to future in their heritage" in August 2000 (unfortunately one to two months after I had left Ghana). They were part of a group named the 'Afrikan Jewels', which meant that they were members of a national youth-outreach program called 'Rites of Passage'. As part of the program they were going to participate in the "tribal rites of womanhood for the Ashanti and Manya Krobo peoples – a ritual gantlet through which African girls have passed for centuries". At their ritual farewell ceremony in America they were told they were leaving as children, but would return as young adults.

So these girls came to Krobo-Odumase for a few days to be initiated in a *dipo* ceremony, especially organised for them, outside of the normal *dipo* season. *Konọ* Sakite received them willingly and let them know accordingly through his welcome address that 'willing pupils with open minds have much to learn from his people and their ways'. The African-American girls were to 'pass through *dipo* to enter womanhood', but what was actually described was the so-called outdooring part of the *dipo* rites. The 'Afrikan Jewels' were dressed in priestess Lako Sakite's house with *kente*, they were given beads to wear and a woman marked their hands with ink to represent the usual twelve small scars in clusters of three. Two or three Krobo teenage girls, who had passed the rites before, were dressed as well to assist the American girls. They were taken to the courtyard in front of the palace to be presented to the paramount queen mother, who had organised a small durbar with other queen mothers. There they were

---

[445] Stories by Mike Harden, columnist of 'The Columbus Dispatch newspaper' online: http://www.Dispatch.com/news/

315

asked to dance, barefoot on the gravel course. Although they were dressed and prepared in Lako Sakite's house, who is the chief *dipo* priestess in Odumase, she did not perform any of the *dipo* rituals for them. They had probably just been taken to her house because she possesses many beads and other items used, and is part of the royal family.

The role that is played by queen mothers in this 'commodification' of *dipo*, to use Nketia's phrase, is remarkable. Whereas in the Asante area the queen mothers supervise *bragoro*, the Krobo queen mothers are not the ones who supervise the *dipo* initiation. Rather this is the duty of the traditional priestesses. The queen mothers may only mediate between family members in conflicts concerning *dipo*. However, they have appropriated the role of supervising the cultural performance of *dipo* for tourists. During my stay in Krobo a number of busloads of (American) tourists, actually mainly exchange students from Legon University, came to visit Odumase a couple of times. Each time a mini-durbar was staged for them in front of the palace with the queen mothers 'sitting in state'. The chiefs and the priests were absent. The 'Afrikan Jewels' story mentions that: "Manye Mamle Okleyo, the paramount queen mother, had agreed to supervise the rituals and welcome the Jewels into womanhood as she had the daughters of her town.". Apparently the author mixed up the Krobo practices with Akan practices. Tourists and outsiders in general have no idea of the local cultural repertoire, and so the *dipo* performance can easily include the queen mothers and represent 'Ghanaian culture'.[446] It is important that this indicates, as I mentioned above, that in the context of tourism, *dipo* is not so much presented as particular 'Krobo culture', but as 'Ghanaian' or even 'African culture'. It has lost its 'religious' local meaning here, which emphasises a belonging to Krobo society. As a 'traditional practice' it is, just as the queen mothers are, a symbol of objectified 'Ghanaian culture' here, also referred to with the term 'tradition'. 'Culture' is positively valued as portraying Ghanaian cultural heritage, which can attract tourists to promote development. The queen mothers act as brokers here between the local community and the outside world and in this way locate themselves in a global political economy.

The limits of discursive space

Basel missionary work and British colonial rule successfully drew a parallel between the contrast 'Christianity' – 'Heathendom' and the contrast 'modern' – 'traditional'/'uncivilised', implying that there was a bounded domain that could be recognised as 'Heathendom', which was 'traditional' and a 'remnant of the past'. Nevertheless, 'traditional religion' has survived within modern Krobo so-

---

[446] See De Jong (2001: 232) about the similar effect of mask performances for tourists in Senegal.

ciety, which indicates both the flexibility of 'tradition' and the creative and dynamic aspects of tradition and cultural identity. In previous chapters it was explained that the importance of *dipo* as *kusumi* in constituting a person and reaffirming ties to the family and hometown in particular remains very important in everyday lives of Krobo people. At the same time, 'traditional' practices such as *dipo*, termed as 'culture', are a hotly debated issue in Ghana.

Even though the government ministries and the Institute of African Studies represent an educated elite's perspective on culture, the view of Pentecostal churches is largely supported by young people in urban areas, while the area of interest of traditionalists can mainly be found in the realm of chieftaincy and 'traditional' ritual practitioners, and the formal standpoints of former mission churches are carried by the old elite, the repertoire of the different discourses is available to many Ghanaians including Krobo people, and they all make use of it. Which perspective they highlight and which value they attach to 'tradition' and 'culture' depends on the context of speech. Presbyterian Church members often just pay lip service to their church's official standpoint, as they continue to perform *dipo* secretly, while Pentecostal churches offer their adherents a way out: people can be delivered from their 'past', which ties them to family relations. However, with the latter's increasing influence, the dissociation from *dipo* and other 'traditional' ceremonies has received a renewed incentive.

In contemporary local vernacular, the dichotomy between Christianity and tradition is upheld. The contrast between 'culture' as something of 'the past' and Christianity as 'modern' and 'civilised' determines the discursive space within which Ghanaians have to organise their view of the world, even though different values are attached to culture in local usage. Different churches show different reactions. The Roman Catholic Church and its members show an inclination towards inculturation. The standpoint that there should be an African-oriented type of Christianity makes the Roman Catholic Church popular for a large segment of people. The state-held notions of conservation and rejuvenation of Ghanaian cultural heritage partly coincide with the quest of the mainline churches for inculturation or 'Africanisation'. However, the Pentecostal Churches remain rather ambivalent if not hostile towards this entire culture project (cf. Van Dijk 2001: 31), and reject all 'culture' and 'traditional practices' as demon-inspired.

Even if people attach different values to traditions, their discussions take place within the same limited discursive space laid out by the missionary and colonial dichotomy between Christianity/modernity and tradition. Krobo people who value 'culture' and emphasise that *dipo* is important to portray 'Krobo culture' and define Krobo identity and do not reject cultural practices as 'satanic', still have to emphasise that culture is 'not just pagan', and admit that contemporary culture has become 'more fetish', that there is need for 'modification' and they place the 'original' culture in the past. For example, the link so often made by the Basel missionaries between *dipo*, as part of Heathendom, and 'immorality' is still prevalent today. Where the Basel missionaries ascribed 'immorality' to the rites they encountered at the time, both Christians and non-Christians today attribute what they perceive as a decline in morality to the weakening of the rites. Both the views of the missionaries and contemporary Christians, however, reflect a Christianised idea of a pre-pagan past, when an ideal 'original', 'authentic' *dipo* was performed on Krobo Mountain without much interference of 'fetish' priests and girls supposedly married right after *dipo* and learned how to become proper wives and mothers. People who perceive culture as a custom (*kusumi*) that cannot be abolished, or as part of a cultural heritage that needs to be preserved, still emphasise that *dipo* should be 'refined' and 'polished'. The 'fetish' elements should be removed, the naked breasts covered, and the 'innocent' aspects such as the decoration with beads, the dancing and the passing on of traditions should be preserved. This 'modification' argument is used by some Christians, the government and traditionalists, but they all reason within the limited discursive space people have to define their position.

Another area where culture loses its local religious meaning and becomes acceptable in Christian terms, is where it is made into 'innocent culture', or folklore, to promote a national identity and tourism. In tourism the aim of preservation of culture and at the same time development and progress overlaps. However, the meaning of 'culture' is transformed, it is objectified and commoditised. Locally, culture articulates cultural identity in this way, but vis-à-vis the Western world culture promotes tourism by creating a different, 'authentic' Other. The performers of 'culture' therefore try to gain access to the resources of the global tourist industry. However, the actual *dipo* initiation cannot be commodified, because most Krobo attribute power to *dipo* and its performance contains basic cultural values. The cultural performance of aspects of *dipo* during festivals and for tourist and other audiences is nevertheless also an example of the fact that *dipo* can acquire new meanings and 'tradition' is very much alive and actualised all the time.

In sum, the different discourses are not neatly separated, but merge. People can, for example, obviously be both Christians and government representatives at the same time. Their usage of culture differs depending on the context of discussion. While there is an overt debate and struggle over the current meaning and practical implications of cultural norms, it coexists with the pervasive conviction that the Krobo have 'a unique culture', consisting of specific institutions, rules and beliefs, which are common to all members of the community and which need to be 'preserved' (cf. Lentz 1997: 71). Debates on the cultural practice of *dipo* with its long history of contestation, reveal different outlooks on what modern identity entails. By rejecting *dipo*, people can at times emphasise their Christian identity. In, for example, the national context, *dipo* is a strong marker of Krobo identity. However, the tradition/culture–Christianity dichotomy determines the discursive space within which Krobo people have to organise their view of the world and therefore at the bottom a deep ambivalence remains.

9

Conclusion

Throughout this study we have investigated the meaning of *dipo*, and the insights its resilience and dynamics yield into responses of the Krobo to modernisation in the form of encounters with colonial intervention, missionary influence and of modern nationalism. It was established that the rites are continually contested and called 'outmoded', 'pagan' and used to stereotype Krobo women as 'promiscuous'. Views on *dipo* are expressed largely through an idiom of conflict between tradition and Christianity. One basic question in this study was how the discursive field, with its keywords 'tradition' and 'culture', in which *dipo* is discussed and contested, evolved. Another question was how *dipo* can be so enduring and at the same time articulate different meanings. By focusing on the centrality of *dipo* in Krobo society, this study aims to contribute to the continuing need to undermine the pervasive idea of unchanging and static traditions in Africa and the notion of homogeneous and bounded cultural wholes. My assumption is that the main themes of initiation remain central in a globalising world, and that 'tradition' cannot be studied in isolation from 'the modern' nor without taking its history into perspective.

Before coming to a final discussion of the main questions, I would like to recapitulate the main findings of this study. In existing literature the *dipo* rites are usually regarded as 'puberty rites', which seems at odds with the fact that even two-year-old girls can pass through them and at the same time ignores the fact that initiation can 'do' many things. Furthermore, the assumption that female initiation deals with domesticity and individual girls and therefore serves the domain of the domestic and the domination of men, was questioned. The fact that female rites may emphasise the future role of a woman as a mother and wife does not necessarily mean that women are 'oppressed'. Relations of authority enacted in *dipo* are first of all based on seniority. Senior women and priestesses perform the rites and their mothers, grandmothers and aunties may accompany the initiands. These women clearly enjoy participating in the rites and feel proud of their daughters. During the rites there is a greater emphasis on a woman's cleanliness and fertility and on becoming a 'real' or 'pure' Krobo than on her future role as a wife. Moreover, the relation with the family and the wider group is established and confirmed, more so than the relationship with a future husband. In addition, Krobo initiation is performed for groups of girls rather than for individual girls. The fact that *dipo* does not just focus on a point in life of an individual girl between two different stages, but that it is also a main event on the social calendar, partly explains its deep embeddedness in Krobo society.

This study shows that the notion of ritual cleanliness is very important in *dipo* and that it is a central theme in ritual activities of the Krobo. This clarifies why girls, even if this somewhat contravenes the other important theme in *dipo* of constructing a female gender identity by emphasising fertility and sexuality, can also be initiated at a very young age. Male initiation rites are almost absent, but men, like women, need to be ritually purified and therefore are circumcised as babies in order to be regarded as clean persons. The emphasis on cleanliness also creates a sense of belonging as it determines who are excluded and who are included into that group of people who consider it important to belong to their family house in their hometowns. The primary unit of social organisation and identity in Krobo society is the patrilineal (extended) family, the lineage or 'the house'. In the situation of economic decline the persistence of 'houses' enables a sense of identity and cohesion to be maintained among their members, who could not cope without effective support from their lineage. Even when they live in remote farming villages or abroad in urban settlements, they still maintain relationships with 'home' by initiating their children. Many attempt to return permanently one day, ultimately at the time of their death. Through *dipo*, the performance of rituals that cleanse and purify, women are included as members of their patrilineage and society. In this way they are able to bear children who belong to their or their childrens' genitor's patrilineage. Even though the occurrence of *yo bi*, children who belong to their mother's father's lineage, is a common phenomenon, the ideal is to include these children in their genitor's lineage. Many people are not married due to financial constraints, but the ideal is therefore to have a full marriage. People generally believe that a successful marriage, which is a family affair, can only be established when a woman has been initiated.

The *dipo* performance is thus a means of expressing individual and group identity, which has to be understood within the context of Krobo notions of personhood and the world, and of what is termed 'traditional religion'. As we saw in chapter six, the ideal Krobo person is a sociocentric person, a 'relational self', whose relations, which extend into the realm of the ancestors and spirits, are created and re-affirmed during the performance of the rites. In chapter five it became clear that *dipo* only takes place during a fixed time of the year, depending on the ritual calendar, which was originally based on agriculture, and at fixed places, namely at and around the shrines in *dom* and is mainly performed by traditional priestesses. The fact that *dipo* can only be celebrated at a fixed place and time, indicates that most (Christian) Krobo recognise the spiritual power of the shrines in and around the hometowns. However, even though *dipo* is firmly grounded in a calendar and territory, it has been adapted to modern demands to make it possible for migrants and school girls to participate. It has been drastically shortened and takes place around the Easter holidays. In *dipo*,

320

distance and difference are subordinate to a sense of belonging to one and the same community. It produces locality to counteract the effects of the villager's dispersal (cf. De Jong 2001: 260). In other words, the rituals have an ongoing relevance to their performers because they enable them to come to terms with the dislocating effects of the global political economy.

The data presented here showed that the ritual symbolization of gender and ethnic identity during the *dipo* rites is an effective procedure for making Krobo identity matter to individuals, affectively and cognitively. Ritual is not something which disappears with modernization. People rather want to distinguish themselves in a globalising world and need markers for difference. As *dipo* rituals express the key cosmological ideas and notions of Krobo people regarding society and the person (cf. Riesman 1986: 94), they comprise a central means of marking a distinct Krobo identity. Only a competing ritual system could have killed *dipo* and the priesthood in general. The Basel Mission was very wary of ritual and what they considered as outward appearance. The Basel missionaries even protested against converted Krobo girls wearing jewellery during their confirmation ceremony. Pentecostal churches today offer an alternative and fill a void in this respect. Their rituals are so strong that in some ways they constitute a more serious rival to 'traditional religion'. However, even though they propagate a complete severance from blood ties and ancestral and other traditional religious practices, they leave room for manoeuvring between traditional religion and Christianity by incorporating traditional spirits and forces in their cosmology as 'devilish and evil' forces, which have to be fought continually. These churches often attract young and urban people who want to break away from traditional authority structures and strive toward a more prosperous future. Many women also attend these churches. However, the old main churches remain powerful as well. Especially the Presbyterian Church has deep roots in Krobo society. It remains the domain of the educated and old authority structures. In Manya Krobo, the paramountcy and the Presbyterian Church have been intertwined since the beginning of the Basel Mission time.

One of the efforts of this book has been to show that in order to understand how the discursive field in which *dipo* is discussed and contested has evolved, it is essential to investigate the history of colonization. In particular the Krobo encounters with the Basel Mission between 1837 – 1917 and with the British colonial administration between 1892 – 1930s have been decisive periods in which the preconditions evolved for current developments concerning *dipo*. The evangelising mission of the Basel Mission can be taken as an early example of globalisation. The Basel Mission has been instrumental in exporting and inculcating 'modernity' by reshaping Krobo society in the process of converting people to Christianity. One of the effects of this modernity was that, even though the Basel missionaries were unsuccessful in their attempts to convert the Krobo for a long time, the Krobo became drawn into conversations whose terms - central concepts and arguments - were set by Europeans, of what was part of what John Comaroff and Jean Comaroff (1992: Ch. 9) call their 'colonization of consciousness'. The Basel missionaries hence successfully 'paganised' *dipo*. It was shown in this book that *dipo* can only be discussed within a framework of particular discursive constructions of 'culture' and 'tradition', and never on its own merits. In this sense, one could even say that Christianity created *dipo*. To many Krobo the practice of *dipo* is an entirely obvious phenomenon, something that happens almost naturally. However, in public speech the only way the *dipo* rites can be referred to now, is either in negative terms in a Christianized idiom, as 'fetish', 'pagan' and 'outmoded, or in more positive terms as 'cultural traditions' where they are objectified as part of a 'cultural heritage'. This way of rendering *dipo* the subject of a particular discursive field in which it is contested, creates a constant field of tension with its actual practice, which has several consequences.

Mechanisms of cultural change therefore cannot be studied in isolation from existing power inequalities. The colonial exercise of power over the Krobo was not only expressed by the many negative views of the *dipo* practice by administrators and missionaries; it was also demonstrated by the fact that the Krobo to some extent internalized these negative meanings and that the Christian discourse became hegemonic. The *dipo* rites are often seen as the catalyst of 'immoral behaviour', teenage pregnancies and prostitution. Whereas the *dipo* rites are contested within Krobo society itself, other groups in Ghana often perceive Krobo women as promiscuous and they are known for supposed prostitution (cf. Akyeampong 1997). The obsessions of Basel missionaries with *dipo* as pagan and immoral have contributed to make women's sexuality emblematic of Kroboness. Eriksen (1993: 155) explains that sexual stereotyping is related to ethnicity in many societies, as gender imagery is often used to describe ethnic groups as a whole. In such a practice gender can be used not only as a symbol of 'objective' cultural differences between ethnic groups, but also as an expression of myths and prejudices that can strengthen those differences (Santen & Schilder 1994: 133).

One response of the Krobo to the colonial encounter was the increasing separation between the public and the private, between the 'frontstage' and 'backstage' in Krobo society. Field (1961) called the *dipo* rituals 'ceremonies of everyday life'. They still are, in the sense that they do not only concern ritual specialists, but also everybody else, as every daughter should ideally pass through the rites. However, as a consequence of the events leading to the ban on *dipo* in 1892 (chapter four), the essential rites, which are now termed 'fetish', have increasingly become part of the backstage of Krobo culture. What comes to the frontstage is the 'dressing up', and the 'harmless culture'. After 1892 *dipo* went underground, as it was criminalized. At the same, it was 'civilized' in public: as became clear in chapters three and four, one of the main objections of the Basel Mission and the colonial administration had been the 'indecency' and 'immorality', supposedly indicative of the 'barbarous' and 'pagan' state of the Krobo. After this, the naked breasts were very cleverly covered up in public and *dipo* became 'just a dressing-up custom'. The main rituals were performed by the priests in secret. When Huber's descriptions of the *dipo* performance are compared with contemporary ones, one difference seems to be that today the performance of the rituals has even more become the work of specialists. Whereas in the past many more rituals, such as the killing of the goat on Saturday, would be performed by the head of a 'house' and the father of a girl, these days it is done by the priests and their helpers. Some parents do not even want to be seen at the scene of the performance, because it is regarded as a 'fetish' place, and they let aunties or grandmothers, usually from *yono*, take care of their daughters during this time (chapter seven). One example of the increasing secrecy, is the 'climbing of the *tɛgbɛtɛ*' performance. According to the 19th century accounts of British colonial agents, they had been witnesses of this performance (chapter four). Even Huber was permitted once to watch this. However, nowadays no strangers are permitted near the tɛgbɛtɛ, and not even the male priests can enter during the performance of the rite. Apart from a move to the 'backstage', this development shows at the same time an increasing awareness on the part of the traditional priests of their minority position and the need to emphasise and protect their identity vis-à-vis Christianity.

Another response of the Krobo to the colonial encounter was to gain conceptual mastery over their changing world (cf. Comaroff & Comaroff 1992: 259). The concept of tradition has not been passively received by the Krobo, but creatively and dynamically appropriated. What is referred to with the term '*kusumi*' is regarded as part of 'tradition'. *Dipo*, as part of *kusumi*, has become emblematic of Kroboness in a positive sense. In Krobo language, the term *kusumi* is usually used when referring to the re-enactment of long-held practices belonging to the realm of the ancestors and ritual ceremonies. As the word *kusumi* is derived from the Portuguese 'costume' (English: 'custom'), we can assume the word has been used for a long time now, but that it was constructed in interaction with 'modernity', as it arrived from Europe (chapter five). Although people complain that *dipo* is not anymore as it used to be, *dipo* is perceived as *kusumi*, and a selective representation of the past has produced an 'original' and 'ideal *dipo*'. Even though the rites have drastically changed, in particular after 1892, imagining tradition and culture this way produces a sense of cultural identity and the continuity of tradition. *Dipo* relates to older idioms of collective identity and together with the feeling that people are members of a group that can identify with these cultural elements, even if contested, it contributes to a feeling of shared identity. The way *dipo* is objectified as 'tradition' is therefore part of modernity and a way of dealing with modernity. Ideas of 'ancient custom' and the oppositional category of modern/traditional have mainly developed from the colonial experience. 'Krobo custom' obtained a particular meaning in the encounter with Europeans.

Reified notions of cultural differences have existed in non-Western societies apart from any European presence (cf. Sahlins 1993: 4), as the Krobo case also shows. Strangers who sought refuge on Krobo Mountain had to accept distinct rules and customs that distinguished the Krobo from the Akan in particular. However, today people consciously mobilise 'culture' and assert a continuity of culture in order to claim an ethnic distinctiveness in the national realm or gain access to the global tourist market (cf. Peel 1994; Sahlins 1993). 'Culturalisation' of *dipo*, that is to say, turning it into 'harmless culture', is one of the contemporary developments with regard to *dipo*. During the *Ngmayem* festival, for example, cultural and ethnic identity is stressed by performing *dipo* dancing outside the usual ritual context. Within Ghana, *dipo* has become an icon of 'Krobo culture'. Here 'culture' is objectified in order to become a powerful resource by serving the strengthening of the Krobo as a political community claiming larger returns from the government. For example, at the *Ngmayem* festival that I witnessed in 1998, the president at the time, J.J. Rawlings, was invited to attend the festival. I was told that at the festival of 2003 the vice-president actually complied with his invitation at the festival of 2003. The reification of *dipo* performances for tourists and politicians is part of an example of the fact that *dipo* can acquire new meanings, and 'tradition' is very much alive and actualised all the time. Contrary to popular thinking, which views globalisation as betraying an idea of the world as a conglomerate of separate and internally homogeneous cultures, it nonetheless does not imply a homogenisation or westernisation. The diversity of human cultures, 'depends less on the isolation of the various groups than on the relations between them' (Levi-Strauss cited in: Sahlins 1993: 16). As the Krobo case also clearly shows, people feel the need to construct and stress boundaries and mark differences only in interaction with others by referring to, for example, ethnicity, gender and religion. Sometimes this happens within the Krobo community, for example, when Christians may want to differentiate themselves from the 'heathens'. At other times the Krobo claim a common identity based on a perceived cultural distinctiveness vis-à-vis other groups in Ghana. Encounters on a global level have in this way intensified the continuous renegotiation of identity and ethnic boundaries (Appadurai 1990; Comaroff & Comaroff 1993).

For anthropologists, ritual has long been a marker of all that separates rational modernity from traditional culture(s), in this way labelling 'other cultures' as 'stuck in tradition' and locality. The seemingly 'traditional' *dipo* rites as a contemporary cultural practice that continues to be perceived as 'unique Krobo culture' that cannot be abolished and needs to be preserved, yet at the same time has been under attack for over 150 years now and changed significantly, urge us to rethink notions of culture and tradition, the persisting dichotomy of 'tradition' and 'modernity' and the interplay of the local and the global. The concept of 'culture' has increasingly come under siege in anthropological writing since the

1980s, as it operates in anthropological discourse to enforce separations that inevitably carry a sense of hierarchy. In other words, culture is the tool for making other. There still is the tacit understanding that anthropologists, who are usually from the west, study the non-west, that is, the Western self studies the non-Western other (Abu-Lughod 1991: 138-139). I agree with Abu-Lughod that we should be conscious of the danger that anthropological discourse 'that elaborates on the meaning of culture in order to account for, explain, and understand cultural difference, (…) also helps construct, produce, and maintain it' (ibid.: : 143), and therefore of the danger to perceive selves and others as given. We should remain aware of a tendency toward essentialism.

However, I do not think we should abandon studying 'culture' altogether. I have tried to overcome the impression of 'culture' as a bounded and largely a-historical universe of shared ideas and customs, by tracing connections between the past and the present of the Krobo community. In this way I have also attempted to fill part of the gap in our knowledge about the Krobo people that has existed in particular since Huber's study, while getting away from his compartmentalized study of 'traditional society'. It thus became clear that the *dipo* practice can only be understood within the complex web of local and global processes. At the same time, in the light of the essentialist, reified conception of 'culture' having passed into everyday Western discourse, and non-Western discourse as well, it is precisely the way 'culture' is debated and the popular use of 'culture' through which claims to particular identities are made that I have investigated. 'A culture' viewed as a 'thing-like' phenomenon provides an ideal rhetorical instrument for claims to identity, phrased in opposition to modernity, Westernisation, or neo-colonialism (Keesing 1994: 30). Seen from this perspective, Krobo people are not just 'trapped' within the modernist discourse of Christianity and nationalism, they also consciously make use of it. However, even though in local usage different values are attached to culture, the 'Christianity-tradition' dichotomy, associating Christianity with the 'modern/civilised' world and 'tradition/culture' with 'the past' and a 'backward' world, still determines the discursive space within which Krobo people have to organise their view of the world. Even if a reassessment of 'traditional culture' has taken place, e.g. as in the 'Africanisation' debate, this is a Christianisation of sorts of the image of traditional Krobo culture.

Despite the vast majority of Krobo being Christians, there are no ready substitutes for *dipo* as symbols of overall communal identity. Most Krobo Christians continue to let their daughters pass through *dipo* because they feel the pressure of family obligations. At the same time ancestral obligations are also felt to be genuine, as many Christians very much share the general presuppositions of Krobo religious culture. *Dipo* continues to express a local ontology of invisible beings and cosmological complexity. Even Pentecostal notions regarding personhood and the world were shown to easily accommodate 'traditional' notions. On the one hand, by taking ancestral and non-Christian spirits very seriously, it offers believers the opportunity to be a Christian without giving up the concerns of traditional religion. On the other hand, local Pentecostalism needs 'traditional religion' as a system of religious alterity to strengthen its Christian identity. At the same time, for those women who do not wish participate in *dipo*, maybe because they want to loosen ties with their relatives, Christianity offers another circle of identification. We can conclude that the so-called traditional *dipo* rites have retained their resilience and have intensified along with modernity's embrace. It is only in a colonial and postcolonial context that the proliferation of the traditional is fully intelligible (cf. Piot 1999: 173). Since rituals such as *dipo* are a conglomeration of symbolic statements about identity and social relations, they remain central foci of both continuity and contestation in processes of change.

To conclude, this study suggests that in order to comprehend why the understanding of *dipo* as traditional culture is so powerful and persistent and why Krobo people, despite a strong adherence to Christianity, continue to perform the rites, we had to study both the practice of *dipo* and investigate history. Moreover, a historical perspective would avoid the pitfall of approaching the notion of culture as fixed and bounded. At the same time, my assumption was that 'tradition' cannot be studied in isolation from 'modernity'. Rather, the fixation of tradition as shown in particular in the *dipo* rites is part of modernity. Therefore, the constant attack on *dipo* ever since modernity arrived on the scene in the form of Christianity and the resultant Western 'civilisation', paradoxically emphasises its power. It is at once one of the most 'traditional customs' in Krobo society and, as a counterpart to modernity, therefore also the most resilient.

Glossary

ablade	native sandals, formerly the privilege of royals
ab_odoi	dwarfs or a kind of fairies, which are seen as the children or messengers of the gods
afugbɛ	Maxwell's Brown Duiker
agbaa	secret knowledge
agbosimi	'knocking the door', a first stage in the customary marriage rites
akpeteshie	'local gin', locally distilled palm wine
aplamdɛ	waist marks
asafoatsɛ	sub-chief or military leader
banku	popular food prepared on the basis of fermented corn
batakari	northern type of dress, also seen as a 'battle dress'
bɛɛmbo	'sweeping marks', cicatrisation designs as proof of initiation
bi-kpo-jemi	outdooring the child
blɛfogbi	'White man's language', usually referring to English
blɛfono	white person
b_o	Roan antelope skin (but also cloth in general)
bragoro	(Akan) puberty rites
boa	reddish dye made of white clay and certain leaves used for bodily decoration
cedi	Ghanaian currency
dade	cutlass
dipo	initiation rites for girls performed among the Dangme speaking groups in Ghana, in particular by the Krobo and the Shai
dipo-yo	(Pl. *dipo-yi*) girl(s) passing through *dipo* initiation
d_om	'in the valley', i.e. the capital towns in the plain
duku	(head)kerchief, scarf
fufui	meal made of pounded cassava or yam, sometimes mixed with plantain (Akan: *fufu*)
gbalo	diviner
gbeje	world of death
gbetsi	spiritual-spouse
hewa	power
huanim	spiritual world
huza	farm settlement
j_otso	the banks of the Volta River at Kpong (jo = Volta)
juju	witchcraft or sorcery

ka	earthen dish with grinding grooves, used in combination with a *kukplatso*, a small wooden pestle
kaba	blouse sewn out of wax print cloth (from *kaba srotu* – cover shoulder)
kasi	clan
kente	long, narrow woven cotton or silk stripes, sewn together to make a ceremonial cloth, mostly manufactured in the Volta Region or the Asante Region
kla	a spiritual entity, closely connected with one's self which bears one's birthday name
klala	(white) calico
kla-tsime	kla shrine
klogbi	'Klo language', the Krobo dialect of the Dangme language
klohuɛ	traditional hairstyle
Klo wem	'Klo home', i.e. Krobo Mountain
klutu	a type of shrine
koli	blue glass bead
komi pee	priestly hat woven from raffia fibre in a conical shape, also worn by the *dipo* initiands
kono	'he who is carried in the shoulders': i.e., title for paramount chief
kpaku-nyo	breast round 'like a calabash'
kpokpoi	festive meal made of yam
kusumi	custom, ceremony, rites, tradition
la	a bracelet with the priestly (black and white) beads, a symbol of ancient cultural and ancestral tradition
labia	messenger of a priest
laventa	perfume (lavender water)
likoko	small drinking cup, usually made of a coconut shell, which is used by the priests to pour libations
manye	queen mother
mantse	chief
mɛnɛ	traditional cosmetics
musu	pollution, evil thing
nguo	white clay (used in rituals)
nyɛ	mother
nyoli	precious white bead
nyo-kpami	'massaging the breast'
nyo-tso	'stick like breast'
nyumu	man
otim	fermented corn dough (Akan: *kenkey*)
piɛm	deity's sanctuary

328

sankofa	(Akan) an adinkra symbol meaning 'return to the roots', also key symbol for the promotion of national Ghanaian culture
sɛ	'stool', also a stool used to symbolise a chief's power
sɛsɛɛ	'parting word' with which one leaves the other world before being born into this world
seyelo	regent for an absent priest
soni	raffia fibre used in ritual
subue	long, red loincloth
sukuufo	'school people', educated people (sukuu = school, -fo (Akan)= people)
susuma	often translated as 'soul', spiritual part of one's individuality
takpa	large, round drinking pot
tɛlimi	libation
totroku	another word for *tɛgbɛɛ*, also the name of a deity worshipped in the Djebiam-Ogomɛ and Manya-Kponguno divisions
tovi	black bead of the fruit of a liana plant
tsɛ	father
tsitsii	dried flower of the palm tree, used as cleansing torch
tsu	'red', or 'fair'(referring to someone's complexion)
yaya	calamity
yereyeli	'yam eating' festival (after the Akan odwira)
yi-hoom	traditional hairstyle
yisi wombo	cicatrisations on the belly
yo	woman
yobu	evil thing
yono	upcountry
yumu	black or dark (in complexion)
wanimo	chief priest
wansam	circumciser
we nokotoma	elder of the 'house'
weku	'house' or 'lineage'
weku-we	family house
wem	house
wenguam	palace and court of paramount chief Sakite I in Odumase
wetso	division
wono	male priest
wotsum	a deity's round one-room clay hut covered with a straw roof
woyo	female priest

Abbreviations

BMA	Basel Mission Archives
CO	Colonial Office
DC	District Commissioner
GNA	Ghanaian National Archives
GSS	Ghana Statistical Services
NDC	National Democratic Congress
NPP	National Patriotic Party
PNDC	Provisional National Defence Council
PRESEC	Presbyterian Secondary School
PRO	Public Record Office London
UNESCO	United Nations Educational, Scientific and Cultural Organization

Appendix: Krobo texts

Libation texts at the 'Putting the millet in the water ceremony', March 1999 (chapter five)

<u>1st woman:</u>

Nana Klowɛki bimɛ, nɛ ke wa fo bimɛ nɛ a wa á, Nana o ngo kɛ wa ma ba nɛ wa ba bi jokwɛ om a gbi. E fo bimɛ nɛ a wa, e ma du a ke ka mɛ. E tsɛ wo nɛ wa ba nɛ kusimi nɛ ngɛ kɛ ma je sisije o wa ba wo ngma nyumi konɛ wa kɛ ma tsa dipo o no. Wa ba wo jokwɛm' boobo no mɛ, mo nitsɛ o maa na boni je o tsuo ba da ha. Wa ba nɛ wa ba ngo wa nine womi nɛ wa kɛ wo ngma nyumi. Wa yi akpla, ngma nɛ wa ma nyumi womi no, e puɛ nɛ wa nu lɛ nɛ wa tso mi. Kaa bonɛ wa peeo ha mo daa no o jaa pɛ wa ngɛ peeo nɛ. Wa kɛ nyɛ ba nɛ hyɛ ba hiɛ, jokwɛ wi ji wo. Wa ngɛ mo pɛɛ kpae konɛ ngma a nɛ puɛ o nɛ wekubi tsuo ba na nɛ a tsomi, konɛ wa ye ayilo.

<u>2nd woman:</u>

Jaa o ja; ejakáá wo nɛ wa ba ngɛ noo peeo wo hu a pee wo Kloyihi. Kloyi nɛ a pee wo wa le kaa e ngoo. Ke a tsɛ wo wa ba pee o. Ke wa pe hu wa yeo nguo pɛɛpɛ kaa bo nɛ mo maa Nana de wo o. Wa da yi no nɛ, nɛ wa ngɛ hae wa ngɛ mo maa Nana hae nɛ o piɛ wa he nɛ e hi pɛpɛɛpɛ kaa bonɛ, wa peeo daa, jokuɛwi ji wo

Libation texts at the 'blocking of the road' ceremony, April 1999 (chapter five)

<u>The priest Ajase:</u>

Mwɛno ji wa kusum nɛ wa kɛ tsuo wa ni ngɛ jojoɛ no. Tsɛ Mau kɛ e yo zugba zu ba jo no, mwɛno ji wa blo tsimi. Konɛ no yaya nɛ ma je wo o se kɛ pa a se kɛ ma ba nɛ e maa ngo e nine ba wo kusim nɛ wa ma tsu ngɛ dipo nya a, Tsatsɛ Mau wa tsi lɛ blo ngɛ hiom no ko nɛ nyɛ ha wo jojoɛ nɛ wa sɛ dipo o nɛ no yaya ko ko da ba ngo e nine ba wo mi.

Ɛee-e mwɛno so tsɛnɛ a so, Tsɛ Mau kɛ zugba zu . Nana Klowɛki ngɛ ba joo nonɛ ma deo no. wa li bo sem loko wa ngɛ bo hɛmi lee. Kɛ je blema ngɛ nimeli a yi no, nɛ a kɛ kple kloyo si o nɛ wa Nɛnɛmɛ a tsu o lɛ no o no wo bibimɛ wa ba su nɛ wa ba tsue nɛ o nɛ. Wa a nyɛ pɛ kpae o daa nɛ e ma su dipo o ngɛ lsta be o mio wa tsi o blo loko wa je dipo o Sisi. Konɛ bonɛ pee nɛ zangmayihi nɛ wa maa sɛ dipo o jojoɛ nɛ ba ngɛ a no nɛ a fo gbo ne a fo gbiɛ. Wa a nyɛ pɛ kpae, ke nɔnɛ wa li nyɛ ko le ha wo; ke nɔnɛ wa pee nɛ e dɛ o nyɛ dla to kla nɔ. Nɛ nyɛ ha nɛ yobu ya se nɛ tslom nɛ ba. Jojoɛ wa a bie o nɛ jojoɛ jojoɛ. Imi wamino Ajase o-o tsua manye ba.

Eee-e mwɛno so libi o, nga kuoli omɛ a da l kɛ wo ji nga kuoli omɛ o nɛ. Mo Nana Kloweki, mo ji mɛ tsuo nokotoma. Loo no nɛ wa a pee nɛ o e da o, e dɛ o wa li bo sem nɛ wa a bo hɛm lee. Wo nga kuoli omɛ ke nɔnɛ e dɛ o nyɛ dla to kla nɔ ha wo nɛ tslom nɛ ba; dede ya dede, kaja a ya kaja, jojoɛ o, jojoɛ, tsua ma- nye ba.

Old lady 'crossing the road' with a baby, October 1998 (chapter six)

Maa Lako:
Nomlo lɛ kɛ a fo lɛɛ pe e nyɛɛ loo wa mo blom poe nɛ ke o ya so nɛ o ba, ke o ya miɛ nɛ o ba, nɛ ke o ya tslo nɛ o ba tslo. Kɛ a bi o si nɛ a de kɛ o ngɛ; o se blo nɛ tsi, o se blo nɛ tsi pɛpɛɛpɛ. O wa nɛ o ba ya pa, o ba ya lɛm, o ba bɛ, o ba hoo ni, o ba ya jua nɛ o ho ni nɛ wa ye. Ke a fo nomlo no nɛ e peeo ji loo nɛ. Wa pɛ kpae a tsi o se ha wo.

Nɛ wa peeo nɛ ke o ya so nɛ o ba nɛ ke o ya miɛ nɛ o ba, o se blo nɛ tsi, o hɛ kpɛ blo gblaa. A deo ke tsatsɛ loko a deo kɛ maa. A deo kɛ maayo, a deo kɛ maa, tsatsɛ lee, maa lee tsatsɛ lee, maa lee jaa a deo nɛ o-o. O wa nɛ o ba ya pa. Yo lɛ pe e duo. O du nɛ o sia mɛmɛ. O hɛ papaapa (3x). A fo we mo ngɛ Nam nɛ o biɛ. Nam no biɛ we kokooko. Ke a de mo tomoku o o de mɛ tomoja. Ke no de we mo noko o a de we noko.

Libation texts at divination, April 1999 (chapter seven)

Maa Lako, April 1999:
Sɛ wono Opata, e bi Tɛtɛbio, e ba kɛ ma du e bimɛ a he ha mɛ nɛ (nyɛ hɛ we bo) wa ya bimɛ he nɛ a je konɛ wa ma kɛ tsu a he ni, a tso a ya he ni o; e ma ni o tsumi; mo we o tsɛ o da ji no nɛ nɛ wa ha mo konɛ ni o nɛ wa ma tsu o e jo gbo, e jo nlɛyu, nɛ a je a kpe a je ayo nɛ a de kɛ imi pɛ lɛ ma pee ha mɛ. Pɛo pɛɛ, jokwɛwi ji wo nɛ wa maa je sisi huo no ke no nɛ wa li o nyɛ ko le ha wo. Nɔnɛ wa li o nyɛ kɛ gu wa nlami mi nɛ wa nɛ wa kɛ pee nɛ e no nɛ jo, pɛo-o pɛɛ, nyɛ gbaa wo. Mo o biɛ mi l ngɛ ni o tsue ngɛ o nɛ. L tsu we ngɛ i hewami nya; da ji no nɛ i ngɛ nyɛ hae nɛ nyɛ joo no. Ke a ya so a ba, ke a ya tslom a ba; Nyɛ hami hewam. Pɛo pɛɛ wa kpae, nɛ je biyo nɛ hi nɛ je yo nɛ hi nɛ wo hu wa himi.

'Papa' Tetteh:

Eee mwɛno hǫ tsɛmɛ a Hǫ Mau jǫ nǫ nɛ o tsɛ Jǫtso kɛ ya pue Akǫle tsuɛpɛ. Domɛyobi Domɛluǫ kpakpao kaa bǫnɛ yamo ǫ de ǫ jeha lɛ su; nǫnɛ ma je kloyom, yagagami, tɛmi kokumi, alaemi, klo pɛ a peeǫ ha mɛ ngɛɛ nɛ. A to ǫ a he so konɛ ke a ma nga nǫ nɛ nga huǫ. E ba kaa imi lasifǫlo ma ba du a he ngǫ ha mɛ nɛ a ya tslǫ nɛ a ba tslǫ dede e ya dede kaja; a ya kaja. Ke a maa nɛ a hiɛ ɛ we nǫko ke a ya a a hiɛ nǫ. A fǫ nɛ a wo a tsɛmɛ kɛ a nyɛmɛ. Nǫko kpɛ suo nɛ e wu bǫ. Pɛo pɛ nɛ ke a bu mɛ bǫ ǫ a hla nyumu kpa nɛ ba wo dipo hiǫ ha mɛ, nɛ kwɛ nǫ jǫm nɛ ba.

Dipo rites, April 1999

Tying of *soni* (*soni muomi*), April 11, 1999:

O tsui titli, o ko nɛ ba o komi, o dɛ nɛ ba o dɛm. Ke o ya tslǫǫ, o ba tslǫǫ, kɛ a bi o si a de kɛ o ngɛ daa. O fǫ gbo kɛ gbiɛ. Ke a fǫ mo nɛ o wa a ma pe mo kloyo, o nyɛmi ji Lawɛ. Lawɛ nǫ tsuo a ma piɛ o nǫ ǫ he ha mo.

Lawɛ mo ji nyumu, wɛɛ o sǫni ǫ, wa ma a piɛ Ata nǫ he ha lɛ. O nǫ fɛe nǫ nɛ sa nɛ a pee ha mo ǫ wa kɛ ma piɛ Ata nǫ ǫ he. Kǫnɛ ke e su ni ǫ womi nǫ wa ma wo ni ha mo. Lǫǫ o jǫǫ mɛ o nu. Ke o ya so nɛ o ba, ke o ya tslǫ ǫ o ba. Lawɛ a ma ngǫ o nǫ ǫ kɛ piɛ Ata nǫ he.

Wrapping the white calico around the girls' waists, Saturday April 17, 1999:

O bo ji nǫ nɛ, nɛ o tsɛ kɛ ngɛ mo Kloyo pee. Ke o ya so nɛ o ba, o tsui nɛ ba o tsuim, o ko nɛ ba o ko nu; O dɛ nɛ ba o dɛ mi. Ke a tsɛ mo ǫ o de kɛ ee. O bo nɛ a kɛ mo Klo yo pee nɛ ke o ya so nɛ o ba; ke o ya miɛ nɛ o ba.

Touching the goat, April 17, 1999:

Doe o tsɛ Tɛwia kɛ e dem to kake ji nǫ nɛnɛ e kɛ ngɛ mo kloyo pee. Ke o ya so nɛ o ba; ke o ya miɛ nɛ o ba. Ke o ya tslǫǫ nɛ o ba tslǫǫ.

Monday 'washing of the head', April 19, 1999:

O ma te si nɛ o ma bɛɛ, kɛ o bɛ taa. O ma ya pa "mini wa ye?" A kɛ wa ma tsi ku, loo wa ma ye nǫ. Kɛ o sa kuada, kɛ o tsi kuǫ, o pee hwonyu fai kɛkɛ wa ye ke nǫko ya jɛ mo kɛ a bu mo bo lo? O ma de lɛ kɛ ɛɛ, oɛ' i bɛmi bǫ ngɛ i nine sem. I dase ji nǫmlǫ nǫ, a sɛm dipo; a pee mi Kloyo.

References

Books, theses, reports, book sections and journal articles

Abedi-Boafo, J. (1978). *Dangme nyaii: Classical and idiomatic Dangme expressions with their meanings in English.* Accra: Bureau of Ghana Languages.

Abu-Lughod, Lila. (1991). Writing against culture. In R. Fox (Ed.), *Recapturing anthropology: Working in the present* (pp. 137-162). Santa Fe, NM: American Research Press.

Adams, W. H. (1908). The tail girl of Krobo Hill. *Blackwood's Edinburgh Magazine, 184*(1116), 517-534.

Adjaye, Joseph K. (1999). Dangerous crossroads: Liminality and contested meaning in Krobo (Ghana) 'dipo' girls' initiation. *Journal of African Cultural Studies, 12*, 5-26.

Agyeman, D. K. (1988). *Ideological education and nationalism in Ghana under Nkrumah and Busia.* Accra: Ghana University Press.

Akyeampong, Emmanuel Kwaku. (1996). *Drink, power, and cultural change: A social history of alcohol in Ghana, c. 1800 to recent times.* Portsmouth and Oxford: Heinemann and Currey.

Akyeampong, Emmanuel Kwaku. (1997). Sexuality and prostitution among the Akan of the Gold Coast c. 1650-1950. *Past and Present: A Journal of Historical Studies, 156*, 144-173.

Akyeampong, Emmanuel Kwaku. (2001). *Between the sea and the lagoon: An eco-social history of the Anlo of Southeastern Ghana c. 1850 to recent times.* Athens, OH and Oxford: Ohio University Press and Currey.

Akyeampong, Emmanuel Kwaku, & Obeng, Pashington. (1995). Spirituality, gender, and power in Asante history. *The International Journal of African Historical Studies, 28*(3): 481-508.

Amanor, Kojo Sebastian. (1994). *The new frontier: Farmer responses to land degradation: A West African study.* Geneva and London: UNRISD and Zed Books.

Ameh, Robert Kwame. (1998). 'Trokosi' (child slavery) in Ghana: A policy approach. *Ghana Studies, 1*, 35-62.

Anderson, Benedict. (1983). *Imagined communities: Reflections on the origin and spread of nationalism.* London: Verso Editions/ NLB.

Appadurai, Arjun. (1990). Disjuncture and difference in the global cultural economy. *Theory, Culture and Society, 7*, 295-310.

Appadurai, Arjun. (1995). The production of locality. In R. Fardon (Ed.), *Counterworks: Managing the diversity of knowledge* (pp. 204-225). London: Routledge.

Appadurai, Arjun. (1996). *Modernity at large: Cultural dimensions of globalization.* Minneapolis, MN: University of Minnesota Press.

Arhin, Kwame. (1967). The structure of greater Ashanti (1700-1824). *The Journal of African History, 8*(1), 65-85.

Arlt, Veit. (1995). *Die Basler Missionare und Krobo zur Mitte des 19. Jahrhunderts: Die Etablierung weltlicher Herrscher in Krobo im Lichte der fruehen Berichte aus dem Archiv der Basler Mission.* Unpublished master's thesis, History Department, University of Basel, Basel.

Arlt, Veit. (1996). *Diplomacy and power politics in mid-nineteenth century Krobo: Krobo chieftaincy and politics seen through the early reports by Basel missionaries.* Paper presented at the Department of History, University of Ghana, Legon.

Arlt, Veit. (1997). 'Come back when the new paramount chief is enstooled, then we will tell you the real story!' In B. Sottas, T. Hammer, L. Roost-Vischer & A. Mayor (Eds.), *Le forum suisse des africanistes* (pp. 128-137). Hamburg: LIT Verlag.

Arlt, Veit. (2002). *Tradition as a resource: Changing forms of political legitimacy in the Krobo states (Southeastern Ghana). BAB Working Paper, 3*, 1-24. Paper presented at Historischen Seminar, Universität Basel, Basel.

Arlt, Veit. (2003a). Making scholars: The Bana Hill Senior Boys' Boarding School. In J. Schneider, L. Roost-Vischer & D. Péclard (Eds.), *Le forum suisse des africanistes 4* (pp. 285-307). Hamburg: LIT Verlag.

Arlt, Veit. (2003b). *A seaboy's tale: The Congo Free State experiences in the autobiography of Gabriel Sikapa (1874-1958)*. Paper presented at the Graduiertenkolleg The Black Atlantic, Zürich and Basel.

Arlt, Veit. (f.c.). *Christianity and culture: The appropriation of global processes in Krobo, Gold Coast Colony, c. 1860-1917*. Unpublished doctoral dissertation, University of Basel, Basel.

Asad, Talal. (1993). *Genealogies of religion: Discipline and reasons of power in Christianity and Islam*. Baltimore, MD: Johns Hopkins University Press.

Ashie, T. T. (n.d.). *The secrecy of dipo customs*. Unpublished manuscript.

Ayi, C. K. (1966). *A study of the music of dipo custom (a puberty rite) among the Shai*. Unpublished master's thesis, Institute of African Studies, University of Ghana, Legon.

Azu, Enoch. (1929). *Adangbe historical and proverbial songs*. Accra: Government Printing Office.

Azu, Noa Akunor Aguae. (1927). Adangbe (Adangme) history. *The Gold Coast Review, 2*(2), 239-270.

Azu, Noa Akunor Aguae. (1928). Adangbe (Adangme) history - concluded. *The Gold Coast Review, 4* (1), 3-30.

Azzu Mate Kole, Nene. (1955). The historical background of Krobo customs. *Transactions of the Gold Coast and Togoland Historical Society, 1*, 133-140.

Baëta, C. G. (Ed.). (1968). *Christianity in tropical Africa: Studies presented and discussed at the Seventh International African Seminar, University of Ghana, April 1965*. London: Oxford University Press.

Barnard, Alan, & Spencer, Jonathan (Eds.). (1996). *Encyclopedia of social and cultural anthropology*. London: Routledge.

Barth, Frederik. (1969). Introduction. *Ethnic groups and boundaries: The social organization of cultural difference* (pp. 9-38). London: Allen and Unwin.

Baumann, Gerd. (1996). *Contesting culture: Discourses of identity in multi-ethnic London*. Cambridge: Cambridge University Press.

Beckwith, Carol, & Fisher, Angela. (1999). *African ceremonies*. New York, NY: Abrams Publishers.

Bediako, Kwame. (1990). *Jesus in African culture: A Ghanaian perspective*. Accra: Asempa Publishers.

Beek, Walter E. A. van. (1998). Identity in African ritual. *Focaal: Tijdschrift voor Antropologie, 32*, 119-140.

Beidelman, T. O. (1997). *The cool knife: imagery of gender, sexuality, and moral education in Kaguru initiation ritual*. Washington DC: Smithsonian Institution Press.

Bell, Sir Henry Hesketh Joudou. (1911 [1893]). *Love in black. Sketches of native life in West Africa*. London: Edward Arnold.

Blakely, Thomas D., Beek, Walter E. A. van, & Thompson, Dennis L. (Eds.). (1994). *Religion in Africa: Experience and expression*. London and Portsmouth: Currey and Heinemann.

336

Boaten, Nana A. A. (1992). The changing role of queenmothers in the Akan polity. *Research Review, 8*(1/2), 90-100.

Borsboom, Ad & Otto, Ton. (1997). Introduction: Transformation and tradition in Oceanic religions. In Ton Otto & Ad Borsboom (Eds.), *Cultural dynamics of religious change in Oceania* (pp. 1-9). Leiden: KITLV.

Borsboom, Ad. (2002). *The Self and Others. Confusing ideology with everyday practice.* Paper presented at the international conference 'Multiple Identifications and the Self', held at Berg en Dal, May 31-June 1, 2002, 1-10.

Bowen, Elenore Smith (pseud. of Laura Bohannan). (1964). *Return to laughter.* New York, NY: Doubleday Anchor. (First published 1954).

Bowie, Fiona. (1999). The inculturation debate in Africa. *Studies in World Christianity, 5*(1), 67-92.

Bowie, Fiona. (2000). *The anthropology of religion: An introduction.* Oxford: Blackwell Publishers.

Braude, Benjamin. (1997). The sons of Noah and the construction of ethnic and geographical identities in the medieval and early modern periods. *William and Mary Quarterly, 54*(1), 103-142.

Brown, Judith K. (1963). A cross-cultural study of female initiation rites. *American Anthropologist, 65*, 837-53.

Carrithers, Michael, Collins, Steven, & Lukes, Steven (Eds.). (1986). *The category of the person: Anthropology, philosophy, history.* Cambridge: Cambridge University Press.

Clarke-Ekong, Sheilah. (1995). Ghana's festivals: Celebrations of life and loyalty. *Ufahamu, 23*(3), 16-33.

Clifford, James, & Marcus, George E. (Eds.). (1986). *Writing culture: The poetics and politics of ethnography.* Berkeley, CA: University of California Press.

Coe, Cati. (2000). *'Not just drumming and dancing': The production of national culture in Ghana's schools.* Unpublished doctoral dissertation, University of Pennsylvania, Pennsylvania.

Cohen, Anthony P. (1994). *Self consciousness: An alternative anthropology of identity.* London: Routledge.

Comaroff, Jean, & Comaroff, John. (1993). Introduction. In J. Comaroff & J. Comaroff (Eds.), *Modernity and its malcontents* (pp. xi-xxxvii). Chicago: University of Chicago Press.

Comaroff, John, & Comaroff, Jean. (1992). *Ethnography and the historical imagination.* Boulder, CO: Westview Press.

Coplan, David D. (1972). *Krobo Klama.* Unpublished master's thesis, Institute of African Studies, University of Ghana, Legon.

Cox, James L. (Ed.). (1998). *Rites of passage in contemporary Africa: Interaction between Christian and African traditional religions.* Cardiff: Cardiff Academic Press.

De Jong, Ferdinand. (1997). The production of translocality: Initiation in the sacred grove in South Senegal. *Focaal: Tijdschrift voor Antropologie, 30/31*, 61-83.

De Jong, Ferdinand. (2001). *Modern secrets: The power of locality in Casamance, Senegal.* Unpublished doctoral dissertation, University of Amsterdam, Amsterdam.

De Witte, Marleen. (2001). *Long live the dead! Changing funeral celebrations in Asante, Ghana.* Amsterdam: Aksant Academic Publishers.

Debrunner, Hans W. (1967). *A history of Christianity in Ghana.* Accra: Waterville Publishing House.

Drucker-Brown, Susan. (1993). Mamprusi witchcraft, subversion and changing gender relations. *Africa, 63*(4), 531-549.

Dumont, Louis. (1986). A modified view of our origins: The Christian beginnings of modern individualism. In M. Carrithers, S. Collins & S. Lukes (Eds.), *The category of the person: Anthropology, philosophy, history* (pp. 93-122). Cambridge: Cambridge University Press.

Elias, Norbert. (1987). *KII: Stage two: Development of a hill-top tribe.* Deutsches Literaturarchiv, Marbach: Reference Norbert Elias 808.

Eriksen, Thomas Hylland. (1993). *Ethnicity and Nationalism. Anthropological Perspectives.* London, East Haven: Pluto Press.

Ewing, Katherine P. (1990). The illusion of wholeness: Culture, self, and the experience of inconsistency. *Ethos, 18*(3), 251-279.

Fabian, Johannes. (1991). *Time and the work of anthropology: Critical essays 1971-1991.* Chur, Switzerland and Reading: Harwood Academic Publishers.

Fasholé-Luke, E, Gray, Richard, Hastings, Adrian, & Tasie, G (Eds.). (1978). *Christianity in independent Africa.* London: Collings.

Field, Margaret J. (1941a). *Some aspects of Manya-Krobo land affairs* (Report).

Field, Margaret J. (1941b). *Memorandum on the dipo custom* (Report). Somanya.

Field, Margaret J. (1941c). *A Supplementary note on Krobo 'dipo' rites* (Report).

Field, Margaret J. (1942). *The Krobo constitution in relation to the Nyewe-Ogome dispute and the significance of priestly stools.* Unpublished manuscript.

Field, Margaret J. (1943). The agricultural system of the Manya-Krobo of the Gold Coast. *Africa, 14*(2), 54-65.

Field, Margaret J. (1961). *Religion and medicine of the Ga people.* Accra and London: Presbyterian Book Depot and Oxford University Press. (First published in 1937).

Field, Margaret J. (n.d.). Research notes by Margaret Field (PhD) - Krobo fetishes (pp. 1-85). Manya Krobo Traditional Archives.

Friedman, Jonathan. (1990). Being in the world: Globalization and localization. In M. Featherstone (Ed.), *Global culture: Nationalism, globalization and modernity* (pp. 311-328). London: Sage.

Geertz, Clifford. (1973). The integrative revolution: Primordial sentiments and civil politics in the new states. In C. Geertz (Ed.), *The interpretation of cultures: Selected essays* (pp. 255-310). New York: Basic Book.

Geisler, Gisela. (1997). Women are women, or, how to please your husband: Initiation ceremonies and the politics of 'tradition' in Southern Africa. *African Anthropology, 7*, 92-128.

Geschiere, Peter. (1997). *The Modernity of witchcraft: Politics and the occult in postcolonial Africa.* Charlottesville, VA: University Press of Virginia.

Geschiere, Peter & Meyer, Birgit. (1999). Globalization and identity: Dialectics of flow and closure: Introduction. In P. Geschiere & B. Meyer (Eds.), *Globalization and identity: Dialectics of flow and closure* (pp. 601-615). Oxford: Blackwell Publishers. (*Development and Change, 29*(4)).

Ghana Evangelism Committee. (1993). *National church survey: 1993 update: Facing the unfinished task of the church in Ghana.* Accra: Assemblies of God Literature Centre.

Gifford, Paul. (1994). Ghana's charismatic churches. *Journal of Religion, 24*(3), 241-265.

Gilbert, Michelle. (1988). The sudden death of a millionaire: Conversion and consensus in a Ghanaian kingdom. *Africa, 58*(3), 291-314.

Gilbert, Michelle. (1989). Sources of power in Akuropon-Akuapem: Ambiguity in classification. In W. Arens & I. Karp (Eds.), *Creativity of power: Cosmology and action in African societies* (pp. 59-90). Washington and London: Smithsonian Institution Press.

Gilbert, Michelle. (1993). The cimmerian darkness of intrigue: Queen mothers, Christianity and truth in Akuapem history. *Journal of Religion in Africa, 23*(1), 2-43.

Gilbert, Michelle. (1994). Aesthetic strategies: The politics of a royal ritual. *Africa, 64*(1), 99-125.

Gilbert, Michelle. (1995). The Christian executioner: Christianity and chieftaincy as rivals. *Journal of Religion in Africa, 25*(4), 347-386.

Gorgendière, Louise de la. (1996). Ethnicity: A conundrum. In L. de la Gorgendière, K. King & S. Vaughan (Eds.), *Ethnicity in Africa: Roots, meanings and implications* (pp. 1-16). Edinburgh: Centre of African Studies, University of Edinburgh.

Grimes, R. L. (2000). *Deeply into the bone: Re-inventing rites of passage.* Berkeley, CA: University of California Press.

Grosz-Ngate, Maria, & Kokole, Omari H. (Eds.). (1997). *Gendered encounters: Challenging cultural boundaries and social hierarchies in Africa.* London: Routledge.

GSS. (2002a). *2000 Population and housing census: Special report on 20 largest localities.*

GSS. (2002b). *2000 Population and housing census: Special report on urban localities.*

GSS. (2002c). *2000 Population and housing census: Summary report of final results.*

Haenger, Peter. (1997). *Sklaverei und Sklavenemanzipation an der Goldküste: Ein Beitrag zum Verständnis von sozialen Abhängigkeitbeziehungen in Westafrika.* Basel and Frankurt am Main: Helbing Et Lichtenhahn.

Hafkin, Nancy Jane & Bay, Edna G. (Eds.) (1976). *Women in Africa: Studies in social and economic change.* Stanford, CA: Stanford University Press.

Hagan, George P. (1993). Nkrumah's cultural policy. In K. Arhin (Ed.), *The life and work of Kwame Nkrumah: Papers of a symposium organized by the Institute of African Studies, University of Ghana, Legon* (pp. 3-25). Trentin, NJ: Africa World Press.

Halldén, Erik. (1968). *The culture policy of the Basel Mission in the Cameroons 1886-1905.* London and München: Kegan Paul and Renner Verlag.

Hampton, Jamie. (1991). *Meeting AIDS with compassion: AIDS care and prevention in Agomanya, Ghana.* London: ActionAid in association with AMREF and World in Need.

Hannerz, Ulf. (1992). *Cultural complexity: Studies in the social organization of meaning.* New York, NY: Columbia University Press.

Hansen, Karen Tranberg. (1999). Second-hand clothing encounters in Zambia: Global discourses, western commodities and local histories. In R. Fardon, W. van Binsbergen & R. van Dijk (Eds.), *Modernity on a shoestring: Dimensions of globalization, consumption and development in Africa and beyond* (pp. 207-226). Leiden and London: EIDOS in association with African Studies Centre Leiden and Centre of African Studies London.

Hansen, Karen Tranberg. (2000). *Salaula: The world of secondhand clothing and Zambia.* Chicago, IL: University of Chicago Press.

Hastings, Adrian. (1993). Were women a special case? In F. Bowie, D. Kirkwood & S. Ardener (Eds.), *Women and missions: Past and present: Anthropological and Historical Perceptions* (pp. 109-125). Providence, RI: Berg.

Hastings, Adrian. (1994). *The church in Africa, 1450 - 1950.* Oxford: Clarendon Press.

Hasty, Jennifer. (2000). Who-leads and who follows: Hegemony and 'house style' at the State Press in Ghana. Unpublished Paper, Pacific Lutheran University.

Hefner, Robert W. (1993). Introduction: World building and the rationality of conversion. In R. W. Hefner (Ed.), *Conversion to Christianity: Historical and anthropological perspectives on a great transformation.* (pp. 3-44). Berkeley, CA: University of California Press.

Henige, David. (1974). Seniority and succession in the Krobo stools. *The International Journal of African Historical Studies, 7*(2), 203-226.

Hill, Polly. (1970). *The migrant cocoa-farmers of Southern Ghana: A study in rural capitalism.* Cambridge: Cambridge University Press.

Hobsbawm, E. & Ranger, T. (Eds.) (1983). *The invention of tradition.* Cambridge: University Press.

Hoch-Smith, Judith, & Spring, Anita (Eds.). (1978). *Women in ritual and symbolic roles.* New York, NY: Plenum Press.

Huber, Hugo. (1958). Adangme purification and pacification rituals (West Africa). *Anthropos, 53,* 161-191.

Huber, Hugo. (1988). La divinité et sa prêtresse: Une image Africaine de la feminité qui sort du cadre? *Genève-Afrique, 26*(1), 67-84.

Huber, Hugo. (1993). *The Krobo: Traditional social and religious life of a West African people.* Fribourg, Switzerland: University Press Fribourg.

Idowu, E. Bolaji. (1973). *African traditional religion: A definition.* London: SCM Press.

Jackson, Michael, & Karp, Ivan. (1990). Introduction. In M. Jackson & I. Karp (Eds.), *Personhood and agency: The experience of self and other in African cultures* (pp. 15-30). Washington and Uppsala: Almqvist and Wiksell and Smithsonian Institution Press.

Jacobson-Widding, Anita. (1990). The shadow as an expression of individuality in Congolese conceptions of personhood. In M. Jackson & I. Karp (Eds.), *Personhood and agency: The experience of self and other in African cultures* (pp. 16-31). Washington and Uppsala: Almqvist and Wiksell and Smithsonian Institution Press.

Jansen, Wihelmina Helena Maria. (1997). *The dynamics of gender: Transformation, context and design.* Nijmegen: Centre for Womens' Studies, University of Nijmegen. (Research Program 1997-2001).

Jell-Bahlsen, Sabine (1997). Eze Mmiri Di Egwu: The water monarch is awesome: Reconsidering the Mammy Water myths. In F. E. S. Kaplan (Eds.), *Queens, queen mothers, priestesses and power: Case studies in African gender* (pp. 103-134). New York, NY: New York Academy of Sciences.

Jenkins, Richard. (1997). *Rethinking ethnicity: Arguments and explorations.* London and New Delhi: Thousand Oaks and Sage Publications.

Johnson, Narh. (1997). *The traditional authority structure of Yilo Krobo State.* Unpublished master's thesis, Institute of African Studies, University of Ghana, Legon.

Kanogo, Tabitha. (1993). Mission impact on women in colonial Kenya. In F. Bowie, D. Kirkwood & S. Ardener (Eds.), *Women and missions: Past and present: Anthropological and historical perceptions* (pp. 165-186). Providence, RI: Berg.

Keesing, Robert. (1994). Theories of culture revisited. In R. Borofsky (Ed.), *Assessing Cultural Anthropology* (pp. 301-312). New York, NY: McGraw-Hill.

Killingray, David. (2000). Imagined martial communities: Recruiting for the military and police in colonial Ghana, 1860-1960. In C. Lentz & P. Nugent (Eds.), *Ethnicity in Ghana: The limits of invention* (pp. 119-136). London and New York, NY: MacMillan Press and St. Martin's Press.

Kirby, Jon P. (1994). Cultural change and religious conversion in West Africa. In T. D. Blakely, W. E. A. van Beek & D. L. Thomson (Eds.), *Religion in Africa: Experience and expression* (pp. 56-71). London: Currey.

Kofi, Quashigah. Edward. (1998). Religious freedom and vestal virgins: the 'trokosi' practice in Ghana. *African Journal of International and Comparative Law, 10*(2), 193-215.

Kölle, Christian. (1936). *Der Kopfjäger und sein Sohn: Erzählung aus dem Kroboland (Goldküste), West-Afrika.* Unpublished manuscript.

Konrad, Dagmar. (2001). *Missionsbräute: Pietistinnen des 19. Jahrhunderts in der Basler Mission.* Münster: Waxmann.

Kratz, Corinne A. (1994). *Affecting performance: Meaning, movement, and experience in Okiek's women's initiation*. Washington and London: Smithsonian Institution Press.

Kropp-Dakubu, M.E. (1973). A survey of borrowed words in Dangme. *Research Review*, 81-128.

Kropp-Dakubu, M.E. (1987). *The Dangme language: An introductory survey*. Basingstoke and London: MacMillan Publishers.

Kropp-Dakubu, M.E. (1999). *Ga-English dictionary*. Accra: Black Mask Ltd.

Kudadjie, J. N. (1997). Some implications of the Dangme concept of 'sësëë' for moral philosophy and moral education. *Quest, 11*, 3-27.

Kudadjie, J.N. (1976). Aspects of religion and morality in Ghanaian traditional society with particular peference to the Ga-Adangme. In J. M. Assimeng (Eds.), *Traditional life, culture and literature in Ghana* (pp. 26-53). Owerri and London: Conch Magazine.

Kuklick, Henrika. (1991). *The savage within: The social history of British anthropology, 1885-1945*. Cambridge: Cambridge University Press.

Kumekpor, M. L., Bredwa-Mensah, Yaw, & Van Landewijk, J. E. J. M. (1995). *The Ghanaian bead tradition: Materials, traditional techniques, archaeological and historical chronology, bead usage, traditional-sociological meaning*. Legon: Ghana Bead Society.

La Fontaine, J. S. (1985). *Initiation: Ritual drama and secret knowledge across the world*. Manchester: Manchester University Press.

La Fontaine, J. S. (1986). Person and individual: Some anthropological reflections. In M. Carrithers, S. Collins & S. Lukes (Eds.), *The category of the person: Anthropology, philosophy, history* (pp. 123-141). Cambridge: Cambridge University Press.

Lamin, Sanneh. (1983). *West African Christianity: The religious impact*. London: Hurst.

Lentz, Carola. (1997). Creating ethnic identities in North-Western Ghana. In H. Vermeulen & C. Govers (Eds.), *The politics of ethnic consciousness* (pp. 31-89). London and New York, NY: MacMillan Press and St. Martin's Press.

Lentz, Carola. (1998). *Die Konstruktion von Ethnizität: Eine politische Geschichte Nord-West Ghanas 1870-1990*. Köln: Köppe Verlag.

Lentz, Carola, & Nugent, Paul. (2000). Ethnicity in Ghana: A comparative perspective. In C. Lentz & P. Nugent (Eds.), *Ethnicity in Ghana. The limits of invention* (pp. 1-28). London, New York: MacMillan Press Ltd, St. Martin's Press, Inc.

Lienhardt, Godfrey. (1985). Self: Public, private: Some African representations. In M. Carrithers, S. Collins & S. Lukes (Eds.), *The category of the person: Anthropology, philosophy, history* (pp. 141-155). Cambridge: Cambridge University Press.

Lincoln, Bruce. (1991). *Emerging from the chrysalis: Rituals of women's initiation*. Oxford: Oxford University Press.

Lutkehaus, Nancy C. & Roscoe, Paul B. (Eds.). (1995). *Gender rituals: Female initiation in Melanesia*. London: Routledge.

Lutkehaus, Nancy C. (1995). Feminist anthropology and female initiation in Melanesia. In N.C. Lutkehaus & P.B. Roscoe (Eds.), *Gender rituals: Female initiation in Melanesia* (pp. 3-29). London: Routledge.

Marcus, George E. & Fischer, Michael M. J. (1986). *Anthropology as cultural critique: An experimental moment in the human sciences*. Chicago, IL: University of Chicago Press.

Marsella, Anthony J., DeVos, George, & Hsu, Francis, L. K. (Eds.). (1985). *Culture and self: Asian and Western perspectives*. New York, NY: Tavistock Publications.

Mauss, Marcel. (1986). A category of the human mind: The notion of the person; The notion of the self. In M. Carrithers, S. Collins & S. Lukes (Eds.), *The category of the person:*

Anthropology, philosophy, history (pp. 1-26). Cambridge: Cambridge University Press. (Translated by W. D. Halls).

Mauss, Marcel. (1990). *The gift: The form and reason for exchange in archaic societies.* London: Routledge. (First published in 1950).

Mbinglo, Meh Nsodu. (2002). *Drama behind the church signboard.* Accra.

Mbiti, John S. (1969). *African religions and philosophy.* London and Nairobi: Heinemann.

McClintock, Anne. (1995). *Imperial leather: Race, gender, and sexuality in the colonial contest.* London: Routledge.

Meyer, Birgit. (1992a). 'Delivered from the powers of darkness': Bekentenissen over duivelse rijkdom in Christelijk Ghana. *Etnofoor, 5*(1/2), 234-256.

Meyer, Birgit. (1992b). 'If you are a devil, you are a witch and, if you are a witch, you are a devil': The integration of 'pagan' ideas into the conceptual universe of Ewe Christians in Southeastern Ghana. *Journal of Religion in Africa, 22*(3), 98-132.

Meyer, Birgit. (1994). Beyond syncretism: Translation and diabolization in the appropriation of Protestantism in Africa. In Stewart & R. Shaw (Eds.), *Syncretism/anti-syncretism: The politics of religious synthesis* (pp. 45-69). London: Routledge.

Meyer, Birgit. (1995). *African Pentecostal churches, Satan and the disassociation from tradition.* Paper presented at the Symposium Religious Revitalization and Syncretism in Africa and the Americas, at the 94th Annual Meeting of the American Anthropological Association, Washington.

Meyer, Birgit. (1995). *Translating the Devil: An African appropriation of Pietist Protestantism: The case of the Peki Ewe in Southeastern Ghana, 1847-1992.* Unpublished doctoral dissertation, University of Amsterdam, Amsterdam.

Meyer, Birgit. (1997). Christian mind and worldly matters. *Journal of Material Culture, 2*(3), 311-337.

Meyer, Birgit. (1998). 'Make a complete break with the past': Memory and postcolonial modernity in Ghanaian Pentecostal discourse. In R. Werbner (Ed.), *Memory and the postcolony: African anthropology and the critique of power* (pp. 182-208). London: Zed Books.

Meyer, Birgit. (1999). *Translating the devil: Religion and modernity among the Ewe in Ghana.* Edinburgh: Edinburgh University Press.

Middleton, John. (1979). Home-town: A study of an urban centre in Southern Ghana. *Africa, 49*(3), 246-257.

Middleton, John. (1983). One hundred and fifty years of Christianity in a Ghanaian town. *Africa, 53*(3), 2-19.

Miller, Jon. (1994). *The social control of religious zeal: A study of organizational contradictions.* New Brunswick, NJ: Rutgers University Press.

Miner, Horace. (1956). Body ritual among the Nacirema. *American Anthropologist, 58*, 503-507.

Moore, Henrietta L. (1994). *A passion for difference.* Cambridge: Polity Press.

Morris, Brian. (1994). *Anthropology of the self: The individual in cultural perspective.* London: Pluto Press.

Mudimbe, V. Y. (1988). *The invention of Africa: Gnosis, philosophy, and the order of knowledge.* London and Bloominton, IN: Currey and Indiana University Press.

Murray, D. W. (1993). What is the Western concept of the self? On forgetting David Hume. *Ethos, 21*(1), 3-23.

Narh, A.J. (1998). *The impact of Christianity on the dipo custom of the Krobos.* Unpublished bachelor's thesis, Department of Sociology, University of Ghana, Legon.

Nketia, Joseph Hanson Kwabena. (1955). *Funeral dirges of the Akan people.* Achimota.

Nketia, Joseph Hanson Kwabena. (1986). *The music of Africa.* London: Gollancz.

Nkrumah, Kwame. (1963). *Africa must unite*. London: Heinemann.

Notermans, Catrien. (2002). True Christianity without dialogue: Women and the polygyny debate in Cameroon. *Anthropos, 97*(2), 341-354.

Notermans, Catrien. (2003). Nomads in kinship: fosterage and the self in Cameroon. *Focaal. European Journal of Anthropology, 42,* 89-103.

Obeng, Pashington. (1996). *Asante Catholicism: Religious and cultural reproduction among the Akan of Ghana*. Leiden: Brill.

Obeng-Assamoa, Peter Kwabena. (1998). *The Mate-Koles of Manya Krobo*. Unpublished master's thesis, Department of History, University of Ghana, Legon.

Odjidja, E. M. L. (1973). *Mustard seed: The growth of the church in Kroboland*. Accra: Waterville Publishing House.

Odjidja, E. M. L. (1977). *Krobo Girls' School: Death and resurrection*. Accra: Waterville Publishing House.

Odonkor, S.S. (1971). *The rise of the Krobos (From an original Ga text by Thomas Harrison Odonkor)*. Tema: Ghana Publishing.

Ofoe, Benjamin Tetteh. (1979). *The Puberty Rites of the Yilo Krobos within the African Traditional Set-up*. Unpublished extended paper in partial fulfilment of the requirement for the award of a Diploma in Theology, Department for the Study of Religions, University of Ghana, Legon.

Olupona, Jakob K. (1991a). *Kingship, religion, and rituals in a Nigerian community: A phenomenological study of Ondo Yoruba festivals*. Stockholm: Almqvist and Wiksell.

Olupona, Jakob K. (Ed.) (1991b). *African traditional religions in contemporary society*. New York, NY: Paragon House.

Omenyo, Cephas N. (2001). *The ongoing encounter between Christianity and African culture: A case study of girls' nubility rites of the Krobos*. Legon-Accra: Adwinsa Publications.

Oppong, Christine. (1974). *Focus on cultural aspects of menstruation in Ghana*. Legon: Institute of African Studies, University of Ghana. (Paper for WHO).

Otto, Ton & Pederson, Poul. (2000). Tradition between continuity and invention: An introduction. *Folk: Journal of the Danish Ethnographic Society, 42,* 3-18.

Parrinder, E. G. (1976). *African traditional religion*. London: Sheldon Press.

Peel, J. D. Y. (1978). The Christianization of African society. In E. Fasholé-Luke, R. Gray, A. Hastings & G. Tasie (Eds.), *Christianity in independent Africa* (pp. 443-455). London: Collings.

Peel, J. D. Y. (1994). Historicity and pluralism in some recent studies of Yoruba religion [Review article]. *Africa, 64*(1), 150-167.

Pels, Peter. (1999). *A Politics of Presence. Contacts between Missionaries and Waluguru in Late Colonial Tanganyika*. Australia, Canada [etc.]: Harwood Academic Publishers.

Pels, Peter. (1999). *A politics of presence: Contacts between missionaries and Waluguru in late colonial Tanganyika*. Amsterdam: Harwood Academic Publishers.

Piot, Charles. (1999). *Remotely global: Village modernity in West Africa*. Chicago: University of Chicago Press.

Platvoet, Jan & Toorn, Karel van der. (1995). Pluralism and identity: An epilogue. In J. Platvoet & K.van der Toorn (Eds.), *Pluralism and identity: Studies in ritual behaviour,* (pp. 349-360). Leiden: Brill.

Prodolliet, Simone. (1987). *Wider die Schamlosigkeit und das Elend der Heidnischen Weiber: Die Basler Frauenmission und der Export des Europäischen Frauenideals in die Kolonien*. Zürich: Limmat Verlag.

Quarcoo, A.K., & Johnson, Marion. (1968). Shai pots: The pottery industry of the Shai people of Southern Ghana. *Baessler-Archiv, 16*(new series), 47-87.

Quarcoopome, E. Nii. (1991). Self-decoration and religious power in Dangme culture. *African Arts, 24*(3), 56-65.

Quarcoopome, E. Nii. (1993a). Agbaa: Dangme art and the politics of secrecy. In M. H. Nooter & S. Vogel (Eds.), *Secrecy: African art that conceals and reveals* (pp. 113-129). New York, NY: Museum of African Art.

Quarcoopome, E. Nii. (1993b). *Rituals and regalia of power: Art and politics among the Dangme and Ewe, 1800 to present.* Unpublished doctoral dissertation, Department of Art History, University of California, Los Angeles.

Quarcoopome, E. Nii. (1994). Thresholds and thrones: Morphology and symbolism of Dangme public altars. *Journal of Religion in Africa, 24*(4), 339-357.

Quarcoopome, E. Nii. (n.d.). *Missionary photography and statecraft in Manya Krobo, c.1860-1939.* Unpublished manuscript.

Ranger, Terence. (1983). The invention of tradition in colonial Africa. In E. Hobsbawm & T. Ranger (Eds.), *The invention of tradition* (pp. 211-262). Cambridge: Cambridge University Press.

Ranger, Terence. (1988). African traditional religion. In S. R. Sutherland & P. Clarke (Eds.), *The world's religions: The study of religion, traditional and new religion* (pp. 106-114). London: Routledge.

Ranger, Terence. (1993). The invention of tradition revisited: The case of colonial Africa. In T. Ranger & O. Vaughan (Eds.), *Legitimicay and the state in twentieth-century Africa: Essays in honour of A. H. M. Kirk-Greene* (pp. 62-111). London: MacMillian Press.

Rasing, Thera. (2001). *The bush burnt, the stones remain: Female initiation rites in urban Zambia.* Münster: LIT Verlag.

Rattray, R. S. (1923). *Ashanti.* Kumasi and London: Basel Mission Book Depot and Oxford University Press.

Rattray, R. S. (1927). *Religion and art in Ashanti.* Oxford: Clarendon Press.

Reindorf, C.C. (1889). *The History of the Gold Coast and Asante (based on traditions and historical facts comprising a period of more than three centuries from about 1500 to 1860).* Basel: Basel Mission Book Depot.

Renne, Elisha P. (1995). Becoming a Bunu bride: Bunu ethnic identity and traditional marriage dress. In J. B. Eicher (Ed.), *Dress and ethnicity* (pp. 117-138). Oxford: Berg Publishers.

Richards, Audrey. (1956). *Chisungu: A girl's initiation ceremony among the Bemba of Zambia.* London: Routledge.

Riesman, P. (1986). The person and the life-cycle in African social life and thought. *The African Studies Review, 29*(2), 71-138.

Roscoe, Paul B. (1995). Conclusion: 'Initiation' in cross-cultural perspective. In N.C. Lutkehaus & P.B. Roscoe (Eds.), *Gender rituals: Female initiation in Melanesia* (pp. 219-238). London: Routledge.

Sackey, Brigid. (1985). The significance of beads in the rites of passage among some Southern Ghanaian peoples. *Research Review, 1*(2), 180-191.

Sahlins, Marshall. (1993). Goodbye to *Tristes Tropes*: Ethnography in the context of modern world history. *Journal of Modern History, 65*, 1-25.

Santen, Jose C.M. Van. (1993). *They leave their jars behind: The conversion of Mafa women to Islam (North Cameroon).* Leiden: VENA.

Sarpong, Peter K. (1971). *The sacred stools of the Akan.* Accra-Tema: Ghana Publishing Corporation.

Sarpong, Peter K. (1976). *Ghana in retrospect: Some aspects of Ghanaian culture.* Accra: Ghanaian Publishing Corporation.

Sarpong, Peter K. (1977). *Girls' nubility rites in Ashanti*. Tema: Ghana Publishing Corporation.

Sarpong, Peter K. (1996). *Libation*. Accra: Anansesem Publications.

Sarpong, Peter K. (2002). *Peoples differ: An approach to inculturation in evangelisation*. Legon-Accra: Sub-Saharan Publishers.

Schlegel, Alice & Barry III, Herbert. (1979). Adolescent initiation ceremonies: A cross-cultural code. *Ethnology, 18*, 199-211.

Schmidt, Wilhelm. (1931). *The origin and growth of religion: Facts and theories*. London: Methuen.

Schramm, Katharina. (2000). *Dancing the nation: Ghanaische Kulturpolitik im Spannungsfeld zwischen Nation und globaler Herausforderung*. Münster: LIT Verlag.

Schroeder, Rose M, & Danquah, Samuel. (2000). Prevention of HIV/AIDS through traditional means: The cultural practice of dipo. *Psych Discourse, 31*(10), 5-7.

Senah, Kodjo Amedjorteh. (1997). *Money be man: The popularity of medicines in a rural Ghanaian community*. Amsterdam: Spinhuis.

Shaw, Rosalind. (1990). The invention of 'African traditional religion'. *Religion, 20*, 339-353.

Shostak, Marjorie. (1983). *Nisa: The life and words of a Kung woman*. New York, NY: Vintage Books.

Shweder, Richard, & LeVine, Robert A. (Eds.). (1984). *Culture theory: Essays on mind, self, and emotion*. Cambridge: Cambridge University Press.

Sikapa, Gabriel T. (1999). *The memoirs of G. T. Sikapa*. Unpublished manuscript. (Written 1937-1943. Translated from Ga into English and annotated by his grandson Evans Sikapa Madjitey).

Sinclair, Karen. (1986). Women and religion. In M. I. Duley & M. I. Edwards (Eds.), *The cross-cultural study of women* (pp. 107-124). New York, NY: Feminist Press, City University of New York.

Smith, Mary Felice. (1981). *Baba of Karo: A woman of the Muslim Hausa*. New Haven, CT: Yale University Press. (First published 1955).

Staring, Richard, Land, Marco van der & Tak, Herman (Eds.). (1997). *Globalization / localization: Paradoxes of cultural dentity*. Nijmegen: Stichting Focaal. (*Focaal: Tijdschrift voor Antropologie, 30/31*).

Steegstra, Marijke. (2002). 'A mighty obstacle to the Gospel': Basel missionaries, Krobo women and conflicting ideas of gender and sexuality. *Journal of Religion in Africa, 32*(2), 200-230.

Stoeltje, Beverly. (1995). Asante queen mothers: A study in identity and continuity. In G. Ludwar-Ene & M. Reh (Eds.), *Gender and identity in Africa* (pp. 15-33). Münster: LIT Verlag.

Tettey, Michael Teye. (1977). *The dipo custom of the Krobo: Its history, practice, and significance*. Unpublished bachelor's thesis, Department for the Study of Religions, University of Ghana, Legon.

Teyegaga, B. D. (1974). Christians must shun dipo custom: It is unchristian and paganistic. *The Christian Messenger, 4*(12).

Teyegaga, B. D. (1985). *Dipo custom and the Christian faith*. Accra: J'piter Printing Press LTD.

Thomas, Nicholas. (1991). *Entangled objects: Exchange, material culture, and colonialism in the Pacific*. Cambridge: Harvard University Press.

Thomas, Nicholas. (1992). The inversion of tradition. *American Ethnologist, 19*, 213-232.

Turner, Victor. (1967). *The forest of symbols: Aspects of Ndembu ritual*. Oxford and London: Clarendon Press and International African Institute.

Turner, Victor. (1979). Betwixt and between: The liminal period in rites de passage. In W. A. Lessa & E. Z. Vogt (Eds.), *Reader in comparative religion: An anthropological approach* (pp. 234-243). New York, NY: Harper and Row.

Turner, Victor. (1991). *The Ritual process: Structure and anti-structure*. Ithaca, NY: Cornell University Press.

Van den Bersselaar, Dmitri. (1998). *In search of Igbo identity: Language, culture and politics in Nigeria, 1900-1966*. Unpublished doctoral dissertation, Leiden University, Leiden.

Van der Veer, Peter (Ed.). (1996). *Conversion to modernities: The globalization of Christianity*. New York and London: Routledge.

Van Dijk, Rijk. (2000). *Christian fundamentalism in sub-Saharan Africa: The case of Pentecostalism*. Copenhagen: Centre of African Studies, University of Copenhagen.

Van Dijk, Rijk. (2001). Contesting silence: The ban on drumming and the musical politics of Pentecostalism in Ghana. *Ghana Studies, 4*, 31-64.

Van Dijk, Rijk. (2002). Ghanaian churches in the Netherlands: Religion mediating a tense relationship. In I. v. Kessel (Ed.), *Merchants, missionaries and migrants: 300 years of Dutch-Ghanaian relations* (pp. 88-97). Amsterdam and Accra: KIT Publishers and Sub-Saharan Publishers.

Van Dijk, Rijk, & Van Rouveroy van Nieuwaal, E. A. B. (1999). Introduction: The domestication of chieftaincy: The imposed and the imagined. In E. A. B. Van Rouveroy van Nieuwaal & R. Van Dijk (Eds.), *African chieftaincy in a new socio-political landscape*. Hamburg: LIT Verlag.

Van Gennep, Arnold. (1960). *The rites of passage*. London: Routledge and Kegan Paul.

Wilks, Ivor. (1956a). Tribal history and myth I. *Universitas, 2*(3), 84-86.

Wilks, Ivor. (1956b). Tribal history and myth II. *Universitas, 2*(4), 116-118.

Wilks, Ivor. (1975). *Asante in the nineteenth century: The structure and evolution of a political order*. London: Cambridge University Press.

Wilson, Alexandra (Ed.). (2003). *The bead is constant*. Accra: Ghana Universities Press.

Wilson, Louis E. (1986). The evolution of paramount chiefs among the Adangme to the end of the nineteenth century: The case of the Krobo (Ghana). *Genève-Afrique, 24*(2), 73-100.

Wilson, Louis E. (1990). The 'bloodless conquest' in Southeastern Ghana: The Huza and territorial expansion of the Krobo in the 19th century. *The International Journal of African Historical Studies, 23*(2), 269-279.

Wilson, Louise E. (1991). *The Krobo people of Ghana to 1892: A political and social history*. Athens, OH: Ohio University Press.

Young, Frank W. (1965). *Initiation ceremonies: A cross-cultural study of status dramatization*. Indianapolis, NY: Bobbs-Merrill.

Archival sources
(full references can be found in the text)

Basel Mission holdings in the archives of Mission 21, Basel:

D-1 Incoming correspondence from Ghana up to the outbreak of the First World War

D-3 Records of the Ghana Mission from the First World War period 1914-1918: in- and out-correspondence

D-8 Church Census Data from 1890

D-10 Miscellaneous MSS concerning Ghana in European languages

D-11 certain categories of duplicated letters and reports
D-30 Photographs and Pictures of Ghana
D-31 Hand-drawn maps and sketches, Plans of buildings, legal documents concerning land

Basel Mission Periodicals:
- Der evangelische Heidenbote (monthly from 1828-1928)
- Deutsches Kollekteblatt
- Evangelisches Missions-Magazin 1857-1928
- Jahresberichte 1853-1917

National Archives of Ghana, Accra

ADM 11/1 Eastern Region
ADM 11/1/1679 Native customs and fetish
ADM 1/9/4
ADM/NP 13/1

Public Records Office (PRO), Kew, Great Britain

Colonial Office (CO) 96 and 98 (Gold Coast records)

Newspaper articles

Abolish outmoded customs. (1998, December 2). *Daily Graphic*.
Absentee chiefs at Krobo. (2002, November 4). *The Ghanaian Chronicle*.
Asiedu, William A. (1999, February 2). Modify cultural practices. *Daily Graphic*.
Dei, Kofi. (1999, June 1). Preserving the dipo culture. *Ghanaian Times*.
Doku, Francis. (2000, June 29 - July 5). Krobo girls told: No more dipo until age 15. *Graphic Showbiz*, 1, 8.
Editorial: Freeing the Trokosi girls. (1998, August 21). *Daily Graphic*.
Editorial: The Gambaga outcasts. (1998, September 11). *Daily Graphic*.
Editorial: 'Toward cultural death (3)'. (1998, August 26). *Ghanaian Times*.
GNA. (2000, June 23). Manya Krobo to review cultural practices. *Daily Graphic*, 16-17.
Kumah, Divine. (1998, May). Our girls on the Internet: Why are we feigning surprise? *The Watchman*.
Noonoo, Ken. (1998, October 27). Tension in Manya Krobo. *The Ghanaian Times*.
Okyere, Joe, & Ampratwum-Mensah, Akwasi. (1998, November 2). Let's strengthen cultural values. *Daily Graphic*.
Oppong Kyekyeku, Oheneba Mensa. (1998, November 10). We must redeem our cultural values. *Ghanaian Times*.
P&P Comment: Let's save Ghanaian womanhood. (1998, 8-14 October). *People and Places*.
(1998, August 22). *The Standard*.
Women take the front. (1998, November 17). *Ghanaian Times*.

Brochures

Appertey, E.K. (1988). *Yilo Krobo Presbyterian Church centenary 1880-1980: Brochure and programme*. Somanya.

Anonymous (1994). *Order of service for the burial and thanksgiving service for the late Rev. B. D. Teyegaga (aged 88 years)*. Accra: J'piter Printing Press LTD.

The Cultural Policy of Ghana. (n.d.). Accra: The National Commission on Culture.

Various. (1990). *Burial service of Oklemekuku Azzu Mate Kole*. Tema: Ghana Publishing Corporation.

Ethnologie:
Forschung und Wissenschaft

Hartmut Zinser
Mythos des Mutterrechts
Um ein Nachwort ergänzte Neuauflage.
Im Anhang: Rezensionen der 1. Auflage
Was ist das Mutterrecht? In welchen Ländern und in welchen historischen Epochen hat es ein Mutterrecht oder eine Gynäkokratie gegeben, wie sahen oder sehen die gesellschaftlichen Verhältnisse und besonders die Geschlechterbeziehungen unter ihm aus?
Die vorliegende Arbeit bedient sich dennoch nicht der psychoanalytischen Methode in der Darstellung ihres Gegenstandes. Sie wählt die Form des Plädoyers, in dem die Argumente für und wider, auch solche, die sich der Symptomanalyse verdanken, dem Urteil des Lesers ausgesetzt und die Urteilsgründe zusammen mit den Interessen und Bedürfnissen, die in ihr wirksam sind, zur Diskussion gestellt werden.
Bd. 1, 1997, 100 S., 15,90 €, br.,
ISBN 3-8258-2554-X

Günther Schlee
Identities on the Move
Clanship and pastoralism in Northern Kenya (second edition 1994, first published in 1989). This is a title distributed by LIT Verlag. The book was first published by Manchester University Press in 1989. The distributed version is part of the second edition published by GIDEON S. WERE PRESS, Nairobi, Kenya in 1994.
Clans are normally thought of as contained within ethnic groups. In the Horn of Africa the pastoral Rendille, Gabbra, Sakuye and some Somalis of northern Kenya and southern Ethiopia have many clans in common. As a result the clans are not always smaller or less important than the ethnic groups. How such inter-ethnic relationships came about is the subject of this study many go back beyond ethnic divisions to over 400 years ago. The book also examines the uses to which they are put, for instance in managing herds.

Oral history is combined with cultural comparison and the analysis of social structure. The many original texts are themselves of linguistic interest. Blending synchronic and diachronic perspectives, the book synthesises historical ethnology in the Continental tradition with social anthropology. Historically it overturns some established ideas about how the Horn was settled. Anthropologically it shows how relations may exceed the bounds of the ethnic group as the conventional unit of study. It will be of interest to anthropologists, sociologists and social geographers or planners concerned with pastoral development.
Bd. 2, 1994, 288 S., 24,90 €, br.,
ISBN 3-8258-4800-0

Wim van Binsbergen
Intercultural Encounters
African and anthropological lessons towards a philosophy of interculturality
This book brings together fifteen essays investigating aspects of interculturality. Like is author, it operates at the borderline between social anthropology and intercultural philosophy. It seeks to make a contribution to intercultural philosophy, by formulating with great precision and painful honesty the lessons deriving from extensive intercultural experiences as an anthropologist. It culminating section presents an intercultural philosophy revolving on the tenet 'Cultures do not exist'. The kaleidoscopic nature of intercultural experiences is reflected in the diversity of these texts. Many belong to a field that could be described as 'meta-anthropology', others are more clearly philosophical; occasionally they spill over into belles lettres, ancient history, and comparative cultural and religious studies. The ethnographic specifics supporting the arguments are diverse, deriving from various African situations in which the author has conducted participatory field research (Tunisia, Zambia, Botswana, and South Africa).
Bd. 4, 2003, 616 S., 40,90 €, br.,
ISBN 3-8258-6783-8

LIT Verlag Münster – Hamburg – Berlin – Wien – London
Grevener Str./Fresnostr. 2 48159 Münster
Tel.: 0251 – 23 50 91 – Fax: 0251 – 23 19 72
e-Mail: vertrieb@lit-verlag.de – http://www.lit-verlag.de

Ethnologische Studien
herausgegeben von Ulrich Köhler
(Universität Freiburg)

Brigitte Hülsewiede
Die Nahua von Tequila
Eine Nachuntersuchung – besonders zur
Struktur und Wandel von Familienfesten
Bd. 21, 1993, 500 S., 35,90 €, gb.,
ISBN 3-89473-360-8

Carola Kasburg
Die Totonaken von El Tajín
Beharrung und Wandel über vier
Jahrzehnte
Bd. 22, 1992, 352 S., 30,90, gb.,
ISBN 3–89473–361–6

Gabriele Robinson
**Akkulturationsprozesse in ihrer
Auswirkung auf die Identität der
Maori**
Bd. 23, 1992, 250 S., 24,90 €, br.,
ISBN 3-89473-383-7

Ursula Bertels
Das Fliegerspiel in Mexiko
Historische Entwicklung und
gegenwärtige Erscheinungsformen
Bd. 24, 1993, 250 S., 24,90 €, gb.,
ISBN 3-89473-635-6

Claudia Kalka
**"Eine Tochter ist ein Haus, ein Boot
und ein Garten"**
Frauen und Geschlechtersymmetrie bei
den Warao-Indianern Venezuelas
Bd. 25, 1995, 460 S., 30,90 €, gb.,
ISBN 3-8258-2132-3

Ralph M. Becker
**Trance und Geistbesessenheit im
Candomblé von Bahia (Brasilien)**
Bd. 26, 1995, 392 S., 35,90 €, gb.,
ISBN 3-8258-2462-4

Eveline Dürr
**Mitla zwischen Tradition und
Moderne**
Wandel einer zapotekischen Gesellschaft
in Oaxaca, Mexiko
Bd. 27, 1997, 392 S., 24,90 €, gb.,
ISBN 3-8258-2648-1

Brigitte Hülsewiede
Die Mayordomías in Tequila
Das religiöse Ämtersystem heutiger
Nahua in Mexiko
Bd. 28, 1998, 560 S., 35,90 €, gb.,
ISBN 3-8258-2649-X

Christiane Bögemann-Hagedorn
Hinter Opuntienhecken
Kulturwandel und ethnische Identität
in einem Otomí-Dorf des Valle del
Mezquital, Mexiko
Bd. 29, 1998, 304 S., 25,90 €, br.,
ISBN 3-8258-2650-3

Ulrich Köhler (Hg.)
Santa Catarina Pantelhó
Ein Dorf von Indianern und Ladinos
in Chiapas, Mexiko. Ansätze zu einer
Ethnographie
Bd. 30, 1997, 424 S., 19,90 €, br.,
ISBN 3-8258-2651-1

Eveline Dürr; Stefan Seitz (Hrsg.)
**Religionsethnologische Beiträge zur
Amerikanistik**
Bd. 31, 1997, 272 S., 35,90 €, gb.,
ISBN 3-8258-3259-7

Maria Susana Cipolletti
**Stimmen der Vergangenheit, Stimmen
der Gegenwart: Die Westtukano
Amazoniens 1637 – 1993**
Bd. 32, 1998, 446 S., 35,90 €, gb.,
ISBN 3-8258-3425-5

Norbert Roß
Bilder vom Regenwald
Mentale Modelle, Kulturwandel und
Umweltverhalten bei den Lakandonen
in Mexiko
Bd. 33, 2001, 304 S., 30,90 €, br.,
ISBN 3-8258-3969-9

Anke Laufer
**Rassismus, ethnische Stereotype und
nationale Identität in Peru**
Bd. 34, 2000, 408 S., 30,90 €, gb.,
ISBN 3-8258-4904-x

Heiko Feser
**Die Huaorani auf den Wegen ins neue
Jahrtausend**
Bd. 35, 2001, 576 S., 45,90 €, gb.,
ISBN 3-8258-5215-6

LIT Verlag Münster – Hamburg – Berlin – Wien – London
Grevener Str./Fresnostr. 2 48159 Münster
Tel.: 0251 – 23 50 91 – Fax: 0251 – 23 19 72
e-Mail: vertrieb@lit-verlag.de – http://www.lit-verlag.de